Gay Life and Culture A WORLD HISTORY

Gay Life and Culture A WORLD HISTORY

Edited by Robert Aldrich

Universe

EDITOR'S ACKNOWLEDGMENTS

I would like to thank all the staff at Thames & Hudson for their help in the preparation of this book, particularly Wendy Gay, who has done splendid research on the illustrations, and Sam Wythe, whose editorial work has been meticulous, sympathetic, and cheerful. I am grateful to several scholars—notably Alastair Blanshard, Mark Seymour, Julie Ann Smith, David West, and Garry Wotherspoon—who kindly read some of these chapters or offered useful suggestions. Finally, I am grateful to my colleagues in the Department of History at the University of Sydney for providing a congenial and stimulating academic home, and for their continued support of my work.

R. A.

Half-title: Brassaï, *Homosexual Couples at the Bal de la Montagne Sainte-Geneviève*, c. 1932

Frontispiece: Rudolf Schlichter, *Women's Pub*, c. 1925

First published in the United States of America in 2006 by
Universe Publishing
A division of Rizzoli International Publications, Inc.
300 Park Avenue South
New York, NY 10010
www.rizzoliusa.com

Originally published in the United Kingdom in 2006 by
Thames & Hudson Ltd
181A High Holborn
London WC1V 7QX
www.thamesandhudson.com

ISBN-10: 0-7893-1511-4
ISBN-13: 978-0-7893-1511-3

Library of Congress Control Number: 2006903208

2006 2007 2008 2009 / 10 9 8 7 6 5 4 3 2 1

Printed and bound in China by C&C Offset Printing Co., Ltd

CONTENTS

Gay and Lesbian History
ROBERT ALDRICH

Since time immemorial and throughout the world, some men and women have felt a desire for emotional and physical intimacy with those of the same sex. Men have lusted after and loved other men; women have lusted after and loved other women. The epic *Gilgamesh* – the earliest complete version of which dates from 1700 BCE – recounts the adventures of a mythical king who, as foreshadowed in a dream, meets a wild man, Enkidu, whom he comes to 'love as a wife'.[1] The ancient Greek and Judaeo-Christian traditions, the fountains of Western culture, also provide tales of the bonding of bodies and souls. Homer's *Iliad* describes the companionship of Achilles and Patroclus in the context of the Trojan War, traditionally dated to the early 12th century BCE, while Sappho, the lyric poet of the 6th century BCE, charts the pangs of female–female love so movingly that her home island, Lesbos, has provided the term 'lesbianism'. The ancient Greek world famously celebrated relations between males, seeing the love of beauty (as vaunted by Plato in his *Symposium*) as an initiation into philosophy. Although Judaism condemned sodomy, the Jewish scriptures (the Christian Old Testament) provided examples of women-centred women and of men passionate for their fellows, including the Israelite Naomi and her widowed daughter-in-law, Ruth, and the shepherd-turned-giant-killer David, who was befriended by Jonathan, son of King Saul. This, Oscar Wilde remarked almost three thousand years later, exemplified 'the love that dare not speak its name'.

A world away from Greece and Judaea is a Chinese story told in the 3rd century BCE of the friendship between Duke Ling, a contemporary of Confucius, and his favourite, Mizi Xia. Because the young man famously offered a peach to his friend as they walked through an orchard, rather than eating it all himself, the 'love of the shared peach' became a description for homosexual intimacy for centuries to come. Meanwhile, in India, the epic *Mahabharata* (probably composed from *c.* 200 BCE) chronicled the friendship between Krishna and Arjuna as the force propelling them to immortality.[2]

In the ancient world, therefore, intimate partnerships between men and between women were recorded and celebrated; they were situated in heroic legends and real-life friendships, seen as part of the culture of the gymnasium or of the court, and even led the way, according to some cultures, to philosophical and spiritual enlightenment. This suggested to many later observers, such as Wilde in his reading of the Bible, scholars translating Greek poets or

In the *Iliad* (composed *c.* 8th century BCE) Homer tells of the close friendship between Achilles and his companion Patroclus. The precise form of their relationship is not made explicit but, for later tradition, its very intensity signified that they were lovers. This cup by the Sosias Painter, made *c.* 500 BCE, shows Achilles binding Patroclus' wounds.

lesbians reading Sappho, that physical and emotional desires for those of the same sex were immanent and essential traits transcending time and culture. However, most historians now emphasize the fact that these basic yearnings have been expressed in various ways, including all sorts of affection and companionship, but also different types of sexual intercourse. Often those who have felt these passions have cohabited with partners, formed networks and cultures of sociability and solidarity, and occasionally engaged in political activism to promote or defend their sentiments.

In some societies same-sex behaviours and attitudes have been generally accepted, even honoured. In other times and places they have been considered reprobate, branded sinful and immoral; legislators have made same-sex acts illegal, while doctors have diagnosed and treated same-sex desires as illnesses. The wide range of sexual feelings – and different societies' reactions to the ways in which they are expressed – serves as a reminder of the inherently unstable nature of both sexuality and social mores.

The contemporary world reveals a panoply of same-sex behaviours, attitudes and identities. Most of the larger cities of Europe, the Americas and Australasia – from San Francisco to Paris, from Buenos Aires to Sydney – host a vibrant, affirmative and public same-sex culture, organized openly around bars, cafés and other commercial venues and concentrated in particular neighbourhoods. Voluntary associations bring together those who wish to mingle with others of similar orientation while they play sport, engage in cultural pursuits, worship or take part in political campaigns. In many European countries, and such nations as Canada, Australia, New Zealand and South Africa, same-sex acts have been decriminalized, while some local governments have passed laws prohibiting discrimination or vilification of those with same-sex preferences, even allowing them to register partnerships or to marry.

This overt sexual culture has spread to a more limited extent beyond Europe and European settler societies to cities such as Bangkok. Yet in these places, and especially outside countries where those of European heritage predominate, many men and women do not fit into the mould of such an identity and lifestyle, preferring to practise their sexuality in different (and often less public) fashions. Thus no less active same-sex cultures flourish elsewhere around the world, though without social and legal approbation, and generally without the public institutions now so common in the West. In India and Singapore, for instance, same-sex acts remain illegal, but gathering places, private circles of friends and sexual contacts, and quietly circulated literature provide opportunities for encounters and exchange. In other societies, including much of the Islamic world, institutionalized public life for those who share same-sex yearnings is notable by its absence: same-sex encounters (and indeed most sexual behaviour outside marriage) are relegated to clandestinity in the face of laws that invoke heavy penalties for deviance from officially condoned norms. In all of these countries women and men may commit sexual acts or harbour sexual feelings for those of the same sex without willingly setting themselves apart or articulating a specific identity. Finally, in a few locations across the globe same-sex acts may still be performed as part of

Although our knowledge of Sappho's life in Lesbos in the 6th century BCE remains scant, she has come to represent an ideal of love between women, with her fragmentary, lyrical poems that praise female beauty and celebrate the daily lives of her young companions. This watercolour of Sappho and fellow poet Erinna, painted around 1864 by Simeon Solomon, is evidence of the painter's own interest in themes of same-sex desire.

The biblical story of Sodom (Genesis 19), a city destroyed – along with three others – by brimstone and fire for its 'sin', is the most commonly cited justification for anti-homosexual sentiment. Although it has prompted centuries of persecution, the story's true meaning has been widely disputed. Mosaic of the 12th century from Monreale Cathedral, Sicily.

age-old rituals of initiation, beyond the parameters of the wider world's very notion of sexuality.

Many names have been ascribed to these acts and attitudes and to the people who adopt them. 'Sodomy' was a common term in Western countries, borrowed from a (probably misunderstood) reading of the biblical story of the cities of Sodom and Gomorrah, allegedly razed by God because of vice. The word was sometimes applied (and thus codified in legal statutes) to bestiality and even to such acts as fellatio and cunnilingus that took place between those of opposite sexes; the word has also been employed more narrowly for anal intercourse between males. Classical historical allusions offered another set of terms in the West: 'sapphism', in reference to the Greek poet of Lesbos, for the desire of women for other women, and 'Greek love' for its male counterpart. Such terms, and the religious and historical allusions they contain, of course had no purchase in cultures in which Judaeo-Christian and Classical traditions did not exist. Societies where Hinduism, Buddhism, Confucianism or animism prevailed had other words for, and different attitudes towards, same-sex engagement and sexuality in general. The pre-colonial Americas, Africa and Oceania maintained their own sexual codes and vocabularies, though the soldiers, missionaries and administrators of Europe's empires tried to stamp out heathen vice. Indeed, the imposition of Western and largely Christian sexual norms on colonized peoples represented one of the major ambitions of imperialists, from the Iberian conquistadors of South America to those who brought 'commerce and Christianity' to people whom they considered the benighted savages of primitive lands.

Meanwhile, through centuries of history, men and women continued to take part in 'sodomitical' or 'sapphic' behaviour and to profess desire and love for others of the same sex. The chapters presented here illustrate romantic attachments and carnal pleasures through the ages: the *paiderastia* of ancient Greece, the friendships of medieval monks, the multifaceted sexual world of Renaissance humanists, the *mignons* of Louis XIV's court, women who passed as men to emancipate themselves from social expectations, and the 'Ladies of Llangollen' in 18th-century Wales. Some paid a high price for their affections or actions. Male sodomites were arrested, tortured, imprisoned and burned at the stake if they became too indiscreet. If women were less often objects of persecution, such relative freedom may be explained by incredulity at the idea of lesbian love or sexual interest among the 'weaker sex' – a view accompanied, paradoxically, by a certain acceptance of female intimacy.

In the late 1860s a Hungarian doctor invented a Greco-Latin neologism – 'homosexuality' – that became a widely adopted appellation for same-sex behaviour. According to Michel Foucault, the act of naming contributed to the formation of a social category and an inherent identity. 'Sodomites' committed sodomitical acts; 'homosexuals' were seen, and increasingly saw themselves, as possessed of an inborn and perhaps immutable identity. The label of 'homosexuals' was not universally accepted, and 'inverts', 'Urnings' and 'Uranians' were proposed as alternatives, each suggesting a different aetiology of 'contrary' passions. Each language, in addition, had its slang terms: a homosexual was a *pédé* in French, *Schwul* in German, *frocio* in Italian, *maricón* in Spanish. Edward Carpenter wrote about 'homogenic' love, and Walt Whitman lauded the 'love of comrades'. For lesbians, there was talk of 'tribadism'. Some spoke of the 'third sex', isolating homosexuals as a different gender from men and women. Discussion about homosexuality – its cause and, for many, its possible cure – provided a subject for the emerging science of sexology in the publications of Karl Heinrich Ulrichs, Ambroise Tardieu, Magnus Hirschfeld and Sigmund Freud. All offered theories, based (so each argued) on incontrovertible scientific evidence, and homosexuals themselves, such as Carpenter, contributed their views. These new discussions prompted demands for law reform, and scandals – notably the trials of Oscar Wilde in 1895 – focused attention on homosexual life.

By the 1950s activists often spoke of 'homophiles', a term largely replaced by 'gay' or the more inclusive 'gay and lesbian' from the 1960s onwards. Terminology and sexual categories were then stretched further. 'Lesbigay', which achieved currency in America, added 'bisexuals' (another relatively new term), and transgender and transsexual individuals joined the abbreviation to form 'LBGTT'. 'Men who have sex with men' (MSM) came into use for males who did not identify as homosexual yet who engaged in homosexual sex. Meanwhile, 'women-focused women' or 'women-loving women' appeared as a comparable term. In the 1990s a new generation appropriated 'queer', a previously derogatory epithet, to cover all non-normative sexual individuals, groups and acts.

Each term corresponds to a particular moment in the history of Western sexuality and to a social perspective on sex between women and sex between men. 'Sodomy' alludes to a religious conception, especially the interdiction of same-sex behaviour by monotheistic religions. 'Homosexuality' was a product of 19th-century scientism, of the medicalization of sexuality, and of a new

„Friederike Schmidt" als Mann, nackt und als Frau in gewöhnlicher Tracht

European travellers to other parts of the world frequently expressed their shock at attitudes towards sexuality that conflicted so strongly with their own Judaeo-Christian notions of sexual sin. This woodcut, attributed to Utamaro, dates from around 1800; just sixty years later Western influences in Japan would begin to erode centuries of toleration.

emphasis on psychological make-up rather than the simple practice of 'unnatural' acts. 'Homophile', which semantically shifted the focus from sex to love, found favour with campaigners promoting tolerance and acceptance, and with those who sought the seamless integration of individuals with same-sex urges into wider society. 'Gay' and 'lesbian' were preferred by activists who, along with feminists, ethnic groups and other minorities, galvanized the new social movements from the 1960s onwards. 'Gay liberation' sometimes revelled in the difference between gay and 'straight' people, proclaimed 'gay pride' and, at least for the more radical, pursued 'lesbian separatism' or a revolutionary challenge to 'heterosexist' society. 'Queer', in turn, reflected the influence of postmodernist and anti-identitarian academic discourse (though 'queer' itself clearly constituted an identity), not unrelated to the opposition of many dissidents to the 'recuperation' of gay men and lesbians into mainstream society and its institutions.

Terminology reveals historical contexts, but words can also become a semantic morass. 'Gay and lesbian' (or variants in other languages), admittedly a culturally loaded and time-bound expression, has nevertheless achieved wide use in the West. It is worth emphasizing, however, that no single term encompasses the variety of same-sex attitudes and behaviours, even in a Western context, that have existed from antiquity to the present. Nor can one label capture fully the changing perspectives of those who felt emotional and sexual preferences for their own sex, and the ways in which society reacted. In Europe alone, the difference between sexual cultures in France, where homosexual acts were decriminalized in the 1790s, and Britain and Germany, where such acts remained illegal until well past 1945, is patent. Variations between sexual cultures in northern and southern Europe persisted until at least the 1970s, and in contemporary Europe there exists no homogeneity in homosexual life. Elsewhere in the world these differences are even more marked.

That 'homosexual' and 'gay' have achieved vernacular usage, and that the words have been widely translated and transliterated, indicates a certain globalization of sexual cultures that began long ago with imperial conquests. This phenomenon has accelerated thanks to long-distance travel and the chat rooms provided by the internet. Guidebooks provide long lists of gay and lesbian establishments around the world, and the music, drinks, clothes and interactions on offer do not surprise those who jet from Miami to Madrid or from Melbourne to Munich. Consumerism has done much to standardize lifestyles, but so too has a brand of activism that sees Western-style liberation and public affirmation as appropriate manifestations of sexual orientation. In the late 20th century AIDS, a medical problem most associated with a specific sexual group (although wrongly so), brought sexual behaviour to the forefront of general attention, dragging many 'closeted' individuals, practices and groups into the public gaze.

Few can now be unaware of sexual practices that, in the medieval formulation, were 'not to be named among Christians', and of groups that once dared not speak their names. Nevertheless, sexual globalization has not effaced differences around the globe, nor should it obscure variation in history. A historical approach can serve to relativize our ideas concerning attitudes and behaviour, as well as our conception of dominant sexual norms and values.

Sex and history

Reference to and the study of different times and places provide keys to an understanding of both sexuality and sexual attitudes and behaviour.[5] The ritualized practice of homosexual acts, for example as part of initiation ceremonies in New Guinea, was based on ancestral traditions. Acceptance of intersexual individuals, such as berdaches among Native Americans or *mahu* in Polynesia, was also based on time-honoured, if to Western eyes unconventional, sexual and social roles. Homosocial and homosexual practices in the Islamic world prolonged a sexual culture that predated Qur'anic injunctions against same-sex intercourse. Modern Japanese and Chinese literature alludes to the 'passions of the cut sleeve' and the warrior customs of a more ancient period. In the Western world, the Classical Romans discussed, copied or rejected Greek practices. During the long centuries in which Christianity provided the ruling Western ideology, men and women with 'perverse' urges looked back to antiquity for legitimation of damned desires and to derive comfort when undergoing tribulations in uncongenial environments. Even contemporary notions of egalitarian sexual partnerships between consenting adults hark back to the 19th-century ideals of Carpenter and Whitman.

Particularly in the 1800s – to stay with the European example – much of the theoretical articulation of homosexuality was historical. Christians with 'contrary' sentiments, despite that religion's prohibitions, particularly revered the biblical friendship between Jesus and John, his 'beloved disciple'. More frequently, historical antecedents were found in Greco-Roman culture, especially since the Classics still provided the common

The ambiguous relationship between Christ and St John – described four times in the Gospels as 'he whom Jesus loved' – has led writers such as Christopher Marlowe and Denis Diderot to the controversial conclusion that they were lovers. Their friendship was celebrated, particularly in the 19th century, by homosexuals seeking to legitimize their 'unorthodox' desires. Sculpture by an anonymous German artist, polychromed wood, *c.* 1320.

This image by Wilhelm von Gloeden (*c*. 1900), coyly described by the photographer as an 'evocation of a scene from ancient Greece', typifies the lure of the Mediterranean for those seeking an easier climate in which to indulge their sexual desires.

culture of educated men and – in so far as they were given access to education – of women. Students learned about Socratic love, at least when texts were not bowdlerized. Real or mythical partnerships – Zeus and Ganymede, Alexander and Bagoas, Hadrian and Antinous – served as icons for gay men searching for ancestors. Furthermore, men with homosexual desires journeyed to the Mediterranean, following in the footsteps of the 18th-century art historian Johann Winckelmann, who mixed appreciation for antiquities with appreciation of Italian youths. Their pilgrimages combined culture and sex, as they admired the ruins of Classical antiquity or gazed on Renaissance art while enjoying the pleasures of olive-skinned *ragazzi* whom they cast in the image of Classical gods. The seduction of the Mediterranean drew men to Rome, Florence and Venice, to Capri and Taormina, in a journey of intellectual and sexual discovery.[4]

Writers in particular looked at foreign societies for evidence of sexual variance. Magnus Hirschfeld edited a scholarly yearbook that published articles about distant places and sexual mores, and he went on a world tour to gather evidence about the 'intermediate sex'. Edward Carpenter wrote a study of sexual life among 'primitives', looking especially at homosexuality and the military tradition around the world; in India and Ceylon, he extolled the charms of native youths. Colonialism facilitated travel and sexual encounters with exotic others. Henry Morton Stanley subsumed his yearnings into a novel about an intimate friendship between a black African and an Arabic Zanzibari.

Like countless adventurers, soldiers and civil servants throughout the colonial period, T. E. Lawrence was to form several close, though presumably chaste, attachments to local young men. This is his photograph of Salim Ahmed (known as Dahoum), to whom he dedicated his masterpiece, the *Seven Pillars of Wisdom* (1935).

Gay and lesbian culture flourished during the Berlin of the Weimar Republic, where bars and clubs for gay and lesbian clients proliferated. These heady – and fleeting – years of pleasure were captured in the novels and memoirs of Christopher Isherwood, as well as by the crueller eye of artists such as Otto Dix and George Grosz. Here, Dix records the famous Eldorado cabaret at its height in 1927.

Lawrence of Arabia developed a passion for an Arab. André Gide wrote of sexual adventures in Algeria and Egypt. E. M. Forster fell in (unrequited) love with an Indian and had his most meaningful early sexual experience with an Egyptian. The American Charles Warren Stoddard's camp short stories related sexual opportunities in Polynesia, and his compatriot Frederic Prokosch wrote a novel plotting a homoerotic journey from the Levant to the Far East. The experiences, and the books in which they were recollected, passed from one generation of homosexuals to another, a veritable archive of sexual lore.[5]

Such engagement, whether in writing or in real life, was not limited to other times or distant places. In the wake of the Wilde scandal, homosexuals fled Britain for Paris, and in the interwar years (until Hitler took power) they joined Christopher Isherwood in Weimar Berlin. After the Second World War, cultural and sexual voyagers followed Paul Bowles to Tangier. In the heyday of gay liberation, men flocked to San Francisco and New York, while those with exotic tastes sought companionship in Bangkok or Manila. Such peregrinations were not limited to gay men. There was a small lesbian 'colony' in Capri at the end of the 19th century, and a circle of lesbians – Gertrude Stein, Alice B. Toklas, Natalie Clifford Barney, Agnes Goodsir – gathered in interwar Paris. Some women went further afield: the Frenchwoman Isabelle de Puygoudeau explored the Sahara, and the Swiss Annemarie Schwarzenbach wrote about lesbian love in Persia.

'Somewhere else', whether in the past or in the wider world, often seemed more hospitable to gay men and lesbians than home. Social scientists and travellers, not all of them homosexual, looked for sexual utopias overseas – a quest that led to the roseate view of Classical Athens held by 19th-century homosexual commentators, or, at a later date, the Samoa idealized by the sexually ambivalent Margaret Mead. Many also made heroes of sexual forebears, concentrating their efforts on outing famous figures and promoting a 'great homosexual man' and 'great lesbian' view of history, perhaps in a necessary

Many émigrés sought refuge in Paris, where homosexuality was celebrated among the artistic elite. Among the women attracted to the Parisian lesbian scene – which centred around the salons of such figures as Natalie Clifford Barney and Gertrude Stein – was the artist Agnes Goodsir, whose *Type of the Latin Quarter*, painted *c*. 1926, evokes the self-confidence and androgynous sophistication of these independent women.

process of affirmation in which a genealogy of homosexual morals was drawn up. If Michelangelo or Shakespeare was or could have been gay, or if Queen Christina or Aphra Behn might have been lesbian, latter-day descendants belonged to a noble family. This version of history has been perpetuated in works that list (sometimes spuriously) 'the greats' of the gay and lesbian past.

Most contemporary scholars have a rather more nuanced view of the complexities of sexual life, as well as of historical study. One of the major academic fields in gay and lesbian studies, though with a lengthier record of publications on gay male than lesbian themes, is history. Jonathan Ned Katz's compilation of documents on American gay history, published in 1976, showed the wealth of material buried in the archives and revealed the homosexual history of a country that championed its puritan virtues.[6] Sir Kenneth Dover's study of ancient Greek homosexuality and John Boswell's volume on Christianity and homosexuality, published in 1978 and 1980 respectively, pioneered scholarship, in the one case challenging a centuries-long effort to efface *paiderastia* as a vital aspect of Greek society, and in the other opening a hotly contested debate about the homophobia of Christianity.[7] Alan Bray's study of Renaissance England recovered from oblivion the cults of friendship and homoeroticism in the early modern world.[8] A ground-breaking work by Lillian Faderman explored romantic friendship and love between women.[9] Since the early 1980s gay and lesbian history has expanded so rapidly that shelves bend under the accumulation of books and articles. Several of them, from Michael Rocke's volume on Renaissance Florence to George Chauncey's work on early 20th-century New York, have been hailed as major contributions not just to the history of sexuality but to history in general.[10] More recently, a scholar such as Louis Crompton has masterfully essayed a broad-ranging interpretation of homosexuality and civilization.[11] References in the present volume testify to the outpouring of scholarship over the past quarter-century.

Gay and lesbian history has pursued many paths: examining the social environments of homosexuality; charting the evolution of *mentalités*; deconstructing representations of attitudes and behaviours; exploring sexualities in societies from pre-Columbian America to post-colonial Asia. The theories of Marx, Freud, Kinsey, Foucault and other social scientists have been applied to the past. The methodologies of gay and lesbian history have been scrutinized.[12] New topics have been explored, including not just *sex* between men or women, but *love*, a curiously neglected aspect of gay and lesbian history on which Jonathan Ned Katz and Martha Vicinus have refocused.[13]

The essays presented here synthesize this burgeoning research, providing original perspectives on sexual cultures in particular times and places, and suggesting the authors' own interpretations and conclusions. Diversity in approach reflects diversity in the situations about which authors write. Human cultures are numberless, and brief chapters cannot provide comprehensive treatments, but this book nevertheless gives overviews of Europe, the Americas, the Islamic world, Asia, Africa and Oceania. Archival records, memoirs, creative literature and artworks are pieced together to form a variegated picture of lust, love, desire and the social reactions they provoked.

Homosexuality in the Antipodes

One way of introducing a global study of homosexuality is to look at a country in which different sexual traditions have intertwined: Australia. Aborigines comprise one of the world's oldest continuously extant societies, and for millennia their culture lay beyond the major developments in Europe, Asia and the Americas. Since 1788, when the British colonized Botany Bay, Australia has received waves of migration. In the 19th and early 20th centuries Anglo-Celts formed the majority, but there were also Chinese working in the goldfields and Melanesian indentured labourers in the cane fields, while a host of people arrived from many other horizons. After the Second World War, Australia sought migrants from Continental Europe, and Scandinavians, Italians, Maltese and Yugoslavs took passage to the Antipodes. In the 1970s, with the end of the 'white Australia' policy that restricted non-Europeans, the field widened further to include Turks, Lebanese and migrants from throughout Asia. Australia's cities grew more cosmopolitan (nearly one-third of Sydneysiders were born overseas), and a policy of multiculturalism encouraged new settlers to retain their traditions and beliefs at the same time as becoming 'true' Australians. The nation has not always proved a migrant paradise, and Aborigines and those from non-English-speaking backgrounds remain disadvantaged. However, Australia displays a mosaic of cultural groups and sexual cultures.

Relatively little has been written about pre-contact Aboriginal sexuality, with early ethnological accounts constrained by disapproval of 'abnormality', writers' discomfort with taboo subjects, the multiplicity of Aboriginal societies and the secret nature of many customs. However, one present-day Aboriginal lesbian wittily rejects the charge that homosexuality was an import: 'I get that all the time … As far as I know, homosexuality has existed here for a long time, it's not a white man's disease – it's probably the only thing we didn't catch off the white man!' Anthropologists concur that homoerotic behaviours existed in pre-contact Australia, from ritualized mutual masturbation among males to the taking of 'boy-wives' – intergenerational homosexual relations with communal domestic arrangements. Evidence for oral, anal and interfemoral homosexual practices between men has been located, and there are indications of lesbian behaviour as well.[14]

When Britain began to settle eastern Australia in the 1780s, its primary aim was the establishment of penal colonies, a moralizing vision that aimed to rid the British body politic of undesirables and to effect their moral regeneration for imperialistic purposes. Transported prisoners constituted the bulk of the population in the first decades of colonial history. British laws in the early 1800s, which allowed capital punishment for sodomy if penetration and seminal emission could be proved, were applicable, and the colonies adopted their own legislation that made sex between men (although generally not between women) criminal. By the time the colonies federated into the Commonwealth of Australia in 1901, laws made it possible for men to be arrested for oral or anal sex, attempted sexual acts, solicitation or other morals offences.[15]

The first homosexual trial in the colonies, which was heard in 1796, resulted in acquittal, but other offenders were not so lucky: during the course

The harsh, homosocial environments of frontier posts in western America and in Australia – such as this sheep station in the outback, painted by Tom Roberts between 1888 and 1890 – facilitated close bonds of friendship and occasional 'situational' homosexuality.

of the 19th century twenty men were executed for homosexual offences, the last in Tasmania in 1863. From 1796 to 1901 there were 439 arrests relating to homosexuality in New South Wales alone. Many brought to court in the earlier decades were former convicts, men from the 'lower orders' arrested for having sex in a public or quasi-public place. In a few cases coercion was clearly involved, but most seemed to have been consensual encounters. One man in Western Australia explained that 'I can't help it. It's a disease. I prefer a man or a boy any time to a woman' – an acceptance of homosexuality as a pathology, but also a forthright avowal of his preference.

Despite laws, arrests and the anti-homosexual ethos of Christianity, various homosexual cultures emerged. Segregation of convicts in barracks and the overwhelming predominance of men over women among Europeans in the early period of colonization led to much 'situational' homosexuality. Moralists thundered that sodomy was endemic in Australian penal colonies,[16] the Roman Catholic bishop of Sydney alleging in 1837 that two-thirds of prisoners on Norfolk Island engaged in the vice. Indeed, the supposed prevalence of homosexual acts provided an argument in favour of ending transportation and the 'unnatural' situations in which perversion thrived.

Transportation of prisoners wound down in eastern Australia from the 1840s (although it was not halted in Western Australia until 1868). Increasingly free immigrants arrived, tempted by the growth of Sydney and Melbourne, the prosperity of sheep-raising pastoralism, the 1850s gold rushes, and the pushing of the European frontier further into the outback. Many were young, and homosexual behaviour, it is thought, was not uncommon among pioneers who lacked female companionship. The idea of mateship – close friendship, unfailing loyalty and intimate social relations – promoted a homoerotic and homosocial culture among working-class men even if, in principle, sex was excluded. Mixing and mingling in pubs, boarding houses and public baths nevertheless afforded temptations.

The story of the notorious bushranger
Captain Moonlight (Andrew George Scott, left) and his close companion James Nesbit – whom he had met in prison – reveals that same-sex relationships in Australia were not the preserve of an educated elited. In 1879, while he was waiting to be hanged, Moonlight wrote several passionate letters describing his love for Nesbit and expressing his wish that they should be buried together.

Nonconformist sexual behaviour and long-lasting partnerships existed at all levels of society. One instance is the story of the bushranger Captain Moonlight – a Robin Hood outlaw vilified and heroized in Australian lore. The son of an English vicar, Andrew George Scott (as he was christened) aspired to become an engineer. He reputedly fought with Garibaldi's redshirts in the Italian Risorgimento, with the British in the Maori Wars in New Zealand, and with the Union Army in Civil War America before landing in Australia in 1867. Initially received in the best society through forged letters of introduction, two years later Scott was implicated in a bank robbery. While in prison he met James Nesbit; the two became fast friends, a relationship that continued, after their release, with complicity in crime. When Nesbit was shot in 1879, a distraught Scott penned letters about 'my own dearest friend': 'We were one in heart and soul, he died in my arms and I long to join him where there shall be no more parting.' Scott's wish that they be buried in a common tomb under an inscription to 'two friends reunited in death' went unfulfilled when Moonlight was hanged.[17]

At the other end of the social spectrum were Robert Herbert and John Bramston, educated at elite English public schools and at Oxford and admitted to the bar in London. They were life-long soulmates (only one eventually married) in Britain and Australia, where Herbert became the first premier of Queensland and Bramston served as a minister. The two gentlemen, who had already shared rooms in London, combined their surnames into 'Herston' for their Brisbane property. Further south, in Sydney, a turn-of-the-century governor, Lord Beauchamp, publicly praised young Australian manhood, enthusing over 'splendid athletes, like the old Greek statues … The life-savers at the bathing beaches are wonderful.' (In the 1930s his wife sued for divorce, threatening to reveal his homosexuality.)

By the 1890s, the embryo of an animated, if clandestine, homosexual culture existed in Australia's premier city. Oxford Street, still today the hub of

Sydney's gay ghetto, was its centre, a boulevard where shoppers at the new department stores – whose shop assistants earned a reputation as dandies – mixed with soldiers from the Victoria Barracks, the ne'er-do-wells who hung around the Darlinghurst Gaol, Italians and Chinese from nearby ethnic neighbourhoods, and loiterers in Hyde Park. Pubs, parks and Mr Wigzel's Turkish baths provided venues for social connection.[18]

The history of lesbians is less well documented than that of homosexual men. Since women were not subject to arrest for lesbian activities, court records – a key source of information about men – are lacking. Some sexually transgressive women did come to public attention when they dressed as men – figures such as Ellen Tremaye, who cross-dressed for much of her life and lived with women lovers. Convict days saw much concern about women consorting in female 'factories' (workhouses) where they were confined. Letters and poems evidence the affections of women. Mary Eliza Fullerton, for instance, penned a sonnet in 1909 to the 'heart of my heart' – Mabel Singleton, the long-term companion with whom she moved to Britain. Lesbia Harford wished in one of her verses: 'Would that I were Sappho, Greece my land, not this!'[19]

In the early 20th century homosexual dalliances continued to fuel rumour, and newspapers featured the scandalous news of arrests, sometimes following police entrapment, of men who solicited or had sex in public toilets, parks or other cruising sites that Australians call 'beats'. Those apprehended ranged from itinerants to pillars of society: in the interwar years, the *Melbourne Truth* reported the arrests of a labourer, an Indian hawker, a police sergeant, a schoolmaster and a doctor. In 1937 a Brisbane baronet and his accomplices were arraigned as organizers of 'a club of jaded businessmen who liked to play around in the nude' after they had allegedly abducted a young man for 'evil' purposes, while the author of a 1932 book on sexuality was himself repeatedly arrested for indecency. Those brought to court generally pleaded that they had been entrapped or unwillingly seduced, or that they had committed homosexual offences under the effects of alcohol. A few in the early 1900s bravely affirmed their homosexual identity.

The Second World War helped loosen morals for both homosexuals and heterosexuals. Post-war consumer society, especially the wider availability of apartments and automobiles, increased mobility and privacy. Not all could feel at home, however, in a place where a police chief could state that homosexuality and Communism were the greatest perils facing the country. Most gay men and lesbians remained closeted; some fled overseas.[20] A handful dared to flaunt their homosexuality, facing social disapprobation and imprisonment. By the 1950s there were regular 'gay balls' in Sydney and in other cities. Busy beats attracted men for sex, particular pubs and cafés developed notoriety as meeting places, and 'artistic' gay men congregated in circles of theatre-goers and music lovers. Homosexuality occasionally surfaced in novels and public debates, as well as in scandals that attended unwanted revelations.

The new militancy of the 1960s, however, prompted demonstrations in Europe and America, with the New Left proclaiming its revolutionary message and new social movements to champion the concerns of women, ethnic minorities and sexual dissidents. Although campaigns for gay emancipation had existed elsewhere for decades, Australia lacked an equivalent to Magnus Hirschfeld's 1890s 'scientific-humanitarian' committee or post-1945 organizations such as the Campaign for Homosexual Equality in Britain. It was the Stonewall rebellion in New York in 1969 that provided a touchstone, and in the following years a gay political movement hit the streets with demonstrations, newspapers and public lobbying for decriminalization of homosexual acts.

In 1970 Australia gained its own gay and lesbian movement: the Campaign Against Moral Persecution, or CAMP Inc. – the name a pun on the notion of specifically gay, 'camp' behaviour. This inaugurated out-and-proud advocacy through petitions, marches and publicity. A political scientist from Sydney, Dennis Altman, in 1971 published *Homosexual: Oppression and Liberation*, a pioneering work of gay theory.[21] The following year a homosexual law lecturer, George Duncan, drowned at a gay beat in Adelaide, provoking speculation that he had been killed in an episode of 'poofter-bashing'; his death provided further impetus to the new gay activism. In 1978 Sydney saw its first parade of musclemen, transvestites, dykes and political militants, who marched through the city until confronted by police – the first instalment of the Gay and Lesbian Mardi Gras that would become a major event in Australia's social calendar.[22]

Despite continued conservative disapproval of homosexuality, gay organizations, publications and social venues flourished in the 1970s and 1980s. In Sydney, Ruby Red's catered for lesbians, mustachioed clones danced at the Midnight Shift, leathermen headed for The Ox, dance queens gathered at Patch's disco, and men looking for Asian partners went to Flo's Palace. Others headed straight for saunas – the classically named Roman Baths and the rather euphemistically signposted Ken's Karate Klub. Many ended their night out in the dim recesses of Club 80 or the back passages of Numbers bookshop. By day, gay men and lesbians proclaimed gay pride, formed political collectives, rallied outside Parliament House and distributed copies of *Campaign*, *Lesbians on the Loose* or *Gay Information*. These years witnessed an era of sexual liberation that seemed to many a long party and an endless round of pleasures, even after the first reports of a mysterious disease affecting homosexuals in America.

AIDS wreaked disaster in Australia, each issue of the gay weeklies filled with obituaries, while the mainstream press endlessly discussed the causes and treatment of the disease. Sensationalist reports spread rumours about the supposed ways that AIDS might be caught, and fear and mourning gripped the gay community. Paradoxically, the medical crisis helped establish a new visibility for homosexuals, who set up AIDS councils, treatment centres and support groups. Explicit safe-sex education campaigns proved remarkably successful in altering dangerous behaviour. Gay men thus became effective partners of the government and of medical practitioners. In addition to bringing together homosexuals and heterosexuals, AIDS helped to build bridges between gay men and lesbians, who volunteered to care for the sick and who demanded greater government commitment to research and medical

An early Gay Pride demonstration in Adelaide, 1973. Although gay liberation movements had taken hold in many countries in the early 1970s, the cause in Australia was given added impetus by the suspicious death in 1972 of George Duncan, a gay academic widely believed to have been murdered by the police. The inquest into his death challenged society's attitudes to homosexuality and prompted the South Australian parliament to decriminalize homosexual acts.

provisions.[25] Ironically, as the AIDS crisis intensified, New South Wales decriminalized homosexual acts in 1984, following a precedent set by South Australia. Other states and territories followed suit (Tasmania as late as 1997).

To many visitors of the Sydney Mardi Gras — which draws hundreds of thousands of spectators to the main parade and tens of thousands to an all-night party — gay and lesbian life in Australia seems a model for a legalized, open and fun-loving culture. Gay men and lesbians play a prominent role in public life: one of the seven justices of the Australian High Court, Michael Kirby, is a much-respected gay man; and the head of the Australian Greens political party, Senator Bob Brown, is openly gay. So is award-winning novelist David Malouf, and the former president of the Australian Medical Association, Kerryn Phelps, is lesbian. Laws in most states protect homosexuals from discrimination and provide penalties for vilification. Gay and lesbian newspapers advertise countless social, political and religious groups, and Sydney has hosted the Gay Games.

Not all is sunny in Oz, however. Some homosexuals suffer from isolation in country towns and the outback. Many 'men who have sex with men' search out sexual encounters far from the established scene because of fear, embarrassment, sexual ambivalence or discomfort with a homosexual identity. Not all lesbians and gay men feel at ease with the prosperous, youth-dominated lifestyle portrayed in glossy magazines. Aboriginal Australians and those from certain other ethnic backgrounds find it difficult to balance ancestral demands

Gay Pride today: the Dykes on Bikes celebrate their sexuality in exuberant fashion as part of Sydney's famous Mardi Gras.

with those of urban gay and lesbian cultures, although Asian gay culture in particular is vibrant in Australia. Public authorities are not wholly supportive: the Archbishop of Sydney refuses to give Communion to open homosexuals; the ageing head of the fundamentalist Festival of Light is regularly wheeled out to lambast the Mardi Gras; and the conservative Australian prime minister, unlike many other political leaders, refuses to send a message of support to the celebrations. Activists complain that the event has lost its edge and that many gays prefer middle-class respectability to social contestation. Sexually transmitted diseases and unsafe sex are on the rise, alcohol and drug abuse remains a problem, and cases of anti-homosexual violence still occur. The major political parties oppose gay marriage or registered partnerships, while homosexuals wishing to adopt children or to bring partners from overseas face formidable bureaucratic and legal challenges.

History and the gay and lesbian future

The gay history of Australia reveals many traits visible in other societies, past and present. It shows the different constructions of same-sex behaviour and the variety of attitudes that have existed throughout history, many of which persist today. Some people have engaged in 'situational' homosexuality; others are 'men who have sex with men' (or the female equivalent); yet others think of themselves as homosexual, or gay, or queer. For some, homosexuality has been diagnosed as a disease or damned as a sin. Others see it as inborn, and scientists have recently searched for a gay gene. Men and women who have desired each other have found places to meet and ways to socialize, negotiating their cultural heritages while creating new identities.

Australia's gay life shows how different sexual traditions have intermeshed in the modern world thanks to migration, the spread of gay liberation and its derivative movements, and globalization. There were centuries-old homosexual practices among Aborigines. Lustful men engaged in backstreet sodomy in colonial society, or sought companionship with mates in suburban pubs or remote sheep stations. Classical allusions appeared in the Antipodes when Governor Beauchamp saw lifesavers as Greek gods or Lesbia Harford invoked Sappho. There were the intimate and enduring friendships of Robert Herbert and John Bramston, and of Maria Fullerton and Mabel Singleton. Later came the in-your-face affirmative gay pride of activists. The varying attitudes of Asians, Mediterraneans and other members of a multicultural society have all contributed to the cultural and sexual crucible. The AIDS crisis provoked a reassessment of homosexuality. Australia shows the tensions between minorities and the mainstream, it reveals the metamorphosis of attitudes about sexuality, and it demonstrates how homosexuality provides a lens through which to view the evolution of institutions and attitudes.

Around the gay world and through its history

The remaining thirteen chapters of this book traverse time and space. The first five look at same-sex intimacy, primarily in Europe, in the centuries before the invention of the word 'homosexuality'. Charles Hupperts discusses the Classical world of Greece and Rome, source of some of the longest-lived references for homosexuals, and in the case of Greece, the society in which same-sex relations were most accepted before the present day. Bernd-Ulrich Hergemöller then takes us through the Middle Ages, a time when Christian interdiction of homosexual relations – and the persecution of sodomites that it mandated – coexisted with a cult of intimate friendship. Helmut Puff examines the Europe of the Renaissance and Reformation, not just the homosocial cultures of humanist Italy, but also the daily life of 'sodomites' in central and northern Europe. Michael Sibalis asks to what extent religious, political and legal views about their behaviour changed with the philosophy of the Enlightenment and the upheaveal of the French Revolution. Laura Gowing provides a survey of women-loving women in early modern Europe, how they articulated desires through friendship, 'passing' and eroticism, and the ways in which broader society tolerated or inhibited their sexuality. In the following chapter Brett Genny Beemyn brings together different continents, diverse civilizations and almost three centuries of history to look at the Americas.

Florence Tamagne examines the 'homosexual age' over the seventy years following the first use of the word 'homosexuality' in around 1870, including the milieux of Marcel Proust and Radclyffe Hall; gay Paris, not-so-prim London and naughty Berlin; the first homosexual emancipation movements; and the gay 'holocaust'. Domenico Rizzo picks up the pieces of this homosexual world in the wake of the Second World War, looking at the relationship between private life and the public sphere, and tracing the metamorphosis of activism from homophile movements of the 1950s, through gay liberation in the 1970s, to the activism made necessary by the AIDS epidemic in the 1980s and afterwards. Leila Rupp then focuses on lesbian experiences of social life, politics and culture in the modern world, providing an investigation of what it was to be a lesbian in the 19th and 20th centuries.

The next section of the book is devoted to different traditions of sexual culture. Lee Wallace inquires into how Europeans 'discovered' varying sexual attitudes and behaviours as they explored and conquered the Americas, sub-Saharan Africa and Oceania. Vincenzo Patanè examines homosexuality in the Islamic societies of North Africa and the Middle East, from practices pre-dating the Qur'an to contemporary manifestations of gay identity. Adrian Carton turns his attention to three great civilizations of Asia – China, Japan and India – and the culture of same-sex experiences in Taoism and Confucianism, Buddhism and Shintoism, Hinduism and Jainism. Finally, Gert Hekma brings us up to date with an investigation of changes in gay and lesbian life since the 1980s under the impact of AIDS, globalization, the questioning of sexual identities and new political struggles.

These chapters lay out the panoply of the various behaviours, identities and lives of those with same-sex desires. They give the lie to any assumption that such desires are aberrations in human history, or that there is a universal set of 'natural' sexual mores from which they depart. They explore the ways in which same-sex sexuality has been conjugated in different historical and cultural circumstances. They provide a reminder of the violence committed against those with 'abnormal' orientations – sodomites burned at the stake in the Middle Ages, those sent to the concentration camps of Nazi Germany, and those decapitated under present-day fundamentalist regimes. They warn of the dangers of imposing any one group's model of sexual normality on disparate populations, whether on the basis of religious precepts, the perceived verities of nature, medical diagnoses or vaguely articulated 'family values'. They show, too, the forms through which men and women have represented same-sex eroticism in art and literature, how they have created webs of social and sexual connections, and how they have continued to invent new types of pleasure. From Theocritus' verses to episodes of *Queer as Folk*, from the symposium at which Socrates spoke about love to the internet sites where men and women chat about sex, the story of homosexuality spans human history. From the eroticism of the Islamic *hammam* to the 'great mirror of male love' in Tokugawa Japan, and from the berdaches of North America to the boy-wives of Aboriginal Australia, here are illustrated both the essential commonality of love and lust, and the variegated ways in which such desires have been constructed through the ages.

Homosexuality in Greece and Rome
CHARLES HUPPERTS

Greece
Themes and sources

It is a precarious undertaking to attempt to describe the sexuality of a people who lived almost 3,000 years ago, and it would be delusory to pretend that we are in a position to grasp fully the significance accorded to sexual experiences by people who had an altogether different cultural and social background from our own today. To begin with, we must bear in mind that ancient Greece was not the unified political entity that exists today. Its cities were independent states with their own governments, and laws and customs could vary greatly from place to place. The greater part of this discussion will be restricted to Athens, since the majority of sources from Greek antiquity concentrate on life in this city. Furthermore, we shall focus principally on a particular period in the history of Athens, namely the 6th to the 4th centuries BCE.

Investigations into homosexual behaviour in the past are always dependent on the manner in which particular contemporary groups or individuals conceptualized and discussed the practice. Such representations of homosexuality could assume various forms, depending on the medium in which they appeared. In Greece, for example, the speeches made during trials in which people were indicted for their sexual behaviour provide strongly moralistic representations of homosexuality that are necessarily legal in tone. Then there were the comedies of Aristophanes, which were intended to amuse ordinary Athenian theatre audiences. There were also philosophical discourses, with their keenly didactive moralizing nature. Erotic poems were recited during parties, and scenes depicted on Greek vases, objects of everyday use, are also a very important source on the homosexual behaviour of the contemporary public. By means of signs and symbols, recognizable to many contemporaries, these vase-paintings tell us something about the Greeks' sexual desires, actions and norms. Finally, we also have at our disposal medical texts by physicians who attempted to understand the biological dimensions of sexuality.

Myths as mirrors

The Greeks imagined their gods anthropomorphically. This meant that the gods were vulnerable to powerful sexual desires and passions just like their human counterparts. In this respect, Greek mythology functioned as a mirror

Homosexuality was an integral part of both Greek and Roman culture, provoking little comment. This Roman silver goblet from *c.* 50 CE – the so-called Warren Cup – shows an intimate moment between a man and a youth in an appropriately Hellenized interior. Erotic scenes in Roman art are largely distinguished by their domestic setting and illustrate sex as an unremarkable aspect of everyday life.

The myth of Zeus' abduction of the young Ganymede to be his cupbearer illustrated to ancient Greeks how even the gods were susceptible to the attractions of beautiful young men. Zeus – here in human form, although later artists would represent him as an eagle – strides forward purposefully with the boy tucked under his arm. Ganymede holds a cockerel, a traditional love-gift from an older suitor. Painted terracotta group from Olympia, *c.* 470 BCE.

upon which Greek men could project their sexual desires and wherein they could recognize themselves. The Greeks were familiar with many tales in which gods, especially Zeus, engaged in extramarital affairs, demonstrated promiscuous behaviour or pursued homosexual relationships. One of these myths relates how Zeus became enamoured of Ganymede, a prince of Troy, who was regarded in his time as the fairest of all young men. Zeus transformed himself into an eagle and took the youth with him to Olympus. Here, to the outrage of Hera, Zeus' wife, Ganymede shared his master's bed each night and spent the day pouring his wine. All the other gods (except for Ares, the god of war) also fell in love with young men. The story of Apollo's tragic love for Hyacinth is well known. The West Wind was also deeply enamoured of this Spartan prince and seethed with jealousy over the attentions bestowed upon the Sun God by Hyacinth. One day, while Apollo and Hyacinth were throwing discus, the West Wind contrived to make Apollo's throw alter its course and strike the youth in the head. The discus killed Hyacinth, and from his blood sprang the flower that was to bear his name. Myths such as those concerning Ganymede and Hyacinth were to inspire many artists, particularly from the Renaissance onwards.

Greek mythology also contained numerous stories about heroes and demigods who pursued youths, such as Hercules, Laïus, Orpheus, Minos, Tantalus and Meleager. The best known of these myths concerned the friendship between Achilles and Patroclus, two Greek heroes who participated in the Trojan War. The poet Homer made Achilles – an invincible, merciless hero and son of a goddess – the protagonist in his epic the *Iliad*. While Homer never describes the friendship between Achilles and Patroclus explicitly in homoerotic terms, there are nonetheless scenes that demonstrate the intensity of their relationship. When Patroclus is killed, for instance, the inconsolable Achilles – crying on the beach – is visited by his friend's ghost, which asks him to arrange for their ashes to be placed together in one urn so that they will be united in death for eternity. From the 5th century BCE, this friendship between Achilles and Patroclus was explained by the Greeks themselves in homosexual terms, and their relationship was regarded by many Greeks as the template for ideal friendship. Achilles was viewed as someone who remained ever faithful to his companion and thereby sacrificed himself, knowing that in avenging his friend's death he would speed the end of his own life.

A Panhellenic phenomenon

The sources clearly suggest that homosexuality and homoerotica were prevalent throughout the Greek world, but not always in the same fashion. For example, there were Greeks who believed that pederasty was first practised on the island of Crete. According to this belief it was not Zeus but rather the legendary king Minos of Crete who had preyed upon Ganymede. Through a historian from the 4th century BCE, we know of a report documenting an intriguing Cretan initiation ritual. Whenever a man wanted to initiate a youth, so we are told, he was expected to 'kidnap' him. The youth was presented with gifts and, accompanied by friends of the 'kidnapper', was taken to a random location in the countryside. After two months the party returned to the city. Thereafter the youth was released and received more expensive gifts, including a soldier's kit, an ox and a beaker. The ox was sacrificed by the boy to Zeus, and at the subsequent feast the youth made it known how his lover had conducted himself: it was, for instance, forbidden for the man to use force in the course of his seduction. It was considered a distinction for youths to be 'kidnapped': it earned them esteem, they received honorary places at dances and races, and they wore a special costume that differentiated them from others. The ritual was not an initiation that brought youths into the world of adult men so much as an induction into an elite group. However, it is noticeable that nothing is said of particular forms of sexuality; in other cultures anal penetration was normally a very important aspect of initiation, whereby the adult man passed on his power to his younger counterpart.

In Sparta, another Doric community like Crete, homosexuality was closely linked to the vigorously militaristic character of the state. Spartan society was organized along the lines of an army in perpetual training. Males left their families at the age of seven and as adults lived separately from their wives in tents and barracks. Husbands, so we are told, secretly visited their spouses, spending brief periods with them before returning to bunk with their friends. Homosexual friendships were frequent and were even encouraged. The Greek verb *lakonizein* means 'to do it the Spartan way', with the connotation of penetrating a youth. A relationship between a mature soldier and a young recruit was also seen as an ideal breeding-ground for the development of the younger man. It must not have been uncommon for the lover and his beloved to stand beside one another on the battlefield. We are told by Xenophon and Plutarch (among others) that in the 4th century BCE the city of Thebes, to the north of Athens, hosted a special military unit of three hundred men, the so-called Sacred Band, that was completely comprised of amorous couples. The close friendship and mutual sense of honour before their partners ensured that the lovers would not abandon each other. The division remained undefeatable for years until 338 BCE, when Philip II of Macedon, the father of Alexander the Great, routed the company and all its men were killed.

Inscriptions on rocks near a shrine devoted to the god Apollo, most probably dating from the 7th or 6th century BCE, have been discovered on the island of Thera (modern Santorini) not far from Crete. The inscriptions mostly refer to a single boy's name, with the addition of words such as 'good', 'excellent' and 'beautiful'. Anal contact between two men is mentioned five times. It is highly improbable that these texts had a sacred meaning, since sexual acts in sacred places were forbidden. Similar inscriptions dating from the 4th century BCE have been found on the island of Thasos, around 35 metres (115 feet) from the beach in the bay of Kalami. It is likely that such locations functioned as cruising places for homosexuals seeking contact with one another or that they were used by prostitutes.

This lion, restored in modern times from ancient fragments, commemorates the site of the battle of Chaeronea in Boeotia (338 BCE). According to several ancient authors, this is where the so-called Sacred Band – formed exclusively of homosexual couples from the city of Thebes – fought alongside other Greek forces until they were overcome by Philip II of Macedon.

Many other cities and islands are mentioned in the sources in connection with homosexuality. Poets who composed homoerotic verses, for instance, came from the island of Samos (where Anacreon lived) and from the cities of Megara (Theognis), Thebes (Pindar) and Rhegium in southern Italy (Ibycus). Apart from in Athens, vases bearing homoerotic imagery were also made in Corinth and Thebes. Other sources indicate that homosexuality was practised in Elis, Chalkis and Sicily as well.

Athens, city of masculine eroticism

The social structure of ancient Athens differed significantly from that of its present-day counterpart. The city was a commune to which male citizens were central and in whose hands power was concentrated. Husbands and wives in many respects lived separate lives. Women spent most of their time indoors, while their husbands frequently lived much of their lives outside. Public and cultural life in Athens was a man's affair, and men had everything well organized for themselves. Many sundry aspects of daily life in the city were geared towards the satisfaction of its male citizens' desires. This means, among other things, that sources on (homo)sexuality in Classical Athens were almost exclusively authored by men and were also destined to be read by men. Our information is therefore very limited and coloured by ideology.

Sex was not regarded as functioning exclusively for propagation and the continuation of the family, but also for pleasure and enjoyment. Sexual gratification in itself was not viewed as something wicked, dirty or forbidden. Greek consciousness had not yet come into contact with Christian morality, in which physicality and sexuality would be associated not only with marriage, but also with shame, abstinence, sin and punishment. The nude male body was ubiquitous in Athenian culture. All over the city there were images that emphasized and glorified the beauty of the male form. Statues of the god Hermes with a large phallus, the so-called 'herms', stood at the city's crossroads; they were credited with apotropaic qualities and were believed to ward off evil. Athenians were obsessed with fitness, sport and bathing. The focus on the body in Athenian culture usually involved nakedness, especially in such places as the gymnasium, a sporting venue that was not accessible to women. Men appeared not to be affected by shyness and prudery; indeed, they were comfortable about watching sexual acts. On all kinds of everyday items, such as drinking cups and oil lamps, erotic scenes were depicted very explicitly. The impression, therefore, is that sex was not always seen as a private matter, something that one should be ashamed of. On the contrary, sex was something that one shared with friends and did in company. During symposia – private parties where wine flowed in abundance – prostitutes of both sexes were engaged. The woman of the house remained upstairs in her rooms with her children and slaves, while her husband enjoyed sex and alcohol with his friends. Sexuality was omnipresent in the world of Athenian men, in their thoughts, activities and conversations.

Athenians viewed the love of a man for a girl or woman as something not altogether different from love for a boy or a man. These were two forms of sexual desire (*eros*), either of which could be more appropriate for particular individuals at certain junctures in their life. Few Greeks took the view that the man who loved a boy had a different nature from the heterosexual man. In the course of an Athenian's life, both forms of sexuality could appear together or in succession. The Greek language had not established separate terms for 'heterosexuality' and 'homosexuality', and so the question of sexual identity was not a pressing concern. There is no mention in the evidence of any discrimination or of a subculture, and there is no sense of 'coming out'.

What does appear to have been of great importance was the role that one assumed during the sexual act. Simply stated, a man was expected to behave like a man. He was expected to be in control and ought not to allow himself to be dominated. The man must be the penetrator, whether it be vaginal, anal, oral or intercrural (between the thighs). All sorts of positive qualities were

In 514 BCE the lovers Harmodius and Aristogeiton attacked the tyrannical dynasty then ruling Athens. Although the motive for the attack was amorous rather than political, the couple were credited with the dynasty's downfall and commemorated by statues in the marketplace – evidence of the special place accorded to homoerotic devotion and civic duty in Athenian political life. Roman marble copy after an original bronze by Kritios and Nesiotes, 477 BCE.

associated with this role, such as masculinity, courage, belligerence, virility, intelligence and reliability. Those who allowed themselves to be penetrated, women and men alike, were thought to be weak, servile, cowardly, submissive, fickle, gullible, insatiable and untrustworthy. This sharp dichotomy, which functioned as an ideology of machismo, was created by men themselves and did not, of course, correspond to reality. It should be seen as a defensive posture of men against their own insecurities about sexuality, gender identity and impotency. Athenian men hoped that women would be incapable of seeing through these constructions and would continue to be impressed by their sexual prowess. Besides, men used these expressions of sexual ideology to convince themselves of their own superiority and thereby hoped to approximate the gods.

Pederasty in Athens

Male homosexuality was central to Athenian culture. A homosexual friendship usually took the form of a pederastic relationship. The junior partner – the beloved, or *eromenos* – was normally between twelve and eighteen years old. Sources indicate that as soon as the youth developed a beard the relationship usually ended, since he became less attractive in the eyes of adult men. The lover – the *erastes* – was traditionally an adult man or a young man with a light down on his cheeks who expressed an erotic interest in a younger counterpart. The lover was expected to take the initiative and to pursue the beloved rather than the other way around. Many vases bear images of an older lover, often with a beard, touching the scrotum of a youth in an attempt to arouse and win him over.

Occasionally, the *erastes* offered beautiful, useful and sometimes expensive gifts, the relationship clearly resting on the *do ut des* principle – 'you do something for me, I'll do something for you.' The beloved could be tempted by a portion of meat, a discus, a flask of olive oil, a flower, an apple, a garland or a pouch of money. Several animals were also popular as gifts, the rooster and the hare being the most common. Greek boys were fond of cockfighting, and besides, the rooster was a symbol of virility. The hare, on the other hand, was of economic value because meat was expensive. Yet it could also have a special significance, representing an androgynous animal with equal measures of masculine and feminine attributes. It was thought that eating the flesh of a hare stimulated a man's willingness to allow himself to be penetrated. Most

A scene of pederastic courtship from
c. 520 BCE: an older, bearded man makes
advances towards a young boy with the
typical gesture of seduction, touching
the scrotum in an attempt to excite him.
The boy responds favourably, touching
the man's beard and (on the reverse)
jumping up to embrace him. The vine
and grapes symbolize Dionysus: wine
and love go hand in hand.

overleaf
Here, the young men being courted
are surrounded by athletic equipment
and lyres, implying accomplishments
that would have made them all the
more desirable to their admirers.
One has a hare on his lap – like the
cockerel a conventional love gift. The
dedication at the rim –'HIPODAMAS
KALOS', 'Hippodamas is beautiful' –
might have been added by a suitor in
an attempt to win the boy's affections.
Cup by Douris, *c.* 480 BCE.

of these animal gifts referred to hunting. In contemporary poetry, homoerotic
seductions were denoted by the terms *diokein*, 'to pursue', and *pheugein*, 'to
flee': the *erastes* adopted the role of the hunter who pursued his quarry, while
the *eromenos* was seen as the prey attempting to escape. The animal that the
erastes presented to his younger friend augmented this symbolism. Besides, he
used it to further impress the boy, suggesting that 'just as I have caught this
beast, so shall I be successful in my hunt for you.' The quarry that the lover
offered to the youth was proof of his masculinity, speed and power, a display of
might and machismo. When young men attained adulthood their roles routinely changed from that of beloved to lover. It was at the very least conspicuous
when lovers were younger than their partners.

Pederasty in Athens was an alternative form of sexuality that was often
highly regarded. There were no laws that forbade pederasty, and it must not
have been unusual for men to have a boyfriend while they were married.
Indeed, it sometimes happened that boyfriends were brought into the family
circle. In pederastic relationships, sexual desire and the search for sexual pleasure were central, and so promiscuity was very common. Men who had had
many partners acquired an enhanced reputation. In relationships such as these,
the youth was often represented as someone who would offer no resistance to
his lover's advances — even as someone with experience, who knew what he
wanted and took the initiative himself in the seduction. Thus vase-paintings

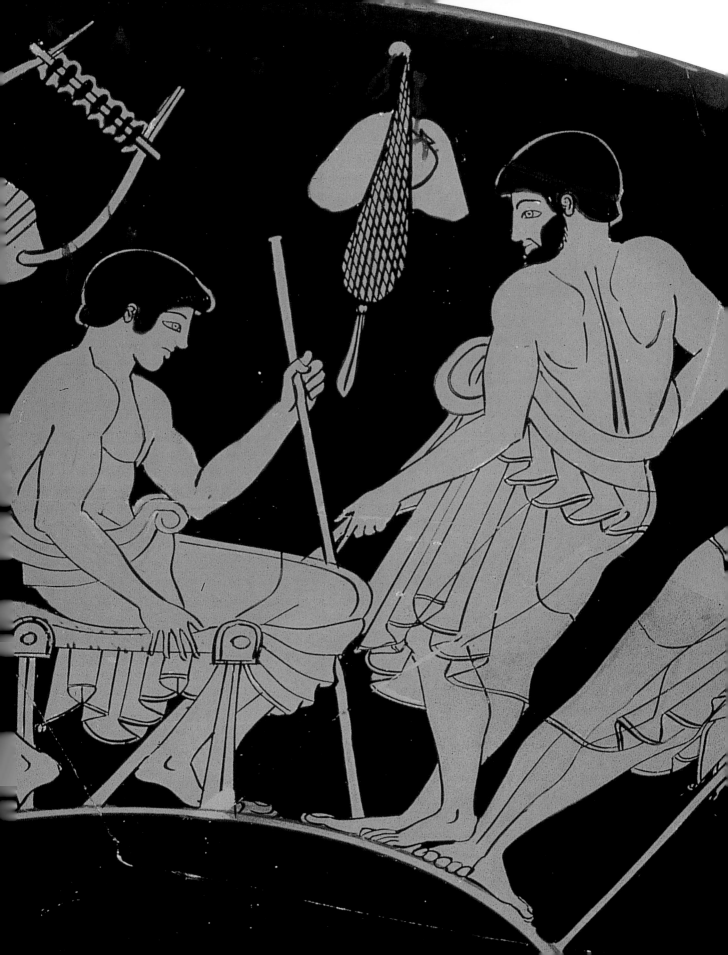

From around 500 BCE, money bags begin to appear in scenes of homoerotic seduction, as in this cup by Makron, painted c. 480 BCE. Whereas money had been just one of several gifts used to tempt young Athenians, it seems that the distinction between their behaviour and that of common prostitutes was becoming blurred. As a result legislation was passed preventing any citizen who had prostituted himself from holding public office.

sometimes portray the youth outsmarting his lover and callously running away with a gift before the man gets want he wants. When the friendship endured, the lover could help his younger friend with certain aspects of his development. To suggest, however, that such relationships had a pedagogical function is to exaggerate the point.

From around 500 BCE, the money pouch appears in homoerotic imagery as well as in scenes of seduction between men and women. In the former case, the pouch initially functioned as one among many gifts, but differences between prostitutes and ordinary *eromenoi* became rather indistinct — that is, the behaviour of Athenian youths had become tantamount to that of prostitutes. From the year 450, the money pouch disappears from homoerotic representations. From this evidence we might deduce the date of a law that explicitly prevented young Athenians who accepted money for sexual services from assuming public office. The underlying assumption was that those who offered their bodies for sale were also potentially capable of trafficking the interests of the wider community. Once this law had been introduced, the young civilians who allowed themselves to be paid for their services could be threatened with court proceedings if they pursued a career in politics. But many apparently had neither the inclination nor the opportunity to fill important positions in the people's assembly. The legislation soon fell into disuse, and in the 4th century a great rift emerged between official morals as reflected in the old law on homosexual behaviour and the sexual practice of everyday life, for we know of various examples of prominent politicians who had acquired a reputation for having prostituted themselves and who were not prosecuted.

Homosexual behaviour did not necessarily depend on a difference of age. Although rarer than other types, some vase-paintings illustrate scenes of courtship between men of roughly equal ages, as in this example by the Affecter, *c.* 550–520 BCE; and there are records of men of the same social class who lived together in adulthood.

Homosexual prostitution took all manner of forms and was not illegal. As a rule, foreigners and slaves would have served as prostitutes, but some boys with civil status also made money in this way. A father or guardian who earned money by allowing his freeborn son or pupil to work as a prostitute could be penalized, as could the client. There was a separate tax for prostitutes, additional proof that the practice was accepted by the authorities. In addition, we must not forget that slavery was central to Athenian society. Many Athenians possessed one or more slaves, who were part of their master's estate and were completely subject to his will. Slaves were thus also sexually available to their masters. Unfortunately, we know little about this issue, and it could well be that a very important part of the sexual life of Athenians consequently remains closed to us.

Other forms of homosexuality

Pederasty was not the only form of homosexual behaviour. Black-figure images on vases provide a relatively large number of examples of adult males courting other adult men. These sorts of scenes occur particularly often in the work of the 'Affecter', a painter who was active in the period between *c.* 550 and 520 BCE. This artist displays a keen interest in images of homosexual seduction, often producing scenes in which a man is portrayed in the midst of pursuing another man or a youth. Sometimes the two figures offer one another gifts, and as a result it is unclear exactly how sexual roles were delegated.

On Athenian red-figure vases, which date from around 530 BCE onwards, there is a noticeable shift in this respect, there being many more examples (around one-third of all homoerotic representations) of seductions between

A cup by Peithinos dating from *c.* 510 BCE showing courting pairs of youths, one of which – the couple at right – are of roughly the same age. Sexual roles were customarily allocated according to age, although in scenes of seduction between equals, as here, the distinction between *erastes* and *eromenos* is often difficult to determine.

boys or youths of the same age. Here, too, the allocation of sexual roles is often difficult to determine, since it is not always possible to differentiate between the *erastes* and the *eromenos*. Similarly, in images that show the god Eros chasing a youth, the age of the pursuer and his prey is often not relevant, although Eros obviously preferred companions of his own age. We know from other sources that adult males could live together. This mostly occurred among men of the same social class, namely Athenian citizens, some of whom even held important political positions. Such relationships were permitted, and so we must conclude that differences in age were not a necessary condition for homosexual relationships.

Euphemisms and coarse language

The manner in which sexual acts between men or youths are represented in words and images differs from the way in which heterosexual relations are depicted. Painters were reluctant to depict homosexual acts explicitly. Sometimes a man is shown thrusting his penis between the thighs of a youth, the so-called 'intercrural' form of penetration. This posture probably refers to anal sex, or functions as a euphemism for it. There are several examples of anal

penetration, masturbation, the use of a dildo, fellatio and analingus. Poets and painters were masters at employing euphemisms in their allusions to sex. Words such as 'cable', 'lance' and 'barley' referred to the phallus. 'Wreath' and 'throat' stood for anus, and 'foal' or 'ship' signified a whore. Painters utilized other symbols: a circle formed with the thumb and one or more fingers is a sign for the anus with which the *erastes* indicates his desires. A dog sniffing the scrotum or buttocks of a man or youth often suggests analingus, since the Greek word for dog, *skulax*, had this secondary meaning.

There was one genre from which euphemisms and flowery expressions for sexual acts were notably absent, namely comedy. In the 5th century the Athenian comic poet Aristophanes was a master of obscene language. Scholars count seventy-five different words used by the poet to signify the male genitalia, and he employed no fewer than one hundred different expressions for the sexual act, which often testified to an aggressive attitude: examples include 'to thread on a spit', 'to jab', 'to bump', 'to bore through', 'to grate' and even 'to wound'. Obscene language was used as a weapon with which to ridicule others – one of the functions of comedy – but also in order to amuse the public. Aristophanes often targeted adult men who assumed passive sexual roles. A man who allowed himself to be penetrated was thought to lower himself, through his behaviour, to the status of a woman. The passive homosexual, known as *kinaidos,* was stigmatized in comedies as a contemptible person who tended toward promiscuity, uselessness, decadence, inferiority, shamelessness and corruption. The public were amused by exaggeration, distortion and satire of this sort. It seems that Aristophanes confronted people with a particular aspect of Athenian culture that was offensive to him personally and to many others besides. However, it appears – and this we can also surmise from other sources – that the effeminate, sexually passive adult man was a well-known and tolerated phenomenon in Athens.

Dionysus

Dionysus, the god of wine, intoxication and experiences of transformation, was also associated with homosexuality. His followers, the satyrs, were regularly portrayed in a drunken state, often sporting prominent erect phalluses as they molested women and, sometimes, boys. Their arousal is a symbol of boundless sexual energy. Their erections suggested that they were ruled by lechery and a desire for penetration and masturbation.

Dionysus, on the other hand, is sexually more ambiguous. It was said that he once descended to the underworld to return his mother, Semele, who had been struck by Zeus' lightning, to the world above. The god did not know the way, and a certain Prosymnos promised to help Dionysus in exchange for a sexual favour. Dionysus agreed and ratified his promise with an oath, and Prosymnos instructed him as to the correct path. Upon his return Dionysus discovered that Prosymnos had in fact died. In order to honour his promise, the god visited Prosymnos' grave, cut a branch from a fig tree growing there, and fashioned it into a male member on which he promptly sat, so fulfilling his promise to the dead man. Phalluses to Dionysus were erected in cities as a monument to this

Once a youth had accepted the initial approaches of an older admirer, relations usually took the form of intercrural sex, which was conducted in a standing position. Although vase-painters fought shy of explicit depictions of homosexual acts, scenes such as the one above – by an artist called the 'Painter of Berlin 1686' and dated to *c.* 550–530 BCE – are not uncommon.

Satyrs – the mythical half-human followers of Dionsysus – symbolized the sexual urge in its full, uninhibited state. Befuddled by drink, they were happy to approach any sexual object or perform any sexual role, and they are sometimes depicted in scenes of same-sex lust. It was said of Dionysus himself that he 'does what men do and experiences what women experience'. Circle of the Nikosthenes Painter, c. 510 BCE.

event. In the cult of Dionysus the phallus also came to represent the desire to be penetrated. This is confirmed by the manner in which satyrs are represented penetrating one another and using dildoes to penetrate themselves. It was also said of Dionysus that 'he does what men do and experience what women experience.' Images on 6th-century vases from Athens, Corinth and the regions around Thebes demonstrate that the cult of Dionysus involved festivals during which *komoi*, groups of dancing men and youths under the influence of wine and music, surrendered themselves to all sorts of homosexual acts. The participants engaged in lewd dances, kissed one another, thrust out their buttocks and penetrated one another. A Dionysian intoxication seems to have aided and permitted the reversal of sexual roles, regardless of the participants' ages.

Homosexuality and sport

In Athens there was a direct relationship between sport and homosexuality. There were three gymnasia in the city, large sports facilities outside the walls and all manner of smaller wrestling schools. Vase-paintings clearly show that these sports facilities were places for men and youths to meet and engage in sexual contact. Competition and rivalry characterized sport, as did homosexual behaviour in the gymnasia. The youths showed off their irresistible beauty, and their lovers fought for their favours. Various scenes show explicitly that the act was also consummated in these locations. Often a copulating pair were surrounded by other men and youths. The oil that young men carried with them

Self-display was an integral part of the culture of the gymnasium: it is not surprising, therefore, that training grounds should also have been places charged with erotic possibility. Men could appraise youths from the sidelines, discreetly strike up conversation, and occasionally even indulge in sexual behaviour. Cup attributed to Douris, from the first quarter of the 5th century BCE.

in *aryballoi* (small, round oil flasks) must also have come into use during these activities. The gymnasia, therefore, had an important function as gay cruising places. One thing, however, is striking: there is nothing in the sources to suggest that particular sports facilities were especially reserved for or characterized by homosexual behaviour. Moreover, there seem to have been no complaints on the part of men or youths who were discourteously treated or bothered by the homosexual activities that occurred during their training in these places. It thus appears that the relationship between sport and homosexuality in Athens was such an intimate one that homosexual behaviour in the gymnasium and the wrestling school was standard. There was no discussion of a homosexual subculture. Rather, sports facilities were public meeting places in a wider homosexual culture. For the Athenian male, therefore, there were certain spheres of life in which homosexuality dominated, or at the very least occupied a position of equality alongside, heterosexuality.

Plato's Symposium

Plato's *Symposium* occupies a special place in the homoerotic literature of antiquity. It is the first text in Western literature that provides an intensive analysis of what constitutes love and passion, and it plainly functions as a defence of homosexual love. In its wealth of philosophical examination and insight, its genial setting and its literary character, the *Symposium* represents an unprecedented masterpiece that has acted as a highly influential source of inspiration to many Western thinkers, writers and poets.

A man attempts to kiss a youth at a banquet: a wall painting from a tomb in the Greek colony of Paestum, Italy, dating to *c.* 480 BCE. Like the gymnasia, the institution of the symposium provided a traditional opportunity for flirtation. The host invited friends to his home for an evening of drinking, talking and singing. Both male and female prostitutes would be hired, and the evening traditionally ended in an orgy.

In the *Symposium*, Plato has two principal subjects — *eros* and Socrates, his teacher — which he combines with great skill. He attempts to prompt his reader to think about the nature of *eros*, and about the place and function of *eros* in human life. The *Symposium* is also intended to provide a portrait of Socrates, who occupies a prominent place in the dialogue. We are told about the peculiarities of his behaviour and character, about his dealings with youths, and about his manner of philosophizing. The context of the dialogue is as follows: on the occasion of his victory at a drama festival, the tragic poet Agathon invites a number of Athenians to celebrate with him. It proves to be an atypical symposium, for the flute-player (a prostitute) is led away, and the attendants declare that everyone is to monitor his own drinking and that the evening should be spent sedately. Furthermore, everyone is to give a speech in praise of the god Eros.

To give an impression of the discussions that take place, let us consider the three most important of the seven speakers. The contribution of the fourth speaker, the comic poet Aristophanes, assumes the form of a myth that contrives to explain the three forms of *eros*. According to Aristophanes, there was originally a triad of human genders: the masculine, the feminine and the masculine–feminine. The human body at that time had the form of a sphere, with four arms, four legs and two faces. After a rebellion against the gods, Zeus cleft humans in two to cripple their strength, and in this manner they arrived at their current form. Yet the two halves retain an irresistible urge to unite with one another. Those who originate from a male sphere desire youths, those who come from a female whole are attracted to women, and those who originate

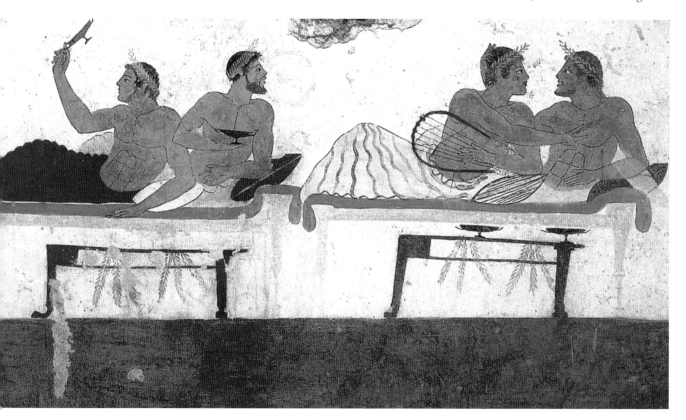

from the androgynous whole are attracted to the opposite sex. Aside from explaining the existence of the three forms of sexual identity, the myth suggests that *eros* consists of the urge to become one with our other half, that love is the desire for two to unite as one. As soon as someone finds a counterpart, he or she no longer wishes to be separated from it, and the two halves want to remain together until death. In his comedy *The Clouds*, Aristophanes had ridiculed Socrates by representing him as a pseudo-philosopher who occupied himself with nonsense. Plato does the same with Aristophanes. In his contribution to the symposium, Plato represents the comic poet, a fervent heterosexual, as portraying homosexual men more positively than heterosexuals: the former display a better character, are more masculine and loyal, and make for superior politicians. The things Aristophanes says are the opposite of what he usually proclaims in his comedies, and he thus gets beaten at his own game.

After the fifth speaker, Agathon, it is Socrates' turn. He reveals that he has become adept in the mysteries of *eros* through a wise woman named Diotima, and that what he is about to disclose has been learned from her. The previous speakers have all spoken eloquently of *eros*, but what Socrates is about to say is, according to him, the truth. *Eros* is a creative force; that is to say, he encourages humans to create, to produce. To be in love is to focus on beauty and goodness. Beauty, for example an attractive body, encourages one to produce and thus constitutes the foundation for the creative urges of those who are in love. *Eros* is therefore equivalent to begetting in beauty, as Plato formulates it. There are men, for example, who find women attractive and are aroused by them. Through this they engender a 'product', namely a child. The progeny bears characteristics of the *erastes* and is a part of him, and is therefore good. The 'product' perpetuates an essential part of him, and so Socrates concludes that *eros* is interchangeable with the desire for immortality because the *erastes* propagates himself via the offspring. With this theory Socrates appeals to the fundamental instinct of every person to extend his (or her) own life. The propagation of children is a way in which to realise *eros*. However, this practice among men who are attracted to women offers only a very limited form of immortality, to which men who prefer other men do not in fact aspire. Homosexual love propagates spiritual offspring that are of greater longevity than children, such as virtue, thought or knowledge. Through their manner of living, homosexual lovers inspire others to pursue the same lifestyle. They might prolong their mortality through means of an artwork, for instance, a philosophical treatise, or laws that guide human behaviour.

According to Socrates, those who realize the highest form of *eros* – people with a philosophical nature – are ultimately destined to encounter the divine and, specifically, divine beauty. In a particularly moving passage, Socrates explains the stages through which one would have to proceed in order to attain such spiritual heights. The first phase involves the body. A philosopher falls in love with the figure of a beautiful boy, and he desires to beget in him. He creates beautiful words. Consequently, he will gradually come to the realization that his friend's outward beauty is essentially related to the beauty of all other bodies. This insight will make the philosopher fall in love with beautiful bodies in general, and will result in his becoming detached from the specific body of his friend. The following phase of his development – which takes several years – begins with the philosopher becoming enamoured of the youth's soul or character. The philosopher's insight henceforth becomes broader and more encompassing, and his *eros* directs him to observe human habits and behaviours. By the third phase, the philosopher must be in a position to free himself from the physical and the personal, able to devote himself exclusively to the study of science, philosophy and knowledge itself until he is finally able to behold the vast sea of beauty that knowledge represents. At the moment of this encounter, the philosopher creates great and beautiful thoughts and reasoning. And so, after lengthy exertion and disengagement from the physical and personal, the philosopher suddenly gains insight into beauty itself and penetrates an eternal, divine and perfect world. The beauty that he now perceives surpasses all standards, in comparison with which handsome youths shrink into insignificance. Entry into this divine world makes the lover immortal in that he now produces everlasting virtue and thought.

Socrates has hardly finished his speech when an intoxicated Alcibiades bursts into the house of Agathon and interrupts the company in its esoteric repose. Alcibiades was renowned for his good looks, his dissolute and immoral behaviour and his political ambitions. In the *Symposium*, Plato suggests that Alcibiades was in love with Socrates, as demonstrated by the speech that he offers to Eros. His contribution, which brings the reader from the heights of divine love back to the reality of the everyday, is a panegyric on Socrates as the embodiment of an ideal, someone who is capable of great self-control, who displays virtue and who possesses knowledge. Alcibiades reluctantly confesses his love for this singular Athenian. His story makes it clear that Socrates has responded paradoxically, creating the explicit impression that he was intrigued by Alcibiades' beauty and has fallen in love with him. Socrates accepted his invitations and regularly trained with him, but failed in his role as *erastes* by making no attempt to seduce the youth. The sexual roles became subverted. At his wit's end, Alcibiades took the initiative to seduce Socrates and offered his physical charms in exchange for his older friend's knowledge and moral beauty. As the two lay together, Alcibiades cuddled up to Socrates, but the latter refused to yield, behaving instead like a demure *eromenos* and resisting all sexual advances. Alcibiades admits that he spent the entire night beside Socrates as though the philosopher were his father or elder brother, and so feels rejected, frustrated and insulted.

Plato elucidates that although Socrates resembled the ideal philosopher in the eyes of Alcibiades, following the standards of Diotima he remained too attached to the personal and physical in that he continued to pursue contact with youths and was most certainly affected by their beauty. Socrates thus seemed arrested in the second phase of philosophical development. Plato chooses to use the mask of Diotima to criticize his teacher, and through this mask he indicates to the reader that the erotic attitude of Socrates limited his intellectual development. Nevertheless, we have to imitate him in his erotic availability, for then we know for sure that we are on the right track.

Lesbian love

Our knowledge of homosexuality among women in Greek antiquity is very scanty. This is not to say that lesbianism was rare or unknown, merely that most of the sources left to us were written by men for male audiences. There are several vase images that allow a lesbian interpretation, but the only explicit mention of female homosexuality in Classical Greek literature occurs in Plato's *Symposium*, in the speech by Aristophanes. In his description of women who originate from a feminine whole, Aristophanes is somewhat reluctant to label them as women who love exclusively women. Moreover, he does not use the term *eros* for the erotic feelings that women harbour for one another, as he does for masculine sexuality, but rather the neutral term *trepesthai*, 'to be focused on'.

The person most associated with lesbian love in Greece was Sappho, the 6th-century poet from the island of Lesbos. Save one poem, only fragments of her work have come down to us. In her poetry Sappho wrote about the world of women, their daily lives, their marriages and their participation in religious ceremonies. She also praised the beauty of women and the love that they shared, and spoke of her own love for girls. We can surmise from her poetry that she kept a group of young women around her for whom she sang verses. In all likelihood these girls had been entrusted to Sappho before their impending marriages and were being instructed by her in all manner of things.

Female homosexuality is referred to only fleetingly in Classical Athenian literature, and vase-paintings – painted by men for a male clientele – do not deal with the sexual life of Athenian women of civic status; the illustration here, of one woman titillating another, is a very rare example. Some scholars doubt a sexual context and read it as two prostitutes at their toilette.

Sappho's frank utterance of lesbian feelings has meant that she and her poetry have not always received the recognition they deserve. Some scholars have gone as far as to alter or elaborate upon the texts in order to make the homo-erotic content disappear. The story told in antiquity that Sappho took her own life after renouncing her passion for girls, falling in love with and subsequently being rejected by the young ferryman Phaon is most likely a fabrication.

Rome
Virtus and stuprum

Central to the life of the male Roman citizen was the notion of *virtus*, a term usually translated as 'virtue' but which literally signified masculinity. *Virtus* represented the qualities that made one a real man. Romans were a people with pronounced military inclinations and therefore power, courage, determination and perseverance formed the basis of their actions. Romans believed that they ought to be in a position to govern the world and dominate others. 'Parcere subiectis et debellare superbos' ('Spare those who have surrendered and fight against those who resist') wrote the poet Virgil in his description of a Roman's duty. In heart and soul, the Roman was a usurper, aggressor and conqueror. A Roman ought to dominate and rule all spheres of life, whether with his weapons, his words, his knowledge or his phallus. He was a devotee of the god Priapus, a fertility deity who was also the protector of roads and entrances. The god's large phallus protected the people against demons, thieves and other evils. Romans often kept an image of Priapus in the hallway as an indication that a real man resided in the house and would protect his family in any circumstances. A man's sexuality was above all the way in which he demonstrated his *virtus*. For a true Roman, sex equated to penetration, and in principle all sexual acts in which he was not dominant were condemnable. This focus on the penetrative role was so pronounced that the sex of those whom one penetrated was actually of no importance: one could have sex with a woman, a youth or an adult man as long as one played the active role.

Hence we can understand that fellatio and cunnilingus, which were seen as passive acts, were rejected by Romans as repulsive behaviour. Furthermore, to have sexual relations with a free Roman citizen outside of marriage, regardless of whether it involved a woman or a man, was generally considered outrageous. It was viewed as a form of *stuprum*, an act that brought into disrepute the *pudicitia* (honour) of freeborn Roman men and women. As a consequence, the term is often translated with words for sexual offences and obscene acts, such as 'adultery' or 'rape'. Adultery was regarded as the worst form of *stuprum*, especially if it was committed by a woman. A man was expected to have control over the sexual experiences of his wife who, in Rome, nevertheless enjoyed greater freedom than her Greek counterpart. When a man was the victim of *stuprum* — for instance when he was raped — the scandal mainly affected the victim and not so much the perpetrator, in that the latter's deed was regarded as proof of his exceptional virility.

Images of the Roman god Priapus were set up in entrances to homes and gardens to ensure fertility and prosperity and to protect property (the erect phallus was endowed with apotropaic qualities). Some images were accompanied by messages that threatened penetration of trespassers, male or female. Wall painting from the House of the Vettii in Pompeii, *c.* 62–79 CE.

An idealized portrait of Antinous, the handsome boy from Bithynia with whom the Roman emperor Hadrian fell in love, made soon after the boy's death. When Antinous drowned in the Nile in 130 CE, Hadrian proclaimed him divine and erected statues throughout the empire in his honour. It appears that the emperor had broken no rules governing sexual behaviour or masculine conduct, possibly because the youth was not a Roman citizen.

Slaves and prostitutes

The Roman attitude towards homosexuality was rather different from that of the ancient Greeks. Various Roman intellectuals who took issue with homosexual behaviour viewed the love of boys as an inappropriate, pernicious effect of the influence of Greek culture, which did not suit Romans. But their view was incorrect, for homosexuality was in fact fundamental to Roman culture. For instance, the comedies of Plautus (*c.* 245–184 BCE) contained many typically Roman allusions to homosexuality, such as jokes about sexual experiences with slaves. Other sources also establish that it was normal for a Roman to have open sexual relations with persons of either sex. Certainly nobody opposed sexual relations with one's own slaves. In this context, a Roman could exercise his power as a full citizen or satisfy his desire to fulfil the passive role. In contrast to the situation in ancient Greece, a large proportion of Roman literature discusses sexual relations with slaves. Young slaves were popular; we know that the poet Virgil had a preference for these. Some slaves belonging to the household of the emperor Augustus were known as his *deliciae*, or 'darlings'. Emperor Domitian had a relationship with his eunuch Earinus. The most famous example was the friendship between the emperor Hadrian, a married man, and Antinous, a boy from Bithynia in the north of present-day Turkey.

We do not know for sure whether Antinous was a slave, but it is certain that he was no freeborn Roman, and for this reason his friendship with the emperor did not cause a scandal. Hadrian was so deeply in love with the young man that he was inconsolable when, in 130 CE, Antinous drowned in the River Nile in obscure circumstances during a journey through Egypt with the emperor. Hadrian endowed Antinous, approximately twenty years old when he died, with divine status; throughout the empire, he erected statues and temples devoted to the boy's memory. Hadrian dedicated poetry to him and built a city – Antinopolis – on the spot where the young man died.

Male prostitution was also a part of Roman life. Indeed, the practice developed to the extent that it became a luxury trade. Most male prostitutes were slaves, but Roman citizens could also earn their money in this manner. The Roman calendar featured a special day that was devoted to male prostitutes, and there were brothels exclusively for men who sought amusement with one another. It is worth noting that there were also many adult men serving as prostitutes who adopted both passive and active sexual roles, the so-called *exoleti*. A perfect example of the double standard with regard to prostitution is found in the reaction of the moralist Cato the Elder, who praised a youth whom he saw exiting one of the brothels on the Forum: it was appropriate that the young man should entrust his passions to professionals rather than other men's wives. However, when he met the youth in the same place again several days later, Cato berated him, saying: 'I praised you because you come here occasionally, not because you live here.'

Despite the fact that it was an acknowledged part of Roman culture before contact with Greece, some critics periodically blamed sex with freeborn young men – along with other examples of loosening morals – on 'bad' Greek influences. Same-sex sexual behaviour remained widespread, however, and myths that touched in the subject persisted in popularity, as shown in this mosaic of Jupiter (Zeus) and Ganymede from the 3rd century CE.

Greek influences

Rome encountered other cultures through conquest, and Greek traditions in particular (especially from the mid-2nd century BCE) exercised considerable influence on Roman lifestyles, ranging from the import of luxury goods and art objects to the introduction of new cults, rituals and other customs – including those of an erotic nature. A loosening of morals also occurred. In many circles of Roman society people adhered less fervently to traditional mores concerning marriage, and even adultery committed by women became more common and was tolerated. Every so often, however, conservative citizens such as Cato the Elder denounced the weakening of morals as a destructive aspect of Greek influence on Roman culture. The historian Livy tells an interesting story about an important event in Rome in the year 186 BCE, when certain practices that took place during festivals in honour of the god Bacchus – which had been brought to Italy from Greece – came to light. By coincidence, a consul discovered what was going on in these observances, and compelled a prostitute who had been initiated into the cult as a slave to tell him what she knew of it. Initially, the cult had been a women's affair. Once men had been permitted entry, however, the festivals were organized at night. Obscenities were committed between men and women, and between men and men. People were sacrificed. Those who did not allow themselves to be initiated were raped or murdered. Many Romans, including people from prominent families, had secretly affiliated themselves with the cult. The movement was eventually stamped out, and we read in Livy that thousands of Romans were executed or thrown into prison. Thereafter, Bacchic festivals were forbidden for an unspecified time.

Loosening of morals

Once Romans had come into close contact with Greek culture and it had become chic in certain circles to adopt Greek behaviour, even the measures mentioned above and the vigilance of moralists such as Cato could not hinder the popularity of relationships between free men. Nevertheless, public opinion reacted fiercely against this form of love, and it was probably in response to the threat of 'bad' Greek influence that a law was passed penalizing homosexual relationships with freeborn Roman boys.

These legal restrictions could not suppress the fact that pederasty was openly engaged in among freeborn young men. One of the most important sources on the manner in which homosexual love was experienced in Rome comes from the poets of the 1st centuries before and after the birth of Christ, such as Catullus, Tibullus, Propertius and Horace. We shall take Catullus as an example. He entertained a passionate love for Lesbia (probably a pseudonym for Clodia), a *femme fatale* with a formidable reputation in all matters concerning love. Catullus dedicated numerous poems, now belonging to the canon of Latin literature, to his feelings for this woman. Men who were his rivals in the sphere of love – his enemies, in other words – were ridiculed by Catullus, often in language brimming with obscenities. He portrayed them as sexually 'abnormal' – that is to say, afflicted by 'passive' desires. Poem 16, directed against two persons named Aurelius and Furus, begins aggressively: 'Pedicabo ego vos et irrumabo' ('I shall fuck you in the arse and in the mouth'). The Romans had a special verb, *irrumare*, for oral penetration, an activity considered suitable for real men. Fellatio was pre-eminently seen as a 'passive' and thus a despicable act. Catullus dubs Aurelius a *pathicus* and Furus a *cinaedus*, words that were both used to indicate a passive homosexual. Catullus also composed a series of eight poems about his love for Juventus, a young male Roman citizen. These poems are characterized by the same emotional commitment as those concerning his love for Lesbia. We cannot but conclude from this that Catullus must have had homosexual experiences, and had thus committed *stuprum*. In the poem he praises the youth's beauty, particularly his lovely eyes, but laments the young man's capricious behaviour in his rejection of Catullus' advances. The poet accordingly makes his apologies and promises to be less insistent. Here we are confronted with a completely different Catullus – not the macho Roman who spews aggressive language and attempts to subdue the object of his desire, but the insecure lover who allows himself to be cowed by his young companion. The usual sexual roles appear to have been reversed. This romantic image of love was typically Greek, and in the poems of Catullus, just as in other Roman poetry, we meet both forms of homosexual *eros*.

The policies of Emperor Augustus

Wars, and especially the civil wars of the 1st century BCE, had greatly depleted the number of Roman men, and morals had become degraded. In response, the emperor Augustus took measures to restore the importance of the *familia* and to make it the cornerstone of Roman society. He enacted a law that ensured Romans could no longer elect to go through life as bachelors. Every man under the age of sixty, and every woman no older than fifty, was obliged to marry. Adultery was punished more severely. However, it is notable that the legislation enacted by Augustus did not address the question of homosexual morality. As long as one always assumed the active sexual role – that of the penetrator – homosexual behaviour was acceptable, even though one's desire might be concentrated on Roman youths.

The story of the tragic friendship between Nisus and Euryalus is significant in this context. The tale appears in the ninth book of the *Aeneid*, the epic written by Virgil under the authority of the emperor Augustus, in which Rome's development as a world power was represented as having been preordained by the gods. According to the *Aeneid*, the Trojans had been destined to build a new city in Latium in Italy, from where the descendants of their leader, Aeneas, would later found Rome. Aeneas was absent from the Trojan camp when it was attacked by Turnus, a prince of Latium. Two soldiers – Nisus, the lover, and Euryalus, a handsome youth with the first traces of a beard – offered their services to alert Aeneas. Nisus did not wish his friend to accompany him on the dangerous expedition, but Euryalus refused to leave the task to his friend alone. When the two arrived in the enemy camp under the cover of night, they provoked a terrible bloodbath, but during the pursuit Euryalus was killed. In his passion, Nisus threw himself at the enemy but paid for it with his

Eros stringing his bow, a Roman copy of an original sculpted by Lysippos in the 4th century BCE. Altars to the god Eros were erected in gymnasia: it was believed that he protected male friendship and he was especially associated with homosexual love. With time Eros lost his connection with homosexuality and gradually became younger and younger: the Romans, who called him Cupido or Amor, often portrayed as a naughty child.

life, falling upon the body of his departed friend. The legend clearly consisted of melodrama wherein mutual love and *virtus* formed central themes. However, the love between Nisus and Euryalus also seems to be an example of *stuprum*, since both young men were freeborn Trojans, the forefathers of the Romans. It is likely that the mythical nature of the tale would have placated Roman sensibilities in this regard.

The effeminate man

At the end of the 1st century BCE, we see a certain tolerance emerge towards men who behaved effeminately and who allowed themselves to be penetrated. Rumour had it that several prominent politicians and generals took the passive role in homosexual relationships. It was said that Caesar fulfilled the feminine role in his relationship with Nicomedes, the king of Bithynia. Caesar was called 'the queen of Bithynia', and his soldiers sang: 'Gallias Caesar subegit, Nicomedes Caesarem' ('Caesar subdued Gaul, Nicomedes [subdued] Caesar'). Catullus dubbed the general a *cinaedus* and called him *mollis*, 'soft' or 'unmanly'. Caesar seemed not to have taken this slander to heart, probably not because there was no kernel of truth in it, but because he commanded sufficient respect from his followers. He had a reputation as a prolific seducer of women, and his skills as both a general and a soldier raised him above all reproach: he was a victor both in bed and on the battlefield.

Augustus was also credited with this dual sexual character. On the one hand he was renowned as an adulterer and a conqueror, while on the other he was deprived of his *pudicitia* by Caesar, his adoptive father; and other anecdotes were told that labelled him as *mollis*. Such stories were also circulated about other emperors, with the exception of Claudius. Nero outshone them all by entering into marriages with men wherein he alternated between playing the role of bride and that of groom. Many – but not all – of these anecdotes were just gossip. In other elevated social circles during the imperial age, sexual morals were also loosening, and passivity among men was increasingly tolerated. An effeminate man would often be called *cinaedus* (as in the poems by Catullus quoted above), which derived from the Greek word *kinaidos*, or *pathicus*, 'he who endures'. These men were labelled as lustful 'non-men' who were incapable of controlling their unusual desires. Often, but not always, the terms were used to denote someone who went too far with his sexual desires by engaging in unmasculine, passive behaviour.

These men, different as they were, were clearly present in Roman society. They were regarded as an outrage in the eyes of respectable, true Romans, however, and throughout the course of the empire's history were often the first to be condemned. In 342 the co-emperors

Constantius II and Constans I passed a law that forbade passive homosexuality. The punishment for infringement was probably castration. In 390 Theodosius I ordained that all passive homosexuals who prostituted themselves in brothels should be burned alive, and in 438 this punishment was extended to all men who assumed passive sexual roles. This growing hatred of homosexuality was closely aligned with the rise of Christianity. Adherents to this religion took a particular view of sexuality in which assessments of goodness were based upon what was deemed natural or unnatural rather than on the sexual role of males. Sexuality that was exclusively directed towards procreation was thought to be in harmony with nature as God had intended. From this time onwards legislation became more vigorously anti-homosexual, and all forms of homosexuality were considered scandalous and unlawful. During his reign, from 527 to 565, the emperor Justinian ordered that all forms of homosexual behaviour should attract the death penalty.

In conclusion, we may say that homosexuality formed a very important aspect of both Greek and Roman society, and that it was probably even more evident in Greek than in Roman culture. Life in Greece, and especially in Athens, was permeated by homosexuality and homoeroticism. Furthermore, in Classical antiquity there were several forms of homosexual behaviour. Preference was given to pederasty – in both cultures, young people were judged as beautiful and attractive, and were not considered forbidden objects of love – but relationships between adult men or between youths of the same age also occurred. The relatively open-minded and tolerant attitude of ancient cultures towards homosexuality has particularly to do with a rather free and easy attitude towards sexuality in general. From the male point of view, sexuality was seen mainly as one of the opportunities afforded by nature for men to enjoy life enthusiastically. The limits society tried to define especially concerned the role one took during the sexual act. When ideas about the function and nature of sexuality altered with the arrival of Christianity, so too did attitudes towards homosexuality – a gradual change, but one that had dramatic results.

The Middle Ages
BERND-ULRICH HERGEMÖLLER

What were the Middle Ages? The concept of a 'middle age' that separated the period of the Western Roman Empire from the present day originated in the humanist circles of the 15th century, while the division of the past into antiquity, the Middle Ages and modern times first gained currency two centuries later. The Middle Ages were thus understood to be a period in the history of the European West that stretched from the 7th to the 16th centuries, from a series of Arab advances around 635–650 until the Renaissance and the Reformation, the initial stage of which concluded with the Peace of Augsburg in 1555. Three themes dominated this thousand-year span: the supreme rule of emperors and popes; faith in Catholic Christianity (and the Bible) as the true religion; and the use of Latin as a lingua franca by scholars and the educated elite.

For practical reasons, it is now customary to subdivide this long epoch into three phases: the early Middle Ages, which ran from late Classical times to the reigns of the Ottonian kings (around 1000 CE); the high Middle Ages, which lasted until the death in 1250 of Frederick II, the last of the Hohenstaufen monarchs; and the late Middle Ages, which ended with the discovery of the New World and the beginning of Luther's Reformation.

As far as the history of homosexuality is concerned, it should be noted that neither for the early nor for the high Middle Ages are there sources specifically relating to the daily life, or the judicial pursuit and execution, of men and women who had sexual relations with others of the same sex. The simple reason for this is that the concept of 'homosexuals' as members of a separate category was at that time completely foreign (the term 'third sex' was known, but only from the works of Plato). Rather, humans were judged, following Classical views, according to their behaviour in relation to 'nature', i.e. on whether their acts led ultimately to reproduction. Those whom we today call 'homosexuals' were grouped together with others who had sex with animals, who engaged in anal or oral intercourse, or who practised contraception or abortion. Uniform legislation governing aspects of sexual morality was not yet in place, and men and women who engaged in these acts instead came under the jurisdiction of local bishoprics, which imposed punishments with an eye to the possible 'reconciliation' of the sinners.

Only in the 13th century did it become common to call homosexual men 'sodomites' and to subject them to the rule of the Inquisition (established by Gregory IX in 1233), which had the right to torture and execute those who

Dürer's woodcut of a men's bathhouse, made in 1497, hints at the possibilities for sexual contact afforded by such all-male environments. The suggestive groupings, male voyeur, waterspout and even the knotted tree trunk all serve to underline a distinctly homoerotic atmosphere.

To the Church, sexual desire was tolerated only as a means of producing children. This miniature from a French *Bible Moralisée* of the early 13th century shows two same-sex couples being encouraged by devils to indulge in forbidden love.

were found guilty. The great cities of Europe – Venice, Florence, Paris, London, Ghent, Bruges and Cologne – also set up special commissions in the 14th and 15th centuries that pursued sodomites and which also pronounced many death sentences. German bishoprics and free cities such as Augsburg, Regensburg and Basel followed suit, instigating witch-hunts of groups of men and bringing individuals to trial. During this wave of persecution, even kings, princes and popes were interrogated and had penalties imposed upon them.

Apart from the religious and legal aspects of homosexuality, however, there also emerges a literary and cultural context for same-sex relationships, at least as far as male-to-male contacts are concerned. This can be seen clearly in several distinct groups whose poems and letters exalted friendship between men and homoerotic culture: the Gallo-Roman circle of the poet Venantius Fortunatus in the 6th century; court scholars and bishops at the time of Charlemagne and Louis the Pious in the late 8th and early 9th centuries; and the clerics and 'Loire poets' of the Anglo-Norman courts in the 10th, 11th and 12th centuries. After a long gap, there was a revival in the 15th century of homoeroticism among Neoplatonic figures in Florence, such as Marsilio Ficino and Pico della Mirandola, and within Pomponio Leto's Accademia Romana. Finally, at the time of the Protestant Reformation, there was the circle of friends grouped around Erasmus of Rotterdam and Jakob Wimpfeling in the Upper Rhine region. Love between friends was expressed by embraces and kisses, by common sleeping arrangements, and by dedications in published works, though never (as far as we are aware) by sexual acts, which would have been regarded as sinful.

The Middle Ages thus had two sorts of men who loved men: the damned 'sodomites', who engaged in 'unnatural' sexual acts, and the prestigious and respected 'friends', who cultivated a sublime *eros* in their letters, poems and philosophical treatises.

The Early Middle Ages
Penitential books and canon law

During the early Middle Ages, Christians in Western Europe were not subject to any centralized papal or imperial bans on particular sexual practices. Punishment of sexual deviations between the 6th and the 10th centuries took place within the communal framework of Christian penitence, and implementation varied considerably, both locally and regionally. In addition to the teachings of the Bible and scholarly interpretation, the Church's treatment of homosexuality was shaped in two ways: through the decrees issued by ecclesiastical councils (which later found their way into canon law), and through the use of the so-called penitential books (*libri poenitentiales*). First used in Ireland in the late 6th century, and later found also in England, the penitential books were manuals for priests whose task it was to keep an account of the everyday transgressions of clerics and lay people. They were private texts, only occasionally endorsed by the authority of bishops or abbots, and dealt with various sexual sins such as contraception, abortion, masturbation, adultery, concubinage, anal, dorsal and interfemoral intercourse, same-sex intercourse, and artificial satisfaction between women or between man and beast (bestiality). These sins were to be expiated through a detailed system of penances that were graded according to length and severity, including fasting, psalm-singing, the giving of alms, corporal punishment, and exclusion from the sacraments or from acts of consecration. Looking at the books' list of offences, one is struck by the wide range of sins that might be viewed as a hindrance to, or avoidance of, the procreative function of the sexual act. As a rule, the penalties for these offences were personal and quantitative and did not result in exclusion from the community. Under certain circumstances, penances could be offset against one another (for example, fasting instead of attending Mass), and the offenders were rewarded – albeit often after several years – with reconciliation.

The Irish and English penitential books made their way across to the Continent during the 8th century, where they received a mixed reception, although they also prompted many similar manuals in the years after their introduction. Perhaps most influential in this context was Burchard, Reichs-Bishop of Worms (d. 1025), who drew from previous penitential books to create his *Decretum*, an attempt to standardize the system of penance. The interpretation of 'unnatural sins' (same-sex sexual acts), however, followed the old pattern. Eventually, these works were superseded by early canon law, the basis for which was laid down by a hugely influential compendium produced in Bologna and known as the *Decretum* of Gratian (*c.* 1140).

In common with the Merovingian kings, Charlemagne surrounded himself with a circle of scholars and poets with whom he shared very close bonds of friendship. They had familiar names for each other, and would write intimate poems in the Classical tradition expressing their admiration and affection for their friends' intellects and bodies. Bronze statue from the early 9th century believed to represent Charlemagne.

The penitential books were also known to the ecclesiastical reformers of the 11th century, chief among whom was Pope Gregory VII (1073–85), whose efforts were directed especially against priests getting married, simony, and the influence of secular rulers on ecclesiastical appointments. In 1049, during the movement's early phase, a cardinal named Peter Damian, on his own initiative and without any known precedent, wrote a long letter called the *Liber Gomorrhianus* ('The Book of Gomorrah'). This tract painted a satirical picture of a generation of sodomitical priests eaten up with cancerous ulcers, and Damian demanded that Pope Leo IX take more severe measures against this 'epidemic'. However, it was not until the Third Lateran Council, held in Rome in 1179, that specific rulings against licence began to appear. The Council decreed that clerics who had acted 'against nature' were to be either barred from priesthood or sent to a monastery, and lay persons were to be 'banished irrevocably from the community of the faithful' (X.5.31.4). This ruling established preferential treatment for consecrated priests, who in the late medieval period would generally be spared, while lay persons could be tortured and executed if the authorities so chose.

Merovingian friendship and the Carolingian Renaissance

The cult of friendship in the Christian West first blossomed in the 6th century, during the time of the Merovingian kings. The late Roman poet and biographer Venantius Fortunatus, who became bishop of Poitiers shortly before his death in *c.* 600, was at the centre of a circle of educated theologians and men of letters to whom he sent erotic poems and letters based on such Roman writers as Horace, Catullus and Ovid. The recipients included Ragnemod (whom Fortunatus called 'Rucco'), later to become bishop of Paris; Chancellor Faramod; and the bishop of Cologne, Carentius, whom he addressed as *carus* ('dear') and *dulcis* ('sweet'). The system of friendship overrode class barriers and created a new, egalitarian community whose members were obliged to offer each other practical aid and support. The nuns of noble birth who were gathered around the former queen Radegund (d. 587) in Arles were also incorporated into this system of friendship, though here the language patterns centred more on admiration and courtly rhetoric.

Under the emperor Charlemagne, this concept of close friendship was revived and intensified. From 777 onwards, long before his coronation in 800, Charlemagne brought selected authors and scholars to his court from all over Europe, commissioning them to write textbooks and gospels, set up libraries, draft ecclesiastical decrees and push through palaeographical reforms. But they also indulged in the art of writing cheerful, erotic poetry, using nicknames taken from ancient mythology or from the Bible. In this charmed circle Charlemagne called himself 'David'; Alcuin of York, the abbot of Tours, was known as 'Flaccus', or 'Albinus' when he wrote to Bishop Arn(o) of Salzburg ('Aquilinus'); Angilbert, who was Charlemagne's son-in-law and lay abbot of St-Riquier, became 'Homer'; and the architect and biographer

Einhard was known as 'Beseleel' (from Exodus 31:2). Many of these poems express pleasure at the bodies and minds of friends who are present, or sorrow at their absence – as with Alcuin's somewhat enigmatic *Ecloga de cuculu* ('Cuckoo Eclogue'), which is evidently addressed to a loved one now far away. Under Louis the Pious, Charlemagne's son, a new circle of friends was established on the island of Reichenau, who carried on the tradition of *Knabengedichte* ('boy poems'), although these also incorporated moral elements. Among the circle were the theologian Gottschalk von Orbais and the scholar-poets Walafrid Strabo and Wetti von Reichenau; the latter's otherworldly *Visio Wettini* (824) provides a vivid picture of the way in which monastic circles envisaged the hellish torments suffered by sodomites. Not even Charlemagne himself was left out of this vision of vice.

The Carolingians and their successors passed no new laws against sodomites; in fact, there was to be no new legislation until the 16th century, when the Habsburg Charles V produced his *Constitutio Criminalis Carolina* of 1532. Since the Frankish and German rulers regarded themselves as successors to the Roman emperors, imperial Roman laws remained in force, although they were not systematically applied. Among them were the *Novellae* ('new laws') of Justinian, passed in 538 and 559 (*Novellae* LXXVII and CXLI), in which he blamed the sodomites and the blasphemers not only for the destruction of Sodom and Gomorrah (Genesis 19), but also for famines, earthquakes and plagues. Justinian expressly recommended torture and other extreme forms of punishment for such sinful people.

These ideas were taken up once more in the middle of the 9th century (when the Carolingian concept of close friendship was enjoying its second golden age) by the pseudonymous 'Benedict Levita'. This cleric either altered or forged a whole series of Carolingian decrees, which were widely distributed through their incorporation into the Fake Decretals of Pseudo-Isidore, a voluminous work of spurious canon law. Benedict played on contemporary fears of invasion by the Saracens by citing the biblical story of the 40,000 Benjamites (freely based on Judges 19–20), affirming that their defeat was God's punishment for the 'sin against nature'. More than this, he dressed it up as a law passed by Charlemagne (who had died some forty years earlier) that required the death penalty for sodomites.

Fear of the Saracens also inspired the poetess-nun Hrotsvith von Gandersheim in the 10th century. In her tragic tale of St Pelagius – which, incidentally, contains a fine description of this beautiful youth – she depicts the martyrdom of a Christian prince who is cruelly executed by the caliph of Cordoba, Abderrahman, because he stubbornly refuses to yield to the latter's unnatural lust.

The Anglo-Norman kingdom and the Loire poets
Just like the Austrian Merovingians and the early Carolingians, the Anglo-Norman kings provided favourable conditions for the development of the cult of friendship and the composition of homoerotic literature. After William the Conqueror had invaded England in 1066, his daughter Adela (d. 1138) ruled

William II flanked by knights: an English manuscript illumination from the early 14th century. William, known as 'Rufus', is the only adult English king never to have married: contemporary chroniclers satirized him as effeminate and described his court as full of 'pathics' and 'foul catamites'. In the regions under Norman control, scholars and writers – both ordained and secular – celebrated an elite homoerotic culture with works that are often surprisingly romantic in style.

over the Continental counties of Blois, Chartres and Meaux, while his male descendants concentrated on England and Normandy. Three of them were caricatured in contemporary literature as effeminate and homosexual: William's sons Robert Curthose ('short trousers') and William II (or 'Rufus', the Red), and his grandson William Etheling, who drowned in the shipwreck of the *Blanche Nef* in 1120.

Throughout the regions under Norman rule were many secular writers, as well as reputable bishops and abbots, who discovered a talent for poetry and a liking for young pupils and intimate friends. Three bishops formed the centre of this 'Loire Circle': Marbod of Rennes (d. 1123), who was a close friend of Adela of Blois; his most able pupil, Baudri (Balderich) of Bourgueil (d. 1130), who was appointed bishop of Dol-de-Bretagne in 1107; and the poet-bishop of Le Mans, Hildebert of Lavardin (d. 1133). Aside from focusing on male–male relationships, this milieu held views that sometimes spilled over into misogyny: for Hildebert, for example, woman ranked as *cumulata infirmitas* ('accumulated infirmity') and was a symbol of temptation, greed and thirst for glory. The philosopher and theologian Anselm of Canterbury, whose ecclesiastical career had begun in 1060 when he was a Benedictine monk in the Norman abbey of Bec, was a prominent writer of homoerotic poetry – a style that was imitated in many late-medieval works once attributed to his name. There are also marked homoerotic tendencies in the letters of Aelred of Rievaulx, author of the programmatic *De spirituali amicitia* ('On Spiritual Friendship'). He belonged to the circle of friends surrounding the Scottish king David I (r. 1142–53), but was also Cistercian abbot of Rievaulx near York, in the north of England, and was in close contact with Anglo-Norman friends. On a par with him was the grammarian Hilary of Orleans ('Hilary the

Englishman'; d. *c.* 1150), who addressed his poems both to nuns and to hand-some youths.

In the works of some theologians from the so-called School of Chartres (for example Bernardus Silvestris, John of Salisbury and Thierry of Chartres), the pendulum swung decisively against the sodomites. Alanus ab Insulis (d. 1203), in his elaborate rhyming *De planctu naturae* ('On Nature's Complaint'), seems obsessed with the various terminologies for unnatural love and perversions of God-given sexuality, but he is driven first and foremost by a vehement hostility towards sodomy. Alanus evokes the allegorical figure of Nature as *Vicaria Dei* ('God's representative'), who has created Man according to the laws of 'Venus' in a dualistic 'grammar': within this system biological reproduction assumes a leading role as the purpose behind cosmic movement and as a possible condition for the achievement of eternal salvation. A violation of the command to reproduce therefore appears as a violation of the grammar of Creation and reality, of what is right and what is lawful.

The 13th century
Theology and theory

The 13th century saw a considerable change in the attitudes of theologians and ordinary citizens towards sodomites. The scholastic theologians turned away from allegorical and Neoplatonic ideas of natural philosophy, and instead constructed a rational system that traced the history of the world from Creation through to Christ's Second Coming, an account based strictly on Aristotle's four causes (matter, form, effect and purpose). There is no place in this teleological world view for types of sexuality that break the chain of cause and effect, thereby throwing into doubt the *causa finalis*, or destination, of the whole history of salvation. This 'scientific' battle against unnatural sexual acts was waged most vehemently by the then bishop of Paris, William of Auvergne (d. 1249), and by university theologians from the two great mendicant orders, the Franciscans and the Dominicans. Among the most prominent anti-sodomite Dominicans were Paulus Hungaricus (d. 1242), Guillelmus Peraldus (d. *c.* 1261), Thomas Aquinas (d. 1274) and Albertus Magnus (d. 1280). Thomas Aquinas, who in his time was the most controversial and is now the most famous of these authors, devised a categorization of the four *peccata luxuriae* (sins of unnatural sex) in accordance with canon law: on the lowest level were simple offences, such as intercourse with prostitutes; next in the hierarchy of sins came adultery; this was followed by incest; and 'unnatural' acts topped the list. Sins against nature, it was universally proclaimed, constituted the worst of all offences – even more terrible than incest between son and mother or between daughter and father – for the reason that they were physically unnatural, whereas incest at least remained within the procreative system. Sins against nature were in turn divided into four categories: (i) self-satisfaction (*mollities*); (ii) zoophilia (*bestialitas*); (iii) anal and oral intercourse (*concubitus indebitus*); and (iv) same-sex intercourse between men (*vicium sodomiticum*).

The Middle Ages did not divide people into homosexual and heterosexual, but into natural and unnatural. In other words, men were burned to death

The Cathars, a heretical sect that had become established in the Languedoc and parts of northern Italy by the 12th century, believed sexual activity to be fundamentally evil and considered family life of little importance – a position that laid them open to accusations of sodomy by the Church. Indeed, so closely were the concepts of heresy and sodomy associated that in several languages the terms were used interchangeably. Here, in a manuscript illumination of the 1230s, the Cathars are shown kissing the behind of a tomcat.

not because they had had sexual intercourse with other men, but because they had violated the laws of nature. That is why criminal records after the late 13th century include the prosecution not only of men who loved men, but also of men who abused animals. Furthermore, after the 15th century there were also wives who accused their husbands of oral and anal practices. However, the vast majority of criminal proceedings because of 'unnatural' acts in the Middle Ages – approximately 80 per cent – concerned men who were prosecuted for sexual acts with other men, for which the terms *sodomita* and *sodomiticus* were commonly used.

Demonization and politicization, c. 1300

The Cathars arrived in Western Europe from Bulgaria during the early 11th century and by the 12th century had established themselves in Toulouse and Provence, as well as in Lombardy and Tuscany. Their centre was the town of Albi in the Languedoc, after which they became known as Albigensians. The first major group to oppose the Church over such a wide area, the Cathars had a relatively unified philosophy. According to their beliefs, it was the goal of the true Christian to pursue a path of purity, knowledge and asceticism: fertility and reproduction belonged to the material world and were therefore evil. From the outset the Cathars relegated marriage and the family to a position of minor importance, viewing them as undesirable, and for this reason they were suspected by the Church of giving their approval to unnatural

By the end of the 13th century the influence of the Knights Templar had begun to wane. In 1307 Philip IV of France, jealous of the Order's riches, had members arrested, passed over to the Inquisition for torture and, with the connivance of the Church, executed. They were accused of apostasy and various acts of sodomy – one of the first instances of accusations of homosexuality being used for political ends. Below left: a satirical illustration of a Templar kissing a cleric, from a manuscript of Jacques de Longuyon's *Les Voeux du Paon*, c. 1350. Below right: Templars burned at the stake, 14th century, from a chronicle by Bernard Guy.

sexual activities. Persecution by the Church effectively destroyed the Cathars by the end of the Middle Ages, but, during a period in which many theologians set about demonizing unnatural sexuality, sodomy and heresy had become linked in the common mind. (The German verb *ketzern*, 'to commit heresy', is derived from the word 'Cathar'; and *bougre*, or 'bugger', alludes to the heresy's Bulgarian origins.)

The first example in Germany of the crusading theologian figure was Conrad of Marburg. He had already earned himself a dubious reputation as the brutal confessor of (St) Elizabeth of Hungary, widow of the landgrave of Thuringia, but in 1231 he was entrusted by Pope Gregory IX with the task of leading the fight against the enemies of the Faith. It was Conrad's belief that such heretics worshipped the Devil in the form of poisonous toads, black cats and pale skeletons, and in the course of their secret assignations committed the sins of adultery, incest and unnatural sex. Pope Gregory IX used Conrad's dark reports as a basis for the papal bull *Vox in Rama*, which he sent to the Hohenstaufen emperor Frederick II (d. 1250) and all the bishops in 1233, urging them to fight these cat-loving heretics who were indulging in unnatural activities. In this way he forged a dangerous link between the themes of heresy, sexual deviancy and devil-worship (not to mention anal and faecal fantasies) that was to have a powerful influence on the course of many inquisitions during the late Middle Ages. Much disliked, Conrad of Marburg was killed on 30 July 1233, but his ideas survived him.

The trial of the Templars can be regarded as the first concrete result of the approach instigated by Conrad. The dissolution of the Order of the Knights of the Temple of Solomon was begun in 1307 by Philip IV (the Fair) of France, who was perhaps jealous of the Order's power and wealth. Philip had all members in France arrested, imprisoned and tortured; although Pope Clement V was initially reluctant, he eventually dissolved the Order by means

of a papal bull (*Vox in excelso*) at the Council of Vienne in 1311–12. Despite the massive amount of literature devoted to this subject, there is no historical evidence that the Templars did indulge in secret rituals or that they allowed homosexual practices. On the contrary, it is clear from the records that even under torture the knights were astonished even to be asked about such things. Just a few did report having had genuine homosexual experiences, but others recounted (not without a degree of pride) that they had paid forbidden nocturnal visits to barmaids and prostitutes. What is more important from a modern point of view is the fact that this anti-sodomitical atmosphere crossed all class barriers and was now so pervasive that it was possible to make political use of the accusation of homosexuality. This 'crime' was coupled with others relating to the invocation of demons and the world of the Devil: it was claimed that during initiation the Templars gave each other 'shameful kisses' on the mouth, navel, spine and buttocks, and that they desecrated the Cross and worshipped a mystic head (which was variously named 'Maffomet' and 'Magometus' – obviously a corrupted form of Muhammad).

Contemporary with the trials of the Templars were the posthumous accusations made against Pope Boniface VIII, who had died in 1303. In 1310–11 Philip IV, who had long quarrelled with Boniface when he was alive, summoned innumerable people to give evidence against him. Some were witnesses from the time before Benedetto Gaetani had been elected pope, and some of them were merely character witnesses whose testimony was based on hearsay. All kinds of accusations were made against Boniface, as they were against the Knights: that he had been guilty of Christological heresy, of 'passive idolatry' (it was said that he had ordered people to worship his statue) and, above all, of sodomy. The scenes of homosexual assault and the words reported in the records are sometimes so detailed that one might assume a degree of historical truth mixed in with the fantasy. In order to prevent the condemnation of a predecessor, Clement V had the whole affair brought before the Holy See to ensure that it would gradually peter out.

The fall of Edward II of England followed a similar pattern. Although he married Isabella, daughter of Philip IV of France, Edward made no secret of his preference for his favourites, initially Piers Gaveston (who was murdered in 1312) and then the two Despensers, Hugh III le Despenser (the father) and Hugh IV le Despenser (the son), both of whom were gruesomely murdered in 1326. Even though there was no 'evidence' (in the strict sense of the term) of sodomy, the king's critics pointed to the ennoblement and material enrichment of lower-ranking men. This may well have been one reason why Isabella played an active part in Edward's downfall, attempting to seize the kingdom with her own lover. Certainly her father must initially have thought that if the king of England had no heir he would inherit the kingdom; but a son – the future Edward III – was in fact born in 1312.

The common denominator between these three cases – the Templars, Boniface and Edward II – was the politically motivated charge of sodomy, specifically as used by Philip IV in his struggle for supreme power within the Holy Roman Empire. By dissolving the Knights Templar he hoped to use their

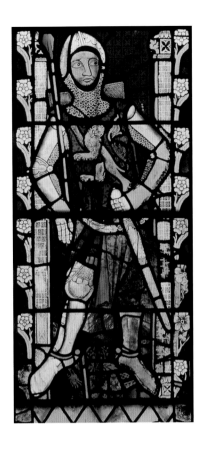

wealth in order to wage war on England as well as to finance a new crusade. The attack on Boniface was engineered to pressure Pope Clement into dissolving the Templars as well as to re-establish his own honour, which had been tarnished by his initial conflict with the papacy. By marrying his daughter Isabella to Edward II in 1308, Philip was possibly hoping to inherit from his homosexual arch-enemy.

Religious and secular inquisition, 13th–14th centuries

One of the most significant changes that took place in the early 13th century was a reform of the Church's penal system. The existing process, which allowed accusations in the form of personal (written) charges and involved a decentralized procedure before the local bishop, archdeacon or other official, was fundamentally altered by Pope Innocent III around 1200, so that an *ex officio* intervention became possible in certain cases, with an *inquisitio* conducted either centrally or by a representative of the pope. The material requirement for a condemnation was no longer an ordeal, which was understood as God's judgment on the case in hand, but a 'voluntary' confession supported by clear evidence. In order to facilitate this system, Innocent IV sanctioned the use of torture as a means of investigation in 1252. Early forms of Innocent III's new principle determined the methods used by Conrad of Marburg and his colleagues, to whom perhaps two hundred people fell victim between 1231 and 1233. But it was only when the use of torture and summary trials became systematic that the Inquisition acquired its reputation

Although painted around 1490, this work by the Spanish artist Pedro Berruguete (opposite) shows the Inquisition at work in the 13th century: a public execution presided over by St Dominic himself. Although created to suppress heresy, the Inquisition also enforced aspects of sexual morality, a task made easier by the zeal with which some cities sought out sodomites. Trials were conducted in secret, with the inquisitor acting as both prosecution and judge; cases were then handed over to the secular authorities for sentencing and punishment.

While passing through Lucca in 1369 on his way back from Rome, Holy Roman Emperor Charles IV and his wife witnessed a young man having sex with a youth. Despite the fact that the young man was a nephew of the town's governor, Charles had him castrated and burnt at the stake (above). The emperor and his wife watch from the window at left. Woodcut after an illustration in the chronicles of Giovanni Sercambi, a local apothecary.

for arbitrariness and cruelty, an approach best represented by the Spanish Inquisition at the end of the 15th century.

It should be emphasized, however, that the inquisitorial attack on sodomites from the 13th until the late 15th century was carried out by secular, municipal authorities and spread from the towns. Very early on, when they were first setting down their written statutes, Italian towns started to formulate penalties for homosexuality: Siena from 1262 to 1270, Bologna in 1288, Florence in 1325, and Perugia in 1342. As a result of these laws, sodomites were hunted down, tortured, mutilated or even executed by the authorities. Castration was common, and so were blinding and the amputation of hands and feet. In Florence, for example, it was decided in 1325 that any sodomite who had intercourse with a younger person should be castrated; in addition, the younger person, if he had not resisted, should be punished with a public whipping and a fine of 50 pounds (*lire*) or 100 pounds if he was between fourteen and eighteen years old. A public beating should also be administered to any woman who 'offered her limbs for the practice of the sodomite pestilence'.

The fact that the Holy Roman kings and emperors had no doubts concerning the execrable nature of sodomy can be illustrated by two examples. Rudolf I of Habsburg, as is succinctly recorded in the Basel Annals, is said to have burned to death a certain 'gentleman from Haspisperch' in 1277 'because of the sodomitic crime'. There is a certain black humour in the more detailed account of a similar case under Charles IV. When the emperor was returning from his second visit to Rome in 1369, he stayed at the castle in Lucca. He, his wife and a cardinal happened to look out of the window and saw a young man having sex with a youth. He had them both brought before him and found out that the young man was a nephew of the governor. Despite the pleas of the parents, he had the young man paraded before the town, castrated and then burned at the stake. The youth was able to buy his freedom.

The Late Middle Ages
Sensational trials and VIPs
It was a characteristic of the persecution of sodomites in the late Middle Ages that all class barriers were broken, and it was a matter of principle that people of

all classes could be prosecuted. Beginning with machinations of Philip IV of France, a number of high-ranking individuals came under suspicion of sodomy. A hundred years after the death of Edward II, the English king Richard II (d. 1400) was also accused of sodomy, which may well have played a part in his downfall. A similar fate befell the Folkung Magnus Eriksson, king of Norway and Sweden: accused by a relative, St Bridget of Sweden, of unnatural behaviour (to be precise, of having intercourse with the knight Bengt Algotsson), he was forced to abdicate in favour of Duke Albrecht of Mecklenburg in 1364. In the context of papal history one should also mention Baldassare Cossa, the antipope John XXIII, who was branded a criminal by theologians at the Council of Constance in 1415 with the aid of some fantastical accusations – the rape of three hundred virgins and of a whole family, including the father.

There was also a good deal of political expediency behind the sodomy charge against Pons Hugo IV of Ampurias (Ampurdán) (1277–1313). This count had brought the wrath of James II of Aragon (1264–1327) upon himself by refusing to follow the king's instructions concerning the Knights Templar and by seizing a Venetian cargo ship. Another case, in Germany, was that of the Duke of Jülich, Wilhelm V – also Earl of Cambridge and a peer of England – who in December 1349 was deposed by his own sons 'because of sodomitic evil'. He was not freed until June 1351, after his brother, the archbishop of Cologne, and others had paid over a large sum of ransom money.

A similarly nasty affair involved the nobleman Konrad von Murach from the Upper Palatinate, who in 1466 was forced to confess to having indulged in the sin of sodomy. In actual fact, he had refused to give the castle and district of Tännesberg back to the Counts Palatine, and this was their way of making him submit.

The persecution of sodomites in urban society

The attitude of late medieval urban society towards homosexuality was extremely ambivalent. Humanistic men of letters and philosophers revived the ethos of Platonic friendship, while painters and sculptors devoted great works of art to the beauty of the male body. However, in many towns – sometimes the very same ones where the artists were at work – the contemporary cultural trend was towards an inquisitorial penal code. This included the active search for sodomites, which entailed financial rewards for those who denounced the culprits; the acceptance of unwritten and anonymous accusations; torture as a method of investigation and as a means of eliciting further names; the application of a differentiated system of corporal punishments and personal degradation; and, finally, the ritual of public exhibition and destruction of the bodies of those condemned.

Venice and Florence hold relatively complete sets of records that document the systematic persecution of sodomites from the 14th century onwards. But there were also many towns on the German side of the Alps that put the sodomites on trial, including Augsburg, Regensburg and Basel. The city of Cologne – an ancient Roman foundation with approximately 35,000 inhabitants, making it the largest town in Germany at that time – was especially assiduous in this regard, sponsoring several secret commissions that actively elicited information concerning the 'unspeakable sin' from confessors during 1484, although there were no penal consequences. We know of no comparable cases from German towns situated north of the Main river, whereas in the late medieval trade centres of Flanders, such as Ghent and Bruges, there was violent persecution of sodomites, on a par with that in Florence and Venice. In the inquisitional records of Montaillou, a small village in the Languedoc that was investigated for Catharist heresy at the beginning of 14th century, sodomy figures prominently. However, there has not yet been any systematic research into similar anti-sodomite proceedings in such important cities as Avignon, Paris and London.

According to the sources mentioned above, the sodomites were brought forth by the town council bailiffs to be banished or executed; they were, of course, given no opportunity to leave behind any record of their own circumstances, thoughts or feelings. Nevertheless, the sources – which bear witness to negation and exclusion – do frequently reflect a more positive side: they depict, indirectly, the sodomites' working and family lives, with all their everyday problems and pressures. The direct speech that these criminal proceedings often put into the mouths of the accused also offers important insights into the views that the youths and husbands had of themselves and others. Here follow a few examples.

Social topography

When the councillors of Cologne visited the parishes of the old city in 1484, the parish priest of St Martin's told them that he knew of a 'foul society' on the Heumarkt, and of some houses on the neighbouring Leinwandmarkt that he would demolish without further ado if he could. The priest believed he had concrete knowledge of what went on in these places, and had evidently been observing one particular group so closely that he was able to estimate their number at two hundred. Other records kept by the council commission also refer frequently to this quarter, as well as to a neighbouring area extending down to the Rhine. Clearly, the priest had discovered an early form of social topography and had pinpointed some type of conduct that did not take place in complete secrecy.

The upper classes in Venice (which then had a population of about 100,000) also had very concrete knowledge of the sodomites' favourite haunts. In 1444 the Council of Ten – specially appointed judges principally in charge of rooting out crimes against the state, but by that time also responsible for the punishment of sodomy – ordered that all establishments in which children and young people learned to play music, sing and dance should close at nightfall. Raids were carried out on apothecaries and the shops of barbers, surgeons and goldsmiths, and several mass trials – most notably between 1422 and 1483 but also at other times – uncovered whole networks of 'apothecary's customers'. The Molo (wharf area) was kept under surveillance, the rulers being particularly afraid of homosexual activity among the sailors because they believed that it would be punished by shipwrecks and floods.

Young men exercising in a gymnasium: a Netherlandish woodcut by the Master of the Banderoles, *c.* 1450–75. Medieval court and civic records give us a partial but sometimes extremely vivid picture of the daily lives of homosexuals who lived in towns and cities. In a particular, we learn of the types of places where homosexuals would meet, which, depending on the city in question, ranged from private houses and exercise grounds (as here) to bathing places, apothecaries' shops and the 'secret chambers' (lavatories) of monastic buildings.

The situation in German towns was quite different. In the old bishopric of Regensburg, for instance, which had a population of about 12,000 in 1500, a man accused of sodomy gave the names of two guest houses as 'scenes of the crime': in the Nuremberg house of 'Guldenkron', he had 'done it' with a nobleman seventeen years previously, and in the Regensburg house of 'Lindwurm', he had committed 'knavery' with another man. Other assignations took place in the 'secret chamber' (the lavatory) of the monastery of the Augustinian Eremites in Regensburg, as well as in the city's chapel of the Holy Cross. There is mention of both 'secret chambers' and church buildings in many other sources, which suggests that these places were used frequently for rendezvous.

The fact that one cannot generalize from these individual glimpses of social topography is made clear by the trial of sodomites in Augsburg in 1532. The homosexual lives of the men – who were all adult and married – for the most part took place not within their own four walls, but outside the city gates.

Those who were 'ready for action' met in three suburban bathing places that were situated beside rivulets and which also offered overnight accommodation. The main culprit, Berlin Wagner, also liked to take his partners to villages around the city such as Hainhofen, where the incumbent priest was a friend of his, or to a special guest house in Friedberg, Swabia.

Social structure

In the late Middle Ages sodomy was an offence committed not only by the aristocracy or the wealthier classes. The information we have from Italian and German towns relates to sodomites who are clearly from the centre or the lower third of the social spectrum. Most people charged with sodomy were middle-class craftsmen and traders, and lower-class servants, retailers and casual workers. But of course the ruling classes and the officials, the noblemen of Venice and the upper-class families of Germany, were also involved, if only on a smaller scale.

Heading the list of the accused in 15th-century Venetian records are glassblowers, goldsmiths, barbers, gondoliers, shoemakers, tailors, carpenters and silk-weavers. About one third of the sodomites were aristocrats, clerics and boys (often from the colonies), all of whom were subject to different penal codes: clerics came under canon law (in which there was no death penalty); boys under the age of twelve were exempt from the maximum penalty but not from torture; and aristocrats were generally given the opportunity to flee before judgment was passed.

Michael Rocke has calculated that between 1478 and 1520 there were 1,119 sodomites condemned in Florence, made up of the following: 232 shoemakers, 134 weavers, 125 clothiers, 97 butchers, 95 barbers, 94 clerics (both secular and in religious orders), 85 tailors, 62 dyers, 61 carpenters and 61 other tradesmen, plus a number of officials, apprentices, servants and artists. Members of the lowest classes – that is, people living on charity, non-taxpayers and those on the fringes of society – do not figure at all in the Florentine or Venetian records. In Avignon, the profession of one Raimundus Pascal, who was charged (probably unjustly) with sodomitical lewdness in 1365, was given as 'money-lender'. The professions mentioned in the late medieval sources of the German-speaking part of Switzerland include cook, verger, court attendant, fisherman, barber and carpenter, while the Augsburg records of 1532 list one grocer, one landlord, one bath-attendant, one gingerbread-maker and a schoolteacher. Strikingly, the Augsburg sources feature several priests, including the curate in charge of St Moritz and a parish priest from outside the city.

If we presume that homosexuality existed as a matter of course at all social levels, these findings are a clear indication that the prosecutors were simply not interested in fringe groups such as beggars or prostitutes (who were in fact already branded), but were out to get the 'pillars of society' responsible for production, economic prosperity and the whole system of family life and procreation. In this respect, the city fathers were guided by the archaic notion that the sin of sodomy would draw the wrath of God down upon the community and for this reason constituted a threat to them all.

In 1475 Johannes Stocker, a curate of Basel Minster, was convicted of repeatedly raping Johannes Müller, a choirboy. His punishment – lenient by the standard of the times – was the confiscation of assets and banishment beyond the Alps. As if in mockery, he signs himself at the bottom of the settlement 'Johannes Stocker, presbiter et sodomita' ('priest and sodomite').

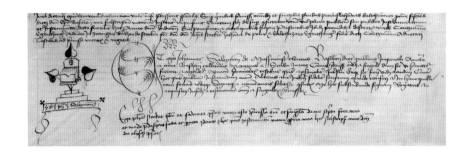

Penal measures

It is one of the little-known facts in the history of criminal law that the penalties imposed on sodomites between the 13th century and early modern times were systematically intensified and diversified. Municipal decrees in the late 13th and early 14th centuries generally imposed corporal punishment on first-time offenders, in the form of castration or whipping, or gave them fines; the death penalty was reserved for repeat offenders. A typical form of execution for those convicted of sodomy was public burning at the stake, a practice associated with the trials of heretics (especially during the Cathar crusades). The example set by the Old Testament, which tells of a rain of fire over Sodom and Gomorrah (Genesis 19), and the edict of Theodosius I in 390 may also have played a part in the establishment of this unwritten law.

As early as the 14th century, there were several spectacular trials of individuals. In Venice in 1354, the judges of public morals convicted and burnt to death a man named Rolandino Ronchaia, who called himself 'Rolandina' and who had worked for years with the prostitutes on the Rialto. Emperor Charles IV, as we have seen, had a 'soddomito' castrated and burned to death in Lucca in 1369. No less spectacular, since it was contrary to canon law, was a trial held in Augsburg in 1381: two monks, who were fellow members of the Beghard brotherhood, and a peasant were publicly burned because of 'heresy that they had performed with one another'.

An example from Augsburg shows the tendency of the persecutors to inflict the greatest degree of physical pain and indeed to revel in the sufferings of their victims. In 1409 four priests were put in a huge birdcage and hung up from the highest tower in the old town until they died of hunger and thirst. The fifth man in their group, a furrier, was 'let off' with mere burning at the stake. We do not know whether the Augsburgers imported the birdcage idea from Italy or thought it up themselves, but it is possible that the choice of the cage as a punishment was meant to preserve the priests' physical integrity and to avoid direct bloodshed. The Bolognese followed a mixed procedure in 1422 when they executed a priest, choosing to shut him up in a thatched hut, pour oil over it and set it on fire. In 1475 the bishop of Basel and his panel of judges imposed a much milder penalty on Johannes Stocker, a curate of the Minster, who confessed to having raped a choirboy several times: all his goods were confiscated, but he was allowed to go into permanent exile on the other side of the Alps.

In 1426 Antonio Masi from Bologna, known as Cantarino, suffered a grisly combination of degradation and physical punishment: he was led naked, with

Knights and nobility seem frequently
to have lacked a guilty conscience when
it came to accusations of sodomy. This
was particularly so with Richard Puller
von Hohenburg from Alsace, who had
the witnesses to his crime murdered
and who submitted appeals to the
emperor and the pope. He was finally
arrested and burnt at the stake in Zurich
in 1482, alongside the barber Anton Maetzler.
This illustration, from Diebold Schilling's
Great Chronicles of Burgundy, shows the
city's mayor outside the city gates, himself
executed in 1489 for various crimes
including sodomy.

a bonnet on his head, through the town to the place of execution, where he was publicly castrated. Stripping, being held up to ridicule, public exhibition, castration, and sometimes an agonizing execution under the scornful gaze of the jeering mob — these were the methods devised for the destruction of the criminal's personal dignity as well as his body.

In Venice and Florence, the persecution of sodomites was accompanied by proactive measures that were unique in form. The public of both cities were offered large financial inducements to hand over the names of sodomites; anonymous denunciations were permitted; those in holy orders were compelled, on pain of being banned from the priesthood, to inform the authorities of even the slightest suspicion; and those who were found guilty were promised a reduced penalty and a reward if they agreed to become 'witnesses for the prosecution' by denouncing their sexual partner. All these were measures that led to a new career: that of the sodomite informer. Apart from the death penalty, cities in Italy and Germany also made use of mutilation (cutting off the right hand), blinding, the imposition of fines, and exile.

A slim falconer, wearing a crown of leaves and dressed in tight, fashionable clothing, out hunting arm-in-arm with an equally elegant companion. This light-hearted image was etched by the Housebook Master in *c.* 1485 and captures well the potential for homoerotic sentiment in late medieval courtly culture.

How people saw themselves

The actual words of the accused as set down in the criminal records often reveal a remarkable degree of self-esteem and self-awareness on the part of the sodomites. Evidently many men, facing certain death and having nothing to lose, threw off all inhibition and told of their own eventful past; they despised their ecclesiastical and secular persecutors who, in truth, could not possibly stamp out sodomy.

Rolandino Ronchaia, mentioned above, made the following statement in 1354. Since childhood he had never felt any 'natural desire' for a woman. He had left the woman he had married in Padua and had settled in Venice. Since he had the voice, face, demeanour and breasts of a woman, people had regarded him only as a woman and had called him 'Rolandina'. He had given men exactly the same pleasure as women gave them.

In 1395 an English equivalent of Rolandina was arrested in London and burned at the stake. John Rykener, alias 'Eleanor', had for years been having intercourse with men in exchange for money, mainly with students and Franciscans; he had dressed either in men's or women's clothes according to the wishes of the client. The fact that he preferred priests was due simply to the fact that they paid him more than anyone else.

Priests were generally spared the death penalty when they were found guilty of such crimes. During his trial in 1326, Arnaud de Verniolles, a wealthy Franciscan and subdeacon of Pamiers caught up in the troubles at Montaillou, described in great detail how he used to entice young students to one of his two houses, on the pretext of hearing their confessions, and then rape them. He used to explain to them that intercourse with men was a lesser sin than intercourse with women, since sex with men corresponded to nature and was good for the health. Mocking his opponent, the then bishop of Pamiers (later to become Pope Benedict XII), de Verniolles maintained that in Pamiers alone there were 3,000 men infected with the vice.

There was an equal measure of self-esteem and lack of a guilty conscience among the knights and nobility. This can be seen from the case of the Alsatian chatelain Richard Puller von Hohenburg. Firstly, he swiftly got rid of an eye-witness to his homosexual activities, and then succeeded in delaying his threatened arrest for several years by appealing to the emperor and the pope. At last he was seized in Zurich, together with his latest lover, and sentenced to death by burning in 1482.

There are many verse epics and rhyming chronicles from the late Middle Ages that reflect the reality of the 'sodomitic sin'. Most of these texts mock the culprits' apparent refusal to procreate and propose the severest penal measures. On the other hand, the ethical value of friendship was revived in the poems and letters of the Italian Renaissance, and, towards the end of the 15th century, on the threshold of the Reformation, humanists such as Erasmus of Rotterdam and Jakob Wimpfeling began to develop their own independent forms of the friendship cult.

The medieval period even conceived of a men-only state from which all women were banished, albeit in an anonymous French prose novel called *Bérinus*, written in the late 14th century. The eponymous hero, governor of the island of Blandie, is threatened by a strange enemy named King Agriano of Gamel. The latter has instructed the knights in his kingdom to bring him all the women so that they can be locked up. The women succeed in fleeing to Blandie, however, and Agriano – the *faulx roys desnaturez* – takes bloody revenge on the Blandie islanders, having their noses cut off and their eyes poked out. After a long war, Agriano finally gets the punishment he deserves: for ten years he must rot in a deep ditch with worms and snakes until the boiling sea carries him off to the gaping jaws of hell. In keeping with the spirit of the age, this homosexual land is viewed not as a paradise but as a tyranny. The 'false, unnatural king' can only celebrate his triumph for a brief moment before being taken down to Hades. Nevertheless, the idea of a men-only state was both thinkable and open to discourse in this age of ambivalence.

Early Modern Europe, 1400–1700
HELMUT PUFF

Scholars of the Renaissance in the 19th century, some of them gay, envisioned the 15th and 16th centuries as an age in which individualistic hedonism reigned and male–male eroticism thrived, a refracting mirror held up to their own 'Victorian' age. Walter Pater (1839–94), John Addington Symonds (1840–93) and other writers forged an eroticized image of the past to reflect their own and their readers' desires. Visions of the Renaissance thus contributed to the construction of modern sexual selves.[1]

This celebratory image of sexual freedom in the Renaissance is a figment, based on the selective use of evidence and inspired by works of art, most of them Italian in origin. Today's homosexuals share much less with their supposed companions in the past than modern theories of sexual desire (which see it as innate) would suggest. In accordance with sexology and other sciences that place sexuality within the realm of nature, historians have traditionally cast the sexual as a stable aspect of life without a particular history. In fact, we must free ourselves of this longing for an erotic utopia in the past and instead strive to approach sexual concepts and erotic lives in history on their own terms.

Recent research on male–male sexuality during the early modern period has uncovered a different history, one replete with contradictions and tensions. It was a period in which terms such as *sodomia* and *vicium sodomiticum*, with their associations of heresy, treason and *lèse-majesté*, designated a vast and confusing array of non-procreative sexual practices. Conventionally, these practices included masturbation, non-vaginal intercourse between a man and a woman, sex between animals and humans, as well as all forms of same-sex sexual acts – the term's most prominent connotation. Yet the much-reviled concept of sodomy was coeval with the celebration of affectionate love between men. It was a period when persecution of sodomites hovered between the haphazard and the systematic; when theological and judicial condemnations of sodomy coexisted with the affirmation of homoeroticism in works of art; when previously neglected sources of homoerotic inspiration, many of them ancient in origin, surfaced in a Europe that was in the process of re-establishing its Christian foundations through a series of religious reforms. Contradictions as fundamental as these cannot, and should not, be resolved into a harmonious overall picture; rather, they inform the historical process. What is more, men (and women) of all classes embraced, negotiated and manipulated the plethora of ideas and institutions that shaped sexual ideas

According to medieval theology, those who indulged in illicit sexual acts, homosexual or otherwise, were doomed to a long and painful afterlife. In Taddeo di Bartolo's *Last Judgment*, a late fourteenth-century fresco from the Collegiata in San Gimignano, a man labelled 'sotomitto' is impaled through mouth and anus while three demons torture adulterous women.

The hideous vision of the 'sin of Sodom' carried over into the early modern period almost unchanged. Above: This woodcut from a text on the seven deadly sins by Georg Wickram (c. 1545) shows the destruction of Sodom and Gomorrah (the sexual sins themselves were deemed unrepresentable in a religious context). Below: The *Constitutio Criminalis Carolina*, the law code promulgated by Charles V in 1532. It prescribed burning at the stake for men or women convicted of 'unchaste behaviour'.

and sexual practices during the early modern period. The presence of historical tensions and contradictory impulses surrounding same-sex sexuality is my starting point for this chapter.

Patterns of persecution

Sodomia, that enigmatic coinage of medieval theologians, continued to gain currency in the early modern period. It yielded ever-new meanings and entered new social and literary contexts. 'Neither now nor on the Day of Judgment', one Leonard of Udine (b. 1400) argued, would sodomites be able to excuse their behaviour, since nature had unmistakably taught humans to procreate. What exactly these sodomitical sins were, however, was hard to gather from this theologian's elusive descriptions.[2] The most revered preachers of the age therefore translated *sodomia* into the realm of social experience. At a time when theologians voiced fears that a mere mention would spread sexual unorthodoxies like a contagious disease and manuals for confessors urged priests to handle the 'unspeakable sin' with the utmost discretion, the sodomite became a stock figure of homiletics. St Bernardino (1380–1444), for instance, a Franciscan friar and popular sermonizer from Siena, openly condemned urban societies in his native Italy that condoned the sexual pursuit of male youths by adult men.[3] The Dominican St Vincent Ferrer from Spain (d. 1419) or the Alsatian Johann Geiler von Kaysersberg (1443–1510) may have been less descriptive. Yet like many other preachers they warned their flock against plagues, famines and other disasters caused by practitioners of the vice 'against nature'. Sodomites in a community's midst would bring about God's wrath. Thus it consistently appeared that individual sexual behaviour was connected to the fate of whole communities.

In addition to being a severe transgression of Christian sexual ethics, *sodomia* therefore became a sign of social disorder. When, at the end of the 15th century, Sandro Botticelli (1445–1510) illustrated Dante's *Divine Comedy*, he rendered the part of hell where sodomites are punished in an angled and skewed perspective, unlike any other image in the cycle. This distortion captures succinctly the profound corruption of the natural and social orders associated with this sin.[4]

At a time when scholastics, legal commentators and poets elaborated on sodomy's utter reprehensibleness, kings, magistrates and ecclesiastics started to formulate laws against those who allegedly defied the natural order by engaging in intercourse with their own sex. Italian cities decreed the death penalty for same-sex eroticism as early as the 13th and 14th centuries, and such anti-sodomy legislation became more common in the 15th century when sermonizers occasioned further laws.[5]

Actual prosecution did not have to rely on express legal stipulations against sodomites, however. After all, many kingdoms, territories and towns seem to have lacked specific legislation and yet persecuted sodomites. In an age when politico-legal authority was predicated on Christian tenets, biblical passages – above all the Old Testament narrative of Sodom and Gomorrah – provided judges with the authority necessary to carry out punishments in cases of

Whether the seventh circle of hell in the *Divine Comedy* includes those punished for same-sex eroticism has been a matter of debate: in keeping with convention, Dante refrains from naming the 'unspeakable sin'. The eccentric perspective of this illustration, painted sometime between 1480 and 1495 by Sandro Botticelli, alludes to 'crimes against the laws of nature'. Botticelli himself would be accused of sodomy in 1502.

sodomy. This notwithstanding, anti-sodomy measures did gain a new legal basis in secular law during the early modern period. The Holy Roman Empire's criminal law code, the so-called *Constitutio Criminalis Carolina* of 1532, both fixed and recast prior legal practice. The relevant statute prescribed burning at the stake for 'unchaste behaviour' committed between men, between women, or between men and animals.[6] In England, Parliament passed a law in 1533–34 'for the punishment of the vice of buggerie'. In fact, this statute paved the way for King Henry VIII's break with Rome: Catholic clerics were its primary target.[7]

Wherever we look, urban courts spearheaded attempts to rid communities of sodomites, be they clerics or laymen; they were viewed as traitors, heretics, or simply as a danger. At one end of the spectrum lies Florence, one of Europe's premier banking centres and the birthplace of the Renaissance. In 1432, the city embarked on an unprecedented experiment when its government launched a campaign to uproot the illicit love between men that supposedly had infested their community. In fact, all across Europe the city was known as much for the greed of its merchants as for its sodomy-prone citizens. The stereotype that troubled the Florentine government was found by the 'Office of the Night', the civic commission set up to fight sodomy, to be not far from the truth. Over the decades commissioners investigated, interrogated and punished a good part of Florence's male population, producing a trail of archival

Execution ober Sodomitig.
der St att BRVG.

'Execution for sodomitical godlessness in the city of Bruges': an engraving
by Frans Hogenberg, *c*. 1578. Having seized control of Bruges's mendicant
monasteries, Calvinists used politically motivated accusations of sodomy
to have the clerics executed. Such slurs were commonly used to vilify
Catholics, especially monks and prelates, and images such as this served
as Protestant propaganda.

records in its wake. According to the Office's findings, erotic bonds between men did indeed pervade the city's social fabric. This highly unusual and ultimately unsuccessful effort in sexual engineering only came to an end in 1502, when the commission was disbanded. Yet sodomy remained punishable.[8]

Venice, a city vulnerable to floods and epidemics, witnessed a comparably systematic campaign against sodomites as urban scapegoats. After 1516, the city's 'Collegium contra sodomitas', first instituted in 1418, even employed agents provocateurs to entrap culprits. In a city governed by an urban elite, patricians commonly went without punishment, while the lower and middle classes bore the brunt of the proceedings.[9] The long-lasting, comprehensive programmes of civic moral reform and the specialized task forces launched by certain Italian communes to eradicate sodomy had no parallels in the rest of Europe, however.

At the other end of the spectrum lay Russia, with its low levels of prosecution. As a rule, male–male eroticism there remained within the jurisdiction of the Orthodox Church. Russian secular law courts and state institutions rarely seem to have been active in cases of same-sex sexual activity. As sins, sexual acts between men remained within the domain of confession and church discipline.[10]

Many parts of Europe experienced relatively moderate levels of persecution. Trials for 'pederasty' were seemingly rare; or, as one might reformulate it, homoeroticism rarely came to court.[11] For instance in Bruges, one of Europe's largest cities, ninety executions for sodomy are reported for the years 1385–1515. Although this constitutes a considerable number, the death penalty for this 'very strong, evil, and detestable crime and sin of sodomy' rarely averaged more than one per cent of all capital punishments.[12] In London, only one man was charged with sodomy in the years between 1420 and 1518.[13] The German city of Frankfurt documented two sodomy trials, one in 1598 and one in 1645 – cases that demonstrate, among other points, how a citizen's erotically suspect actions were sometimes the matter of conversation long before they reached the courts.[14]

Importantly, execution was not the only punishment for sodomitical acts. Judges regularly took into account potentially mediating factors such as a suspect's young age, the use of force, or the number of sexual encounters. According to the gravity of the offence, the convicted was reprimanded, fined, exiled, sent to the galleys, beheaded or burnt at the stake. In Florence, the attempt to rid the city of sodomy met with resistance to upsetting the status quo; as a result, the authorities intervened cautiously, in most cases imposing fines on the guilty.[15] But even in the North, where death sentences for adult and repeat offenders were common, responses to same-sex eroticism were not unequivocal. In Cologne in 1484, the city council's investigation into the 'spread of sodomy' proceeded with caution, despite some clerics' advocacy of a more stringent response: a deceased council member had emerged at the centre of allegations.[16] Attitudes towards and persecution of sodomy were thus more contradictory than the gruesome record of executions leads us to believe.

However, in an age of state-building across Europe, persecution did intensify. Across Europe, relative laxity in medieval ecclesiastical courts gave way

be Gottlosigkeit in

The true por-
traiture of   the Earle of
                               Castlehaven.

Although rare, trials for sodomy in 17th century England caused great scandal. In 1631 the Earl of Castlehaven was accused of being sexually involved with two male servants and of allowing them to rape his wife; he was found guilty and beheaded, while the two servants in question were hanged. The case's lurid details were reported in full at the end of the century and circulated in pamphlet form as late as 1710.

The 'Office of the Night' was established by the government of Florence in 1432 for the purpose of stamping out illicit vice. Yet so entrenched was the tradition of homoerotic behaviour in Florentine culture – despite preachers who railed against the temptations of pretty boys – that the experiment was abandoned seventy years later. This detail from the *Presentation of the Virgin* (opposite), painted by the Florentine Fra Carnevale in 1467, shows a church interior frequented by elegant young men in intimate conversation.

to stricter standards. On the Iberian peninsula, the early modern Inquisition tightened the rhetoric against sodomy and the enforcement of sexual discipline. But these standards were not nearly as deadly as commonly assumed. In Portugal, only a tenth of the sinners who confessed to the so-called 'ineffable sin' between 1587 and 1749 were put on trial. Overall, the Inquisition's handling of homoeroticism was 'marked more by compassion than justice', as long as subjects cooperated.[17] Practices, and levels of discipline, nevertheless varied. A high number of sodomy proceedings in Aragon, for instance, contrasts with lower numbers in other parts of Spain.[18] However, it does seem that secular authorities in Spain simultaneously stepped up their efforts in bringing suspected sodomites to trial: 147 sodomy proceedings before the secular courts of Seville and Granada led to the burning of 65 men between 1578 and 1616.[19]

As public events, sodomy trials and executions that concerned members of the nobility attracted particular attention. The story of Gilles de Rais's murderous lust for children has been notorious ever since his execution in 1440.[20] The 'sodomitical knight' Richard Puller von Hohenburg and his servant died at the stake in Zurich in 1482. According to contemporary chroniclers, this constituted a formative event for the Swiss Confederacy with its anti-aristocratic outlook.[21] Cross-class sodomy and rape became the potent signifiers for patriarchy's demise in the trial against Mervin Touchet, the second Earl of Castlehaven, who was executed in 1631.[22] In manifold ways, these spectacles of the law figured politically as well as sexually.

Trials and executions raised awareness that in a community's midst were sexual actors who threatened to harm the commonwealth – or at least that is what many believed. Not surprisingly, community members took an active interest in sexual matters. They not only stood on the sidelines, but at times actively partook in the early modern 'persecuting society' (to use Robert Moore's phrase). This was especially so if the targeted persons had no or little social capital, as was the case with foreigners, migrants and outsiders.

Court records – the basis of much of our knowledge about sexual cultures in early modern Europe – are notoriously hard to interpret. Trials often privilege the exceptional over the ordinary; as documents, they reduce a complex reality to the needs of bureaucratic formulae and due process; and in court, defendants and witnesses often reinvented themselves as they told their stories. Despite these limitations, court records are not the fictive accounts that some historians have made them out to be. Much information entered the record accidentally; the formulae of persecution are a window into the mentality of the experts; statements themselves can be read against the grain; and conflicting witness accounts provide insights into the way in which sodomy was perceived and lived.

But who were the targets of persecution? Only in the eye of some modern polemicists did sodomites form a group. If tempted, any man could be brought to act in the sodomitical fashion, or so one believed. Although medical commentators expounded that a particular sexual taste, bodily complexion or individual 'nature' might induce a person to stick with his own sex, sodomy

Albrecht Dürer had a particular interest in subjects of a homoerotic nature, even alluding to male–male eroticism in works that are obviously religious. Here, in Dürer's *Betrayal of Christ* from 1508, Judas' kiss is almost shockingly intimate.

was not thought of as a lifelong orientation, let alone a social identity. The excesses of the high life, such as feasting and the consumption of luxurious foods, for instance, supposedly led men to desire or commit same-sex sexual acts.[23] Yet within this assumed general susceptibility for erotic temptations of all kinds, lust for the same sex was considered a particularly dangerous and contagious form of desire – one whose grip on the person was relentless.[24]

How do we reconcile the harsh logic of persecution and the unforgiving rhetoric surrounding sodomy with findings that show that same-sex eroticism was embedded in men's ordinary lives? In the aftermath of Anabaptist rule (1534–35) in the northern German city of Münster, the authorities rounded up a certain Franz von Alsten – a quack whose confession exposed an active sex life among male artisans, some of them married, in the small nearby town of Hamm.[25] To pick a different and well-documented example (touched upon in the previous chapter), a scandal in Augsburg exposed a thriving cross-class network of male sexual trade.[26] To consider this conundrum we need to frame same-sex eroticism in the 'structures of feeling' (as Raymond Williams said) that have been lost – the affective bonds that tied men to their like. In order to contextualize same-sex sexual activities in the everyday homosocial milieux where they occurred, we need to depart from the concept of sodomy that was prevalent in pre-modern Europe. After all, *sodomia* was a word whose very essence sought to cast a horror on the various sexual activities grouped under its heading.

Intimate matters

In early modern Europe, women and men lived a good part of their lives in separate domestic and social spheres. Men spent much time with other males: at work, in leisure activities, journeying. Artisans, labourers, travellers and sailors lived in close quarters, guilds denied apprentices the right to marriage, and others did not have the means to wed. These spatial and socio-sexual conditions reinforced affective bonds between men. Early modern men were likely to experience emotional and, sometimes, erotic attachments to other men.

In Florence, the Commissioners of the Night discovered a code that shaped homoerotic camaraderie. These rules prescribed that adult men, whether married or bachelors, should take part in the erotic pursuit of youths and adolescents. While some men showed a lifelong preference for their own sex, the behaviour of other males proved to be more cyclical: after youthful attachments to older men, they moved on to marriage and do not appear in sodomy investigations thereafter. Strikingly, these socio-sexual patterns between men complemented the clan-like, hierarchical social networks of Florentine male society, which were organized along the lines of neighbourhood and profession, political allegiances and membership of certain confraternities.[27] But these patterns conflicted with concerns in the same urban community over procreation and moral probity.

Male–male sexual activity frequently crystallized in certain locales. The 15th-century noble Hermann von Landenberg occasionally picked up sexual prey in toilets.[28] Public baths, often associated with male–female sexual licence, served as a meeting place for some men who became the subject of sodomy investigations. When meeting an attendant in a bathhouse, Werner Steiner, a Protestant theologian in 16th-century Zurich, was so overcome with desire that he felt nauseous, or so he confessed under interrogation. At least on this occasion, Steiner claimed to have repressed the impulse.[29] Inns regularly brought strangers together who would share the same bed. On one of his journeys the Alsatian artisan Augustin Güntzer (1596–*c.* 1657) found himself at night in the company of Italian fellow travellers who threatened to rape him. When he wrote down an account of his life, Güntzer thanked his Protestant God profusely for having miraculously saved him from this onslaught of Italian, Catholic rogues.[30] Bathhouses, toilets and inns were places where men socialized with each other. There and elsewhere a masculine culture flourished that hovered between the potential for physical contact and the potential for violence, one of the possible responses to an unwanted erotic advance.

Historical accounts of early modern sexual behaviour have made much, perhaps too much, of the fact that in many instances sexual activity was intergenerational and that sexual roles were tied to age as well as class. According to this paradigm, older men penetrated younger males, as in Florence. This is indeed how homoeroticism was commonly imagined, a perception that itself must have shaped actors' desires and practices. Yet court records bespeak the fact that male–male sex did not always fit this pattern. It would be misleading to project this scenario of sexual domination and subjection onto early modern Europe as a whole. Sexual activity took place in a variety of locations and between a variety of individuals: among adolescents, among adults, and between actors of different ages. Lived eroticism did not always conform to the rules of social hierarchy.

Those who had acted sodomitically were not, as a rule, sexual rebels. Once in the dock, most of the people who had defied sexual morale confessed to their wrong-doing whether torture was used or not. Such admissions of guilt were certainly strategic, meant to assuage the judges. Yet the offenders' stories also show how they had competently hushed up their affairs, or asked their partners to keep silent and to destroy their love letters; how they bribed lovers with gifts; or how, like the Swiss Melchior Brütschli, they had gone on pilgrimage to repent for having 'lost themselves' in anal intercourse.[31] Viewed thus, their actions betray fear. But these same men were also comfortably negotiating their sexual activity. Actors frequently convinced themselves and others that homoerotic activity was negligible or common, a mere trifle of an enjoyment, a lesser sin. Johannes Stocker, a cleric, persuaded Johannes Müller, a youth with whom he was in love, to have sex with him. He mustered physical force as well as the force of argument, reasoning with the youth that 'If everybody who committed this [the act of sodomy] were burnt at the stake, not even fifty men would survive in Basel.' Stocker thus invoked and inverted the biblical narrative of Sodom's end, with its reference to the fifty just individuals whom God wanted to find in the city. This somewhat unusual statement is typical, however, in that the act itself remained unnamed, so insulting was its mention.[32] The term was so heinous, in fact, that it was rarely ever suitable for describing oneself.

In Giovanni di Paolo's vision of Paradise
(c. 1445), new arrivals in heaven are
warmly embraced by those of their
own sex. It is possible that the artist
was seeking to avoid associations of
sexuality (i.e. heterosexuality) by showing
predominantly same-sex couples, but
the cavorting cupids and hares – which
belong to secular images of courtly
'gardens of love' – confuse our response.

Eulogized by Cicero and, later, by
such writers as Aelred of Rievaulx
and Michel de Montaigne, the institution
of friendship was believed to surpass
all other attachments. In this portrait
by Pontormo, one of the men holds a
passage from Cicero's 'On Friendship'
that discusses the superiority of
friendship over wealth, honour,
sensual pleasure and health.

Wherever we look, the sodomite was another, not the self. Not surprisingly, those accused of sodomy frequently denied ever having acted in this way and drew a firm line between their own behaviour and that of sodomites.

Male intimacy also crystallized around friendship as a social practice. Unlike the reviled sodomite, the friend was a celebrated icon.[33] In his essay 'On Friendship', Michel de Montaigne (1533–92) monumentalized his beloved deceased friend Etienne de la Boétie. Intriguingly, this work discusses the highly idealized social institution of friendship alongside other social, emotional and erotic bonds. The essay describes sexual passion as fickle, for instance; by contrast 'the love of friends' generates 'a general universal warmth ... a warmth which is constant and at rest, all gentleness and evenness, having nothing sharp nor keen'.[34] Following the ancients, Montaigne postulates that friendship should be predicated on equality. In this context 'Greek love', that is pederasty, is characterized as having 'a great disparity and divergence of favours between the lovers'.[35] Given the inequality of age and sexual roles, pederasty could never aspire to equal friendship as a practice among equals, despite the fact that the partners share the same sex. Apparently, Montaigne did not conceive of same-sex sexual acts among men of the same age and the same social station.

In early modern Europe the bond of friendship signified far more than the voluntary ties we associate with the term today. Among the privileged classes, friendship was a social institution to complement other social bonds, kinship and marriage most prominent among them. Friendship thus came with obligations: friends erected funerary monuments after their companions' deaths, for example, or they were buried together. In the words of Alan Bray, friendship was an 'ethical praxis'.[36] In fact, what one friend felt for another was described with the same word that characterized amorous ties between the sexes: 'love'.

Upon his accession to the French throne in 1573, Henri III abandoned a distinguished military career, instead cultivating a courtly circle of writers and surrounding himself with handsome, ambiguously dressed favourites. These *mignons*, taken with Henri's love of jewelry and transvestite costume, led his opponents to denounce him for tyranny, heresy and sodomy. He was assassinated by a Dominican monk in 1589. Portrait by François Clouet, *c.* 1571.

Henri III was vilified in an extraordinary number of pamphlets, cartoons and engravings, most of which seem to have been politically motivated. In the example show opposite, Henri's effeminate court forms the subject of a contemporary satire called *The Island of Hermaphrodites*. The epigram on the frontispiece reads: 'I am neither male nor female / and if I confuse / Which of the two I ought to choose / it doesn't matter in the least. To have them both is much the best / For then the pleasure will be double.'

While male–male companionship thrived in all social classes, not only among the elite, friendship as a social pursuit flourished most conspicuously at court, be it ecclesiastical or secular. Popes surrounded themselves with younger family members, furthering their careers and bestowing favours on them.[37] Some rulers were notorious for conspicuously embracing the politics of friendship. Henri III, king of France (r. 1574–89), surrounded himself with a troupe of loyal minions, promoting his troubled rule by forging powerful bonds with close allies. Against the background of a royal marriage that remained childless, an Italian presence at court, and the political tensions between Catholics and Huguenots, the stylishly androgynous appearance of the king's favourites encouraged critics to equate favourites with ganymedes – a view elaborated in thousands of pamphlets directed against the monarch.[38]

King James I of England (r. 1603–25) addressed George Villiers, the first Duke of Buckingham, as 'my onlie sweete & deare chylde'; he signed the same letter 'your deere daide & husbande James R[ex]', after having offered to 'mak … a new marriage' between them.[39] James authored the letter at a moment of political crisis for the English monarchy, reinforcing their bond of friendship by drawing on notions of fatherhood, kinship, marriage and royalty. That the Dutch Stadtholder William III of Orange (1650–1702), later king of England, had a lifelong preference for the company of male friends over that of his wife

PARS EST UNA PATRIS, CÆTERA MATRIS HABET

Martial.

A TOUS ACORDS

Je ne suis male, ni Femelle
Et si je suis bien en cervelle
Lequel des deux je dois choisir
Mais qu'importe à qui on ressamble,
Il vaut mieux les avoir ensemble,
On en reçoit double plaisir.

Like a number of monarchs from the early modern period, William III of England (also Prince of Orange) acquired a reputation for favouring close male acquaintances. Although some of this speculation was politically motivated, his relationship with two men in particular was notably intimate: Hans William Bentinck, who was created Earl of Portland (shown here, on the king's right), and Arnold van Keppel, who became Earl of Albemarle. The king himself found it 'a most extraordinary thing that one may not feel regard and affection for a young man without its being criminal'.

was well known. He had his own likeness painted with the twin image of his favourite, Hans Willem Bentinck, as his self's shadow.[40]

Ties of friendship had the potential to cut through existing social hierarchies, and favouritism regularly incited criticism. A lowly count, Caspar Gottfried of Pappenheim (d. 1650), turned to non-aristocrats for companionship – much to the chagrin of his family, who initiated legal proceedings to depose him for sodomy, among other reasons.[41] In the hands of political leaders and commentators, suspicions of sodomy were a convenient weapon that could be wielded against kings, foreign peoples and opponents in general. These accusations were all the more powerful since no writer at that time – theologian, legal expert or scientist – seems to have questioned the premise that same-sex eroticism was deserving of the severest penalties.

While certain friendships were certainly an exclusive affair, the amorous rituals of such 'voluntary kinship' (as Alan Bray puts it) were often played out in public. Attempts by modern critics to break through the polite and politic façade of friendships to determine whether friends were erotically involved have relied on mainly circumstantial evidence: an unhappy marriage, lack of children etc. On the one hand, the question of whether friends had sex or not is ours. To ask it is a reflection of the way we moderns accord sexuality a central position in a person's life. As historians, we need to accept that our forefathers did not share the same concern. On the other hand, these questions are not ours exclusively, as rumours, criticisms and litigations from the past clearly reveal. It is not that sex was of no consequence in pre-modern societies. Increased awareness of sodomy during this period made homosocial alliances erotically suspicious.

Renaissance traditions and their discontents

The cult of friendship was not new in early modern Europe. It had thrived in monastic circles during the Middle Ages. Yet in the Renaissance, there was an influx of new ideas and new practices. Since the 14th century Italian humanists, artists and princes had striven to revive the world of the ancients in order to renew their own society. This movement, which began in Italy and resonated throughout Europe, unearthed, among other discoveries, a trove of sexual unorthodoxies in antiquity — finds that would inspire the formation of a homoerotic idiom. In the allegations made against the English playwright Christopher Marlowe (1564–93), one of his companions charged that Marlowe had described St John as Christ's 'Alexis'. Derived from a homoerotic poem by Virgil, this name functioned as a codeword for a male lover.[42]

Referring to the representation of beautiful women's bodies, the scholar Robert Scribner once spoke of an all-pervasive eroticization of art before the Reformation.[43] One could make a similar argument, however, for the visual representation of men. To be sure, realistically portrayed naked male bodies lent themselves to erotic responses. Yet other interests, such as anatomy or

A lesser-known aspect of the Orpheus myth tells how, after the death of his beloved Eurydice, the poet spurned the love of other women and turned his attentions to young men instead – behaviour that caused the women of Thrace to kill him for having introduced homosexuality to their land. French woodcut from a 1531 edition of Boccaccio's *Genealogiae Deorum*.

Donatello's famous bronze of David, made *c.* 1440, represents him as a nude ephebe, combining a biblical subject with a startlingly sensual – even erotic – treatment. Some critics, rather controversially, have viewed the statue as a celebration of pederastic love.

what Albrecht Dürer termed the 'art of measurement', also stimulated changes in representational styles. The homoerotic code that emerged in this context was anything but transparent. Many of the figures (and texts) that modern viewers may see as evidently erotic signified in complex ways.

Such was the case with medieval and Renaissance readings of Orpheus, for instance. According to ancient legend, the bard had turned to boys for sexual satisfaction after having lost his beloved Eurydice. In light of contemporary allegories, this amorous metamorphosis could be seen as a form of progress: after all, the love of men for men was held to be superior, whereas male–female love pointed to lowly sexual love.[44] Ganymede, the beautiful boy whom Zeus had abducted to serve as the gods' cupbearer, was another figure who invited a plethora of interpretations; Neoplatonists, for example, turned him into an emblem for the love of the divine. The homoerotic themes and figures in Renaissance mythology thus occupy a space between clearly erotic narratives and deeper levels of meaning. It may prove impossible to separate out these meanings neatly: after all, it was this ambivalence that set the associative games of the cognoscenti in motion.

In humanist circles on the fringes of established academic institutions, Christianity and paganism merged in novel ways. The beautiful bronze sculpture of David by Donatello (*c.* 1386–1466), ostensibly a religious image, resembles a Ganymede, for instance, and invites a sensual response. When sculpting the statue of David as a symbol of Florentine republicanism, Michelangelo (1475–1564) fused the figure of the Old Testament youth with that of the ancient Hercules; both connoted homosexual love, at

Giulio Romano's pornographic woodcuts for an edition of *I Modi* ('The Sexual Positions') inspired a flood of erotica during the early modern period and created a climate in which male–male love could be represented. Here, in a series entitled *The Loves of the Gods* (1527), Jacopo Caraglio depicts Apollo's amorous relationship with the young Hyacinth (note the cupid in the background). Compared with Giulio's model drawing, this print is less explicit. The straddling position conventionally connotes sexual intercourse, however.

overleaf

Two sensuous images of Love personified from the turn of the 17th century. Caravaggio's provocative *Victorious Cupid* challenges the rules associated with the artistic treatment of homoerotic love, while Giovanni Baglione's riposte, *The Triumph of Sacred Love over Profane Love* – despite its more exalted theme – still unsettles the modern viewer with its fields of naked flesh and themes of domination and submission.

least for some viewers.[45] These examples serve to demonstrate that homoeroticism was not strictly inherent in a work of art. Rather, it emerged from contemporary modes of reading, viewing and debating.

In this climate of the revival of ancient culture and of artistic innovations, works of pornography (re)emerged. Featuring woodcuts by Marcantonio Raimondi (*c.* 1480–*c.* 1530) based on drawings by Giulio Romano, Pietro Aretino's *I Modi* ('The [Sexual] Positions', *c.* 1524) is prime example of the genre. Although focused on heterosexual couplings, this text, with its subversive messages much concerned with (heterosexual) sodomy, was the first stirring of a culture of libertines in which verbal and visual representations of male–male intercourse would find a place – one protected by the anonymity of print readership.[46]

Such artistic provocations did not – or at least not necessarily – reflect socio-sexual practice. Primarily, they occasioned delight by upsetting representational conventions. A sexual masquerade such as *Hermaphroditus* (1420), Antonio Beccadelli's collection of satirical poems *à la* Martial, circulated freely only among a small circle of Italian literati and their protectors.[47] Certain works of art were thus apt to reinforce the bonds that tied humanists, artists and patrons together. The paintings of Michelangelo Merisi da Caravaggio (1573–1610) derived their shock value not least from the fact that his adolescent youths subverted the elite and idealizing codes associated with male–male love in 16th-century Italian art. Among the low life that populates his canvases, Caravaggio's males often betray a crudely sexual impulse. In his *Victorious Cupid*, the young boy's cheeky smile invites a sexual response from the viewer. We can even follow his hand to where it disappears suggestively

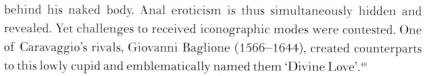

Accused in the presence of Cosimo de' Medici of being a 'dirty sodomite', Cellini cleverly distanced himself from the 'noble art' of pederastic love, claiming that it was the preserve of gods and 'the greatest kings'. Yet during the years he spent working for Cosimo (1545–53), Cellini produced three marble sculptures that attest to an interest in homoerotic themes: *Apollo and Hyacinth*, *Narcissus*, captivated by his own beauty, and *Ganymede*, shown here.

behind his naked body. Anal eroticism is thus simultaneously hidden and revealed. Yet challenges to received iconographic modes were contested. One of Caravaggio's rivals, Giovanni Baglione (1566–1644), created counterparts to this lowly cupid and emblematically named them 'Divine Love'.[48]

Occasionally, Renaissance homoeroticism extended beyond the elite. In English stage drama, a public medium par excellence, double entendres and word play served to hint at male–male desire. William Shakespeare (1564–1616) gave Mercutio, for instance, a rapport with Romeo that reverberates with a phallic bawdiness: 'If love be rough with you, be rough with love./ Prick love for pricking, and you beat love down' (*Romeo and Juliet*, I. iv. 27–28).

Artistic and literary creations emerged from, and in turn fostered, the masculine culture of the Renaissance with its mostly male circles of artists, humanists, scientists and patrons.[49] Against all decorum, the 16th-century Sienese painter Giovanni Antonio Bazzi (1477–1549) daringly adopted the sobriquet 'Il Sodoma',[50] while Michelangelo adapted the Ganymede myth to mythologize his infatuation with Tommaso de' Cavalieri.[51] This masculine milieu has conventionally been described as bisexual – a term that conveys a boundless, free spirit in sexual matters (many of the artists and humanists associated with the homoerotic code were married, like Il Sodoma). But bisexuality as a blanket term fails to convey the sexual particulars, the social exclusivity and the vulnerability of early modern men to homoerotic scandals – in short, the various and proliferating limits of 'sexual freedom'.

The great goldsmith and sculptor Benvenuto Cellini (1500–71) bragged in the *Vita* about his life as a rogue and an artist. The same autobiographical text ignores the fact that its author had been convicted for sodomy, however. In 1557 Cellini received a sentence for keeping a certain Fernando da Montepulciano, an assistant in his workshop, 'in bed as if he were his wife' (as the trial document words it). Upon the accused's meek plea to pardon his 'youthful folly' (Cellini was fifty-seven at the time), Cosimo I, Tuscany's Medici duke, commuted a four-year prison sentence into house arrest of the same duration.[52] As a result, Cellini practically lost his patrons' support. The severe repercussions the artist faced in the wake of the trial spurred his turn to autobiography and poetry as modes of self-expression. Yet Cellini's bold literary invocations of male–male love are remarkably slippery when it comes to his own desires. Cellini's writings invoke sodomy primarily in the registers of defamation, satire and humour. When he was publicly insulted with an accusation of sodomy by a fellow artist, Cellini supposedly responded by playfully distancing himself from that 'noble art' of lovemaking – the practice of ancient gods and rulers but not of a 'humble' artist like himself.[53] According to his own version of events, everybody present sided with Cellini and his witty retort. And the resounding laughter at the anecdote's end might be taken to testify to the age's transgressive spirit. After all, to laugh at sodomy, that most ignoble of sins, defied the prescribed response, which was one of horror. Yet in light of Cellini's biography, the anecdote also conveys unease.

Indeed, a deep-seated ambivalence ran through contemporary engagement with homoeroticism. Some ancient authors, such as Virgil and Ovid, were revered as linguistic models as well as artistic and scientific authorities, and they inspired contemporary poets to emulate the homosexual content of their poetry in exemplary Latin. While such reverence for the ancients minimized the incidence of censorship, overtly sexual passages nonetheless had to be excised for reception in certain quarters, such as the classroom, or in translations of ancient texts into the vernacular, which were widely read.[54]

Although it has come to represent a whole age, Renaissance art consisted of intellectual and artistic endeavours whose reach was limited both socially and geographically. Many parts of Europe outside Italy never fostered an analogous milieu of social camaraderie-cum-eroticism or experienced a similar transformation of aesthetics. Where the Renaissance became an import, as in Hungary, France, England and Germany, it changed in character. North of the Alps, admiration for Italian arts and sciences was often coupled with rejection of Italian mores. In the hands of Martin Luther (1483–1546), the German reformer, a satirical poem on the sodomitical papacy, for instance, turned into clear proof of Italian depravities.[55] Polemicism allowed no respect for a text's original register with its deliberate distortions of reality. Perceived Italian sexual licentiousness, especially between men, formed the background of the North's ambivalent attitude towards Italy. It is this xenophobic and homophobic mindset that fuelled the religious reformers' ire against things Italian. Their equation of Italy with Catholicism and depravity – a trend that had begun well before the onset of the Reformation – confirmed commonly held beliefs about Europe's South.[56]

In an age that witnessed increased religious divisions and the formation of new belief systems (which crystallized around statements of faith called 'confessions'), homoerotically charged representations fell from favour. In the 16th and 17th centuries, these emerging confessions each claimed probity, righteousness and sexual propriety in an attempt to distinguish themselves from one another. Whether Lutheran, Zwinglian, Calvinist or Catholic, religious leaders advocated strict standards of sexual discipline. They promoted marriage as a social panacea and marital sex as the only legitimate sexual outlet. They sought to instil norms of 'biblical' sexual behaviour into their followers, thus forging a sense of belonging among believers.

One result of the religious upheaval of the 16th century was that standards of visual representation shifted. Protestant iconoclasts, reformers and magistrates rid churches of Catholic art. The movement against images was particularly aimed at false idols – images that were themselves thought to be revered – but it also did away with many works of art that lent themselves to sexual fantasy, a danger that humanists and reformers had repeatedly warned against. The 'Reformation of the Image' (as Joseph Leo Koerner termed it) aimed to turn religious art into a vehicle of religious instruction.

This rupture may have been more gradual in Catholicism, yet the mid-16th century also saw the emergence of lists of books prohibited by the Church. Although censorship was aimed primarily at works written by the

The new piety and respectability fostered by the Counter-Reformation saw depictions of pagan mythology and nudity fall from official favour. Artists continued to produce highly impassioned paintings of saints and martyrs, however, and St Sebastian – a passive body penetrated by arrows – provided a justification for numerous representations of the male nude. This example was painted in 1618 by Guido Reni who, according to contemporary biographies, was very 'particular' in manner and refused to be left alone with female models.

Protestant reformers or those suspected of Protestant leanings, the lists later also included texts that were deemed to be obscene. In the wake of the Council of Trent (1545–63) and its reform of Catholic iconography, even Italian Ganymedes became more respectable.[57] In 1623 the French author Théophile de Viau faced an obscenity trial for having authored sodomitical verse, even though similar satire had gone unchallenged a generation earlier.[58] Events such as this encouraged conformity with (if not internalization of) the newly enforced standards of behaviour. But attempts at censorship also linked works of art more firmly to the actual lives of their creators, thus paving the way for modern notions of literary and artistic authorship that often view artistic products as expressions of an author's subjectivity.

It would be erroneous, however, to picture a unified movement away from a carefree atmosphere of intellectual, artistic and sexual experimentation towards the sober spirit of a rationalizing world. Change was gradual and uneven, affecting different places and social groups at different times. Trials for sodomy continued throughout the early modern period. Even communities that had placed their hopes on Protestantism as the gateway to a religiously and sexually more upright society had to face the fact that they could not effectively control sexual activity, though they certainly tried. Instead, they proceeded to limit public exposure of same-sex acts in various ways. 'It seems inadvisable to mention sodomitic sins' was the recommendation of a committee to reform the law in Protestant Sweden, counsel that echoed similar cautionary statements across Europe.[59] The enforcement of this new modesty contrasted with the behaviour of some royal courts, which continued to adhere to a code some commentators understood as homoerotic. In a letter of 1695, Liselotte von der Pfalz (1652–1722), wife of Philippe, Duke of Orleans, the brother of Louis XIV and renowned lover of favourites, even alleged that the climate of pious sobriety at court under the Marquise de Maintenon had led not only to the demise of *politesse* between the sexes, but also nursed what she described as 'debauchery among men'.[60] Importantly, the pace of change varied according to geography, a situation that contributed to vast and persistent discrepancies in sexual cultures across regions and across class. Yet, with the emergence of societies that were religiously more unified, deviations from the norm were more closely guarded against. What is more, circles in which representations of homoeroticism continued to be created and consumed were increasingly endangered. These developments paved the way for the history of homosexuality during the Enlightenment.

Male Homosexuality in the Age of Enlightenment and Revolution, 1680–1850
MICHAEL SIBALIS

The years from the 1680s to the 1850s witnessed important developments in same-sex relations (especially those between men) in Europe. First, a distinct subculture, which some historians anachronistically label 'gay', appeared in the major urban centres of Western Europe. Second, 18th-century intellectuals began discussing sodomy in secular rather than religious terms. And third, the revision of criminal law codes in the late 1700s and early 1800s changed (and generally improved) the legal status of sodomites in most countries.

The homosexual subculture

Sodomy knew no national frontiers in early modern Europe, even if people in most countries tended to ascribe such behaviour to outsiders and foreigners, such as the 'uncivilized' Turks and Russians or, at the other extreme, the overly refined Italians. Indeed, Italy's reputation was such that 'Italian vice' or 'Italian school' were common code words for sodomy. In 1749, for instance, an English pamphlet described Italy as 'the *Mother* and *Nurse* of *Sodomy* ... where the *Master* is oftener intriguing with his *Page*, than a *fair* Lady'.[1] In fact, casual sex occurred across the whole of Europe among both adult men and adolescents, many of whom were probably not even aware that their activities constituted that abomination called sodomy. Most men lived, worked and socialized almost exclusively with other men – a situation especially true for the clergy, unmarried apprentices and journeymen, soldiers and sailors, and boys at boarding school – with the results that one might expect. In addition, family members, workmates and even total strangers shared beds without a second thought. An English verse of the 1770s humorously warned travellers of the dangers of sleeping with someone else at an inn: 'Observe this rule: – ne'er pull your Breeches off. – / From Health restoring Slumbers strive to keep, / Or ten to one you are B[ugger]'d in your Sleep.'[2] Many adolescents apparently regarded sex between themselves as no more than a naughty but pleasurable game. Thus four sixteen-year-old farm boys, arrested in the Dutch Netherlands in 1751, considered what they had done no different from what they had seen older males and females do with each other.[3] Similarly, in a small Spanish town in the late 1760s, six boys (aged nine to fourteen) spent a day stacking wheat, then stripped naked and masturbated one another. They did the same the next day, after which the oldest 'started to throw [the others] face down over the wheat and sodomize them'.[4] Boarding schools were notorious for

Two great Enlightenment figures:
Voltaire and Frederick the Great at Sanssouci, an engraving by Pierre-Charles Baquoy. Voltaire surprisingly regarded same-sex desire as an 'infamous outrage against nature', yet did not let his personal distaste stop him from recommending law reform or from maintaining friendships with many homosexuals. Frederick, his one-time host at Sanssouci and himself most probably homosexual, drafted a law abolishing the death penalty for homosexual acts.

such sexual mischief, especially (but not only) in England. On arrival at Charterhouse in 1822, the eleven-year-old William Makepeace Thackeray was invited by another student to 'Come & frig me', while John Addington Symonds later recalled the 'animal lust' and 'the sports of naked boys in bed together' at Harrow in the 1850s.[5]

A number of early modern monarchs had a reputation for sodomy, like William III of England (r. 1688–1702), Frederick the Great of Prussia (r. 1740–86) and Gustav III of Sweden (r. 1771–92). Louis XIV of France (r. 1643–1715) pursued women, but his brother, the Duke of Orleans (1640–1701), ostentatiously surrounded himself with male favourites. At the courts of such monarchs, networks of friendship and sex among men helped determine the distribution of patronage, preferment and rewards.[6] Beyond the closed world of aristocratic courtiers, half-hidden coteries of sodomites drawn from all social classes could be found, at least in major cities. Many people claimed that sodomy was more widespread than ever before, although this was already an old refrain. Samuel Pepys, writing in London, reported hearing in 1663 'that buggery is now almost as common among our gallants as in Italy, and that the very pages of the town begin to complain of their masters for it'.[7] A French observer remarked in 1783 that 'this vice … has become so fashionable that there is today no order in the State, from dukes down to lackeys and common people, that is not infected with it.'[8]

Although this urban subculture became visible only around 1700, it may already have existed for two or three generations. Almost everything we know about it comes from the records generated by repression – police reports, judicial proceedings and denunciations by moral crusaders – and because surveillance was at best sporadic before the late 17th century, information is sparse for earlier years.[9] A homosexual subculture was most apparent in Paris,

By the beginning of the 18th century, most major cities in Europe had developed sizeable homosexual subcultures, complete with social networks and meeting places. Allowing for the peculiarities of particular urban geographies, the records compiled in the 18th century through surveillance and repression reveal a strikingly uniform picture of the habits of urban sodomites. Here, two Parisian men take advantage of a stormy night and a sequestered location. Pair of engravings from *The Cloistered Whores*, a satirical tract of 1793.

London and Amsterdam precisely because the forces of order were more vigilant there than elsewhere. Paris got an effective police force in 1667 and by the 1690s policemen were patrolling 'cruising' sites (outdoor places where sodomites hunted for sexual encounters) and keeping a watch on the venues where sodomites met.[10] In England, the Societies for the Reformation of Manners (the first founded in 1690, the last disbanded in 1738) set out to purge the country of immorality. In 1699 one of their tracts threatened to reveal the 'scandalous haunts' of London's sodomites (or 'mollies'), which is exactly what the societies did.[11] Authorities in the Dutch Netherlands launched a campaign (a 'witch hunt' or even 'gay genocide' according to some historians) in the 1730s to uproot sodomy in the United Provinces. Dutch sodomites became scapegoats in a period of social panic precipitated by long-term economic and political decline and by a series of disastrous floods (the dikes collapsed in the winter of 1731), which aroused fears that God had abandoned the republic because of the people's sinful ways.[12]

The subculture uncovered through repressive measures was strikingly similar in all three countries. Sodomites picked each other up and sometimes even had sex in city parks and gardens, along streets and thoroughfares, and in squares and public toilets, such as the latrines under Amsterdam's bridges or the bog-houses at Lincoln's Inn in London. Each city had its own unique places, of course: the banks of the Seine in Paris, the arcades of Covent Garden in London or the ground floor of the Town Hall in Amsterdam (at least until better lighting was installed there in the 1760s). Smaller towns must also have had their own cruising grounds, but no one has studied them in France or England. In the Dutch Netherlands, however, court records mention the toilets of Rotterdam, Schiedam and Gouda, a wood just outside The Hague, the banks of a canal in Leiden, and a church tower in Utrecht.[13] Sodomites also regularly patronized certain drinking establishments, where enterprising owners might even reserve rooms for their exclusive use. One of London's 'molly houses' was Mother Clap's, raided by the constabulary in 1726. An informant who visited it found (he said) 'between 40 and 50 Men making Love to one another, as they call'd it. Sometimes they would sit on one another's Laps, kissing in a lewd Manner and using their Hands indecently. Then they would get up, Dance and make Curtsies, and mimick the voices of Women … Then they'd hug, and play, and toy, and go out by Couples into another Room on the same Floor, to be marry'd, as they call'd it.'[14] Parisian sodomites behaved in the same way, according to a 1748 police report about goings-on in several of that city's more disreputable taverns: '[They] put handkerchiefs on their heads, imitating women, mincing like them. When there was some new young man there, they called him the Bride, and in this case, he becomes the object of everybody. They choose each other in these gatherings for mutual fondling and to commit infamies.'[15] The sodomites engaged most usually in masturbation and anal intercourse; contemporary documents rarely mention oral sex or kissing.[16] One British historian attributes this to poor hygiene – 'the smell from accumulated bodily secretions, fecal and urinary traces, perspiration, bacteria, dust and dirt under the foreskin restricted forms of sexual gratification' – while a Dutch historian suggests a 'lack of sexual sophistication among the lower classes', such that 'sex for most people meant penetration: no more, no less'.[17]

There is little trace of a subculture among sodomites in other 18th-century cities – a fact that does not prove its absence, merely that surveillance was less intense. A French pornographic novel published in 1784 does allude to sodomitical practices in Rome, St Petersburg, Berlin, Vienna and Stockholm, where 'depraved men who have a taste for buggery can satisfy themselves for little money'.[18] Berlin's 'warm brothers' had certainly established an incipient subculture there by the end of the century.[19] And although a historian of Hamburg's sodomites has contended that this large port city (with 130,000 inhabitants by the end of the 18th century) had no similar subculture, the arrest of two dozen sodomites in a tavern in 1790 suggests at least some degree of socializing among them.[20]

The most apparent feature of the sodomites' subculture was the blatant effeminacy manifested by some participants, who imitated women's dress, mannerisms and speech, and sometimes adopted female nicknames. Black-eyed Leonora, Pretty Harriet and the Duchess of Gloucester, for instance, belonged to the Vere Street Coterie, broken up by London's police in 1810, although these men may not have appeared woman-like in their day-to-day lives: Fanny Murry, for instance, was 'an athletic Bargeman', and Lucy Cooper 'an Herculean Coalheaver'.[21] Of course, not all sodomites approved of such transgressive behaviour. 'Can't you act like men rather than women?', one Parisian sodomite wanted to know of his fellows in the mid-18th century, while another asked incredulously, 'What! You're men and you give yourself women's names?'[22] This effeminacy is hard to interpret. Was it just having fun ('camping it up', in today's jargon), a way to signal availability to other men, or

The Earl of Rochester, the notorious English libertine, *c.* 1675. As the Restoration court of Charles II reacted against the strictures of Puritanism, Rochester composed numerous bawdy verses that reveal an almost omnivorous sexual appetite. One such relates how: 'There's a sweet page of mine, / does the trick worth forty wenches.'

merely a mocking acceptance of society's view that sodomites were not real men?[23] Whatever the case, effeminacy made at least some sodomites recognizable in the streets. A Dutch author claimed in 1768 that anyone could distinguish a sodomite by his beardless cheeks, peculiar speech, swaying hips and the whorish look in his eyes.[24] Parisian police in the 1780s routinely stopped men with 'the appearance and the tone of pederasts' (which they never bothered to define in detail), and in some instances hostile passers-by assaulted obvious *rivettes* ('fags').[25]

Randolph Trumbach, among other historians, has argued that the new subculture was the most salient aspect of a 'gender revolution' that occurred in northwestern Europe in the years 1690–1725. Until then, any man might, in certain circumstances, desire another male and act upon that impulse. The typical sodomite was the rake or libertine who took an 'active' (or 'insertive') role in sexual relations with both women and adolescent boys; the most cited example is the Earl of Rochester (1647–80), who paraded 'his mistress on one arm and his catamite on the other'. In contrast, by the mid-18th century most men expressed a sexual desire only for women. Sodomites separated themselves

A Dutch 'friendship glass', from which companions would drink together. This example, from the middle of the 18th century, shows one cockerel copulating with another and is inscribed with the words 'DE SOTE VRIENDSCHAP' – 'sweet [or 'foolish'] friendship'.

from the majority of men and in effect surrendered their manhood by joining a contemptible minority of effeminates who mimicked women and had sex almost exclusively with other (usually adult) males.[26] Not everyone, however, accepts Trumbach's interpretive framework. There is no hard evidence that the majority of 16th- or 17th-century sodomites had an equal sexual desire for both women and boys. Indeed, it seems likely that throughout the early modern period, as in other times (including our own), different types of same-sex desire coexisted.[27] The Duchess of Orleans described the situation in France in 1705 as follows: 'There are [sodomites] of all kinds. There are those who hate women and can love only [adult] men. Others love both men and women ... Others love only children of ten or eleven, others youths of seventeen to twenty-five, and the last are the most numerous.'[28]

The law

Almost everywhere in early modern Europe, the law prescribed death for sodomy, usually by burning at the stake, although the British hanged their sodomites and the Dutch abandoned fire in the mid-17th century for garrotting or drowning in a barrel.[29] In the words of one French jurist in 1715, 'The penalty for sodomy cannot be harsh enough to expiate a crime that makes nature blush', while in the 1760s the influential British jurist William Blackstone thought sodomy 'a crime not fit to be named', which 'the voice of nature and of reason, and the express law of God, determine to be [a] capital [offence]'.[30] Sodomites did more than flout God's commandments and defy nature: they also undermined society. As a Danish jurist explained in 1791, unnatural sexual intercourse 'makes the guilty [party] incapable of business of mind and body, inculcates abhorrence of marriage, the foundation of the state, causes either barrenness or produces an offspring that cannot be called anything but wretched ... These are the miserable consequences for civic community.'[31] In the course of the 18th century, however, there was a growing sense that the death penalty for sodomy was too harsh, as well as a pragmatic concern that publicity engendered by the trial and punishment drew unwarranted attention to deeds best left in obscurity. The authorities in most countries preferred to avoid trials whenever possible, and when they did take place, judges began to impose more moderate punishments. Many rulers modified their penal codes to provide for penalties other than death.

In Prussia, Frederick William I (r. 1713–40) ordered that all sodomites in his realm should be burned at the stake, and at least one perished in Potsdam in 1730. In contrast his son, Frederick the Great (r. 1740–86), himself a reputed sodomite, allegedly remarked that 'in his states he granted freedom of conscience and of cock'. This was not quite true, but the General Prussian Code, drafted during his reign and promulgated in 1794, did replace the death penalty for sodomy with imprisonment for at least one year, flogging on entering and leaving prison, and banishment for life.[32] Empress Maria Theresa (r. 1740–80) decreed in the *Constitutio Criminalis Theresiana* (1768) that sodomites in her hereditary domains (Austria, Bohemia and Hungary) should be 'exterminated from the earth by burning to death'; but her son,

A sodomite being led to execution in Rome (right) and a second man being burnt at the stake in Paris (far right): two engravings from a French edition of Rousseau's epigrams, 1791. Within twenty years of these works being printed, Napoleon's Penal Code was extended to cover the whole of the Italian peninsula, although the Papal States soon reverted to harsh, reactionary social policies.

Anti-homosexual sentiment was especially virulent in Britain during the 18th century. *The Women-Hater's Lamentation* (opposite), published in 1707 following a number of raids on London's molly houses, depicts the suicide of several of the men who were awaiting trial: 'Shop-keepers some there were, / And Men of good repute, / Each vow'd a Batchelor, / Unnat'ral Lust pursu'd.'

Joseph II (r. 1780–90), promulgated a new code in 1787 that made 'disparag[ing] humanity' through 'carnal desire with the same sex' a 'political crime' that earned imprisonment, forced labour and flogging.[33]

Elsewhere, in Germany, the last execution (by decapitation) for sodomy in Hamburg occurred in 1726 (the accused had raped a boy). The city magistrates usually preferred banishment without trial, or at the very least to hold trials in secret. When Hamburg's pastors preached about an ongoing sodomy case in 1749, the Senate warned them that this would let common people learn that such crimes were possible.[34] Only one case of sodomy came to trial in 18th-century Württemberg. In 1762 a cloth-maker was beheaded for his 'satanic instructions' to apprentices, with whom he had engaged in masturbation and anal intercourse over a twenty-year period.[35] Magistrates in Antwerp (the Austrian Netherlands) sentenced a man to death in 1781 for sodomy with four youths aged eighteen to twenty-one. In order to avoid publicity, the judges issued instructions 'to have him secretly strangled in the prison'. His 'four accomplices' were to witness the execution, then be sworn to eternal silence. The privy council in Brussels overturned the verdict and substituted banishment for death.[36]

There were only six executions in France in the 18th century, for the most part when the accused was guilty also of assault or murder. The exception was the burning in 1750 of two simple workers whom the night watch had caught (literally) with their pants down in a Paris street. The police ordinarily released arrested sodomites with a simple warning or, at worst, after a few weeks of administrative detention.[37] In Spain, the penalties imposed by the Inquisition for the 'nefarious sin', which ranged from reprimand to galley-service or burning at the stake, grew increasingly lenient from the late 17th century.[38]

The Women-Hater's Lamentation:

OR

A New Copy of Verses on the Fatal End of Mr. *Grant*, a Woollen-Draper, and two others that Cut their Throats or Hang'd themselves in the *Counter*; with the Discovery of near Hundred more that are Accused for unnatural dispising the *Fair Sex*, and Intriguing with one another.

To the Tune of, *Ye pretty Sailors all.*

I.
YE injur'd *Females* see
  Justice without the Laws,
Seeing the Injury,
  Has thus reveng'd your Cause.

II.
For those that are so blind,
  Your Beauties to despise,
And slight your Charms, will find
  Such Fate will always rise.

III.
Of all the Crimes that Men
  Through wicked Minds do act,
There is not one of them
  Equals this Brutal Fact.

IV.
Nature they lay aside,
  To gratifie their Lust;
Women they hate beside,
  Therefore their Fate was just.

V.
Ye *Women-haters* say,
  What do's your Breasts inspire,
That in a Brutal way,
  You your own Sex admire?

VI.
Woman you disapprove,
  (The chief of Earthly Joys)
You that are deaf to Love,
  And all the Sex despise.

VII.
But see the fatal end
  That do's such Crimes pursue;
Unnat'ral Deaths attend,
  Unnat'ral Lusts in you.

VIII.
A Crime by Men abhor'd,
  Nor Heaven can abide
Of which, when *Sodom* shar'd,
  She justly was destroy'd.

IX.
But now, the sum to tell,
  (Tho' they plead Innocence)
These by their own Hands fell,
  Accus'd for this Offence.

X.
A Hundred more we hear,
  Did to this Club belong,
But now they scatter'd are,
  For this has broke the Gang.

XI.
Shop-keepers some there were,
  And Men of good repute,
Each vow'd a Batchelor,
  Unnat'ral Lust pursu'd.

XII.
Ye *Women-Haters* then,
  Take Warning by their Shame,
Your Brutal Lusts restrain,
  And own a Nobler Flame.

XIII.
Woman the chiefest Bliss
  That Heaven e'er bestow'd:
Oh be asham'd of this,
  You're by base Lust subdu'd.

XIV.
This piece of Justice then
  Has well reveng'd their Cause,
And shews unnat'ral Lust
  Is curss'd without the Laws.

LONDON: Printed for *J. Robinson*, in Fetter-Lane, 1707.
Licensed according to Order.

The pillory at Charing Cross, London. In England, hostility towards same-sex
eroticism had steadily increased during the 18th century, so that accusations
of sodomy frequently ended in public disgrace, prison or the pillory – a vicious
punishment in which the convicted could expect a savage attack by the mob.

The records of the Portuguese Inquisition for 1547–1768 indicate 278 arrests and 12 burnings for sodomy in the 17th century, but only 23 arrests and no burnings in the 18th century.[39]

Danish law prescribed 'death by burning' for 'intercourse against nature' from 1683 to 1866, but no Dane ever died for the crime, although perhaps two foreigners (from Scotland) did in 1628.[40] Sweden first criminalized sodomy between men in 1608, but the National Law Code of 1734 made no mention of the crime. Even so, judges continued to condemn sodomites under the law against bestiality, which they extended by analogy to other 'unnatural' sexual acts. Twenty court cases in 17th- and 18th-century Sweden resulted in several executions.[41] Russia had no state law against sodomy until 1716, when Peter the Great, in the process of westernizing his empire, included a clause against 'men lying with men' in his Military Articles, which applied only to the army and navy. Flogging was the penalty for consensual sodomy; rape could bring death or life in the galleys.[42] Finland had no legal sanctions against same-sex acts before 1889.[43]

The picture was grimmer in Britain, where hatred of sodomy was particularly virulent. *The Women-Haters' Lamentation*, a broadside published in 1707, mocked several sodomites who had committed suicide while awaiting trial: 'Nature they lay aside, / To gratifie their Lust; / Women they hate beside, / Therefore their fate was just.'[44] The death penalty for sodomy dated from 1533, but few trials took place before the 18th century. Statistics from 1749 onwards indicate about one execution per decade in 18th-century London and one per year in Middlesex. The naval authorities also flogged or hanged men for sodomy aboard ship (eighteen executions in 1756–1806).[45] Because conviction for sodomy required evidence of penetration and/or emission of semen, magistrates found it easier to bring a charge of 'assault with the intent to commit sodomy', for which the penalty was a fine, prison (for between one month and two years) or, until 1816, the pillory. The pillory exposed the 'miscreant' or 'monster' – common newspaper terms for convicted sodomites – to the fury of the mob, which jeered its immobilized victims while pelting (and often injuring) them with brickbats, rotting vegetables, eggs, offal, and dead cats and dogs.[46] After the mob killed a sodomite in 1780, Edmund Burke proposed abolition of the pillory to the House of Commons, for which the *Morning Post* rebuked him: 'Every *man* applauds the spirit of the spectators and every *woman* thinks their conduct right.'[47]

In the Dutch Netherlands some provinces punished sodomy with death under imperial legislation that dated back to the 16th century, while others, including Holland, the largest and richest, had no specific laws against it before 1730. (The country received a national penal code only in 1809.) Executions for sodomy were rare (twelve from 1680 to 1729), until the discovery of a nationwide network of sodomites in 1730 led to seventy-five executions, with more than one hundred other men sentenced to death in absentia. There were later waves of prosecution in 1764, 1776 and 1797, and a total of perhaps one thousand sodomy trials between 1730 and 1811. Most convicted men were sentenced to a prison term, sometimes as long as thirty or fifty

Social panic in the Dutch Netherlands during the 1730s caused a wave of repression against homosexuals. Seventy-five men were executed in 1730, and it is estimated that up to one thousand sodomy trials were held during the following eighty years. This contemporary engraving shows two men leaving a tavern together, abandoning their families, being arrested and suffering burning at the stake.

years, or were banished for life, but about two hundred executions also took place. In fact, the very last execution for sodomy in Continental Europe occurred in the Dutch Netherlands, in 1803.[48] By then, however, thanks to the Enlightenment and the French Revolution, such drastic punishment seemed very much out of tune with the times.

Sodomy and the Enlightenment

The Enlightenment was an 18th-century intellectual movement whose exponents, the *philosophes* ('philosophers' in the broad sense of 'lovers of wisdom'), championed individual reason free of the constraints of historical tradition or religious dogma as the best guide both to understanding the natural world and to reforming government and society. The *philosophes* subjected existing institutions and systems of belief, including Christianity, to critical scrutiny. The conservative Abbé Barruel accused them in the 1780s of thereby encouraging 'hideous vices' such as incest, adultery and 'love most contrary to nature'.[49] Sodomy had already been dubbed 'the philosophical sin' in the 1720s, and although the term referred to ancient Greek philosophers, it implicitly impugned the morals of their 18th-century counterparts.[50] In reality, the *philosophes* were not particularly concerned with sodomy but could hardly ignore the subject. In studying nature and society, they had to explain how it came to be that some people felt attracted to others of the same sex. Even if they rejected religious teachings, *philosophes* still had to assess the moral implications of same-sex activity within their secular world-view. As part of

Notions that the sin of sodomy might draw the wrath of God down upon a community were as archaic as they were tenacious. This anonymous engraving, known as *Justice Glorified by the Discovery and Punishment of Rising Sin* (1730), depicts the Dutch Netherlands being destroyed by fire and water as allegorical figures of Truth and Virtue reveal a group of sodomites.

their quest for fairer and more humane law codes, they also had to decide what penalties (if any) should apply to sodomy. That they examined such questions in the light of objective reason in itself constituted significant intellectual progress, quite apart from any specific conclusions they eventually reached.[51]

In the event, few *philosophes* entirely broke free of social prejudice and came out in favour of sexual freedom. Even masturbation, while no longer sinful, seemed decidedly unhealthy.[52] Immanuel Kant (1724–1804), the great German philosopher, summoned his contemporaries to think boldly ('Dare to know!'), and yet described sodomy as 'contrary to the ends of humanity' because it did not lead to procreation; for him, 'the end of humanity in respect of sexuality is to preserve the species.' In committing sodomy, moreover, 'the self is degraded below the level of the animals, and humanity is dishonoured'. Kant considered such activities to be 'unmentionable' because they were 'nauseating', and also because 'frequent mention would familiarize people with them and the vices might as a result cease to disgust us and come to appear more tolerable'.[53] The Enlightenment's watchword was 'nature', and most *philosophes* assumed that sexual pleasure was nature's incentive for men and women to perpetuate the human race, which meant that same-sex desire must be 'unnatural' or 'anti-physical'. And yet it did exist. As Johann Wolfgang von Goethe (1749–1832) observed, 'Greek love' was somehow both 'rooted in nature and at the same time against nature'.[54] The *philosophes* wriggled out of this paradox by attributing same-sex desire to social or psychological causes rather than to nature herself. This allowed them to vilify sodomy – usually

A novel explanation for the destruction of Sodom: this French Revolutionary pamphlet (*The Little Buggers of the Riding School*, 1790) describes how the city of the plain was set afire when a cook was distracted by sexual amusements.

sincerely, though sometimes to avoid the charge of promoting immorality – while simultaneously maintaining that repression was cruel, misguided and unnecessary because social and moral reform were enough to eliminate the problem. Any defence of sodomites they proffered was half-hearted at best.

In his *Philosophical Dictionary* (1764), Voltaire (1694–1778) described 'the love called Socratic' as 'a vice destructive of the human race', 'an infamous outrage against nature' and 'a disgusting abomination', at least between adults. It sometimes developed between adolescents only because 'for two or three years a young boy ... resembles a beautiful girl'.[55] Denis Diderot (1713–84) described sodomitical passion as 'trampl[ing] underfoot ... honour, virtue, decency, integrity, blood ties and patriotic feeling' because Nature 'has ordained everything for the preservation of the species'. He ascribed the 'anti-physical taste' that was allegedly prevalent among indigenous Americans to unattractive women, male 'contempt for the weaker sex', separation of the sexes during the long hunting season, and the hot climate. He thought that elsewhere sodomy resulted from mental defect, senility, fear of venereal diseases (presumed transmissible only by heterosexual contact), the quest for new pleasures to satisfy jaded appetites and the pull of male beauty. (Diderot confessed in a private letter that 'in the public baths among a number of young men, I noticed one of astonishing beauty, and I could not help drawing near him.'[56]) Only a radically unorthodox thinker like the Marquis de Sade (1740–1814) took Enlightenment principles to their logical conclusion by defending sodomy as both universal, with 'disciples and shrines the world over', and entirely natural: 'If [the sodomite] truly is a scoundrel or a monster, ... then why has Nature created him partial to this pleasure?'[57]

In 1764 Cesare Beccaria (1738–94) published *On Crimes and Punishments*, one of the most influential treatises on law reform ever written. Translated from the Italian, it won the applause of *philosophes* and rulers across Europe. Beccaria wanted to replace existing criminal law – 'the dregs of utterly barbarous centuries' – with fairer judicial procedures and more humane penalties. He mentioned 'pederasty' only in passing, as a crime 'of frequent occurrence in society yet difficult to prove'. Without actually urging decriminalization, Beccaria maintained that sodomy had social causes and concluded that 'one cannot call any punishment of a crime just ... so long as the law has not made use of the best means available ... to prevent it.'[58] More explicit calls for decriminalization were rare. One came from the Marquis de Condorcet (1743–94) in a footnote to the 1786 edition of Voltaire's *Prize for Justice and Humanity*: 'Sodomy, when there is no violence, cannot fall within the competence of the criminal laws. It does not violate the rights of any other man. It has only an indirect influence on the good order of society, like drunkenness, [or] love of gambling. It is a vile, disgusting vice whose true punishment is scorn.'[59]

Several pamphlets published at the start of the French Revolution purported to speak for the country's oppressed sodomites. *The Little Buggers of the Riding School* (1790), for instance, argued that, according to the principle of 'individual liberty, decreed by our most august and most respectable representatives' in the National Constituent Assembly, sodomites should be free to do what they wished: 'I can dispose of my property, whatever it is, according to my taste and whims. Now my cock and balls belong to me and whether … I put them in a cunt or an ass, no one has the right to complain.'[60] The editors of a recent anthology describe this and similar pamphlets as 'the first time lesbians and gay men organized as such to address a national government' and claim their rights.[61] This is a fundamental misunderstanding. In fact, these publications were satirical and counter-revolutionary. Their intent was not to defend sodomites, but rather to demonstrate the logical absurdity of the concept of individual human rights. And yet the pamphlets proved strangely premonitory: within a year sodomy had ceased to be a crime in France.

Decriminalization

It is widely believed that the Code Napoléon (1804) decriminalized sodomy in France – a milestone usually credited to its principal architect, Jean-Jacques-Régis de Cambacérès, who was almost certainly a homosexual himself. This is entirely wrong. The Code Napoléon was a compendium of civil law and said nothing about criminal offences. The relevant Napoleonic legislation was in fact the Penal Code of 1810, which was not Cambacérès's work and which in any case merely confirmed earlier legislation. The French Revolution deserves the credit for enacting, in September 1791, a criminal code that omitted any mention of sodomy. The deputy who presented it to the National Constituent

THE TRIAL AND
EXECUTION
OF
CAPT. HENRY NICHOLS,
Who Suffered this Morning,
AT

MY thoughts on awful subjects roll / Damnation and the dead ; / What horrors seize the guilty soul / Upon a dying bed ! / Ling'ring about these mortal clores, / She makes a long delay, / Till, like a flood, with rapid force / Death sweeps the wretch away

Then wrapt and rizen (to be descends / Down to the fiery coret, / Amongst abominable fiends, / Himself a frightful ghost. / There endless crowds of sinners lie, / And darkness makes their chains ; / Tortur'd with keen despair they cry, / Yet wait for fiercer pains.

HORSEMONGER LANE GOAL, SOUTHWARK.

'Heinous, horribly frightful, and disgusting was the crime for which the above poor Wretched Culprit suffered the severe penalty of the law.' A London broadsheet relating the execution for sodomy of Captain Henry Nichols in 1833. His entire family abandoned him, refusing either to see him in prison before his execution or to claim his body.

Assembly observed that the code outlawed only 'true crimes' and not 'those phoney offences, created by superstition [i.e. religion], feudalism, the tax system and despotism'. These apparently included blasphemy, heresy, sacrilege and witchcraft, as well as victimless sexual acts such as bestiality, incest and sodomy.[62]

French territorial expansion during the Revolution and under Napoleon subsequently spread French criminal law and its principles across Europe both by conquest and by example. For instance, when Napoleon annexed Holland to France in 1810, he replaced the Dutch code of 1809, which condemned sodomy, with the French Penal Code. It remained in force even after Holland regained independence in 1813, although there would be several failed attempts to recriminalize same-sex activity until the 1840s.[63] In contrast, Napoleon did not impose his Code on Spain, ruled by his brother Joseph from 1808 to 1813, but in 1822 a short-lived liberal regime adopted a penal code inspired by the French one and thereby decriminalized sodomy in that country.[64]

The situation was particularly complex in the many Italian and German states. Napoleon extended his Penal Code to the entire Italian peninsula, but after his fall some states reverted to earlier legislation (Piedmont-Sardinia and the Papal States), others came under Austrian criminal law (Lombardy and Venetia) and a few adopted codes modelled on the French (the Kingdom of the Two Sicilies in 1819; Parma, Piacenza and Guastalla in 1820). Piedmont-Sardinia eventually instituted more liberal codes, in 1839 and 1859, punishing 'unnatural lust' with up to ten years of prison or forced labour, but only – a significant reservation – in cases causing public scandal. After the unification of Italy under the House of Savoy in the 1860s, Piedmontese law prevailed everywhere except in the south (the former Kingdom of the Two Sicilies), where the central government did not apply the clause penalizing sodomy in acknowledgement of the region's more tolerant legal tradition. Italy as a whole finally decriminalized sodomy between consenting adults in 1889.[65]

Annexation to France during the Revolutionary Wars also brought the Rhineland under French criminal law, which remained in force in the Grand Duchy of Luxembourg and also in six other Rhineland territories that were incorporated into various German states in 1814–15.[66] Meanwhile, in 1800, Elector (later King) Maximilian of Bavaria ordered the drafting of a penal code based on 'proper principles of reason and civil life'. Sodomy was absent from the final product, the Bavarian Criminal Code of 1813, because, according to Anselm Feuerbach, its principal author, 'masturbation, sodomy, bestiality, [and] extramarital consensual intercourse are serious contraventions against moral commandments, but, as sins, they do not belong to the domain of internal law codes.' Not everybody agreed, of course. 'There are acts that do not harm rights', one jurist countered, 'but could occasion such harm directly or indirectly, like smoking on the street, sodomy, and so on – … they should be forbidden by law.'[67] In 1839 Württemberg followed Bavaria's example, as did Brunswick and Hanover in 1840,[68] whereas several other German states that adopted codes based on Bavaria's nevertheless kept sodomy as a criminal offence. Most importantly, Prussia, the largest and most powerful German state, retained its law against sodomy, although reducing the penalty to a simple prison term in 1837. In the Prussian Rhineland, however, sodomy continued to be omitted from the criminal code (a situation inherited from French rule) until 1851, when a new Prussian penal code applied the same penalty across the entire state. As the driving force behind German unification, Prussia ultimately determined the shape of penal law for the North German Confederation (1869) and then the German Empire (1871).[69]

In Austria, the Penal Code of 1803 punished 'unnatural lust' with a prison term of six months to a year (an improvement over the law of 1787); the Code of 1852 increased this to one to five years.[70] Russia, which had punished only soldiers and sailors for sodomy, finally imposed penalties ('birching and exile') on civilians in 1835.[71] Britain still stood out for the savagery of its anti-sodomy legislation in this period. England and Wales hanged fifty-five men for the crime between 1805 and 1835 (figures are missing for 1818–19), one-seventh the number executed for murder. Sodomy remained punishable by hanging until 1861 (1889 in Scotland), but after 1835 the government routinely commuted death sentences. The Offences Against the Person Act of 1861 (repealed only in 1967) reduced the penalty to a prison term of ten years to life, which was still more severe than anywhere else in Europe.[72]

The 19th century

Of course, the letter of the law is one thing, enforcement quite another. Where sodomy remained a crime, there were probably relatively few prosecutions, although we frequently lack statistics. On the other hand, in countries with no penalties for sodomy the police could still use laws against public indecency to

William Beckford, then the wealthiest man in England, who in 1785 was obliged by a homosexual scandal to flee to the Continent for ten years. On his return he maintained a household of young male servants (known by such names as 'Miss Butterfly' and 'Mr Prudent Well-Sealed-Up') and diligently kept a scrapbook of newspaper cuttings relating to the homosexual scandals of the time. Portrait by George Romney, c. 1781.

harass those men who cruised for sex in public places and to close down their drinking establishments. That was the situation in France, for example. Graham Robb argues, however, that on balance 'nineteenth-century homosexuals lived under a cloud, but it seldom rained.' They suffered less from legal persecution than from 'the creeping sense of shame, the fear of losing friends, family and reputation ... the social and mental isolation, and the strain of concealment'.[73] Society's homophobia was most evident whenever scandal broke. In 1785 the 25-year-old William Beckford left England because of rumours about his relationship with a young boy; he spent ten years in exile, 'acting the part of the Wandering Jew and being stared and wondered at as if I bore the mark of God's malediction on my countenance'.[74] Percy Jocelyn, Bishop of Clogher, fled to the Continent in 1822 after being discovered in a compromising position (his breeches round his ankles) with a soldier at a public house in Haymarket, London.[75] That same year Lord Castlereagh, British Foreign Secretary, committed suicide in the paranoid belief that he was about to be denounced (probably unjustly) as a sodomite.[76] In France in 1825, after word got out that a band of soldiers had thrashed the Marquis de Custine for propositioning one of them, people literally turned their backs on him. 'Never', wrote a friend, 'have I seen a greater outburst of indignation ... high society as a whole is furious.'[77] Not surprisingly, many 19th-century sodomites fell victim to extortion, which became a significant problem for the police, who disliked blackmailers even more than sodomites.[78]

Very few men had the courage (or effrontery) to stare down the scandalmongers. One was Joseph Fiévée, an adviser to Napoleon, who lived openly with his lover. 'When one has a vice,' he declared, 'one should know how to wear it.'[79] Sometimes, too, ordinary men spoke out in their own defence. For instance, a 'gentleman' caught in flagrante delicto in London in 1726 insisted that 'there is no Crime in making what use I please of my own body.'[80] A tailor arrested for sodomy in Paris in 1785 similarly told police 'that he was not the only one, that he was harming nobody but himself, that he had given himself over to it very young, and that it was in his blood'.[81] And a Dutch pamphlet of 1817 stated: 'Everybody knows that these scoundrels among their equals openly speak of their gruesome lusts as something that is natural and proper to them.'[82]

Two written defences of sodomy remained unpublished during the lifetimes of their authors (both of them heterosexual). One was by the philosopher Jeremy Bentham (1748–1832), who drafted hundreds of manuscript pages on the subject over a fifty-year period (1774–1824).[83] Bentham argued that society had no valid reason for punishing sodomy – he refuted the religious, philosophical and judicial arguments regularly put forward for treating it as a crime, but did so only because of 'the antipathy with which the persons who had punishment at their disposal regarded the offender'. This was obviously insufficient justification: 'To destroy a man there should certainly be some better reason than mere dislike to his Taste, let that dislike be ever so strong.'[84] In 1818 the poet Percy Bysshe Shelley (1792–1822) penned a more cautious 'Discourse on the Manners of the Antient Greeks Relative to the Subject of Love', which finally appeared in 1931.[85] Only an obscure Swiss

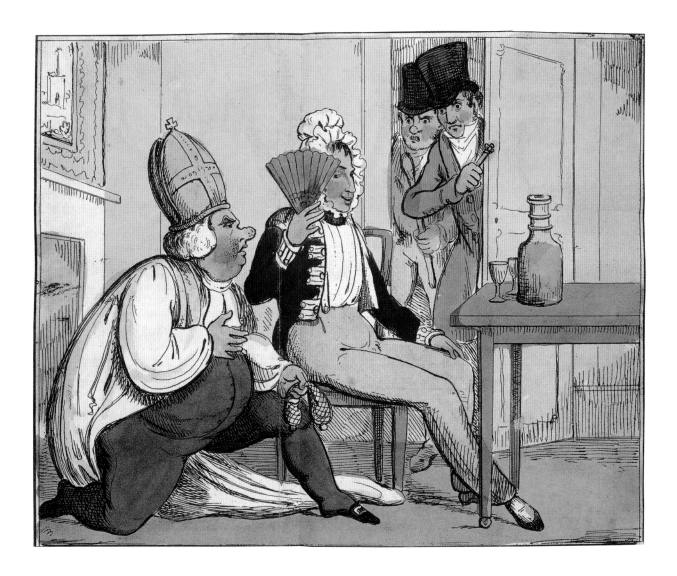

In 1822 Percy Jocelyn, Lord Bishop of Clogher, was caught with his trousers down in the company of a guardsman at the White Lion public house, Haymarket, London. One casualty of the ensuing scandal was the Foreign Secretary, Viscount Castlereagh, who confessed to George IV that he was 'accused of the same crime as the Bishop of Clogher' and committed suicide shortly after.

One of the most notorious Paris cruising grounds of the 1840s, the
Galerie d'Orléans in the Palais Royal. In 1843, the gallery's shopkeepers
sent a petition to the police, complaining that 'the Galerie d'Orléans
has been infested by a crowd of good-for-nothings who have chosen it
for carrying on their hideous business, which one is ashamed to name.'

milliner named Heinrich Hössli (1784–1864), who may have been homosexually inclined (as was his son), dared publish and be damned. Poorly written, rambling and repetitive, *Eros: The Male Love of the Greeks* (2 volumes, 1836–38) was nonetheless a heartfelt plea for tolerance, arguing that same-sex love was entirely natural and citing as evidence its existence in different cultures throughout history. Other writers would take up Hössli's themes later in the century.[86]

Medical science began showing an interest in sodomy from the late 18th century, not in order to construct the 'homosexual' or 'invert' as a distinct type, as would happen one hundred years later, but rather to discern the physical traces that sodomy left on the body: dilation of the sphincter, abrasions around the anus, penile deformation. This was because courts looked to forensic medicine for proof of anal penetration, whether consensual (in states where it was illegal, as in England) or forced (in cases of sexual assault).[87] Probably the most influential medical specialist was Ambroise Tardieu (1818–79), whose *Medico-Legal Study of Indecent Assaults* went through seven French editions (1857–78) and numerous translations. Tardieu maintained that passive sodomites had feminine buttocks and funnel-shaped rectums, while the penises of active sodomites were either 'dog-like' (slender and narrowing to a point) or thick, club-shaped and often twisted; men who practised fellatio had crooked mouths, short teeth and thick lips.[88] For Tardieu, men who indulged in sodomy had made a moral choice, but other medical experts, beginning with an article published by the German doctor Johann Ludwig Casper in 1852, were already shifting medicine in another direction by trying to understand the physiological and/or psychological causes of same-sex desire.[89]

The growing interest in sodomy was most likely prompted by a subculture that was increasingly visible as Europe became more urbanized and small cities grew in size. A shocked Parisian complained to the police in 1850 that during his evening strolls along the boulevards he regularly saw 'scenes of the most shameful immorality … offered by those nameless creatures, those hideous hermaphrodites!'[90] An 1855 guide to London claimed that there were more 'monsters in the shape of men, commonly designated *Margeries* [and] *Pooffs*' in the city than ever before, to the point that certain streets were 'thronged with them'.[91] In 19th-century London, Paris and Amsterdam (other cities await their historians), cruising grounds known in the previous century – parks, squares and public urinals – still turn up in records, but there are also some new ones, such as covered shopping arcades and railway stations. Drinking establishments catering to sodomites were more numerous, or at least less hidden, than in the past. Transvestite balls, especially during the carnival season, were also a new feature of sodomitical life.[92] By mid-century, the homosexual (a term coined only in 1869) was in the process of becoming an inescapable presence in modern urban life.

Lesbians and Their Like in Early Modern Europe, 1500–1800

LAURA GOWING

One of the epithets attached to lesbianism in early modern Europe was *amor impossibilis*, the impossible love; for scholars of this period 'lesbian' has sometimes seemed an impossible word. One recent work denotes the gulf between modern and early modern understandings of the term by italicizing *lesbian* throughout.[1] Despite this difficulty, 'lesbian' has been used since at least the 10th century to connect the story of Sappho with sexual relations between women (its first printed use in English dates from the 1730s).[2] There is no evidence of women using the term to describe themselves: it was a slur, not an identity. Unlike male sodomy, which was widely prosecuted, the concept of lesbianism was not based on a clearly defined sexual act. Few early modern people would have known the word, and those who did would not have understood it in the way we do today – something true of many historical terms, such as friendship, love and sex, which also had different meanings. Judith Bennett suggests using the category of 'lesbian-like' in our examination of the premodern past.[3] Women who did not marry, or who chose to work, live or sleep with other women, may not be identified as modern lesbians; but to ignore the possibility that they were, in some way, *like* lesbians, that their lives offered the potential of lesbian acts is (Bennett suggests) to write heterosexist history.

Recent work has countered the tradition that before 1900 sexual relations between women were almost unimaginable. Critical readings of Renaissance culture have demonstrated the proliferation and the complexity of representations of desire and sex between women.[4] Scholars of gender have developed concepts – such as 'female masculinities' – that make sense of the past as well as the present. Histories that once seemed too threatening to modern identity to be explored – the history of butch–fem, of passing women – are finding a new place.

Long before the end of the 18th century there were words and images that articulated the potential for sex between women. Classical literature, remade into contemporary verse and drama, offered tales of women changing into men to marry women, and of men changing into women to seduce innocent maids; pastoral poems and paintings showed, for example, the embraces between Diana and her nymphs, simultaneously chaste and highly eroticized.[5] More explicitly, St Paul's definition of sodomy, the basis for its criminalization as a capital offence, was quite often interpreted as including women as well as men. Medical and travel literature discussed women who had sex with other

One of the most popular myths for codifying the love of women for others of their own sex was that of the nymph Callisto, seemingly seduced by her mistress Diana (in fact Jupiter in disguise). Such stories of transformation and concealment allowed what was taboo to be depicted openly – and often in a highly eroticized manner, as in this work by François Boucher of 1757.

women as exotic, deviant others, whose difference was marked on their bodies. An English pamphlet of 1734 decried Sappho's role as introducer of 'a new Sort of Sin, call'd the *Flats*, that was follow'd not only in *Lucian's* Time, but is practis'd frequently in *Turkey*, as well as at *Twickenham* at this Day'.[6]

In this world, the distinction between homosexual and heterosexual did not apply: 'lesbian', 'sapphist' and 'tribade' described practices more than identities. But the practices of the early modern period can no longer be seen as the inchoate, inarticulate forerunners of modern sexual identities. Long before sexologists theorized about homosexuality and heterosexuality, sexual acts still influenced ideas of identity. Women who performed lesbian acts might identify themselves, or be identified, as hermaphrodites, as chaste virgins, or as instruments of God or of the Devil. Sometimes, it is the most unfamiliar, unmodern parts of the past that offer the most promising terrain for the history of sexuality. Although stories of tribades, hermaphrodites, dildoes, passing women (women who passed as members of the opposite sex) and romantic friends do not lead directly to modern lesbian, bisexual or transgender identities, and although all of them demand multiple interpretations, these ambiguous and fragmentary stories are the ones that leave most room for our queer imaginations.

The clitoris and the tribade

Female sexuality in the early modern period was understood very differently from the sexless chastity that became the ideal for Victorian women. Before the middle of the 18th century, the prevailing understanding of the gendered body derived from the Classical traditions of Galen and Aristotle. According to the Galenic model, male and female were posited as opposite poles of a spectrum of gender, with hermaphrodites in the centre. A woman's genital organs were compared to the inverted form of a man's organs: the womb (or sometimes the vagina) was the penis, the fallopian tubes the testicles, and so on. Like men, women had seed which, emitted at the moment of orgasm, contributed to conception. The humours, not fundamental physiological or skeletal differences, were what differentiated the sexes; and in extreme circumstances female could turn into male. Femininity, in this world view, did not mean natural chastity and passivity: rather, women were driven by temptation and lust, and sexual activity was essential to their health. Lack of sex resulted in the dangerous retention of seed, in the wasting disease of greensickness or in melancholia.

In this context it was not difficult to believe that women, who required sexual satisfaction and who were fundamentally not naturally chaste, could and would turn to each other. The earliest printed pornography, which by the 17th century was circulating in Latin, French, Italian and eventually in English, mixed scenes of sex between women with heterosexual encounters, depicting married women seducing maidens, bawds initiating prostitutes and nuns amusing themselves with masturbation and flagellation. And while many such works treated sex between women as an arousing preliminary to heterosexual completion, they also created a suggestive and quite complex discourse about women's desires and their ability to satisfy themselves, and each other, without men.[7]

Ignored by medieval medical writers, the clitoris had been 'rediscovered' in the mid-16th century by European anatomists who returned to Classical texts. In keeping with the Galenic tradition, which represented female bodies as inverted versions of the male body, popular medical books – among the most accessible depictions of sex – described the clitoris as the female equivalent of the penis. Given the perceived mutability of gender, this view allowed for the possibility that the clitoris could be used in the same way as a penis. In this context, even a phallocentric model of sex was able to accommodate the idea that women could please each other: female masculinity was not just a performance, but a real physical possibility. The proof was the tribade, who used her clitoris to rub against or penetrate another woman's genitals. Clitorises that acted like penises were, it was thought, extremely unusual, but they were not impossible. In the words of Jane Sharp, a 17th-century English midwife: 'sometimes it grows so long that it hangs forth at the slit like a Yard [penis], and will swell and stand stiff if it be provoked, and some lewd women have endeavoured to use it as men do theirs.'[8] The clitoris was, Katharine Park has argued,

A female hermaphrodite, from George Arnauld's *Dissertation on Hermaphrodites*, 1750. When women were discovered having sexual intercourse with other women in the early modern period, the habitual explanation was that some degree of hermaphroditism was to blame. Any overdevelopment of the clitoris – and its association with the male organ – provided a neat, medically plausible reason for lesbian-like behaviour.

The Classical model of the human body as set down by Galen and Aristotle was still current in the early modern period. It imagined male and female at opposite poles on a scale of sexual difference, with hermaphrodites occupying the central ground. Illustration of a hermaphrodite from *Of Monsters and Prodigies* by the French physician Ambroise Paré (1573).

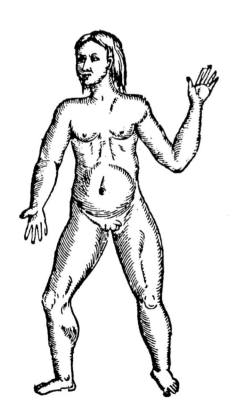

the trigger for a host of cultural anxieties about female sexuality; medical authorities, including Vesalius in the mid-16th century, were reluctant to accept its rediscovery, insisting that it was a pathological development confined to hermaphrodites.[9]

Authorities often attributed the extended clitoris to foreign climates and to the heated blood of Africa and Asia. In the Indies and Egypt, Jane Sharp noted, lewd women who used it like a penis were 'very frequent': she knew of only one in England. In the 19th century the prevailing understanding of inversion was noticeably influenced by ideas of race, a type of sexology that had a long prehistory.[10] One of the most widely circulated stories in the 16th and 17th centuries came from Leo Africanus's *Historical Description of Africa* (1526). Africanus recorded how women in Fez feigned illness or possession by devils so that they could enjoy the sexual attentions of female diviners; they were reputed to use their own husbands as go-betweens.[11] In Egypt, other texts claimed, women's genitals grew so long that they had to be circumcised. Ideas such as these, circulated first in travel literature and later embedded in medical treatises and pornographic volumes, located unnatural sexual practices firmly outside Europe. Some of these stories suggest the familiar idea that sex between women was only possible, or significant, when it involved penetration. Others, as we shall see, offered different possibilities.

By 1600, the phallic use of the clitoris was no longer being discussed solely in relation to African and Asian women; it had become a European phenomenon. European texts from the 17th century featured a series of notorious examples of women whose overdeveloped genitals enabled them to have penetrative sex with other women, passing as men in order to do so. In France in 1601, Marie Le Marcis was charged with male impersonation and sodomy with her female lover. She defended herself, with eventual success, by claiming to be a man with a concealed penis, although medical inspections produced differing conclusions, one doctor defining her as a predominantly male hermaphrodite, another as a woman guilty of sodomy. Her lover testified that Marie had satisfied her better than the husband who had fathered her children.[12]

Hermaphrodites

The Classical model of sex that prevailed in the early modern period also allowed room for those of intermediate sex, whose bodies upset the rules of heterosexual intercourse. Hermaphroditism was widely known, and, according to medical thinking, hermaphrodites occupied the middle ground in the spectrum from male to female; they were, at least in theory, literally central to the understanding of male and female as reversible. In accounts such as *Of Monsters and Prodigies* (1573), by the French surgeon Ambroise Paré, the line distinguishing women with overdeveloped clitorises from hermaphrodites was a fine one, and hermaphroditism was the first suspicion when women were found having sexual relations with other women.

Despite medical acceptance of the existence of hermaphrodites, the social response in Western Europe was almost always to force them to take one gender or the other. Those who were thought to be possible hermaphrodites

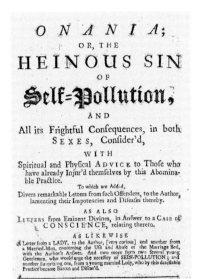

ONANIA;
OR, THE
HEINOUS SIN
OF
𝕾𝖊𝖑𝖋=𝕻𝖔𝖑𝖑𝖚𝖙𝖎𝖔𝖓,
AND
All its Frightful Confequences, in both
SEXES, Confider'd,
WITH
Spiritual and Phyfical ADVICE to Thofe who
have already Injur'd themfelves by this Abomina-
ble Practice.
To which are Added,
Divers remarkable Letters from fuch Offenders, to the Author,
lamenting their Impotencies and Difeafes thereby.
AS ALSO
LETTERS from Eminent Divines, in Anfwer to a CASE of
CONSCIENCE, relating thereto.
AS LIKEWISE
A Letter from a LADY, to the Author, [very curious] and another from
a Married-Man, concerning the Ufe and Abufe or the Marriage Bed,
with the Author's Anfwer. And two more from two feveral young
Gentlemen, who would urge the neceffity of SELF-POLLUTION; and
another Surprizing one, from a young married Lady, who by this detectable
Practice became Barren and Difeas'd.

*There fhall in no wife enter into the Heavenly Jerufalem, any Thing that de-
fileth, or worketh Abomination.* Rev. xxi. v. 27.

The Sixth EDITION, Corrected and Enlarged.

LONDON: Printed for, and Sold by T. Crouch, Bookfeller, at the Bell,
over againft the Queen's-Head-Tavern, in Pater-Nofter-Row, near Cheap-
fide. 1722.   [Price 1 s. 6 d. Stitch'd.]

The rediscovery of the clitoris in the 16th century as an unexceptional part of the female anatomy – one that belonged to ordinary women – caused medical experts to fret over the physical possibilities it presented. They were concerned that women with an enlarged clitoris might be able to penetrate other women, and concluded that masturbation only served to make clitorises phallically enlarged. This English pamphlet of 1722 warns of the 'frightful consequences' of self-pollution.

were subject to medical inspections to decide with which sex they were most identifiable. In most cases hermaphrodites were living as men but suspected of being biologically female; one Spanish hermaphrodite, born a slave, was identified first as male, then as female, and was finally prosecuted for magical practices in concealing her real sex and transforming herself.[13] In cases such as this, the distinction between hermaphrodite and tribade was demonstrably unclear, and medical texts about hermaphroditism and female genital overdevelopment were among the first printed materials in early modern Europe to devote attention to sex between women.

The definition and treatment of hermaphrodites presented difficulties. Medical writers' continued reliance on a certain body of Classical theory made hermaphroditism comprehensible: it provided a physical, medical rationale for sex between women. At the same time, the rediscovery of the clitoris as an ordinary organ blurred the line between ordinary women and hermaphrodites who had clitorises so overdeveloped as to function as penises. What if any woman could use her clitoris in this way? By the 18th century, anti-masturbation literature was developing these concerns still further, creating a circular process of worry about female sexuality: overdeveloped clitorises provoked women to masturbate, and masturbation made clitorises obscenely and phallically enlarged. Masturbation was readily elided with lesbian sex: cautionary examples ranged from the two Roman nuns whose clitorises had grown so large by unusual exercise that they had been ordered to leave their convent to the London gentlewoman who corrupted herself with her maidservant until she made herself ill.[14] The casting of masturbation as a female sin represented, in part, a transition in the way female sexuality was viewed, a move from the concept of women as naturally given to pleasure to one in which they were naturally chaste. But the continuing circulation of stories about tribades and hermaphrodites created a world in which these physical possibilities were surprisingly familiar — at least to those who read journals and pamphlets or had contact with the world of medicine.

Hermaphroditism was not the only physical explanation available for lesbian sex. One woman in late 17th-century London was said to have an infirmity that meant 'no man can lie with her, and because it is so she has ways with women, as well as with her old companions men, which is not fit to be named but most rank whorish they are'.[15] What these 'rank whorish' practices were we can only guess. In early 17th-century France, a doctor was employed by the Paris parlement to investigate a woman who was alleged to be one of several 'tribades or subigatrices', in order to discover 'with what part she had abused several maids and enjoyed many women, giving them great pleasure and enjoyment in the course of carnal intercourse'.[16]

Women on trial

It has been a historical convention that lesbian sex has never been criminalized, has never been treated with the gravity that, particularly in the pre-modern period, attached to sex between men. Yet despite the conviction — apparently firmly cemented by the 19th century — that sex between women was not culpable in the same way as sex between men, pre-modern lawmakers were in fact often prepared to include women in the laws that made sodomy a capital offence. In this period sodomy, in its broadest sense, meant unnatural sexual acts, and in most contemporary definitions it could include sex between two men, between two women, or between a man or a woman and an animal. Medieval and early modern lawyers interpreted Roman law, the influence of which remained pervasive in much of early modern Europe, as penalizing women for sodomy as well as men. In Spain, the standard 16th-century commentary on the medieval laws cited St Paul in order to demonstrate that, like men, women guilty of sodomy were to be punished by burning. In the Holy Roman Empire, the *Constitutio Criminalis Carolina* (1532) formulated by Charles V stated that 'if anyone commits impurity with a beast, or a man with a man, or a woman with a woman, they have forfeited their lives and shall, after the common custom, be sentenced to death by burning.' In Italy, the town of Treviso, near Venice, passed a statute providing that women committing 'this vice or sin against nature' should be 'fastened naked to a stake in the Street of the Locusts and shall remain there all day and night'.[17] Even in England, where sodomy laws were used exclusively against men, two 17th-century dictionaries defined it as an act that could be committed between two women.[18]

What the practical implications of these laws were is still uncertain: there are very few records of women being prosecuted under the sodomy statutes, and many of them are unclear about the precise grounds for prosecution. Most often, the offence was for a woman to have impersonated a man and married a woman; and where sex was concerned, courts were explicitly concerned with penetration, either with the enlarged clitoris characteristic of hermaphrodites or with an 'instrument'.[19] A German trial that took place in Speyer in 1477 follows a familiar pattern. Katherina Hetzeldorfer was prosecuted on the information of a number of women who said that she had had sex with them 'like a man'. One had been her lover for at least two years.[20] One said to the court that Katherina had tried to 'seduce her and have her manly will with her'; another claimed that she had 'whored like a man, and she grabbed her just like a man … with hugging and kissing she behaved exactly like a man with women'. They also talked about the 'huge thing' Katherina used in order to have sex with them 'just like a man': one woman talked of her urinating through it, while another said that 'her semen is so much that it is beyond measure, that one could grab it with a full hand'. The stories suggest that it was impossible for them to imagine that this man could have been a woman. Perhaps, to them, she was always like a man: or perhaps to represent Katherina as unshakeably, potently male was their best defence against accusations of complicity. Katherina herself confessed that she 'made an instrument with a red piece of leather, at the front filled with cotton, and a wooden stick stuck into it, and made a hole through the wooden stick, put a string through, and tied it round'. The sex itself was of critical importance to the court investigators. In response to one interrogation, Katherina said 'she did it at first with one finger, thereafter with two, and then with three, and then at last with the piece of wood that she held between her legs.' None of the judges or the witnesses were concerned to find out, as they might have been in later centuries, whether she was a hermaphrodite; it was accepted that she was a woman who 'tried to have her will' with other women. Katherina was found guilty and sentenced to be drowned; two of her lovers were also arrested, questioned and exiled from the city.

Two hundred and fifty years later, Catherina Margaretha Linck and her 'alleged wife', Catherina Margaretha Mühlhahn, were prosecuted for 'various serious crimes' in Halberstadt in 1721. The record of their trial constitutes the fullest known document for this period. According to her mother, Catherina Linck first dressed in men's clothes to protect her chastity. As a young man, she was baptized with a new name by a female prophet, and travelled and preached for several years. She had gone on to join the army as a musketeer but deserted, escaping punishment when she revealed her sex. Moving on again to different troops, she dressed sometimes as a man, sometimes as a woman, and at least once was inspected by local authorities uncertain of her sex. While working as a stocking-maker she met Mühlhahn, courted her and married her.

Crucial to Linck's prosecution was the 'leather instrument' that made her a man. She had fashioned it herself, she said, when she was in the army, using stuffed leather and attaching two testicles made from pig's bladder; she tied it on with a leather strap. Linck confessed that 'using her ingenuity, she had used it with several girls when she was a soldier'. She had had sex with many prostitutes and sometimes 'ran for miles after a beautiful woman and spent all her earnings on her'.[21] Even widows, she said, played with the leather dildo without realising what it was. Once, she admitted, she put the dildo in her wife's mouth. This was a crucial admission: fellatio was, like sodomy, a capital offence. But the court did not know what to do with the evidence, and the archive records a debate on the question of whether Linck's crime was worse because no semen had been spilled in the criminal acts she had committed, or whether that made it less heinous. Also crucial was the allegation that Catherina Mühlhahn, Linck's wife, had known for some time that her husband was a woman. When she had torn the leather penis from Linck's body, 'and was therefore fully aware that she was no man, she nevertheless later let

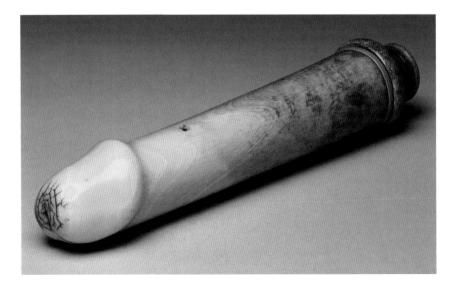

An ivory dildo in the form of an erect penis, complete with a contrivance for simulating ejaculation; possibly French, 18th century. Such objects may have been common in early modern culture: apart from according with the general conception of women as sexually insatiable, they appear in several accounts of cross-dressing or passing women, who fashioned their own versions from leather or wood.

The famous Catalina de Erauso, a Basque woman who passed as a soldier and fought in the Spanish colonies in the early 17th century. Although Catalina took great pains in her memoirs to stress her purity and virginity, she did not eschew flirting with and pursuing other women. Only once she had been arrested for murder did she reveal her true sex, after which she became something of a celebrity in her native Spain.

herself be tickled with it and they lived together even more intimately'.[22] For wearing men's clothes, for marrying her wife and for 'acting as a man' with her, as well as for counts of theft and heresy, Linck was sentenced to execution by beheading; her wife, it was decided, would also be punished for her complicity in sodomy.

The meaning of these offences and the sexual nature of Catherina Margaretha Linck were not obvious to 18th-century lawyers. They discussed at some length the whole question of whether women could commit sodomy, concluding that they could; but it was also suggested that sodomy with 'a lifeless leather device' was not actually genuine sodomy. On the other hand, Linck had been found to be in no way hermaphroditic, nor did she seem to have the enlarged clitoris that had been identified as provoking 'Eastern women' to abominations: her crimes were therefore worse, because they had no 'natural' reason to them. By the 18th century, it would seem, the literature about tribadism, clitoral hypertrophy and hermaphroditism had made its mark: if women were to be accused of sodomy, it would raise a whole series of questions about the meaning of such an act. And what of their partners? In both these cases, the courts were concerned to establish precisely what they had known and when they had known it; their complicity in the crime made them guilty too.

The 'device' that Linck used was not a wholly unfamiliar one. Other crossdressing women fashioned instruments for themselves, and some also made tubes through which they could urinate in public. Catherine Vizzani, a crossdressing woman in 18th-century Italy, had a 'leathern contrivance' fastened around her waist, which, when it was torn off by her investigators, turned out to be stuffed with paper. Dildoes were surprisingly established objects in early modern culture. They featured in erotica and pornography from at least the mid-17th century: in a culture that frequently satirized men as impotent and women as insatiable, they were imagined as the last resort for lewd women looking to satisfy themselves. But dildoes could also be the product of relatively simple, individual technologies. Rarely did their use have lesbian connotations, but they nonetheless signified the autonomy of female sexuality.

Female husbands

The marriage of two women was a familiar story in early modern culture, and only occasionally did it lead to the serious consequences described above. From the picaresque tales of women who travelled away as soldiers or sailors, to Henry Fielding's *The Female Husband* (1746) — a dramatized version of the life of Mary Hamilton, who disguised herself as a physician and married another woman — passing women and female husbands paraded through pamphlets, plays, ballads and broadsheets.[23] In many such tales, sex was peripheral or invisible: the sexual role of a man seemed to be just one of several male privileges claimed by passing women. Catalina de Erauso, a notorious 17th-century Basque transvestite who spent most of her life as a man called Antonio, left an autobiography that records the details of a rampaging life of adventure in

Mexico; only in passing does she mention her encounters with women, in which she always managed to stop short of marriage. Like other renowned cross-dressers, she was eventually celebrated for her virginity. But her chaste behaviour also encompassed flirting with women, as she recounts with pleasure. With one of her employer's daughters, for example, Catalina sat with 'my head in the folds of her skirt and she was combing my hair while I ran my hand up and down between her legs'.[24]

In other cases the focus of the story was on marriage. In London in 1680, Amy Poulter took the name of James Howard and married Arabella Hunt, a young musician at the royal court. Less than a year later Arabella began a plea for an annulment, alleging that Amy had a husband who was still alive, that she had misrepresented herself as a man, and that she was, in fact, a hermaphrodite, or 'of a double gender'. Amy denied this accusation: she was, she said, a 'perfect woman' (a claim confirmed by five midwives who later examined her), and the whole affair had been nothing more than a joke. To make matters more complicated, she had rarely actually cross-dressed — instead, she had presented herself to her bride's household as a man who was disguising himself in women's clothes to escape problems with an inheritance. And Amy's joke, if that is what is was, had involved cohabiting with her wife, and her wife's mother, for six months. Yet the defence of a 'frolic' is, perhaps, an important one: the couple were married in a church (St Mary-le-Bow) of dubious reputation, whose clergy might well avoid awkward inquiries.

Unlike earlier tales of cross-dressing women, the story of Catherine Vizzani (shown below, in disguise as her alter ego Giovanni Bordoni) makes no attempt to conceal the issue of her homosexuality. The surgeon who examined Vizzani's body after her death expected to find a case of hermaphroditism that would explain her 'unnatural desires'; but instead he found a normally formed woman and was obliged to look to her personal history for other possible causes. Vizzani's father had accepted her as his 'son', subscribing to the view that 'Nature must e'en take its Course.'

The pirates Anne Bonny and Mary Read, from Daniel Defoe's *A General History of the Robberies and Murders of the Most Notorious Pirates* (1724). Mary Read had gone by the name of Mark since childhood and much preferred the role of a young man. Once she and Anne had assumed a rough life of piracy, they were always by each other's side and took turns to dress in male clothing. Both were arrested in Jamaica in 1720. Although the evidence does not allow us to come to any firm conclusions regarding their sexuality, Bonny and Read's subversion of gender roles and their clearly intimate relationship make a lesbian reading of their story more than possible.

The complications of this story also suggest important differences in interpretation. To contemporaries, and to later commentators, such a marriage could be at once an innocent game; a case of gold-digging on the part of Arabella and her mother, keen to unite with such a promising young heir; and an unfortunate case in which a man turned out to be impotent, incomplete, or 'of a double gender'.[25]

Despite the apparent familiarity of the idea of persons 'of a double gender', female husbands were often hard to categorize. Hendrickje van der Schuyr was tried in Amsterdam in 1641 for her relations with other women; she had served two years as a soldier, and lived partly in men's clothes, partly as a woman. Her lover, a 42-year-old widow with three living children, described a sexual relationship in which Hendrickje was 'lustful and ever eager for sex'. She suggested, and midwives confirmed, that Hendrickje had signs of hermaphroditism; but other lovers claimed that she menstruated just like other women, and in the end Hendrickje was condemned as a tribade.[26] The extensive medical examinations that Hendrickje and other female husbands endured says something of the persistent need to explain women who had sex with other women as physically marked.

By the 18th century, other stories were circulating in which women's sexual desires could be explained by more than physical abnormality. The story of Catherine Vizzani, published in 1744 and translated into English in 1751, put sexual perversity at the heart of a tale of cross-dressing. In this fictionalized version of her life in and around Rome, Vizzani started off as a teenager enchanted by a friend, spending two years in a 'whimsical amour', 'viewing Margaret's captivating charms and saying soft Things to her'. Once she had learnt to dress as a man, she embarked on a career of pursuing women and ended up being shot in a fight over one. Vizzani, as her biographer pointed out, showed no evidence of abnormal physical development. Rather, she is identified right from the start as a woman corrupted into particular, lesbian, tastes after listening to bawdy stories: 'our Times afford a girl, who, so far from being inferior to Sappho, or any of the Lesbian Nymphs, in an Attachment for

Recent research has suggested that close bonds of friendship (at least between men) were consecrated in church services for hundreds of years, and there are many examples of monuments commemorating same-sex couples. The Chapel of St John the Baptist in Westminster Abbey, London, contains the tomb of Mary Kendall, dated 1710; the inscription records 'that close Union & Friendship, In which she liv'd, with The Lady Catharine Jones; And in testimony of which She desir'd, That even their Ashes, after Death, Might not be divided.'

those of her own Sex, has greatly surpassed them in Fatigues, Dangers, and Distress.'[27] Earlier tales tended to gloss over the marriages and sexual relations of women who passed as men, but this one treats the perversity of Catherine Vizzani's desires as its central theme.

There are still stories today of female husbands and passing women; there are still ways in which desire for women looks like a male prerogative. But these early modern stories and their particular contexts help illuminate the wider world in which relations between women took place. In early modern society, marriage was not primarily an emblem of heterosexual union: it was a bond that provided social and economic security and strengthened ties of kinship, and it was a necessary step for male adults. For at least some cross-dressing women, marriage and sex may have come as an adjunct to all the other male privileges and responsibilities acquired through wearing breeches. In some ways the terms 'transgender' and 'transsexual' provide more useful categories

than 'lesbian' for people like Catalina de Erauso. In other ways they do not: it is rarely clear whether women who lived as men were pursuing an internal conviction that they were not women; and sex in itself was a more flexible category than it would become in modern Western culture. Most of all, perhaps, these cases demonstrate how what Judith Halberstam has called 'female masculinity' was a place where women claimed male privileges of *all* sorts.[28]

It was also the case that in the early modern period church ceremonies such as marriage carried wider, older meanings. Spiritual rituals could consecrate friendship and kinship as well as marriage. As the recent work of Alan Bray has shown, pre-modern culture had a long history of recognizing bonds of friendship between men: some men were buried in the same grave, and some used religious ceremonies to cement their relationships. Intimate bonds between women were much less likely to achieve any public recognition. Sometimes, however, women were buried together in the same way as male friends: there is a monument in Westminster Abbey, London, recording the 'close Union & Friendship' in which Mary Kendall and Catharine Jones lived until the former's death in 1710.[29] Among the most telling and perplexing scraps of evidence for early modern women's lives are two enigmatic entries in the marriage register for the parish of Taxal, Cheshire, which record the marriages of 'Hannah Wright and Anne Gaskill' in 1707 and 'Ane Norton and Alice Pickford' in 1708.[30] It is at least possible that, in a time when clandestine and illegal marriages were a notorious problem, and marriage meant much more than heterosexual sexual union, the notion of marriage was one or two degrees more flexible than it would become in the modern age.

Friendship

For many years, 'lesbian' histories of the pre-modern period focused not on sex, but on love and intimacy. The model of platonic female friendship, elevated in writings across early modern Europe, seemed to demonstrate the innocence and chastity of relations between women. Elite women, particularly in literary circles, celebrated their networks of friendship and their intimate bonds with other women. Many expressed their love in rapturous language that in later centuries was reserved for heterosexual passion. 'I confess I have been most deadly in love with her as ever lover was', wrote the gentlewoman Constance Fowler of her prospective sister-in-law in 1636. In the 1670s Mary Stuart, heir to the English throne, and her close friend Frances Apsley wrote to each other as 'husband' and 'wife'.[31] Such friendships could represent a refuge from, or an alternative to, marriage: for example, Katherine Philips's passionate poems to her female friends in late 17th-century England fashioned a world of feminine eroticism from which men were entirely excluded.

Since romantic friendships were often represented as chaste unions, and since any sexual expression that might have existed is unlikely to appear in written records, they have generally been treated as asexual.[32] But friendship could be both chaste and eroticized, and the language of romantic friendship gave women a way to express erotic love while proclaiming themselves pure. Nor, to contemporaries, did friendships between women or within female communities always look entirely non-sexual. Nuns in Catholic countries had been advised since at least the 13th century to avoid the dangers of particular friendships, and in Protestant countries convents became objects of sexual fantasy. In both Catholic and Protestant societies, more emphasis was placed on companionship and intimacy within the model of heterosexual marriage, and affectionate relationships outside it were beginning to look more peculiar. By the 17th century, the tribade might not seem worlds apart from the chaste friend.[33] A hundred years later the potential disrepute and even criminality that might attach to female friendships were being discussed more explicitly; the scandalous allegations made against Queen Anne and her bedchamber-women in early 18th-century England were only the most public among many other such cases. When she was ousted by the queen's new favourite, Abigail Masham, Sarah Churchill circulated suggestions of 'dark Deeds at Night' and wrote to the queen: 'nor can I think the having noe inclination for any but one's own sex is enough to maintain such a character as I wish may still be yours.'[34] Later in the same century, Hester Thrale's diaries, which gossiped about the society of 18th-century London, commented regularly on suspicions of women with intimate female friends: the sculptress Anne Damer, among others, was 'much suspected for liking her own Sex in a criminal way'.[35]

The eroticization of female friendship shifted the way in which lesbianism was represented: it meant that the tribade, the focus of so much medical and legal attention, no longer sustained the whole weight of condemnation. Gossip about Queen Anne, Marie Antoinette or society women made it publicly clear that lesbian acts did not necessarily involve the performance of 'female masculinity' or the transformation of female organs into male or hermaphroditic ones.

Daily life

Most central to lesbian history are the circumstances of daily life that made same-sex relations possible, likely or difficult. What literary critics and historians have reconstructed of early modern European culture suggests that lesbianism was very far from being an unknown concept. The literate might have access to Classical, contemporary, medical and erotic representations of same-sex desire. Although the majority of women could not write – until the 18th century, at least – many may have been able to read. Even without access to print, oral culture surely carried some traces of Classical and contemporary stories of homoerotic desires, and stories of women marrying women certainly circulated widely.

With or without knowledge of such stories, how might women have experienced and pursued lesbian desires in early modern cultures? Outside the spheres of law and medicine, theatre and poetry, and below the social world of female poets and court friendships, possibilities for lesbian relationships existed in a much wider realm than is suggested by tales of female husbands, tribades and their partners. Perhaps the first thing to note is the proportion of women who, by choice or by compulsion, remained single. Although marriage was conceived as central to social and economic structures, in many parts of Europe and at many times it was far from ubiquitous, and women established

Upon her Knees fam'd Somerset receives,
An Office which another D____ss leaves.

Sarah Churchill, later Duchess of Marlborough, rose to a position of great influence, largely on account of her close relationship with Queen Anne. They conducted a passionate – and sometimes stormy – relationship by means of countless letters, using pet names for one another. It seems likely that Sarah – jealous at the queen's apparent intimacy with a new favourite – was behind a ballad of 1708 that told how the queen 'dearly loved / A Dirty Chamber-Maid' called Abigail. Portrait by Godfrey Kneller, *c.* 1700.

Queen Christina of Sweden (opposite), in a portrait by Sebastien Bourdon, *c.* 1652. Upon her birth in 1626 Christina was thought to be a boy; undeterred, her father ordered that she should be educated in the princely pursuits of political and military science, riding and hunting. Christina herself later claimed 'an ineradicable prejudice against everything that women like to talk about or do'. Rumours of lesbian affairs were perhaps inevitable, although some have also posited hermaphroditism as a reason for her mannish dress, deep voice and refusal to marry.

alternative domestic arrangements in its stead. In England in the later 17th century, married women were always in a minority: many women remained single, and many were widowed. In rural France in the 18th century, groups of single women set up house together and shared costs. Even when people did get married, they generally did so late; the average age for marriage in this period was between twenty-five and thirty years of age. That left a good decade of single adult life, which most young women spent in service, working in a variety of households and experiencing a multitude of different sleeping arrangements with other servants, daughters of the house or with the mistress herself. There were all sorts of opportunities for sexual intimacy.

Single women in early modern Europe were sometimes marginalized, but they were also familiar figures. With or without children, women regularly headed households; many single women took lodgers, and some were able to establish their own businesses. Particularly in north-western Europe, all-female domestic arrangements were neither unusual nor necessarily problematic.[36] Poor single women might spend years living together, moving from lodging to

Despite the centrality of marriage to early modern society, many women remained single. Those in domestic service might find themselves living and working in close proximity to mistresses or other serving women; and the less fortunate might belong to workhouses, prisons or brothels, all of which provided opportunity for sexual intimacy. Engraving of a young woman being initiated into a brothel, from a 1766 edition of John Cleland's *Memoirs of a Woman of Pleasure*.

lodging; their relationships are largely invisible in history but had great economic and social significance. Tim Hitchcock points out that, from the 18th century, workhouse provision ensured that large numbers of poor women lived together, sharing beds and domestic accommodation.[37] Despite the apparent ubiquity of heterosexual marriage in the early modern world, there were also other paths.

Of course, lesbian acts did not take place only in domestic contexts — although women's relative lack of social and spatial freedom in most early modern communities meant they were more likely than men to keep their intimacies behind closed doors. By the mid-18th century, as a whole range of urban subcultures was developing in European cities, there is still no evidence of lesbian communities, although the use of such words as 'tommy' and 'sapphist' in England, for example, suggests a developing sense of sexual identity.[38] In Amsterdam, a series of trials for tribadism provides rare evidence of sexual contacts, seductions and relationships among working women. Two women aged fifty and sixty were denounced in 1750 by their landlady for 'living as if they were man and wife … feeling and touching one another under their skirts and at their bosom'. Others were arrested by nightwatchmen, and a group of five women were reported after their neighbours saw them together through a keyhole and started a riot. Anna Grabou, arrested in 1797, was said to have courted one of her lovers by telling her, as they stood watching a boy swimming naked in the canal, 'you do have something in you that attracts male and female.' Some of her carefully reported speeches suggest a sexual idiom that may not have been exclusively lesbian, but which was open to interpretation as the articulation of female desire: she talks of waking up her maid early in the morning to 'scratch her poverty', and she tells another woman: 'Pretty flower, you're not as pretty above your skirt as below.'[39]

Brothels might have been one place for lesbian connections (some of the women arrested in Amsterdam were prostitutes). Prisons, as they developed across Europe in the 18th century, certainly offered opportunities. In 1750 Geneviève Pommier, a 34-year-old Parisian embroideress, was imprisoned for hawking newssheets. She was helped out by another woman, known as 'la Maréchale', who professed to have fallen desperately in love with her, telling her she was surprised that Geneviève had not learnt in the Salpêtrière prison what 'a good friend' was, or about 'the friendly favours they gave each other' — both of which she demonstrated with kisses, tender caresses and 'brisk and violent movements'.[40] In the Royal Prison in late 16th-century Seville, women were reputed to make their own dildoes and to strut about, crowing 'like roosters'.[41]

For many women, sex and intimacy had a spiritual dimension. It was hard to separate religion from early modern sex: divine or satanic inspiration explained desire, lust and sin; angels, devils and familiars acted as sexual personae or intermediaries; and possession drove women to acts they would never have committed themselves. In an Italian convent in the early 17th century, Benedetta Carlini began to see visions and to receive the stigmata. When her claims were investigated and found to be false, another revelation emerged:

that her cellmate had been forced to engage with her in 'the most immodest acts'. Lying on top of her 'as if she were a man', and speaking words of love, Benedetta would move 'so much that both of them corrupted themselves'.[42] It was a male angel, she told her companion, that was doing those things; they were a form of special divine intervention. It was the presence of the male angel that explained to the two nuns their sexual contact and which gave Benedetta a new, powerful identity. Religion, as well as the performance of masculinity, was key to their sexual expression.

For many early modern women, religious commitment made it possible to forsake men for women and families for friends and sisters. In Catholic Europe, convent life could bring the opportunity to study and meditate apart from men and free from the obligations of marriage. In Protestant countries, radical sects often depended on the commitment of women and on their close bonds with each other; some of them left husbands and children in order to travel and preach with each other.[43] Even without any evidence of sexual expression, such relationships matter for lesbian history: they provide the raw material for a history of 'lesbian-like' behaviours.

Identities and communities

Conditions such as these created a world in which the impossibility or invisibility of lesbian sex was a cultural trope, not a reality. There was a language, both verbal and physical, for lesbian desire. Categories such as hermaphrodite and tribade bore a weight of moral condemnation and medical concern; stories of female husbands and erotic friendships presented a means of creating and concealing intimacies. Actual sexual and emotional practices did not, of course, depend on representation: we have only the scarcest hints of how women pursued their desires. The sexual acts that came to public attention were penetrative and phallic; less phallocentric acts, such as the 'bosom sex' that two 19th-century women shared, will generally escape the historian's eye.[44]

Equally scarce are women's own descriptions of what we would now call sexuality. Called upon to explain themselves, women accused of unnatural sex might say that the Devil drove them to it, as did Catherina Margaretha Linck; but Catherina also argued that dressing as a man was not wrong, because it was only married women, not maidens, who were forbidden to do so. Despite being married, she defined herself as a maid. Yet under interrogation she admitted that 'often when a woman touched her, even slightly, she became so full of passion she did not know what to do.'[45] This statement, even filtered through the clerk's mediation, carries a hint of the dilemma posed by her desires. Amy Poulter insisted that she was no hermaphrodite and that she had married Arabella Hunt for a 'frolic'; Arabella said that she believed her husband to be a man. Benedetta Carlini insisted that her sexual acts with her cellmate were part of a spiritual experience. The familiar story of the 'female husband' made it a potent model of relations between women, but many other sexual scripts remain hidden. Even our concept of sexual intercourse is not consistent with early modern mentalities. The spilling of male or female seed was a moral and social crime against the family, but intimate touch could also be part of

complex homosocial relations. However familiar it might look, the pre-modern sexual past was shaped by different concepts, languages and meanings.

This is not, therefore, a story of slow progress towards a modern lesbian identity. Throughout the early modern period in Europe, a variety of expressions of lesbian desire was possible. Ideas were changing. The association between tribadism, clitoral hypertrophy and hermaphroditism, which gave lesbian desire a recognizable body, lost much of its power, but the perverse, foreign figure of the tribade remained. By the 18th century, stories of female husbands were no longer so easy to associate with maidenhood and heroism. At the same time, as more and more women were living single lives, the renewed ideals of heterosexual marriage conspicuously marginalized them and their relations with other women. Yet by the end of the 18th century, the notion that lesbianism was the 'impossible love', the 'silent sin', retained its power, reinforced by the newer notion that women were naturally chaste or asexual. It was this idea of chastity, perhaps, that allowed so many different ways of being a lesbian, or lesbian-like, to flourish – often in secret, and rarely leaving a historical trace. In 1840 Anne Lister, who had grown up among Yorkshire gentry, left detailed diaries of her sexual exploits with other women; she was quite clear that she, and others she knew, were 'too fond' of women. But she was also quite capable of claiming to friends that she could make no sense of the rumours of Marie Antoinette's lesbian activities; she listened approvingly to sermons on the text in which St Paul anathematizes women's unnatural acts; and she did not define herself as a sapphist.[46] Much of what we might identify with lesbianism had no personal meaning to her, and this must have been true for most early modern women who had sex with women. These qualifications and complications do not make a history of early modern lesbianism impossible: they simply remind us to listen for its many voices.

Having held a kissing competition with her fellow nymphs, the young Amaryllis chooses a winner: a painting of 1630 by the Dutch artist Jacob van Loo. An educated elite familiar with the late 16th-century play from which the story comes – Guarini's *Il Pastor Fido* – would have recognized that the young girl being crowned is in fact the shepherd boy Mirtillo, but a casual observer might well have come away with a different impression. Recent research by historians has suggested that the concept of lesbianism was not as unknown as we might have thought.

The Americas: From Colonial Times to the 20th Century
BRETT GENNY BEEMYN

Sexual and gender practices in indigenous American cultures

The earliest recorded accounts of same-sex sexual activity in the Americas were written by Spanish and Portuguese conquerors, explorers and missionaries, who reported that 'sodomy' was widespread in many indigenous cultures. Such narratives have to be approached with caution, however, since the dominant Christian doctrine of the 15th and 16th centuries considered sodomy to be an abominable sin, and European observers sometimes characterized other cultures as engaging in sodomy and other 'vices' in order to portray themselves as superior and to justify colonial expansion.[1] But these reports cannot be dismissed entirely, especially in cases where a number of chronicles provide similar accounts and where a narrator's descriptions of other aspects of the culture have proven largely reliable.

For example, several narratives noted the prevalence of same-sex sexual behaviour in the region of Mexico that now forms the state of Vera Cruz. When the conquistador Hernán Cortes arrived in the area in 1519, he commanded the local inhabitants to 'give up your sodomy and all your other evil practices'. He subsequently wrote to his monarch, Emperor Charles V: 'We know and have been informed without room for doubt that all (Veracruzanos) practice the abominable sin of sodomy.'[2] A number of Portuguese chroniclers likewise found same-sex sexual practices common among the Tupinambá Indians of Brazil in the 16th century. Pêro de Magalhães Gândavo commented in 1576 that the Indian men near present-day Rio de Janeiro engaged in sodomy 'as if they did not have the reason of men', and, writing about a decade later, Gabriel Soares de Souza described how the young men regularly indulged in sodomy in order to prove and boast about their virility.[3]

Prior to European conquest, attitudes towards same-sex sexual activity varied widely across Latin America, even in cultures under common rule. While sodomy was condemned by Inca leaders and villagers in the Andean highlands, it was apparently considered an acceptable practice in the northern coastal region of the Incan empire. Writing in the mid-16th century, the Spanish conquistador and historian Pedro Cieza de León stated that Popayán men in the area 'pride themselves greatly on sodomy'.[4]

A number of reports of same-sex sexual behaviour in the Americas involved individuals who adopted cross-gender roles, which included having

In 1939 photographer Weegee (Arthur Fellig) captured this drag queen stepping elegantly from a New York police wagon. Despite having been arrested, the 'Gay Deceiver', as Weegee labelled him, is unrepentant, hitching up his skirt and giving a large smile to the camera.

The Spanish and Portuguese conquerors of the Americas, who came from a world in which same-sex sexuality was taboo and vehemently condemned, found not only evidence of widespread 'sodomy' among local cultures, but also a tradition of cross-gender roles. On a journey through Florida in 1564, the French artist Jacques Le Moyne de Morgues noted that 'hermaphrodites' were 'quite common', and described how they would transport the dead and take care of the sick.

sexual relations with and marrying people of the same biological sex. In the earliest known European description of multiple genders in a Native American culture, Spanish explorer Cabeza de Vaca wrote in about 1530 of the Coahuiltecan Indians of what is now Texas: 'I saw one man married to another, and these are impotent, effeminate men and they go about dressed as women, and they do women's tasks, and shoot with a bow, and carry great burdens … and they are huskier than the other men and taller.' De Vaca called the practice 'a devilish thing'.[5]

Because these women-men (biological males who partially or completely assumed the roles culturally defined as female) were often described as stronger and bigger than the men of the group, many European observers initially thought that they were 'hermaphrodites'. For example, Jacques Le Moyne de Morgues, an artist who accompanied a French expedition to Florida in 1564, noted that 'hermaphrodites' among the Timucua Indians were 'quite common'.[6] Due to their strength, they carried provisions when a chief went to war and transported the sick and the dead from the field of battle, a task depicted by Le Moyne in one of his paintings. The work was subsequently reproduced by the engraver Théodore de Bry.

European explorers and conquistadors did not just describe and condemn the gender diversity they found in the Americas. Another of de Bry's engravings depicts Vasco Nuñez de Balboa and his troops having their dogs tear apart forty Cueva Indian women-men, whom they considered to be 'sodomites', during Balboa's trek across the isthmus of Panama in 1513. Similarly, Nuño de Guzmán burned alive a woman-man, whom he thought was a male prostitute, while travelling through Mexico in the 1530s.[7]

Subsequent European chroniclers also assumed that women-men cross-dressed because they were the passive, effeminate sexual partners of other men, commonly referring to them as 'berdaches', an 18th-century French adaptation of the Arabic and Persian words for a male prostitute or 'kept boy'. However, within their respective societies, women-men and men-women (biological females in men's roles) were viewed as neither men nor women, but as additional genders that either combined male and female elements or existed completely apart from other gender categories. Among Native North Americans, for example, the Cree referred to women-men as *ayekkwew*, 'neither man nor woman' or 'both man and woman', and the Zuni called a man-woman *katsotse*, 'boy-girl'. Thus a cross-gendered man or woman whose sexual partner was a non-cross-gendered

Attitudes towards same-sex sexuality differed widely in the pre-contact Americas. This ceramic jar (right), depicting two male figures in an erotic position, was made by the Mochica culture of northern Peru in around 100–800 CE. Yet the Incas who invaded the same region in the mid-15th century were known to have enacted harsh, repressive campaigns against sodomites.

individual of the same biological sex was considered to be in what anthropologist Sabine Lang characterizes as a 'hetero-gender' relationship, and not in a same-sex sexual relationship, as European cultures would define it.[8]

Like Native American cultures, the West African societies from which most Africans in the Americas came exhibited a wide range of sexual and gender practices, including some societies that accepted and, at times, institutionalized same-sex sexual activity and cross-gender roles. Numerous European observers reported that young men and women in highly sex-segregated African cultures engaged in same-sex sexual behaviour, especially before entering heterosexual marriages. In some societies, these same-sex relationships continued well into adulthood. For example, accounts from 17th-century Angola described cross-dressing adult men who had sex with and sometimes married other men.[9]

The preponderance of African men forced into slavery in the Americas in the 16th and 17th centuries, first in Brazil and then in the Caribbean and the United States, likely encouraged same-sex sexual activity within the slave population. At the same time the enslaved Africans, both women and men, were subject to sexual violence from slaveholders. While most of these assaults went unacknowledged and unrecorded, a few were documented, such as the case of the owner of a large sugar mill in Brazil, who confessed to Inquisition authorities in the early 1590s that he had committed sodomy with four men, including two slaves and a free black servant.[10]

Colonial laws and punishments

As part of the conquest of the Americas and the subjugation of indigenous populations and enslaved Africans, colonial authorities enacted Christian legal codes adopted from Europe that often prescribed the death penalty for sodomy (which was typically defined as anal sex). For example, when the Portuguese colonized Brazil, they imposed on the new territory their country's sodomy law, which dictated that a man found guilty of the crime 'be burnt and made dust by the fire so that his body and burial never have memory'.[11] In addition, the offender's property was confiscated and his children and grandchildren forced to live in infamy. Mexico's early colonial authority, the Apostolic Inquisitor, likewise put men convicted of sodomy to death by burning, among them fourteen men who were executed together during a crackdown on male same-sex sexual activity in Mexico City in the mid-17th century. According to the court record, the men 'had nice homes in which they received one another and in which they called one another by the kind of names used in this city by prostitutes'.[12]

Fewer men were executed for sodomy in the North American colonies than in colonial Latin America; legal records document five capital cases from the mid-16th and the 17th centuries — one in the Spanish colony of Florida, two in the Dutch colony of New Netherland, and one each in the English colonies of Virginia and New Haven.[13] As in Brazil and Mexico, however, these executions could be quite gruesome. Jan Creoli, a 'negro' in the New Netherland Colony, was executed in 1646 by being choked and then, after being 'tied to a stake, and faggots piled around him', set afire.[14]

Osh-Tisch, or 'Finds Them and Kills Them' – the last of the Crow women-men, photographed in 1928. Like other Native North American cultures, the Crow recognized individuals who wore the clothes and adopted the roles of the 'opposite sex' as belonging to additional genders completely distinct from male and female.

The sodomy laws in British North America were based on the English buggery statute of 1533, which required proof of penetration, and often two witnesses, for someone to be charged with the crime. The difficulty of meeting these standards in what were typically consensual and clandestine relationships meant that even when same-sex sexual behaviour came to the attention of authorities, the evidence did not support a sodomy charge.[15] In Plymouth, Massachusetts, a court in 1637 found John Allexander and Thomas Roberts 'guilty of lewd behavior and unclean carriage one with another, by often spending their seed one upon another, which was proved both by witness and their own confession'. The two avoided the death penalty, however, because the court lacked evidence to substantiate penetration. Allexander, who was found 'to have been formerly notoriously guilty that way', was sentenced to be severely whipped, burnt in the shoulder with a hot iron and forever banished from the colony, while Roberts, an indentured servant, was whipped and returned to his master.[16]

Opposition to execution also restricted its use. In the first reported death penalty case in New France (Lower Canada), a young drummer who was convicted of a 'crime against nature' in 1648 had his sentence commuted after protests from Montreal's Jesuit priests.[17] New England authorities also at times remitted the sentences of individuals who confessed and repented, believing that same-sex sexual behaviour, like other perceived sins, was a temptation inherent in all people. Puritan leaders may have been reluctant to apply capital punishment to an offence that anyone might commit and that they feared was commonly practised.[18]

Despite harsh legal and religious sanctions against sodomy, New England colonists also seem sometimes to have tolerated the same-sex sexual activities of privileged men who were otherwise respected members of the community. One such individual was Nicholas Sension, a prosperous resident of Windsor, Connecticut. Settling in the colony around 1640, Sension became well known for his often violent sexual advances towards his young male servants and neighbours. Complaints from relatives of the men who had been approached by Sension led town leaders to investigate his behaviour in the late 1640s and then again in the late 1660s. In both cases he was privately reprimanded rather than being brought to court. Only when Sension's solicitations became too frequent to be publicly ignored was he charged with sodomy. At Sension's trial in 1677 numerous men testified to his sexual assaults. But because only one witness would attest that Sension had succeeded in committing sodomy, he was found guilty of the lesser charge of attempted sodomy. As punishment, his estate was placed in bond for his future good behaviour. Sension's lenient sentence, passed despite clear evidence that he had been pursuing sexual relationships with other men for more than thirty years, suggests that the same-sex sexual behaviour of leading New England citizens could be overlooked or dealt with discreetly through non-judicial means if their actions did not become socially disruptive or involve those outside the master–servant relationship.[19]

Although few people were executed for sodomy in the North American colonies, many more individuals, like Sension, were convicted of lesser sexual offences. At least two of these cases involved women. The New Haven Colony was the only American settlement to include sexual relations between women in its sodomy law, but women were prosecuted elsewhere under other statutes. In the earliest such documented case, Elizabeth Johnson, a servant in the Massachusetts Bay Colony, was found guilty of a number of insubordinate and illegal acts, including 'unseemly practices betwixt her and another maid' in 1642. She was fined and severely whipped. In Plymouth, Massachusetts, two married women, Mary Hammon and Sara Norman, were accused in 1649 of 'lewd behavior each with [the] other upon a bed'. Perhaps because Hammon was only fifteen years old at the time, the charges against her were dropped. Somewhat older, Norman was required to confess her 'unchaste behavior' publicly.[20]

Besides policing same-sex sexual activity, Puritan leaders also sought to maintain strict gender boundaries by punishing individuals who cross-dressed or who led cross-gendered lives. While the laws prohibiting same-sex sexual relationships in British North America largely ignored women, both men and women were included in statutes banning cross-dressing and were subject to prosecution. For example, in 1652 Joseph Davis of New Hampshire was fined and ordered to admit his guilt to the community for 'putting on women's apparel', and in 1677, Dorothy Hoyt of Massachusetts was sentenced in absentia to receive a severe whipping when she returned to the colony for 'putting on man's apparel' unless her father immediately paid a fine on her behalf.[21]

More difficult for colonial authorities to adjudicate was the case of Thomas/Thomasine Hall, a servant from Warrosquyoacke, Virginia, who claimed to be both a man and a woman and who, at different times, had adopted the traditional roles and clothing of men and women. Unable to establish Hall's 'true' gender and unsure of whether to punish him/her for wearing men's or women's apparel, local citizens asked the General Court at Jamestown to resolve the issue. Perhaps because it, too, was unable to determine Hall's sex conclusively, or perhaps because it took Hall to be what we would refer to today as intersexed, the court ordered him/her in 1629 to wear both a man's breeches and a woman's apron and cap.

In a sense, this unique ruling affirmed Hall's dual nature and subverted traditional gender categories, but by fixing Hall's gender and denying him/her the right to switch between male and female identities, the court's decision punished Hall and reinforced gender boundaries.[22] Moreover, for the citizens of Warrosquyoacke, the court's judgment only added to their uncertainty over how to treat Hall and further challenged their ability to discern what constituted appropriate sexual and gendered behaviour for him/her. Like the leniency shown to Sension, the ruling in the Hall case demonstrates that Puritan society dealt with sexual and gender transgressions in complex ways that were not always in keeping with legal codes and official pronouncements.[23]

Sodomy prosecutions in the early United States

As Puritan fervour declined in British North America and as the colonies moved towards becoming more secular states in the late 17th and 18th centuries, the citizens of New England became less concerned about enforcing laws on public morality and even more reluctant to punish same-sex sexual behaviour severely. A growing belief in the right to privacy also meant that community members were not anxious to prosecute their neighbours for sodomy and other sex offences. The courts likewise became less interested in moral matters as financial and commercial cases began to proliferate.[24]

The only known execution for sodomy in the North American colonies during the 18th century occurred in 1743 and involved an unnamed Irish doctor in Fort Frederica, Georgia. It was also the last use of the death penalty for sodomy in what became the United States, since the new states began to abolish capital punishment for sexual offences after the American Revolution. By the turn of the 19th century, Pennsylvania, New Jersey, New York and Rhode Island had eliminated executions for sodomy, followed by seven other states by the mid-1820s. Among the thirteen original American colonies, only North and South Carolina kept sodomy on their books as a capital crime throughout the Civil War, abolishing the death penalty in 1868 and 1869 respectively.[25]

The end of executions for sodomy did not mean that the offence was no longer severely punished, however. All of the states that abolished the death penalty imposed new penalties, ranging from compulsory life imprisonment in Connecticut and Georgia to solitary confinement and from one to ten years' hard labour in New Hampshire and Massachusetts. The most leniency was shown by Rhode Island, where someone convicted of sodomy could be imprisoned for no more than three years. However, the death penalty there remained in effect for a second conviction, and, perhaps to emphasize this fact to a first-time offender, the law required that the guilty individual be set upon the gallows 'for a space of time not exceeding four hours and thence to the common gaol, there to be confined for a term not exceeding three years'.[26]

Romantic friendships

Although sodomy remained a criminal offence throughout the country in the late 18th and 19th centuries, people in the United States accepted and even idealized passionate, loving and physically affectionate friendships between members of the same sex. These 'romantic friendships', as they have come to be called, often lasted throughout the individuals' adult lives and, while normally not taking the place of marriage, frequently superseded matrimony in importance, particularly for women. As first described by Carroll Smith-Rosenberg in her ground-breaking article 'The Female World of Love and Ritual: Relations Between Women in Nineteenth-Century America', romantic friendships 'possess an emotional intensity and a sensual and physical explicitness that are difficult to dismiss'.[27]

Typical were the experiences of Sarah Butler Wistar and Jeannie Field Musgrove, who met in 1849 and became close companions while together at boarding school. In their many letters to one another they commented frequently on their mutual affection, which seemed only to grow after Wistar's marriage and her physical separation from Musgrove. Writing in 1864, by which time she was a wife and mother, Wistar described how much she longed to be with '[her] dearest love': 'I can give you no idea how desperately I shall want you.' Musgrove's correspondence was likewise filled with expressions of desire: 'Dear darling Sarah! How I love you and how happy I have been! You are the joy of my life … My darling how I long for the time when I shall see you.' She ended another letter: 'I will go to bed … [though] I could write all night – A thousand kisses – I love you with my whole soul.' Their relationship remained extremely close into old age.[28]

Historical evidence suggests that, in the 18th and 19th centuries, romantic friendships were more common among middle-class whites. However, what would appear today to be same-sex sexual relationships were also recognized and approved of by African-American and working-class white communities. For example, schoolteacher Rebecca Primus and domestic servant Addie Brown, two African-American women in Hartford, Connecticut, had an intense, deeply passionate relationship in the 1860s.[29]

But romantic friendships were acceptable in US society precisely because they were seen as non-sexual. While colonial America considered women as likely as men to succumb to sexual temptation, if not more so, a growing belief in the late 1700s that the sexes were fundamentally different led to the characterization of white middle-class women as innocent and lacking sexual desire, in contrast to the lasciviousness of men. Two women could hug, kiss, caress and share a bed openly without social stigma because their behaviour was viewed as a sign of emotional intimacy rather than sexual attraction.[30]

Yet despite popular perception, romantic friendships were not always non-sexual. The extent to which these relationships were sexual in nature is difficult to determine because many women may have avoided being explicit in their letters. But what contemporary observers would characterize as sexual acts were part of the intimacy that developed between some women. Primus and Brown's relationship involved at least the touching of breasts, and, as indicated by one of Brown's letters, there was an expectation among the young women at the school in Farmington, Connecticut, where she worked of sleeping together, referred to as 'bosom sex'. Brown wrote to Primus that she did sleep with one of the women, but that her bed partner 'got sadly disappointed injoying it, for I had my back towards [her] all night and my night dress *was* butten up so she could not get to my bosom'. Further seeking to allay Primus's concerns, Brown added that she would allow only Primus to touch her breasts: 'I shall try to keep your f[avored] one always'.[31]

Even though Primus and Brown were more intimate than was considered proper for a romantic friendship, their family and friends acknowledged, accepted and facilitated their relationship. Mrs Primus allowed Brown to read the letters her daughter wrote home, Primus's aunt and uncle had Brown to stay with them several times, and all three Primus family members found her jobs. When a neighbour of the Primus's expressed concern that the couple were inappropriately close, Mrs Primus even defended their relationship. As

Thomas Eakins's *The Swimming Hole*, painted *c.* 1883. Although his personal sexual preferences are unknown, Eakins's approach to depicting the (male) body was informed by ideals of 'beauty, fitness and camaraderie' borrowed from ancient Greece. This, his most famous work, aptly illustrates how some men's idealized notions of 'comradeship' could cut across normal barriers of age and class.

Brown told Primus: 'She said I thought as much of you if you was a gentleman. She also said if either one of us was a gent we would marry.'[52]

Yet because neither was male, they were expected to find husbands. Brown's and Primus's families and other members of the Hartford black community may have recognized the depth of their commitment to each other, but it was still assumed that the women's devotion would not preclude or interfere with relationships with men. Primus's aunt, for example, warned Brown not to reveal to a male suitor that she loved Primus more than she would ever care for him. Brown apparently heeded the advice, for the man proposed to her, and, reluctantly, she accepted, which led to the end of her relationship with Primus.[53]

The dissolution of a romantic friendship following the marriage of one or both partners was a more common pattern among male companions. Like female same-sex relationships, romantic friendships between men were loving, passionate and intimate, and might include kissing, caressing and sharing a bed.[54] At times, these relationships could also include sexual acts, as indicated by the surviving letters of Thomas Jefferson Withers to James H. Hammond – young white men from South Carolina who would become two of the South's most prominent defenders of slavery and states' rights. Writing to Hammond in 1826, the 22-year-old Withers enquired 'whether you yet have the extravagant delight of poking and punching a writhing Bedfellow with your long fleshen pole – the exquisite touches of which I have often had the honor of feeling?' Hammond's reply appears lost to history, but a subsequent letter from Withers suggests that Hammond's response was to brag about his sexual prowess, for Withers gently teased his former partner: 'your fleshen pole … has captured complete mastery over you – and I really believe, that you are charging over the pine barrens of your locality, braying, like an ass, at every she-male you can discover.'[55]

While young men might form close emotional and, at times, sexual ties, these relationships were expected to end with adulthood. Indeed, one mark of becoming a grown man in the 19th century was to leave adolescent male bonds behind in order to pursue marriage and a career. Romantic friendships offered male youth a sense of security and comradeship during the uncertainties associated with coming of age; when their lives became more settled, many had little time for what they came to perceive as unmanly attachments.[56]

'True Comrades'

Some men, though, did not relinquish romantic friendships when they became adults, but incorporated intimate same-sex relationships into their concept of manhood. These men continued to revere male companionship and considered what poet Walt Whitman called 'the beautiful and sane affection of man for man, latent in all young fellows' to be the most natural and the purest form of male love.[57] Homoerotic friendships between men, often crossing lines of race and class, were a predominant theme in the work of a number of white male writers and artists in the 19th century, including Henry David Thoreau, James Fenimore Cooper, Herman Melville, Thomas Eakins and Bayard

Taylor. But the most ardent spokesperson for male intimacy was Whitman, whose 'Calamus' poems, first incorporated into the 1860 (third) edition of *Leaves of Grass*, 'celebrate the need for comrades'. In the fifth 'Calamus' poem, for example, Whitman imagined a future world in which love between men would be 'invincible' rather than invisible:

> It shall be customary in all directions, in the houses and streets,
>> to see manly affection,
> The departing brother or friend shall salute the remaining
>> brother or friend with a kiss.[38]

Whitman apparently wrote the 'Calamus' poems after falling in love with Fred Vaughan, a teenager who lived with him in the late 1850s. Like Vaughan, all of Whitman's subsequent sexual partners were young working-class men, and in his diary he catalogued and described the many youths he met on the streets of New York and Washington, DC, and sometimes took home with him.[39] Whitman had even greater opportunities to develop intimate, sexual relationships with young men while serving as a nurse to Union soldiers in Washington's hospital wards during the Civil War. As he told a friend in 1863, 'O how one gets to love them ... so manly and affectionate ... lots of them have grown to expect as I leave at night that we should kiss each other, sometimes quite a number, I have to go round.'[40] Some of the relationships went beyond kissing and continued outside of the hospital, for Whitman proposed to one sergeant that they settle down together. The man apparently did not share Whitman's dream of becoming 'true comrades and never be separated while life lasts', but in 1865 Whitman met Peter Doyle, who became his lover for almost a decade.[41]

Sexual relationships in all-male communities

While administering to the sick, Whitman moved in an all-male environment where war, the loss of close friends and the ever-present danger to one's own life fostered the development of tightly-knit same-sex relationships. But even outside the confines of battle men often formed intense bonds in sex-segregated settings. In the mid- and late 19th century, many middle-class white men found same-sex love and friendship through their involvement in the work of the Young Men's Christian Association (YMCA).

Given its adherence to conservative religious and moral values, the YMCA would seem an unlikely supporter of intimate relationships between men, but, as an early YMCA leader explained in his 1896 history of the organization, one of its primary aims was to address 'the craving of young men for companionship with each other'.[42] Same-sex romantic friendships attracted men to the YMCA and fostered intense loyalty to the organization and to its leaders, many of whom were also 'men-centred'. From the time that YMCA chapters began to form in the United States and Canada in the 1850s, a disproportionate number of group secretaries were lifelong bachelors who devoted their lives to other men and to YMCA service. These men not only worked together, but also ate,

Walt Whitman was one of the most important champions of 'manly love' of the 19th century. His poems, which advocate masculine intimacy and celebrate an ideal of (working-class) male beauty, influenced several generations of writers and social thinkers. Whitman is shown here with Peter Doyle, a horsecar conductor whom he met in 1865 and with whom he had a eight-year relationship. Doyle would later recall their meeting: 'We were familiar at once – I put my hand on his knee – we understood.'

travelled and lived together, and in some cases slept in the same bed. While the extent to which YMCA leaders might have been sexually involved with each other and with the young men they recruited to the organization may never be known, association officials began to warn about friendships becoming excessive and too familiar by the turn of the 20th century, a time when close same-sex relationships were increasingly associated with homosexuality.[43]

The young, urban middle-class whites who constituted the vast majority of YMCA leaders and members were not the only group of men who developed intensely emotional and perhaps physical relationships with each other in the mid-19th century. While historical evidence is limited, research suggests that intimate friendships and same-sex sexual activity were commonplace in many all-male, working-class rural environments, such as mining, logging and railroad camps, cowboy societies and western frontier homesteads.[44] A number of these relationships were presumably prompted by the absence of women, but more than a few men seem to have preferred male companionship, and the opportunity to be surrounded by other men in an environment that was largely free of the dominant society's constraints may have attracted some men to these isolated communities.

The prevalence of same-sex sexual behaviour in exclusively male settings was nothing new. In the 17th century, pirates in the Caribbean became known not only for capturing and plundering ships, but also for partnering solely with other men. Buccaneers largely avoided women, choosing instead to pair off with each other in devoted, long-term relationships that were recognized by

In the sexually segregated life of the frontier towns, the sight of cowboys, miners or other men dancing together for pleasure must not have been unusual. Although the absence of women was an obvious reason for compromise, there were undoubtedly some men who were attracted to all-male environments for this very reason. An 1882 issue of the *Texas Livestock Journal* wrote that 'if the inner history of friendship among the rough and perhaps untutored cowboys could be written, it would be quite as unselfish and romantic as that of *Damon and Pythias*.' The photograph opposite shows a cowboy 'stag dance' from c. 1910, while the lithograph above, depicting a dance in California, was published in 1887.

their shipmates. According to pirate custom, if one of the men died, his property and share of the booty was inherited by his companion. In some cases a partner was also allowed to take the punishment meted out to the other, and in battle they often fought as a team and, at times, died together.[45]

In the 19th century two cowboys might likewise become 'partners' or 'sidekicks' out on the range, where they spent most of their time far from mainstream society's laws and expectations. Even cowboys who paired off initially for protection, companionship or owing to the demands of the work found that their relationship often became deeply emotional and sexual over time. The bond between two partners, an Oklahoma cowboy wrote, 'was at first rooted in admiration, infatuation, a sensed need of an ally, loneliness and yearning, but it regularly ripened into love'.[46]

Sex between men was also an accepted fact of life in mining, logging and railroad camps on the western frontier in the United States and Canada during the 19th century. For example, the Gold Rush of 1849 transformed San Francisco from a frontier settlement into a wide-open town — a place where anything goes — as thousands of single young men from across the United States, Europe and China flocked to the area to seek their fortunes and often to pursue adventure. With women and social restrictions both in short supply, men entertained each other in the city's saloons, gambling places and boarding houses. At the time of the Gold Rush, a number of men at dances would wear a dress or wrap a bandana around their arm to indicate that they would assume the traditional women's part. Presumably more than a few of these same-sex couples went further than dance together, and the opportunities for male–male relations in a freewheeling frontier town like San Francisco might have been an inducement for some men to migrate to the West Coast.[47]

Sexual relationships between men were also common in the work camps on the western frontier of Canada in the late 1800s, as indicated by references to sodomy cases in local police reports, court records and newspaper accounts.[48] While it is not unexpected that men in all-male environments that stressed physical prowess should have turned to each other for emotional support and sexual gratification, it is surprising that western provincial authorities typically avoided passing judgment on their behaviour. An unofficial system of law prevailed in many work camps, and when the formal criminal justice system did intervene, Canadian judges and juries were often reluctant to convict men for same-sex sexual activity or to impose the severest penalty. In 1891 two men in Victoria were sentenced to fifteen years in prison for sodomy rather than the maximum penalty of life imprisonment (their sentences were subsequently commuted to seven years). But like the frontier itself, this community form of justice was rapidly disappearing. As western Canada became more settled by white middle-class families at the turn of the 20th century, unmarried working-class men were increasingly seen as a threat to 'respectable' society, and same-sex sexual activity became more heavily policed and more severely punished.[49]

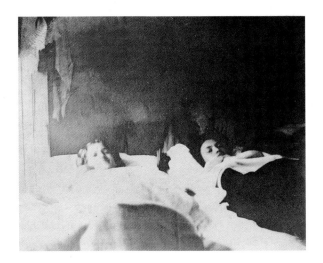

Sexual relationships in all-female communities

Among the few women on the US and Canadian frontiers were prostitutes. Although principally attracted to western towns to make money serving the sexual needs of men, some prostitutes had sex with female customers and privately with each other. For example, a tale popular in the Nevada territory was that Calamity Jane, who became legendary for her sharp shooting and horse-riding skills as well as for dressing and living as a man, had been ejected from a brothel for 'corrupting the inmates'.[50]

The West was not the only location where prostitutes were known for their private sexual relationships with other women. In the late 19th century women having sex with each other for the gratification of male customers was a featured attraction of a number of brothels in Storyville, New Orleans's renowned vice district. But some of these prostitutes also engaged in same-sex sexual acts in their off-hours. 'We got to like it so much', recalled one prostitute, 'we'd lots of times do it when we was by ourselves.'[51]

While even the private sexual lives of these working-class prostitutes, most of whom were women of colour and women from ethnic minority groups, were open to public discussion, the race and class privileges afforded to white, middle-class women in the 19th century meant that their sexuality was beyond mention — in so far as they were even thought of as having a sexuality. In their article on female same-sex sexuality in New Orleans at the turn of the 20th century, Katy Coyle and Nadiene Van Dyke contrast representations of the Storyville prostitutes with portrayals of the young, white society women who attended Newcomb College, a women's college less than a mile from the red-light district. Whereas the prostitutes could only be seen in sexual terms, the Newcomb students were presumed to be innocent and asexual, even though they pursued romantic relationships with each other and apparently often slept together by combining their single dormitory beds.[52]

The Newcomb women, like students at other women's colleges and boarding schools in the mid- and late 19th century, commonly engaged in 'smashing'. As described by a member of an alumnae investigative committee in the 1880s, smashing involved female students

Two contrasting views of all-female communities in New Orleans. The brothels of Storyville (opposite, photographed by E. J. Bellocq) were widely known to offer female same-sex sexual activity for the entertainment of patrons, while the young middle-class students of Newcomb College (above), less than a mile away from the red-light district, were presumed to be innocent of any sexual inclinations whatsoever. In fact, the young students frequently conducted romantic relationships with each other and shared dormitory beds.

falling violently in love with each other, and suffering all the pangs of unrequited attachment, desperate jealousy etc., etc., with as much energy as if one of them were a man … If the 'smash' is mutual, they monopolize each other and 'spoon' continually, and sleep together and lie awake all night talking instead of going to sleep.

Although the committee's aim was to disprove the then popular theory that advanced education was physically damaging to female students, the investigators felt that smashes were detrimental to their health because 'if it isn't mutual, the unrequited one cries herself sick and endures pangs unspeakable'.[53]

While similar to romantic friendships in their intensity and in their emotional and physical passion, many smashes were short-lived and did not extend beyond the women's school years. But some of these romances blossomed into sustained relationships. For example, M. Carey Thomas, the president of Bryn Mawr College in Pennsylvania for nearly thirty years, smashed with a boarding-school classmate in the 1870s. After graduating, the two lived together and considered themselves married. Another leading women's rights activist, Jane Addams, founded Hull House (a settlement house for Chicago immigrants) in 1889 with her long-term partner, Ellen Gates Starr, whom she had met while attending a female seminary. In a similar way to the YMCA leaders who devoted their lives to each other and to helping other men, social reformers such as Thomas and Addams made lifelong personal and professional commitments to other women.[54]

'The World of Sexual Inverts'

Same-sex relationships among middle-class whites in the United States escaped examination and condemnation for much of the 19th century because propriety and discretion placed these couples above suspicion. The same cannot be said of relationships involving people of colour and working-class whites. In the mid-19th century medical practitioners and researchers increasingly turned their attention to sexuality, particularly sexual behaviour that they considered to be perverse, as they began to note the emergence of subcultures of men and women who sought same-sex sexual partners in the poor neighbourhoods of major US cities. A Chicago physician told an audience of other doctors in 1889 that 'a colony of male sexual perverts [who] are usually known to each other, and are likely to congregate together' could be found 'in every community of any size'.[55]

Since effeminate men and masculine women often presented the most visible face of same-sex sexual subcultures, early sexologists considered same-sex attraction to be a symptom of a larger condition that they called 'sexual inversion' — the feeling that one belonged to a gender 'opposite' to or 'inverted' from one's assigned birth sex. Even the term 'homosexuality', which was introduced into US medical literature in 1892 from European writing on sexology, initially referred to someone whose 'general mental state is that of the opposite sex'.[56] Not until the turn of the 20th century did US doctors begin to separate

In the honourable tradition of passing women, Deborah Sampson, known to her fellow soldiers as Robert Shurtleff, bound her breasts and in 1782 enlisted to fight in the American War of Independence. A late 18th-century account of her story concludes that she had affairs with women – 'it must be supposed … more from necessity, than a voluntary impulse of passion' – although there is no real evidence to suppose that this was the case. Portrait by Joseph Stone, 1797.

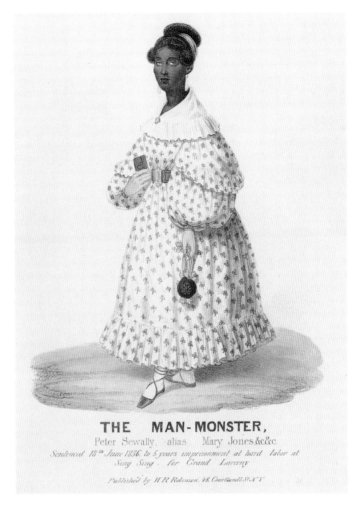

THE MAN-MONSTER,

Peter Sewally, alias Mary Jones &c&c.

Sentenced 18th June 1836, to 5 years imprisonment at hard labor at Sing Sing, for Grand Larceny.

Published by H R Robinson, 48 Courtlandt St N Y

The 'Man-Monster' Peter Sewally, also known as Mary Jones, worked the streets of New York as a female prostitute and pickpocket in the 1830s. He was arrested in 1836 and sentenced to five years' hard labour for 'grand larceny', although the mere fact that he was dressed as a woman when he was apprehended would have been enough to secure a conviction. This lithograph's lurid title contrasts strongly with the rather demure image of Sewally wearing a printed cotton frock.

the concept of same-sex sexuality from cross-gender identities and behaviours, but – owing perhaps to the ongoing significance of drag to 'homosexual' communities – the terms 'inversion' and 'homosexuality' were sometimes used interchangeably. For example, English sexologist Havelock Ellis, echoing the findings of US medical observers in the late 1800s, wrote in the 1915 edition of his landmark study *Sexual Inversion* that 'as regards the prevalence of homosexuality ... the world of sexual inverts is, indeed, a large one in any American city, and it is a community distinctly organized – words, customs, traditions of its own; and every city has its numerous meeting-places.'[57]

Among the US cities that had extensive same-sex sexual subcultures in the late 19th century were Chicago, New York, Philadelphia, San Francisco and Washington, DC. 'Perverts of both sexes maintained a sort of social set-up in New York City, had their places of meeting, and advantage of the police protection for which they could pay', remembered Charles Nesbitt, a physician who explored the city's nightlife in the 1880s and 1890s. He discovered that effeminate men and masculine women gathered at beer gardens, drag balls and on city streets, both in New York and in Philadelphia.[58] Vibrant same-sex sexual communities also existed among African Americans and whites in Washington, DC. A St. Louis doctor reported on a 'drag dance' in the nation's capital in the

When the police of Mexico City raided a private ball in 1901 they discovered forty-one men dancing together, half of whom were dressed as women. The case of 'The 41' provoked a stream of popular prints (such as the one above, by José Guadalupe Posada) and sensationalist news stories, which confirmed anti-homosexual prejudices, but also allowed those attracted to the same sex to recognize the existence of a homosexual community.

1890s, where black men 'lasciviously dressed in … low-necked dresses and … feathered and ribboned head-dresses, garters, frills, flowers, ruffles, etc. … deport themselves as women'. According to the physician's informant, the 'queen' of the group, who was naked except for a ribbon around his penis, was 'subject to the gaze and osculations in turn, of all the members of this lecherous gang of sexual perverts and phallic fornicators'. Same-sex gatherings of a different sort took place in the capital's parks; police records from the 1890s indicate that both black and white men were regularly arrested for engaging in oral sex, especially in Lafayette Square across from the White House.[59]

By the late 19th century extensive male same-sex sexual subcultures had also developed in a number of large cities outside of the United States, including Toronto, Mexico City, Havana, Buenos Aires and Rio de Janeiro.[60] As in the United States, some of these subcultures were quite visible and well defined. In Buenos Aires, for example, the 'inverts' who gathered in one of the city's main public squares had their own language, fashion and rituals. According to an Argentine sexologist, when a man entered what was called the 'cofradía', or confraternity, he was said to have '"thrown the slipper" … he dresses as a woman, he paints himself, adopts a feminine name … and frequents dances' with other men interested in same-sex sexual relationships.[61] Similarly, effeminate men in Rio de Janeiro developed their own slang, gestures and ways of dress to identify themselves to other men in the city's streets, parks and entertainment venues. However, because Brazilian law prohibited 'disguising one's sex [by] wearing inappropriate clothes', men in Rio who cross-dressed in public had to be ever mindful of the police except during the city's Carnival season, when drag was so widespread as to be unofficially sanctioned.[62]

Although neither cross-dressing nor private same-sex sexual acts were specifically illegal in Mexico, state authorities still did not tolerate expressions of same-sex sexuality. In Mexico City in 1901 police raided a private party and arrested forty-one men, half of whom were dressed as women. Although many of the participants were apparently from upper-class families, their privileged social position did not protect them from receiving severe sentences. After being publicly humiliated by being made to sweep the streets, at least some of the men were forced to labour in the Yucatán, where the Mexican army was fighting a Mayan uprising. The case of 'The 41', as they came to be known, became a long-running national scandal fuelled by sensational newspaper reports, derisive fictional narratives and engravings of the supposed facts by a popular Mexican artist. While the publicity given to the raid stigmatized male—male intimacy in the popular imagination thereafter, it made same-sex sexuality a part of public discourse in Mexico and let men who were attracted to others of the same sex know that they could belong to a community, even if it was one that was often ridiculed and persecuted.[63]

In her history of same-sex sexuality in the United States, *A Desired Past*, Leila Rupp argues that 'the emergence of urban subcultures of men and women who acted on their desires for same-sex sexual encounters paved the way for the development of the concept of a homosexual identity.'[64] The same could be said about the subcultures that formed elsewhere in the Americas in

Between-the-wars Harlem developed a reputation for exotic nightlife and bohemian culture. With a mixed and sexually ambivalent clientele, its nightspots hosted a lively homosexual subculture. Here, James VanDerZee has captured the 'Beau of the Ball', a young man on his way to one of Harlem's numerous drag dances in 1926.

the late 1800s. Whether it was attending drag dances in Mexico City, cross-dressing on the streets of Rio de Janeiro or congregating in public squares in Buenos Aires, people attracted to others of the same sex created communities based not just on a shared sexual-object choice, but also on a common sense of themselves as different from other people. The widespread adoption of the categories 'homosexual' and 'heterosexual' by sexologists throughout the Americas at the turn of the 20th century reinforced the concept of specific sexual identities. Moreover, by publicly raising the subject of same-sex sexuality, the medical literature helped some women and men who pursued same-sex sexual relationships to find both themselves and a community with which they could engage.

The Homosexual Age, 1870–1940
FLORENCE TAMAGNE

The years 1870–1940 constitute a turning-point in the history of European homosexualities. The term 'homosexuality' itself appears to have been used for the first time in 1869, by the Hungarian writer Károly Mária Kertbeny, in an open letter addressed to the Prussian Minister of Justice demanding the abolition of criminal laws against 'unnatural acts'; it gradually found its way into medical works and newspapers and, eventually, everyday usage. The establishment of the first militant homosexual movements and the appearance of an active gay and lesbian scene, as well as the new visibility of homosexuality in literature and the press, should not, however, lead us to underestimate the reality of repression and the lasting influence of the vehemently homophobic discourse that continued to make its mark in different ways throughout this period, according to the class, gender and origin of the individuals concerned.

The construction of homosexual identities

It was during the 19th century that the sodomite – a 'criminal before God', guilty of an infamous act that deserved the supreme penalty – gave way to the 'homosexual', who did wrong against society, but was also 'sick', 'perverse', 'degenerate', and as much a case for medical treatment as for the law courts.

In fact, it was medical and psychiatric theories more than any other factor that contributed to the 'specification' of homosexuality, to use Michel Foucault's terminology. For a long time, medical literature on the subject was marked by a clash of contradictory definitions and by a multiplicity of competing terms, all claiming to come closest to what actually constituted homosexuality (inversion, uranism, unisexuality, bisexuality, psychic hermaphrodism, contrary sexual feeling and so on). In their effort to establish a proper classification of homosexuality, doctors and psychiatrists set out in search of physiological 'proofs' that would pinpoint the sexual orientation of the patient. In his pioneering work *A Medico-Legal Study of Indecent Assaults* (1857), the Frenchman Ambroise Tardieu, medical adviser to the courts of law, drew up a list of 'signs of pederasty' that placed emphasis on the person's physical appearance (make-up, flashy clothes, uncleanliness); Tardieu also distinguished between active and passive homosexuality, which, he believed, could be discerned by way of an 'infundibular deformation of the anus'. At the end of the 19th century it was the theorists of degeneracy who held sway:

Perhaps more than any other city, it was Berlin that was known for its thriving homosexual subculture between the wars. Otto Dix's portrait of Sylvia von Harden, from 1926, illustrates an independent, androgynous woman typical of this Berlin *demi-monde*; Dix had approached her in the street, saying: 'I must paint you! I simply must! You are representative of an entire epoch!'

figures such as Richard von Krafft-Ebing (*Psychopathia Sexualis*, 1885) and Albert Moll (*Contrary Sexual Feeling*, 1891), followed by thinkers who included Otto Weininger (*Sex and Character*, 1903) and Max Nordau, a disciple of Cesare Lombroso (*Degeneration*, 1895).

Around this time, homosexuality was defined as a 'perversion', which might be innate (the 'born invert') and could therefore not be viewed as a criminal activity, but which might also be acquired (through seduction, prostitution and vice) and should therefore be given appropriate treatment. Although some psychiatrists, such as Jean-Martin Charcot and Victor Magnan (whose article 'Inversion du sens génital et autres perversions sexuelles' appeared in the *Archives de neurologie* in 1882), stressed the virile qualities of their patients , the majority of doctors agreed that there were incontrovertible signs of femininity in homosexuals.

In this context it was certainly the homosexual activist and sexologist Magnus Hirschfeld who did most to popularize the stereotype of the effeminate 'invert', following K. H. Ulrichs's definition of the homosexual as belonging to a 'third sex' and having 'a woman's soul trapped in a man's body'.[1] According to Hirschfeld, the combination of four criteria (one's sexual organs, physical characteristics, sexual instincts and moral character) placed one on a scale somewhere between the 'perfect male sexual type' and the 'perfect female sexual type', thereby determining whether one belonged to a category of *sexuelle Zwischenstufen* (sexual intermediates). According to this reasoning, the 'number of sexual varieties imaginable or real is therefore almost infinite'.[2] Hirschfeld's conclusions were not that far removed from Freudian theory. Indeed, Freud rejected the idea of degeneracy as well as that of a psychic hermaphrodism, emphasizing that 'the most complete psychic virility is compatible with inversion', and he refused to consider homosexuality as a disease, instead supporting the hypothesis that human beings were originally bisexual.[3] Nevertheless, his theories of 'seduction in childhood' and the 'castration complex', as well as his definition of homosexuality as resulting from 'arrested development' and immaturity, could hardly be seen as positive, and homosexuals were still regarded as inferior. The connections frequently made between masturbation and homosexuality (some writers believed that onanism could lead to mutual masturbation, especially among adolescents) also meant that the latter was viewed as a similarly narcissistic and antisocial activity.

Although male homosexuality, degeneracy and criminality were frequently linked, the view regarding lesbianism was more specific. In his book *Sexual Inversion* (1897), the British sexologist Havelock Ellis distinguished 'true' masculine lesbians from 'pseudo-homosexual' feminine lesbians who were supposed to have been seduced. This latter category in fact comprised women whose inability to attract and seduce men would have led them to settle for female partners. However, by comparison with male homosexuality, lesbianism was of little interest to doctors, who either considered it be of marginal significance or cast doubt on its very existence. Deprived of male semen, a woman could not achieve satisfaction, and so relations between women, if they aroused the senses, condemned the lesbian to frustration or even to madness.

After a disappointing trip to Lesbos in 1904, the American heiress and writer Natalie Clifford Barney resolved to establish a school of Sapphic poetry in Paris. Although the project failed to come to fruition, she nonetheless staged pagan rituals and Sapphic 'theatricals' in her garden at Neuilly, where guests included Colette, Mata Hari and Sarah Bernhardt. Barney's weekly salon, which she hosted for over fifty years, was of central importance to lesbian life in Paris in the early years of the 20th century.

Frederick Park (left) and Ernest Boulton (right) – otherwise known as Lady Stella Clinton and Miss Fanny Winifred Park – were arrested in 1869 at the Strand Theatre, London, while in full evening gowns. The police had been monitoring their behaviour for a year, during which time they had been seen soliciting men in shopping arcades and outside theatres while dressed in women's attire.

Despite their often defamatory nature, some lesbians and homosexuals identified themselves with medical stereotypes, perhaps because they provided both a model and a justification. A few novelists even integrated medical thinking on the subject into their works in a highly original fashion. Marcel Proust, in *Sodom and Gomorrah* (1921), presented a complete panorama of the different medical theories regarding homosexuality that prevailed at the beginning of the century, while E. M. Forster's *Maurice* (1914; not published until 1970) described medical treatments, such as hypnosis, that were supposed to 'cure' homosexuality. Similarly, Stephen Gordon, the heroine of Radclyffe Hall's novel *The Well of Loneliness* (1928), doomed to solitude and rejection, was depicted according to Havelock Ellis's theory of the 'congenital invert'.

This medical model was far from being accepted by all, however. The poet Natalie Clifford Barney objected to the masculinization of women, which she regarded as submission to male domination, and preferred instead to look to antiquity for positive references. With her companion, fellow poet Renée Vivien, she undertook a pilgrimage to Mytilene with a view to founding a school of Sapphic poetry in Paris. For men, too, the ancient traditions of pederasty, which had been revived by the works of Winckelmann, the freedoms of the Grand Tour, and by the Hellenistic milieux at Oxford University,[4] cast a positive light on homoerotic desire, offering an alternative in the Victorian Age to the constraints of marriage and domestic life.[5] Christian traditions also

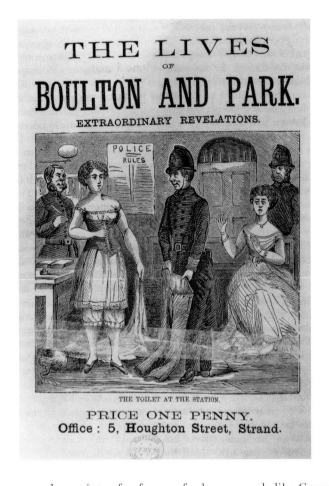

served as points of reference for homosexuals like Gerard Manley Hopkins, who sublimated their erotic impulses into passionate friendships or religious ecstasy, and for lesbians such as Radclyffe Hall, who wrapped the heroine of *The Well of Loneliness* in Christ-like imagery, linking lesbianism with martyrdom and celebrating the virtues of compassion.[6] The idea of chaste but passionate spiritual companionship, as exemplified by the biblical story of David and Jonathan, found acceptance in the Anglo-Catholic Oxford Movement: it also aroused hostility towards Newman and the Tractarians, who were suspected of idealizing homosexuality.

Even more than medical theories, it was scandal that frequently brought homosexuality to the attention of the public at large, notably through the workings of the new mass media. By means of a skilful mixture of facts and accounts of 'perversions', newspapers sought to capture the minds of their volatile readers.[7] In England the first major trial to be covered by the popular press was in 1871 and concerned Ernest ('Stella') Boulton and Fred ('Fanny') Park, who were arrested for appearing in public in women's clothes and later suspected of sodomy.[8] These two young men, who were involved in male prostitution in London – among the 'mollies' and the 'Mary-Annes' – had been dressing as women for about ten years, initially just on stage but subsequently also in their daily lives. They had never had any cause for alarm; they shared an apartment, went out with other young transvestites and accosted passers-by

Hundreds of letters between Boulton, Park and numerous admirers were read out in court during their trial for 'conspiracy to commit a felony' (i.e. sodomy). The letters' slang – such as 'living in drag' and 'getting screwed' – was not, it seems, properly understood by the court. The jury were unable to find a clear connection between Boulton and Park's cross-dressing and illegal sexual behaviour, and both were acquitted. The case was widely reported in the popular press, whose salacious stories were partly responsible for raising public consciousness of homosexuality.

Oscar Wilde with Lord Alfred Douglas
in Norfolk in 1892, three years before
Wilde's disastrous trials. His public
humiliation was of enormous importance
in establishing Britain's concept of
and attitudes towards homosexuality.
According to one recent scholar,
Wilde had escaped censure before
his trial because his contemporaries
had no idea how a homosexual man
should look or act. After his conviction,
however, the public was left with a clear
and lasting image of the effeminate,
dandified homosexual.

France had its own flamboyant figures
at the end of the 19th century: the
aesthete Robert de Montesquiou,
shown opposite in a portrait by Giovanni
Boldoni (1897), served as the model for
two notable decadents in *fin-de-siècle*
literature. Yet even the salons of the
French capital were not unaffected by
the events unfolding across the Channel.

in the arcades of the West End.[9] Their arrest could certainly be construed as a
warning to all those whose provocative conduct went beyond the bounds of
public order. However, the outcome of the trial, in which both men were
acquitted, showed how difficult it was for the prosecutors to draw conclusions
about sexual practices from the confirmation of Park's and Boulton's 'gender
inversion'. Similarly, the sexual conduct of those accused in the Cleveland
Street scandal (1889–90) – which centred on a male brothel and implicated
Prince Albert Victor, son of the Prince of Wales, as well as certain well-known
aristocrats and some telegraph boys – was assessed more in terms of the age
and social position of the accused rather than their sexual identity, and during
the trial no mention was made of new medical findings.[10] The class factor in
particular was deemed to be of prime importance, and the boys, who were
from a working-class background, were seen as the victims of aristocratic corruption, with its stock images of the 'rake' and the effeminate 'fop'. The same
approach was to be seen in France, where in 1903 Baron d'Adelswärd-Fersen
and his friend Albert Hamelin de Warren were accused of 'public offence
against decency' and 'inciting minors to debauchery', having invited school-
boys from the Lycée Condorcet to their bachelor apartment on the pretext of
holding poetry readings and tableaux vivants.[11]

The link between effeminacy and homosexuality suggested by doctors and
psychiatrists was therefore formed only gradually. So it was that, before the
scandal broke, few people believed Oscar Wilde to be homosexual; it was
assumed instead that he was simply adopting the generic pose of the effeminate aesthete and 'playing' the homosexual.[12] The Marquis of Queensberry,
Lord Alfred Douglas's father, said as much when he left his card accusing
Wilde of 'posing as a Somdomite [*sic*]'. For Alan Sinfield, it was Wilde's trial in
1895 that made 'effeminacy, idleness, immorality, luxury, insouciance, decadence and aestheticism' the hallmarks of 'sexual inversion',[13] although it also
allowed many homosexuals the opportunity to identify themselves with the
defender of the 'love that dare not speak its name'.[14] The scandal therefore
unfolded on various levels: it contributed to the adoption of certain modes of
identification (such as the green carnation); it reinforced the feeling of normality in the average reader of the popular press (who was outraged and/or
titillated by all the references to morals that were foreign to him); and, lastly, it
caused homosexuals to react against the danger now facing them by either
withdrawing into the private sphere or by demanding recognition of their
rights. Although in France the figure of the decadent dandy was embodied
perfectly by Jean Lorrain and by Robert de Montesquiou, who inspired J. K.
Huysmans's Des Esseintes and Proust's Charlus, Wilde's fate came to haunt
salons such as that hosted by Winnaretta Singer, Princesse de Polignac, who
had received Wilde on many occasions.[15]

In Germany, however, it was the Eulenburg Affair of 1907–8 that shook the
aristocracy and the military, spreading throughout Europe the image of homosexuality as a 'German vice'.[16] Following a series of military scandals, the
journalist Maximilian Harden launched an exposé of a 'ring' of homosexual
advisers surrounding Kaiser Wilhelm II in the periodical *Die Zukunft*. Harden

As had happened in Britain in 1895, Germany's Eulenburg Affair, a series of trials and scandals that culminated in 1907–8, crystallized the public conception of homosexuality through a flood of newspaper reports and cartoons. Above left: 'Since when is an about-face order given for inspections?' 'At your service, Captain – reporting that the division is being inspected by Count Hohenau today.' Above right: 'Hero-Worship', a cartoon referring to the powerful erotic appeal of a cuirassier's uniform, which apparently made any soldier who wore it in public certain of being propositioned.

named one of the Kaiser's counsellors and friends, Prince Philipp zu Eulenburg, and Count Kuno von Moltke, military commander in Berlin. The affair was not devoid of political implications: Eulenburg, who was generally in favour of closer ties with France, had aroused hostility among the military during the crisis surrounding the fate of Morocco. The real target was certainly not the prince but Wilhelm himself, yet Harden, despite being in possession of compromising documents concerning the sexuality of the Kaiser, refused to make use of them. One sensational trial succeeded another, and together they helped to fix homophobic and anti-Semitic prejudices in the minds of the public (Magnus Hirschfeld, who was called as an expert witness, was a Jew). All these insinuations had an effect. During the First World War the rejection of homosexuals as outsiders led to the suspicion that they were traitors – all the more so since the 'invert', often assumed to have all the vices inherent in the opposite sex, was depicted as a coward and a gossip and therefore a danger to national security. In *Time Regained* (1927), Marcel Proust evokes the climate of suspicion that surrounded homosexuals (Baron de Charlus is nick-named 'Frau van den Bosch'), while in England, *The English Review* of May 1916 denounced 'the moral and spiritual invasion of Britain by German Urnings for the purpose of undermining the patriotism, the stamina, the intel-lect and the morals of British navy and army men, and of our prominent public leaders'.[17] Leading the homophobic crusade, the MP Noel Pemberton Billing declared that the German secret service kept a 'black book' containing the names of some 47,000 homosexuals in high places who were suitable for blackmailing; and in an article entitled 'The Cult of the Clitoris' he directly

One aspect of the cult of health and physical discipline that swept Germany in the early decades of the 20th century was the popular nudist movement known as the FKK (Frei Körper Kultur). Seen as a means of regenerating the German *Volk*, it also appealed – perhaps not surprisingly – to many homosexuals, who were attracted to the movement's celebration of virile athleticism. Here, a still from Wilhelm Prager's *Ways to Strength and Beauty* (1924–26) illustrates how the vogue for nude exercise could carry undercurrents of homoeroticism.

accused the dancer Maud Allan, who was playing the role of Salome in Oscar Wilde's play, of spreading lesbian propaganda.[18]

Even though homosexual relations in the army were denounced and rooted out, the First World War brought men together in the face of extreme danger, creating fertile ground for the development of homosexual friendships, more or less idealized, between soldiers and sometimes between soldiers and officers.[19] Furthermore, by focusing on the male body and accentuating its masculinity (through the wearing of uniforms and the cult of the muscular naked body), the war aesthetic brought with it a strong element of homoeroticism. Far removed from the world of the stereotypical 'effeminate invert', the 'comradeship of the front' was in keeping with the tradition of male societies bound together by a code of honour and by shared experience – groups that included youth movements such as the Wandervögel in Germany and the Boy Scouts in England, boarding schools (military academies in Germany and public schools in Britain) and homosocial institutions such as gentlemen's clubs and sports associations. These relationships were not without their own tensions and neuroses, and sometimes desire and violence merged inseparably, as can be seen from the poems of Wilfred Owen.[20] The psychologist W. H. R. Rivers, who most notably treated the poet Siegfried Sassoon, encountered several cases of officers who were torn between their sexual desires and a strict concept of duty and military discipline, which forced them to sublimate their emotions into a more impersonal concern for the welfare of their men. The

24/8
Verlag „Ross" Berlin SW 68

Die Freundschaft ('Friendship') was one of several homophile publications that were aimed specifically at homosexual men and women during the 1920s and 1930s. It was later banned by the Nazis.

war also brought about an increased awareness of lesbianism. Some women chose to enlist in the ambulance corps, for instance, which elicited mixed reactions: although the press worried about the possibility of 'unnatural' feelings that this would introduce, at the same time it praised the masculine qualities of the women who were actively helping in the defence of the nation.

The First World War was indeed a turning point in the way in which homosexuality was represented. According to Joanna Bourke, 'a world of men was opening up, revealing the wide range of roles played by males and exposing the fluidity between masculinity and femininity.'[21] The radiant beauty of the English poet Rupert Brooke, the voice of 'forever England', who died off the island of Lemnos in 1915, became a focal point in this change of paradigm and helped to popularize an androgynous aesthetic which, in the eyes of the public, was linked as much with the cult of sacrificed youth as with the aspirations of the modern world.

Homosexual practices, lifestyles and cultures

The period 1870–1940 was marked by the rise of homosexual militancy in Europe.[22] In Germany, the Wissenschaftlich-humanitäres Komitee (or WhK), which was formed in 1897 on the initiative of Magnus Hirschfeld, took on the task of educating the public about homosexuality in order to overcome its prejudices. Immediately after its foundation the WhK circulated a petition signed by such luminaries as Thomas Mann, Albert Einstein, Emile Zola and Leo Tolstoy demanding the abolition of Paragraph 175, a German law that imposed a prison sentence on men who indulged in homosexual relations. In 1919 Hirschfeld founded the Institut für Sexualwissenschaft ('Institute for Sexual Science') in Berlin, a centre for scientific research that aimed to assemble all existing records of homosexuality and which incorporated a library and museum. It soon attracted large numbers of visitors from Germany and abroad, including Klaus Mann (son of Thomas Mann), André Gide and Christopher Isherwood.

The WhK was far from being the only such institution. During the 1920s other movements were formed, some of which brought lesbians and homosexuals together under the same umbrella, along the lines of Friedrich Radszuweit's Bund für Menschenrecht (BfM). Generally, however, they were more concerned with promoting homosexual cultures than with waging a political battle; they tended to arrange meetings and soirées, and to publish magazines catering specifically for the homosexual and lesbian public, like *Die Freundschaft* and *Die Freundin*.[25] Other organizations, such as Adolf Brand's Gemeinschaft der Eigenen, founded in 1903, chose a more individual route. Brand favoured a concept of masculine comradeship, which drew in equal measure on Greek pederasty, medieval Germany and the writings of Nietzsche, and he was bitterly opposed to Magnus Hirschfeld's medical view of homosexuality and his desire for social integration. A passionate misogynist and anti-modernist, Brand wanted to create an ideal masculine, chivalrous society, a *Männerbund* united by bonds of honour and dedicated to the cult of friendship and of adolescent beauty. Brand's vision had a degree of influence on certain nationalist institutions and youth movements such as the Wandervögel.

Homosexuality in England was seen as the preserve of an intellectual and social elite – a tradition bolstered by such homosocial institutions as public schools, the universities of Oxford and Cambridge, and the civil service. For the arisfocratic 'Bright Young Things' of the interwar years homosexuality was de rigueur: this portrait of 1927 shows Cecil Beaton, renowned society photographer, and Stephen Tennant, who possibly provided the model for Sebastian Flyte in Evelyn Waugh's *Brideshead Revisited*.

The gains made by homosexual militancy during the 1920s were only moderate, however. Although in Germany it unquestionably offered thousands of homosexuals the chance to emerge from their isolation, to build up an identity of their own and to claim their rights in a generally unfavourable atmosphere, it nevertheless failed to achieve its main objective, which was the decriminalization of homosexuality. Furthermore, any signs that it had fostered a more tolerant attitude proved for the most part to be only superficial. Magnus Hirschfeld was the permanent target of the extreme right and was the victim of several violent assaults. In France, the influence of a German-style militancy remained very limited, partly because homosexuality was not in itself against the law, and partly because any attempt by homosexuals to assert themselves as a community always came up against the republican, *universaliste* model of the state, which recognized only individuals and not minority groups. Although André Gide's *Corydon*, published in 1924, made the author a mouthpiece for French homosexuals, the work was confined to a defence of 'pederasty' as opposed to 'inversion', and it reinforced the notion of an elitist, intellectual homosexuality that bore little resemblance to day-to-day reality. Following the examples established in Germany, a magazine called *Inversions* was founded in 1924 by Gustave Beyria and Gaston Lestrade, an office clerk and postal worker respectively, but it received no support from the intellectual and literary milieux apart from one or two exceptions and soon fell victim to censorship.[24]

In England, although Magnus Hirschfeld encouraged the formation of the BSSSP (British Society for the Study of Sex Psychology) in 1914, presided over by Edward Carpenter and Lawrence Housman, the decriminalization of homosexuality was only one of several objectives. The movement was not very active, and its influence, as in France, was limited to intellectual circles.[25] In any case, the English model of homosexuality appears to have been unusual. Homosexuality was branded a criminal offence, as in Germany, but it was also regarded as being mainly confined to an intellectual and artistic elite. This may be partly explained by the predominance in Britain's upper classes of homosocial structures like public schools, universities (Oxford and Cambridge in particular), clubs, civil administration abroad and the secret services, which legitimized relations between men, made male bonding the cement of national unity, and projected an image of loyalty and patriotism.[26] Pupils at the public schools were encouraged to detach themselves from the influence of women, to suppress their emotions and to work off their sexual drive in the practice of sport. Nevertheless, despite the admonitions of headmasters and chaplains' sermons, the charged atmosphere and sexual tensions provided fertile ground for romantic friendships as well as rough sexual experiences.[27] The years at university only reinforced the myth of male communion. At the beginning of the 20th century a group in Cambridge known as The Apostles, which soon developed into the Bloomsbury circle of intellectuals, celebrated male homosexuality as the highest form of love. In 1920s Oxford the 'cult of homosexuality' (to use Noël Annan's expression) reached its zenith.[28] Aesthetes such as Brian Howard and Harold Acton flaunted their eccentric garb and their

As in other large cities, there were numerous well-established venues in London where homosexuals could meet prospective partners. Urinals were scattered throughout the West End (shown below is 'MacFarlane's patent model for two persons', from 1870); theatres such as the Criterion (below right) had galleries and promenade bars that were ideal for socializing and making new contacts; and the Savoy Turkish Baths on Jermyn Street (opposite) provided a discreet and tolerant atmosphere right up until the 1970s.

intellectualism in order to distinguish themselves from heterosexual sportsmen who, in turn, would vandalize their rooms. After the Second World War, novels such as Evelyn Waugh's *Brideshead Revisited* helped to promote both a nostalgic view of those years of insouciance and the myth of a homosexual liberation that had almost been achieved.

The visibility of certain networks of intellectuals should not, however, disguise the fact that the large European cities had played host to a variety of homosexual subcultures since the end of the 19th century. The connection between homosexual identities and specific places was first made possible by the elaboration of particular sexual geographies, which had as much to do with imagined desires as much as any real social setting.[29] Through a subtle game involving signs of recognition, there would arise in the heart of the town a private space where meetings and exchanges could take place. One person might use an ambiguous phrase when speaking to a stranger, whereupon the other might reply in a particular argot. While the term 'homosexual' was rarely used (and was not even known by some people), there were countless popular expressions for gay men and women, such as auntie, pansy, nancy, queen, queer and faggot (for the former), and pervert and dyke (for the latter). There were also special signs: the colours lilac and mauve, for instance, and dress codes that included (particularly between the wars) suede shoes and camel-hair coats for men, and an exaggeratedly boyish look for women – the more masculine of whom would opt for an Eton crop, sport a monocle, wear men's clothes or even smoke cigars.[30] Although the majority of homosexuals went out of their way not to be noticed and adapted their appearance to suit

Fig. 18.

THE CRITERION BAR.

places and people, the flamboyance of the Wilde type of dandyism was continued through the 1920s by the 'Bright Young Things' – figures such as the photographer Cecil Beaton and the model Stephen Tennant, who dyed his hair and wore make-up, and Quentin Crisp, who as a camp 'queen' caused crowds to gather in the streets of London. 'Cruising' went on around the parks of the capital and in its toilets, stations and pubs,[31] but also homosexual prostitution was to be found in the West End and in the main shopping areas of Regent Street and Oxford Street, with soldiers from the Guards being particularly sought after on account of their fine appearance and uniform. Sports clubs – especially those specializing in boxing – where gentlemen mixed with lads, and public swimming baths also offered plenty of opportunities for friendly and/or sexual encounters.[32] While 'Lady Malcolm's Servants' Ball' – a masked ball that was held annually at the Albert Hall – attracted hundreds of people, private soirées, sometimes transvestite, were held in furnished rooms in Bayswater, Paddington and Notting Hill. These, too, served as meeting places for groups of regulars who often came from the lower classes (servants, waiters, porters etc.) and who knew how to merge into their urban environment and use it for their own purposes.[33]

Even more than London, however, it was Paris and Berlin that between 1870 and 1940 established themselves as the gay and lesbian capitals. Although the police organized unofficial surveillance of the main areas of soliciting – the parks, the banks of the Seine, public baths, theatre galleries, and the

In districts such as Montmartre, Pigalle and Montparnasse, Parisian men and women could socialize in relative freedom. Large balls would attract thousands of cross-dressing revellers to dance halls like the Magic-City and the Bal de la Montagne Sainte-Geneviève. In around 1932 Brassaï, incomparable chronicler of the Parisian *demi-monde*, captured this image of a ball in full swing in the Latin Quarter. As long as customers maintained a certain amount of decorum and refrained from blatant cruising, the police would leave such places alone.

arcades of the Palais Royal and the Champs-Elysées — the French capital was irresistibly attractive to both homosexuals and lesbians eager to escape to the anonymity of the great city from the moralistic conformity of the provinces or from the inquisitorial hounding that took place in their own countries. Paris offered space on its fringes, and so the homosexual subculture mingled with that of the underworld and the seamier elements of society around Montmartre, Pigalle and Montparnasse. There were plenty of homosexual and lesbian bars in these areas, although their life expectancy was rarely more than a year because of raids, frequent scandals that ruined their reputation, and a constant demand for something new by a clientele that liked to go out but also wanted to vary its pleasures. The great masked balls, such as the one at the Magic-City dance hall, which every year saw thousands of men and women dressed in each other's clothes dancing together on Mardi Gras, offered a unique opportunity to declare, at no risk to oneself, one's allegiance to a subculture that still bore the stamp of indecency. In fact, there was also in the smarter clubs a *demi-monde* of prostitutes, queens and thieves: the gigolos had *noms de guerre* (la Crawford, la Mae West) and girls' names (Paulette, Georgette), used the argot of the area, and they often worked independently. Some tricksters would entice their naïve customers and then rob or blackmail them. The rue de Lappe near the Bastille was the setting for *bals musette* (dancing to accordion music) and for other establishments where men could dance together and find a partner for the night — muscular lads from Les Halles, or sailors on shore leave looking to earn a bit on the side. The middle-class man on a trip to Paris from the provinces would often choose not to expose himself to the dangers of anonymous soliciting and preferred the security of established bathing places, the male brothels described by Proust, or regular meetings with a gigolo from the suburbs.

While many emigrants sought refuge in Paris — from Oscar Wilde and Klaus Mann to Romaine Brooks and Radclyffe Hall — it was Berlin that, according to Magnus Hirschfeld, had the largest number of homosexual meeting places from the beginning of the 20th century.[34] As well as chic clubs like the Eldorado, which presented transvestite shows and were frequented by such stars as Marlene Dietrich, there were bars in the less classy districts where homosexuals and lesbians from the middle or working classes could drink, dance and make their pick-ups. Homosexual prostitution reached its peak between the wars: there were 22,000 known male prostitutes in Berlin in 1929, many of them young workers who had fallen victim to the economic crisis and who (most of the time) did not even regard themselves as homosexual. Christopher Isherwood, W. H. Auden and Stephen Spender were among those who sampled the delights of Berlin during those heady years, and they helped develop the myth of the 'working-class boy'. This is a recurrent theme in homosexual literature between the wars, and it can be interpreted as a rejection of Puritan education, as a desire to defy the social and sexual conventions of the bourgeoisie, and also as an attempt to promote the body above the intellect by emphasizing the value of male strength and manual labour. Although the search for sexual partners outside one's own class was not peculiar to the

Located on a corner in Berlin's Schöneberg district, Eldorado was the most famous of all the city's gay nightclubs. During its heyday in the Weimar period, gay men, lesbians and transvestites would dance in some style and watch cabaret acts by female impersonators such as the glamorous Muguette (opposite). It was one of the first such establishments to be closed down by the police after Hitler came to power and became, somewhat ironically, a propaganda centre for the Nazi party.

1920s (either in homosexual or heterosexual relationships), the theme of the 'ideal friend', which is especially prominent in E. M. Forster's *Maurice* and which implies equality between the two partners, is typical of that period, whereas at the end of the 19th century the taste had been more in favour of pederastic liaisons and the celebration of the adolescent body.[35]

Urban geographies, foreign geographies: going elsewhere offered the attraction of a temporary escape from the eyes of others. At the end of the 19th century it was the Mediterranean and the pastoral charms of Sicily, as photographed by Baron von Gloeden and Wilhelm von Plüschow, that formed the focus of desires, appealing as much to Thomas Mann and E. M. Forster as they had to Winckelmann and Hans Christian Andersen.[36] Capri became the main rallying point of the intellectuals, artists and socialites who had broken with their own society. Thus the exoticism of foreign places and people became mixed up with the pleasures of the senses in the form of sex tourism, the exploitative nature of which was often ignored at the time.[37] André Gide, in his autobiography *If It Die* (1926), describes his venal seduction of young North African boys, who revealed his own nature to him. For countless homosexuals, adventurers, soldiers and civil servants, the colonies provided a means of indulging their desires in the anonymity of a homosocial culture.

Even outside the context of particular ways of life such as those described above, one can probably speak of the rise of a 'homosexual culture' during this period, in the sense of common references and shared representations. The classic texts (Plato's *Symposium* and Shakespeare's sonnets) were joined by other literary works such as Thomas Mann's *Death in Venice* (1912), Marcel Proust's *Sodom and Gomorrah* (1921–22), *Confusion* by Stefan Zweig (1926), Virginia Woolf's *Orlando* (1928), and more popular books including Radclyffe

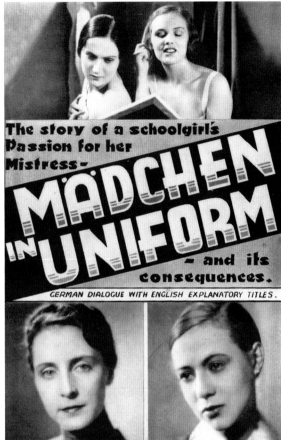

The early 20th century gave rise to a new homosexual visibility: books, films, ballet and popular songs all touched on homosexual themes more or less explicitly. Suzy Solidor (opposite, painted by Tamara de Lempicka) was one of several performers who contributed to the emergence of a gay identity, while the groundbreaking *Different from the Others* (above left, 1919) – partly written by Magnus Hirschfeld – and the overtly lesbian *Mädchen in Uniform* (above right, 1931) are considered landmarks of early gay cinema.

Hall's *The Well of Loneliness* (1928) and *The Scorpion* by A. E. Weirauch (1919). Romaine Brooks's portraits and the works of Gluck (Hannah Gluckenstein) also bear witness to the increasing independence of lesbian themes in art, which were no longer merely a supporting act for the erotic fantasies of male onlookers. Songs (especially those performed by Damia and by Suzy Solidor, who for a while was the lover of Tamara de Lempicka), the theatre (plays by Noel Coward), the Ballets Russes and the cinema all played their part in fostering a new awareness of identity. In 1919 appeared Richard Oswald's film *Different from the Others*, which depicted Conrad Veidt in the role of the homosexual victim of a blackmailer and constituted a plea for the abolition of Paragraph 175. (Magnus Hirschfeld himself appears at the end of the film to advocate its repeal and deliver a message of tolerance.) Leontine Sagan's *Mädchen in Uniform* (1931), based on a play by Christa Winsloe, traces the history of a girl who falls in love with her female teacher at a German boarding school.

In the artistic world at large, writers, painters and photographers all witnessed and recorded this new homosexual visibility, either fascinated or simply entertained by it. At the end of the 19th century decadence, an extreme form of Romanticism, saw itself as a reaction to modernity and to the social upheavals that had resulted from the Industrial Revolution. The movement's attraction to the exotic, its taste for the bizarre and its desire to 'astound the

A **self-portrait** by Romaine Brooks
(1923), one of the expatriates who
gravitated towards the society of Natalie
Clifford Barney, Gertrude Stein and
Djuna Barnes in Paris. Her depictions
of this circle's unconventional members
chart the emergence of a specifically
lesbian identity.

bourgeoisie' help explain the seductive power that homosexuality, and especially sapphism, had over the art and literature of the period.[38] In addition, by choosing homosexual dandies or lesbians as heroes and heroines, decadent artists made clear their rejection of a male identity based on materialistic and imperialistic values. After the First World War homosexuals and lesbians came to symbolize modernity, embodying as they did the aesthetic and moral upheavals of the *années folles*. Alongside cocaine addicts and 'Negro' dancers, 'modern' novels featured homosexuals or lesbians as representatives of the age. While Parisian nights were being immortalized by Brassaï, and Berenice Abbott was photographing the 'Amazons of the Left Bank',[39] their Berlin equivalents were being sketched by George Grosz, Jeanne Mammen, Christian Schad and Otto Dix. For the younger generation of the 1920s, apolitical and Americanized, celebration of the androgynous body symbolized a breakaway from the generation that had dragged the world into war. Underlying this attempt at detachment one can discern a desire to narrow the distance between the sexes and to create a new type of beauty free from stereotypes. And so the 'masculinization' of women (exemplified by the image of the 'garçonne' or 'flapper'), financially independent and aesthetically liberated from the constraints of femininity (long hair and corsets), seemed to go together with the movement for female emancipation, while at the same time the 'feminization' of one section of the new male generation may be interpreted as a rejection of militaristic values in favour of a pacifist and democratic ideal – a trend that continued until Nazism once more exploited the eroticism underlying the glorification of the male body.

Repression and social control: language and practice

At the end of the 19th century legislation on homosexuality varied throughout Europe.[40] Two general trends can be distinguished, each a result of historical heritage and a particular cultural context. On the one hand were the countries whose culture was basically Latin and Catholic (e.g. France, Italy, Spain and Portugal), which had come under the influence of Napoleon's penal code and which lacked any laws criminalizing homosexual practices; on the other hand were Germanic, Anglo-Saxon and Slav countries, mainly subject to Protestant or Orthodox influences, which at the end of the 19th and beginning of the 20th centuries tended to adopt legislation specifically punishing homosexual relations between men.

The social climate of these latter countries was marked by harsh measures against 'sexual offences' and by the reaffirmation of sexual and gender norms. Thus, in 1871, Paragraph 175 of the German Empire's penal code – ultimately based on the Prussian model – specified that 'unnatural acts' between men or between men and animals were punishable by imprisonment and loss of civil rights,[41] while in England the Labouchère Amendment, hastily voted into force in 1885 in the context of the debate on female prostitution, stipulated that 'any act of gross indecency with another male person' was punishable by a prison sentence 'not exceeding two years, with or without hard labour'. In 1898 the Vagrancy Act penalized male soliciting.[42] By contrast, attempts in Germany

(1909) and Britain (1921) to criminalize homosexual relations between women were defeated. Social control by the family or by the Church appeared to suffice when it came to regulating female sexuality, and above all it was feared that a change in the law would inform women of practices about which they were supposed to be ignorant. In fact, during this period it was rare for any European country to impose legal sanctions on lesbianism.[43] According to Jan Löfström, however, it was the mainly rural, pre-industrial nature of Finland and Sweden, linked paradoxically with the absence of any marked polarization between the sexes, that explained why in those countries lesbianism was criminalized alongside male homosexuality.[44] Finnish women, whose qualities of toughness and endurance were much admired, worked alongside men on the farm and enjoyed a degree of authority within the family. Female sexuality and desire also played an important part in traditional culture and were recognized in their own right. Political factors were probably also significant: feminist movements joined in the fight for Finland's independence (gained in 1917), and this led to the early achievement of suffrage for Finnish women, but they did not oppose the new penal code of 1889, which imposed a prison sentence of up to two years for homosexual relations between both men and women.[45]

On a more general level, the efficiency of the judicial machine when it came to controlling homosexual practices was undermined by the difficulty of fixing a legal definition of homosexuality. Between the wars, there were on average 702 arrests a year in Britain for homosexual offences, with a clear increase from 1931 onwards – a strengthening of oppression resulting from the social, economic and political crisis that the country was going through. However, the proportion of people sentenced fell from just over 80 per cent in 1918 to around 50 per cent in 1938, which demonstrates how difficult it was for the courts to apply the law. The figures were very similar in Germany, with an annual average of 704 arrests between 1919 and 1934. There were, however, marked differences between individual states as well as between the towns: Dresden and Munich were extremely repressive, whereas Berlin and Hamburg were far more lax, apparently a result of tacit agreements between the police and various homosexual organizations. Since Berlin and Hamburg were cities with particularly active homosexual subcultures, this local tolerance gave the impression that homosexual practices were carried out with impunity in the Weimar Republic.

In Germany as in Britain, special police forces were assigned to keep watch on cruising grounds such as parks and public toilets. In London during the 1920s, plain-clothes agents from the Metropolitan Police worked in pairs for a maximum of two months because of the risk that they would be recognized, but also for fear of 'contagion'. Frequently regarded as agents provocateurs, they were supposed to catch suspects in the act so that the prosecution could convince the judges of their guilt; often, however, police came up against the reluctance of witnesses to testify, since they considered these intrusions an infringement on their privacy and civil liberties. Police reports in both countries would list meticulously the comings and goings of the suspect, record the few words exchanged, and sometimes note the dress and posture of the person concerned, as well as listing objects regarded as significant (powder, eau de toilette, face cream, mirror etc.); these accounts served as the basis of an often fastidious analysis of the suspect's conduct, which was meant to determine the gravity of the offence and the severity of the punishment. Caresses, masturbation, fellatio and sodomy each had their own positions on the scale of offences, while the age of the partner and the number of times the act was performed would also be taken into consideration. In fact, as H. G. Cocks has pointed out, the legal system, while acting as a regulator of practices that were considered unacceptable, at the same time publicized homosexuality by creating a would-be authoritative discourse that was then taken up by the press.[46]

Not all homosexuals were equally affected by police and judicial repression: the most vulnerable were those who, through necessity or personal inclination, favoured risky conduct such as soliciting in toilets, or whose appearance and deportment were perceived – especially by the police – as conforming to the stereotypes of 'inversion'. In many cases the chief aim of the police was to put pressure on a group of recidivists (particularly prostitutes) and to ensure that homosexual activities were kept under cover by confining them to certain areas that were already classified as marginal or criminal on account of the presence of prostitutes, dealers or gambling houses. The police were less concerned with making systematic arrests, since in the absence of specific legislation these often led nowhere. Consequently, homosexual practices that took place in private, and also semi-public behaviour such as the frequenting of bars and homosexual clubs, were relatively immune. This explains why the working and lower-middle classes, who through lack of time or private accommodation often conducted their affairs in public places, play a disproportionately large role in the statistics. In fact, the perceived link between homosexuality, corruption and degeneracy was still sufficiently strong that many found it difficult to imagine an otherwise respectable man indulging in such practices. So it was that celebrities and people in high places often escaped prosecution.[47]

While homophobic legislation did not prevent the existence of spaces that allowed some liberty or the development of avoidance strategies, neither did the decriminalization of homosexual relations guarantee immunity. In France, even though such relations between consenting adults conducted in private were not against the law, there were certain practices that could be prosecuted under charges of public offence against decency or immoral behaviour, notably in cases that involved minors. Furthermore, there were regular raids by vice squads on gay bars and saunas, which led to the compilation of police files.[48] The closest watch of all was the surveillance of military prostitution in homosexual bars in Paris as well as in ports like Toulon and Brest. On the borders of legality and in the absence of any real means of taking action, these campaigns by certain police prefects could end in disciplinary measures being taken against sailors (details being passed on to the military authorities, demotion or dismissal), prosecutions for indecency (with punishments ranging from a fine to two months in prison) and pressure on landlords to exclude homosexuals (although the establishments themselves could not be closed).[49]

Developments in the way homosexuality was presented after the First World War and the new visibility of male and female homosexuals in the great European capitals should not delude us into thinking that attitudes underwent any profound change. Stigmatizing stereotypes, social exclusion and the threat of police action all point to the homophobic feelings and practices that constantly confronted homosexual men and women, though in different forms and to different degrees. Moreover, it was during periods of crisis that these attitudes had the greatest resonance. A return to order and to social cohesion was accompanied by a stricter definition of the frontiers of 'normality' and by the exclusion of groups regarded as a threat to this order. Thus the homosexual was described as 'asocial' and his sexuality as not 'reproductive', even though he might be married and have children. Homosexuality and paedophilia were frequently bracketed together, and the charge of corrupting young people – which plays on notions of contagion – was one of the most common. A supposed risk of depopulation was also emphasized, for example in France during the 1870s, when the war against Prussia, the loss of Alsace-Lorraine and the trauma of the Commune were still on people's minds. After the First World War, when the demographic situation showed a 'surplus' of women and when the resumption of male and female roles accompanied the desire for a return to order, lesbians were the target of repeated attacks – especially in Britain, where Radclyffe Hall's *The Well of Loneliness* was the subject of a law suit in 1928 and was finally banned.[50] In France, the popular press indulged more and more in caricature through such magazines as *Fantasio* and *Le Rire*, but the main charge levelled against lesbians was their alleged collusion with feminist

Despite homosexuals' increased visibility in Europe in the years following the First World War, anti-homosexual sentiment was still widespread. Social pressure to conform was strong, and the popular press poked fun at nonconformist lifestyles with varying degrees of wit and venom. In this German cartoon from 1924 a mother is trying to coerce her decadent daughter into marriage: 'How should I put this to my child ... Paula, you've now reached that age when one ... with men ... .' The daughter replies, 'Leave it, mother – I'm a pervert.'

Popular humour of the period was full of stereotypes that played on fears of national weakness and anxiety surrounding gender roles. In this cartoon from a British newspaper, printed in 1929, effeminate sailors gossip about their fellows and worry about their complexions. In the scene bottom left, one sailor exclaims: 'This work is awfully bad for my hands. I must get a manicure as soon as I've finished!', to which the other replies: 'Yes – but this bending is good for my figure.'

movements, even though the latter refused to back the demands of lesbians for fear of being discredited themselves.

The homosexual was also defined in terms of class, with each social category rejecting the notion that homosexuality resided within its ranks: the middle classes at the end of the 19th century considered homosexuality to be the result of urbanization and industrialization, and therefore the vice of the working classes, whereas the latter preferred to see it as the perversion of degenerate aesthetes and depraved aristocrats who had fallen prey to sloth, boredom and luxury. In other words, the homosexual was always someone else. His identification as the 'enemy within' was another recurrent theme in homophobic discourse. He was seen as a marginal figure who lived in a ghetto, delighted in secrecy and duplicity, and created particular links with his fellow homosexuals that were invisible to the uninitiated – hence the myth of a 'freemasonry of vice', as described at the end of the 19th century by the Paris prefect of police Félix Carlier.[51] Accusations of homosexuality were also

frequently used to discredit an opponent in public debate, irrespective of his actual sexual orientation. During the 1930s in France, political leader Léon Blum was the subject of vicious caricatures in the extreme right-wing press (the weekly *Gringoire* and twice-weekly *Candide*, for example), which systematically portrayed him with feminine features and in positions that suggested submissiveness, passivity and cowardice.[52] Homosexuality was also frequently linked to the Communist Party; this was due to the façade of tolerance shown by the USSR towards homosexuals, as well as to the support given by the German Communist Party to campaigns waged by homosexual movements. In England, a group of intellectuals that included poets and authors such as W. H. Auden, Christopher Isherwood and Stephen Spender was given the sobriquet 'Homintern', a means of revealing to the public both their Communist sympathies and their membership of a homosexual network that had begun at university.[53] In France, surveillance records compiled in some military ports listed 'public establishments frequented by Communist sailors and homosexual sailors'.

Fear of the invisible, and of the 'weakening' of society through homosexual desire, found its apogee in Nazi Germany.[54] In spite of the homoerotic imagery promoted by certain Nazi groups such as the SA, Hitler's seizure of power coincided with the destruction of the homosexual subculture, a trend typified most notably by the pillaging of Magnus Hirschfeld's Institute for Sexual Science. After 1933 the homosexual bars were closed and all movements and magazines banned. This repression accelerated after the Night of the Long Knives the following year and the elimination of Ernst Röhm, a well-known homosexual – mainly for political motives, although Hitler cleverly presented his execution as part of a crusade for moral order. The following years once more saw accusations of homosexuality used as a propaganda weapon to remove all opponents of the Nazi regime in both the Catholic Church and the army. In 1935 Paragraph 175 was extended to include all expressions of homosexual desire; lesbianism was not criminalized, however, no doubt because women were forced to revert to their traditional roles of wife and mother, and female sexuality was regarded as being merely passive and easily controllable.

From the Nazi point of view homosexuals were of no social value. If they refused to conform to the demands of the German nation (to get married and have children), they had to be eliminated. It was Heinrich Himmler who developed the homophobic Nazi rhetoric, mixing traditional stereotypes with detailed analysis that focused on the survival of the Aryan race. In a speech addressed to the generals of the SS on 18 February 1937, he distinguished between 'true' homosexuals and those who had been 'seduced', who could, according to him, therefore be 'cured'.[55] During the war he maintained an interest in 'medical' experiments (psychiatric and hormonal treatments, castration), by means of which he hoped to send homosexuals to the front without the risk of 'contagion'. Himmler also claimed that homosexuality was a foreign import, resulting from mixed race, and traced a direct link between homosexuals and Jews, rejecting both groups as 'feminine'. The homosexual was a coward, a liar, irresponsible and disloyal. He was the perfect target for blackmail and was possessed by an 'insatiable need for confidence'. This made

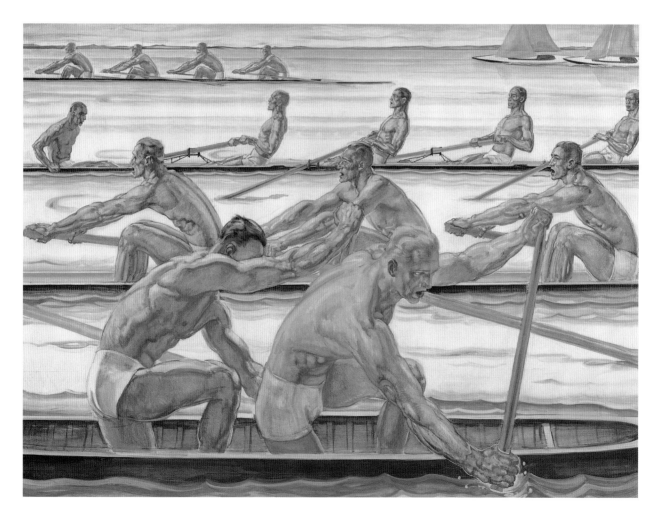

A chart of markings used to identify types of prisoner in Dachau concentration camp, c. 1938–42. Alongside symbols for political prisoners, professional criminals, Jehovah's Witnesses and Jews appears the pink triangle, which identified homosexual prisoners. Interned under Paragraph 175, homosexuals were given strenuous tasks designed to 'cure' them of their unnatural inclinations.

Himmler especially concerned about homosexuality in the SS: it was supposed to represent the elite of the nation and was destined to regenerate the country, so could not therefore be a place for 'perverts'.

Even if it is possible to discern some continuity between the repression of homosexuals during the Weimar period and during the Third Reich, it must be emphasized that the Nazi policy towards homosexuals was clear-cut: totalitarian discourse, police terror, punishments disproportionate to the deed. Those deemed to pose any sort of threat (such as prostitutes, paedophiles and reoffenders) could be placed in preventative detention or even sent to concentration camps after they had served an official sentence. Nearly 100,000 homosexuals were put on file by different surveillance organizations between 1937 and 1940, and the number of people sentenced rose from 872 in 1934 to 9,479 in 1938. Almost 92 per cent of those accused were found guilty. Although lesbians generally tended to escape prosecution, some were arrested under Austrian law, which criminalized female homosexuality, or on various other pretexts, and were interned as being asocial or Communist.[56] Some were made to work in camp brothels and were subjected to systematic rape, thus reaffirming the hierarchy of the sexes and the patriarchal order of things. In total, between 5,000 and 15,000 homosexuals were sent to concentration camps, where most of them died in terrible conditions. In spite of that, after the war the internment of homosexuals was not officially recognized, and Communist propaganda, which from 1934 established a Soviet view of homosexuality as a 'fascist perversion',[57] added to its list of homophobic stereotypes the figure of the Nazi homosexual.[58]

While other countries (Germany and Britain in particular) persecuted homosexuals with vigour, the more laissez-faire attitude of the imperial Russian police allowed a distinct, if discreet, subculture of homosexuality to develop. Bathhouses, which were staffed by youthful attendants, were typical meeting places; this example in St Petersburg, photographed around 1910, catered for an exclusive and well-to-do clientele.

The Russian (and, later, Soviet) situation was in fact somewhat strange.[59] In the Tsarist empire from 1832 onwards the crime of *muzhelozhestvo* ('men lying with men') was punishable by deportation to Siberia for four to five years, accompanied by the loss of all rights. After a reform of the penal code in 1903, the sentence in the case of consenting partners was reduced to a period of at least three months' imprisonment. Prosecutions were rare, and a homosexual and lesbian subculture – 'People of the Moonlight', according to the title of a book by Vasili Rozanov published in 1899 – was able to develop in the first two decades of the 20th century, especially among intellectuals and aristocrats, as can be seen from the works of Mikhail Kuzmin (*Wings*, 1906) and the poets Sophia Parnok and Marina Tsvetaeva. In 1917 the laws against sodomy were abolished, as was the entire Tsarist penal code, which seems to suggest that the Bolshevik regime was particularly tolerant in sexual matters. However, from 1934 onwards homosexuality was once again punishable by a sentence of up to five years' hard labour. According to Simon Karlinsky, repression existed before that date: it simply got worse. Homosexuals (*goluboi*, 'light blues') risked imprisonment or being sent to the Gulag, where they were frequently sexually abused by other detainees who considered them to be *opush cheny* ('degenerate'), while lesbians (*rosovaia*, 'pinks') were generally sent to psychiatric hospitals in order to receive 'treatment'.[60]

Increased repression was not peculiar to totalitarian regimes. Democracies also witnessed a hardening of sanctions during these critical years. The Second World War in particular represented a turning-point in the history of homosexuality in France. The Vichy government introduced the first penalties for homosexual relations on 6 August 1942: a fine and a prison sentence of between six months and three years for any homosexual or lesbian act with anyone below the age of twenty-one (the age of consent for heterosexuals was fixed at thirteen). Various hypotheses have been put forward to explain this legislation. The historian Anthony Copley places it in the context of the

programme for youth regeneration, whereas the jurist Jean Danet suggests that homosexuality may have been considered one of the factors in the fall of France in 1940.[61] Michael Sibalis emphasizes the role played by Admiral Darlan, a senior figure in the Vichy government, in drawing up this legislature, and the desire of the police and judicial authorities to regain control over homosexuality, which had already become a sensitive issue during the 1930s.[62] The Second World War also saw the deportation of homosexuals from Alsace and Moselle – departments that were under German control and therefore subject to Paragraph 175. A taboo subject until relatively recently, this aspect of France's past began to attract attention with the publication in 1994 of the autobiography of Pierre Seel, who as a young homosexual had been imprisoned in Schirmeck and forcibly enlisted in the German army.[63] Nevertheless, when homosexual associations demanded representation at the annual ceremonies commemorating deportation, they came up against fierce resistance from both associations of deportees and from public authorities.

From the end of the 19th century, a specific kind of homosexual culture developed in the United States – particularly in the large cities such as New York – that was not without parallels to European subcultures.[64] Thus Christopher Isherwood, a leading figure in the homosexual scene in Britain between the wars, chose in 1939 to emigrate to California, where he would align himself with the gay liberation movement of the 1970s. His itinerary provides a good illustration of the change in perspectives that occurred from the 1950s onwards. Indeed, following the destruction of homosexual life in the Second World War and the 'return to order' of the Cold War, the United States would become the centre for homosexual militancy and the point of departure for a new movement affirming a gay identity.

CONFIDENTIAL EXCLUSIVE:
Homos On The March
THE DAY THEY PICKETED THE WHITE HOUSE
EQUAL OPPORTUNIT
FOR ALL ....
ALL MEANS ALL
U.S. CLAIMS NO SECOND CLASS CITIZENS
WHAT ABOUT HOMOSEXUAL CITIZENS

Public Spheres and Gay Politics since the Second World War
DOMENICO RIZZO

This chapter considers the relationship between homosexuality and the public sphere from the 1940s to the 1980s. I have interpreted the phrase 'public sphere' in two ways, hence the plural. In the first instance, I have taken it to mean politics on a national level, and in this context I shall assess the importance that the issue of homosexuality assumed in democratic Western states in the decades following the Second World War. The phrase's second meaning, as used here, suggests a political and social arena – the field in which homosexual organizations set themselves up as political actors, putting forward an agenda that sought to combat the causes of discrimination.

These decades were characterized by intense and accelerated social change. Between the 1950s and 1960s, what Eric Hobsbawm defined as 'the great transformation' took place on a world scale: the economy, the geography of human settlements, material culture, identity and gender roles all underwent profound changes.[1] Many of these changes bring to bear on the topic of homosexuality, being connected as they are with the history of the state and democratic citizenship, and with the relationship between 'micro' and 'macro' levels of social experience.

Social networks

We begin in Zurich in 1943, with the two hundred subscribers to a bilingual monthly magazine, *Der Kreis / Le Cercle* ('The Circle'), which was targeted at homosexual men of middle- to upper-class backgrounds.[2] The magazine published articles of literary and artistic criticism, short stories, a large amount of homoerotic poetry and also – consistent with the importance given to medical knowledge about 'sexual inversion' since at least the second half of the 19th century – medical and scientific essays. In fact, the publication in October 1943 of a piece of medical journalism led many readers to write in and recount (anonymously) their own experiences.

This article presented a new therapy designed to cure men of their homosexual inclinations. The treatment consisted of electric shocks, hypnosis and exposing patients to erotic images, and it was based on the principle of 'aversion'.[3] A programme of behavioural stimulation, 'aversion therapy' was supposed to encourage a person to unlearn (or at least avoid expressing) sexual deviation, which was attributed to unhealthy family relationships. The cure promised to 'restore' patients to 'normality', making marriage and procreation possible.

In the decades that followed the Second World War, gay men and women began to organize themselves into political groups with the aim of ending discrimination against homosexuals. The series of demonstrations organized by the Mattachine Society outside the White House in 1965 represented the first time that a gay activist organization had used picketing as a protest tactic. The story is here reported by *Confidential*, a popular tabloid.

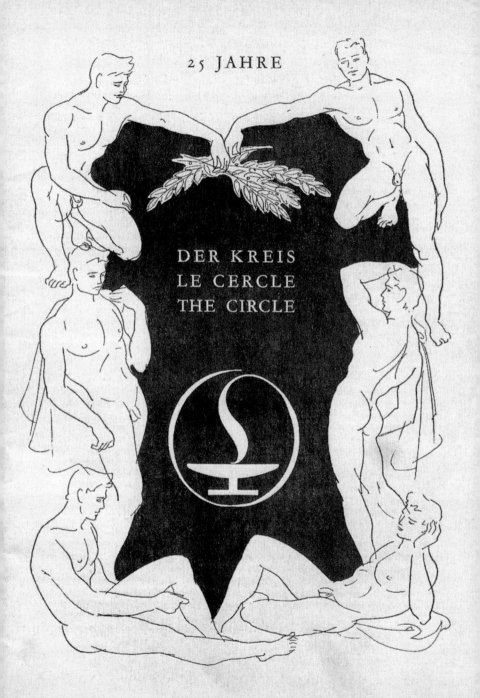

25 JAHRE

DER KREIS
LE CERCLE
THE CIRCLE

The sober Swiss periodical *Der Kreis* / *Le Cercle* was aimed primarily at homosexual men and claimed an international readership. Featuring short stories, literary criticism, homoerotic poetry and essays on the latest developments in medical thinking, it played an important role in the development of homophile organizations in Europe and the US. Shown here is the publication's twenty-fifth anniversary issue from 1957.

First used to treat alcoholism in the 1930s, aversion therapy had become a popular tool during the 1950s and 1960s for psychoanalysts seeking to 'cure' patients of homosexuality and transvestism. Most notorious was electroconvulsive therapy (ECT), in which a machine like the one shown here administered painful electric shocks as part of an attempt to change sexual orientation.

The magazine's readers, judging from the letters published in November 1943, asked themselves two questions while reading this article: whether the cure could work, and if a cure was indeed desirable. The responses help illuminate the point at which the private dimension of homosexual experience met a wider public context. The most dramatic letter came from a reader in Lausanne. 'It would be wonderful', he wrote, 'if a complete healing could put an end to the torment of our lives.'[4] Such an expectation explains why he was immediately interested by this new therapy. However, the author of the letter also felt the need to explain what his 'torment' consisted of. In the first place, he was discriminated against by society and persecuted by the police 'in all countries': entry to the public sphere, he implied, was thus barred. Secondly, 'even setting aside' this disadvantage, it was 'impossible' to find someone who shared the 'same ideal of love, of friendship and of altruism' as he did. Moreover, he added — switching to medico-anthropological language to evoke other handicaps — that 'more often than not economic interests play[ed] a central role' in his relationships, since (he goes on to explain) homosexual men possess the worst qualities of both men and women. Thus to him, in a position of extreme social and private distress, the cure appeared a panacea.[5]

This was, however, the only letter that was so pessimistic and so open to the idea of a 'cure'. The other readers, notwithstanding references to the difficulties they faced in public life, seem rather more positive about their private lives. To some, a desire to be 'cured' seemed absurd, since it meant a person would feel different from the way he had felt since birth and would effectively become a *tabula rasa*; others speak explicitly of a 'destiny' that should be accepted. Many readers of the magazine, therefore, defined their identity around their sexual desire. They did not seem at all to hate themselves, as a 1970s stereotype about earlier generations of homosexuals would have us believe.

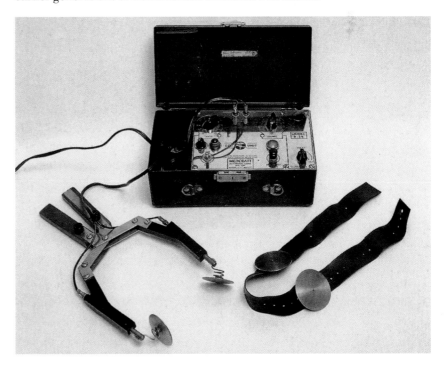

It is particularly interesting that social relations constitute the real point at which the positive and negative experiences recounted in *Der Kreis* differ. Thus, for a reader from Berne, 'the goodness and depth' of sentiments he had felt towards 'the friends with whom [he has] corresponded' did not make the possibility of fathering children – through sexual reorientation effected by shock therapy – worthwhile.[6] A reader from Zurich was similarly optimistic, stating that it was precisely 'in our dear circle' that he found tranquillity and balance in the 'the dark hours' of his life.[7]

Here, the term 'circle' is used ambiguously, standing for a group of friends but also alluding to the magazine's name. This double meaning provides an important insight: between the private sphere (often thought of as isolated and self-contained) and the public sphere (in which people act politically) are many other levels, such as social networks organized around sexual orientation. They form an 'alternative public sphere', a concept not fully encompassed by the term 'closet'.[8]

The readers of *Der Kreis* therefore represented a cross-section of men who through personal experience were aware of the limits placed on the free expression of their sexuality. Although fearful of exposing themselves publicly and 'in a struggle with their own destiny' (as one of them wrote), these men were nevertheless able to close up the gap between their ideals and reality, searching above all for mutual recognition and solidarity with fellow homosexuals. The name of the magazine was therefore symbolic, and the titles of many homosexual newspapers from the 1950s onwards evoked friendship. This situation represents a pre-political or proto-political response to a group need. That said, such steps towards recognition and solidarity need to be considered in the light of the relationship between the state and the sexuality of the individual – a relationship that proved highly resistant to change.

Homophobia and the state

In 1948, the Universal Declaration of Human Rights by the United Nations affirmed equality for all, 'without distinction of any kind, such as race, colour, sex, language, religion, etc.' (Article 2). Yet in many ways the declaration failed to translate into a break with past attitudes, even in countries that were members of the United Nations and governed by liberal-democratic systems. If the declaration provided a mandate for equality between men and women in public life, the issue of sexual orientation posed more complex problems. For some activists, the Declaration of Human Rights became an immediate point of reference. For instance, a group of young Danish homosexuals founded an organization called Forbundet af 1948 ('League of 1948'), which was followed by similar groups in Norway and Sweden. For many years to come, however, activists had to confront discriminatory laws and a repressive political climate that made it very hard even for their demands to be accepted as legitimate.[9]

At mid-century, sexual relations between men (and, less frequently, between women) were considered crimes and were subject to heavy penal sanctions in large parts of the world. The fact that homosexual acts were still

Essentially the first European homophile organization, the Danish Forbundet af 1948 ('League of 1948') was founded by Axel Axgil (see page 360) in response to the Universal Declaration of Human Rights. Here, the organization's emblem, two hands entwined under a four-leafed clover, is shown on a tie-pin.

criminalized in many nations must not be underestimated: the menace of arrest, conviction and imprisonment was a real and constant reminder of a homosexual's social impotence. This knowledge formed part of daily reality for such people, and contributed to the formation of their social identities.

But various legal systems embodied differing conceptions of the relationship between the state and the private sphere of the citizen. The first type of legal regime obtained in states with a convention of law codes that had been influenced by the French Revolution, under which homosexual acts, like many other private practices, were not penalized. As was the case with heterosexual acts, homosexual acts were punished only if they involved violence or sex with underage partners or took place in public space. By and large, the state was unconcerned with the morality and sexuality of its citizens, as long as they were expressed in private; lawmakers, the police and the judiciary did intervene regularly, however, to ensure that what they considered decent behaviour in public was maintained. The implicit duty of the citizen under this system was one of discretion: public space was an arena from which sex must be excluded. In exchange, the citizen obtained freedom of private conduct. This arrangement, in force in such countries as France (after 1791) and unified Italy (after 1861), evolved from a largely middle-class notion of citizenship, in which the separation between public and private spheres was fundamental.[10]

The second legal approach, more common in states with a system based on common law and with a strong Protestant tradition, implied a completely different conception of sexual behaviour. According to this view, there existed intrinsically immoral acts that should be punished as such, regardless of the place or circumstances (such as situations of violence) in which they were committed. These were acts forbidden to human beings because they contravened natural law, and those who committed them therefore warranted exclusion from social citizenship: such 'unnatural' practices included anal and oral sex, whether heterosexual or homosexual.

The distinction between these two types of legal approach is fundamental to the way in which states intervene in the private life of the individual. For instance, as recently as 1998 two adult men were brought to trial in the United States for having committed sodomy in a private house; they were taken by surprise by the police, who had been alerted by a neighbour.[11] Such an arrest would not have been possible in states such as Italy or France.

From the beginning of the 1950s, law reform movements in countries such as the United States and Britain demanded that consensual homosexual acts committed in private should be decriminalized, thus rendering private lives free from public judicial intervention. The American Law Institute proposed legal changes in 1955 in the wake of Alfred Kinsey's reports on male sexuality in 1948 and female sexuality in 1953, which suggested that homosexual practices were widespread and denied their pathological nature.[12] Legal changes, however, were not immediately forthcoming. In Britain, the Wolfenden Committee advanced a similar proposal for reform in 1957, although Parliament changed the law to decriminalize private, consensual homosexual acts only ten years later.[13]

ALLIED FILM MAKERS present

DIRK BOGARDE
SYLVIA SYMS

IN MICHAEL RELPH AND BASIL DEARDEN'S Production

VICTIM

Also Starring
DENNIS PRICE

Original Screenplay by
Janet Green and John McCormick

Produced by Michael Relph
Directed by Basil Dearden

Basil Dearden's *Victim* (1961) was the first British film to tackle the subject of homosexuality explicitly. Dirk Bogarde plays a homosexual lawyer who risks his marriage and career to track down a group of blackmailers. By focusing on the British legal situation, which made homosexuals vulnerable to blackmail and exposure, the filmmakers consciously set out to change public opinion. Here are the suitably dramatic film poster (above) and a front-of-house still (opposite).

The existence of legal sanctions against homosexual acts committed in private not only constituted a major threat that hung over homosexuals' lives, but also permitted blackmail, which played on fears of scandal and revelation. Nevertheless, law reform was strongly resisted because it would effectively have affirmed the principle that homosexual acts were not in themselves morally or socially dangerous. The legal changes that did eventually take place had to wait for a new cultural and political climate, and for the evolution of attitudes towards homosexuality.

One level on which the two different conceptions of the role of the state — abstentionist and interventionist — converged was police surveillance of the public sphere. Notwithstanding different countries' penal codes, police attitudes on the subject of 'indecency' and deviations from a vague concept of 'good behaviour' facilitated widespread surveillance and intervention. Nonetheless, the pressure exerted by police on public expressions of homosexuality varied from country to country, and definitions of indecency were subjective, dictated by local culture and politics.

All Western societies in the 1950s witnessed an increase in homophobia, a result of the idealization of the nuclear family as the dominant social model, which was based on marriage and a rigid division of gender roles. In the decades following the Second World War this value system was particularly rigid, and sexual deviance was seen as a major threat. In the political climate of the Cold War, Communism and homosexuality were frequently lumped together: both risked destabilizing the state and the very structure of society. Yet it is also interesting to note how homophobia in the Soviet Union and the 'people's democracies' of Eastern Europe paralleled that in the West. Homosexual acts were punished for being profoundly antisocial and individualistic, and therefore the expression of an individual's capitalist and middle-class values.[14] This similarity between ideologically opposed systems does not reveal any kind of consistent anthropological behaviour so much as a political truth common to all nation-states founded on the family. Threatening the family was equivalent to threatening the state; likewise, when the national community was under threat, defending and strengthening the family became a patriotic mission, one that shored up social consensus. The law therefore became more stringent for 'deviants', who were identified as being outside the family and therefore outside the nation.

During the period of McCarthyism in the United States, the identification of homosexuals with Communists led to inquiries and purges in the civil service. Similarities between the two groups were pointed out: both homosexuals and Communists moved in a secret underworld; they had specific meeting

The witch-hunts of McCarthyism were directed not only at those suspected of
Communist sympathies. Since homosexuals and Communists were frequently
conflated in the popular mind as 'security risks', the 'Lavender Scare' came
into being. In June 1950 the US Senate authorized an investigation into the
'employment of homosexuals and other sex perverts in government', to be led
by Senator Clyde Hoey (second from right).

places; they produced their own literature; and they shared a sense of mutual loyalty – that is to say, they formed a network of relations on the boundary between private life and the public sphere. During the most acute phase of the Lavender Scare, as it is known, action against homosexuals included purges of the armed forces, the forced resignation of federal employees, FBI surveillance, persecution by the police force and witch-hunts by the media.[15] The phenomenon did not end with the demise of Joseph McCarthy's political career in 1955, however, but continued unabated under the Eisenhower administration, which (as its own records document) classified homosexuals – in so much as they were targets of blackmail – as 'unintentional security risks'. In Britain, meanwhile, there was a notorious case involving double-agent homosexual (as well as heterosexual) spies in the pay of the KGB; when, in 1951, the scandal broke and they realized they would be arrested, several fled to the USSR.[16] The incident seemed to confirm suspicions on both sides of the Atlantic that 'deviants' were ultimately not trustworthy or loyal citizens.

Even though they lacked the tense ideological circumstances of the events described above, there were other cases elsewhere that brought homosexuality to the public's attention and fuelled homophobia. For example, in 1950 the Swedish public was stirred up by a clergyman's accusations that the government was controlled by a type of homosexual 'freemasonry'; this formed the background to revelations – for a long time suppressed by the Swedish royal court – that King Gustav V had been blackmailed by a waiter who had been his lover. That immorality, danger to the nation's security, criminal behaviour, blackmail and prostitution were integral parts of homosexual life was a deeply-rooted conviction of middle-class Scandinavian citizens in this period. They were not alone in this belief, however. Despite the fact that private homosexual acts had not been penalized in France since the Revolution, President de Gaulle's right-wing government kept on the repressive anti-homosexual provisions of the wartime Vichy government – which in the name of a 'national revolution' had promoted 'work, family and fatherland' – and in 1960 categorized homosexuality, together with tuberculosis and alcoholism, as a 'social plague'.[17] Three years earlier, the British Parliament had refused to adopt the legal reforms proposed by the Wolfenden Committee against the background of a virulent press campaign that defined homosexuality as a depraved abomination and a threat to British youth.[18]

The readers of *Der Kreis* whose letters were published in 1943 would not, in the decades that followed, have suffered from merely minor social and institutional pressures like the reader from Lausanne. In many places, homosexuality was still not only a crime, but was also labelled (and considered by some homosexuals themselves) as an illness. On the other hand, by the 1950s those who were inclined to form a 'circle', such as the Swiss readers of a homosexual magazine, had invented ways of meeting with each other and participating in groups that attempted to pursue a homosexual political agenda.

Homophilia

Immediately after the Second World War, homosexual networks and political groups gradually began to present themselves in the public arena with the declared objective of combatting discrimination. In some cases, notably in those countries governed by Communist regimes, in which the margins of all political action were severely constrained, homosexual political activism remained unthinkable until the regimes collapsed. Yet in Western Europe and America, the emergence of homosexual groups campaigning for political change was a major phenomenon of the period from the 1950s onwards.

Everywhere in the 1950s and 1960s, the view that ignorance was a root cause of discrimination was central to the arguments of associations that called themselves 'homophile'. The term itself demonstrated explicitly their rejection of an identity based solely on sexual practices, suggesting instead more generic feelings of attraction and friendship with others of one's own sex. These organizations' members shared the notion that wrong information, or misguided understanding, lay at the heart of the problem of anti-homosexual discrimination. Deep-seated prejudices and disgraceful stereotypes scared the public and government, and triggered repressive mechanisms. Prostitutes and blackmailers, sexually promiscuous and the corruptors of youth, 'inverts' who went against the natural order: these images, homophile groups maintained, prevented the granting of equality to those whose inclinations for intimate friendship and love were directed towards those of their own sex.

If the cause of discrimination was ignorance, then the political objective for homophiles was to demonstrate to people at large their conformity, their compatibility with dominant social values. The way to achieve this was twofold: first, by promoting and disseminating scientific research on homosexuality, which took up ample space in the periodicals of various homophile organizations; and second, by ensuring that homosexuals, even if they had their own lifestyles, were seen as men and women like everyone else (men who were not effeminate and women who were not masculine), and loyal citizens (not potential spies in the pay of the enemy) who were morally respectable (thus not inclined to break the law). According to this viewpoint, the difference between heterosexuals and homosexuals belonged very much to the private sphere; what was necessary, therefore, was to protect personal freedoms through the application of the principles of liberal politics. The homophiles' primary objective was therefore the reform of penal laws.

'We know we are the same', proclaimed one member of the Mattachine Society, the first homophile organization in the United States, to great acclaim in 1953.[19] The Mattachine Society had been founded in Los Angeles almost three years earlier by Henry Hay, a militant Communist reacting against his own party's ardently conservative stance on sexual issues. Hay nevertheless based the structure of his own movement on that of the revolutionary struggle, using secret cells and a strict hierarchy. This militancy was designed to provide an experience of responsibility and a personal and social transformation: homosexuals, an oppressed minority, could place themselves at the forefront of all other minorities.

The first homophile organization in the United States was the Mattachine Society, founded in Los Angeles in the winter of 1950. Originally organized into secret cells along revolutionary lines – a hangover from its Marxist founders – the society called for a movement of gay people to challenge anti-homosexual discrimination.

Founded in 1955 as part of the homophile movement, the
Daughters of Bilitis were the first lesbian political organization in
the United States. Like the Mattachine Society, with whom they
were closely associated, the Daughters advocated assimilation
into heterosexual society, even recommending that lesbians
should dress in recognizably feminine ways. Above are its
monthly magazine, *The Ladder*, which was launched in October
1956, and (left) a membership card of the San Francisco chapter.

The success of a political campaign by the society to acquit a member who had been arrested (by a plain-clothes policeman pretending to solicit him for sex) led to a multiplication of the society's activities and the number of cities where it was represented. However, the widening of its support base also led to the emergence of internal tensions, particularly surrounding the society's hierarchical structure and fears that homosexuals would be persecuted as Communists on account of Hay's background (the *Los Angeles Mirror* had suggested such a possibility in a highly aggressive manner). Campaigners also feared increasing isolation from an already hostile culture. Internal dissent produced a complete reorganization of the Mattachine Society and a redefinition of its aims: 'We know we are the same' formed part of this move away from radical militancy and clandestinity and acted as an invitation to campaigners to fall into line with a 'pattern of behavior that is acceptable to society in general and compatible with the recognized institutions of home, church, and state'.[20]

The Mattachine Society's sister association, the Daughters of Bilitis, held similarly assimilationist views, as did various homophile organizations in Europe. Indeed, there was a great deal of communication among these various groups, and exchanges of ideas regularly filled the columns of their magazines. The first issue of *One* magazine, published by the Mattachine Society, contained the translation of an article that had appeared some months earlier in *Die Insel*, a magazine in Germany; it was presented to American readers to confirm 'how similar are its purposes to ONE's and how international are all of our aims'.[21] *Die Insel*, meanwhile, made ample reference to *Der Kreis*; to *Der Ring* and *Hellas* (both published in Hamburg); to the various Scandinavian magazines of Forbundet af 1948; and, from 1954, to *Arcadie* — the most important homophile magazine of francophone Europe, published in Paris by an association of the same name founded by André Baudry, an ex-seminarian and collaborator on *Der Kreis*.

Homophile societies in Europe and the United States exhibited a great deal of solidarity. In their various periodicals they would swap news, share translated articles and encourage discussion. Below are the exotic-looking *Die Insel* ('The Island'), which was founded in 1925 but did not outlast the Nazis' rise to power, and the Paris-based *Arcadie*, established in 1954.

New Year's Eve at the DOK bar, Amsterdam, in 1955. Opened by the
city's homophile Center for Culture and Recreation, the highly
successful DOK occupied the basement of a theatre and offered a
large space for dancing and socializing. The attitude of the city's
police seems to have been that it was better for homosexuals to dance
behind closed doors than cause trouble in public places.

Not all states shared the enlightened pragmatism of Amsterdam. In 1964 the Florida state government released a brochure entitled 'Homosexuality and Citizenship in Florida' with the avowed intent of making 'every individual concerned with the moral climate of the state ... aware of the rise in homosexual activity'. This surveillance photograph of a 'homosexual act' was, confusingly, accompanied by an exhaustive glossary of gay slang. Such lurid treatment merely ensured that the booklet acquired the status of pornography.

These homophile organizations tended to create a 'reference system' for their members, a social framework facilitated by fellow subscribers to the magazines. Meetings, dinners and charity functions represented their principal activities, and in some cities the societies also set up social centres. (As with private clubs, it was often necessary to be introduced by a member to gain admittance.) All of these initiatives offered real and metaphorical spaces in which homophiles could discuss common themes and socialize. Above all, they reinforced the idea that homosexuals were by no means sinful, sick or criminal.

With the sole exception of Amsterdam – where the homophile movement organized dance nights from 1946 onwards and where, nine years later, it even opened a bar[22] – associations resolutely distanced themselves from the commercial homosexual scene, which was growing rapidly during these years despite waves of persecution by the police. Commercial venues in which homosexuals could interact socially – even if it exposed them to homophobic reactions – were stigmatized by organizations that sought to better homosexuals' lives by fighting homophobia through respectability. Bars, restaurants, saunas and magazines of the male physique followed their own, separate, path of evolution.[23]

A second reason for the homophiles' critical attitude towards the homosexual subculture was their rejection of the particular social model that could be found in semi-clandestine clubs and pubs (often operated by local crime gangs). These venues were thought to be frequented by 'queers' – for the most part effeminate men from the middle and upper classes who seduced members of the working class in exchange for various favours. Another model was provided by the young *folles* who frequented the Parisian neighbourhood of Saint-Germain-des-Prés in the late 1950s. André Baudry, irritated by newspaper reports that emphasized the anti-conformist climate of the Existentialists' *quartier*, wrote that homophiles did not want to be confused 'with these caricatures, these traders in love and lust, these exhibitionists, these young men who no longer are really men'.[24]

Although they rejected effeminacy, the homophiles did not succeed in establishing a 'virilist' model;[25] abandoning the butch–fem, working class–middle class dichotomy required a change in habits that only happened later and in such a way that made the homophile stance seem extremely reactionary. In the 1970s a new stereotype was to appear: the muscled, mustachioed clone, which sprang from an interest in health, athleticism, nature and youth – ideals more in harmony with a consumer culture than with the austere and conformist respectability of the homophiles of the 1950s.

'Is the bitter end approaching?' read the title of an editorial published by *Der Kreis* in August 1967. For the first time in thirty-five years, the magazine was finding it impossible to continue publication: the 1,900 subscribers it boasted at the end of the 1950s had progressively shrunk over the years, and by as much as a quarter since 1965. To subscribers who criticized the editors' politics, the magazine answered by setting down its own, broader view of recent social changes: 'Especially among younger homosexuals, the "problem" of homosexuality has lost much of its urgency through our less restricted way of living today. To make personal contacts is much easier today than it used to be. The countless gay bars everywhere catering to our minority of well-paying customers have also encouraged these contacts.'[26] In the following months, ever more dramatic news about the magazine's financial state foreshadowed the publication of a final issue in December 1967. Although bitterly lamented by European homophiles, the disappearance of *Der Kreis* was a sign of the changing times. On one point the editors proved not to be prophetic, however: their assumption that new lifestyles would make political engagement unnecessary in the eyes of future generations.

Gay liberation

In the summer of 1969, a political organization called the Gay Liberation Front (GLF) was formed in New York, the result of an encounter between gay life and the radical political culture of the New Left. At the end of June of that year, a police raid on the Stonewall Inn in New York sparked a revolt that was led by transvestites and which lasted for several days – a protest without precedent in gay history. At the same time, however, the incident belongs in the general context of confrontations between police and emergent radicals, such as the Black Panthers and feminist and anti-war activists, which were erupting moderately frequently.[27]

The GLF had been established a few weeks after Stonewall. Influenced by the principles and discourse of other forms of radicalism, it provided a means of expression for a new generation who rejected the post-war political and social order and who were willing to take to the streets to manifest their discontent (as had occurred in Paris and in many American cities the previous year). Youth movements were in search of authenticity, sensuality and community, rebelling against what they saw as social alienation produced by a bureaucratic and consumerist society. These young men and women refused to be straitjacketed by the nuclear family, with its attendant roles and the submission to authority that it embodied.[28]

The speed with which the model provided by the Gay Liberation Front was adopted in various Western societies is partly explained by their common experience of significant cultural changes and political agitation. In Britain, an association of the same name was set up in October 1970 by youths who had been part of the American hippie, Black Panther and Gay Activist Alliance movements.[29] In Paris in the same year, the Front Homosexuel d'Action Révolutionnaire (FHAR) was established.[30] In August 1971, the German Homosexuelle Aktion Westberlin group was set up,[31] and a few months later the Fronte Unitario Omosessuale Rivoluzionario Italiano appeared in Italy (its acronym, FUORI, also means 'out').[32] Similar organizations were established in other European countries, as well as in Canada and Australia.

The situation in Germany serves as a good illustration of the general climate. In 1970 Rosa von Praunheim (a drag name), unaware of contemporary movements in America, made a film whose censorship sparked the formation of the local gay rights movement. *Nicht der Homosexuelle ist Pervers, sondern die Situation in der er lebt* ('It is not the homosexual who is perverse but the situation in which he lives') is the story of a young provincial man who moves to Berlin and makes his way through its gay subculture, meeting a range of negatively portrayed characters adversely affected by the circumstances under which they are obliged to live. (Homosexual acts were still illegal under Paragraph 175 of the German penal code, and homosexuality was subject to widespread disapproval.) In the end, he finds his personal liberation in a gay commune, whose members teach him to admit his own homosexuality publicly and to understand that the real problem is not his sexuality but socially sanctioned homophobia.[33]

'Liberation' became a key theme of these movements; it implied a certain vision of the nature and causes of homophobia, of the arguments to use against it and the means by which it could be combatted. Whereas the homophiles had favoured an integrationist approach, the gay liberation fronts assumed a very different political perspective, one based on a comprehensive analysis of political, economic, social and cultural structures and strongly influenced by Marxism and by Marxist criticism of psychoanalysis.[34] The causes of homophobia were inherent in the middle-class, capitalist ethic: racism, imperialism and sexual repression were all expressions and instruments of the exploitation of one social group by others. Alliances with other oppressed groups – the working class, women, ethnic minorities – were therefore seen as fundamental to the struggle. If the entire system (the Establishment) was the root of oppression, liberation could not be achieved by

Loosely based on the 'Black is Beautiful' slogan, 'Gay Is Good' became an affirmation of public pride and liberation during the early 1970s. Badge from around 1969.

A visible community and a demand for political change: what is considered the first gay pride march took place in New York on 28 June 1970. The Gay Liberation Front and many other organizations marched from Greenwich Village to Central Park to commemorate the Stonewall Riots of the previous year and to protest against discriminatory legislation.

homosexuals' requesting a separate 'room of their own'; the zones of toleration created in some cities, in fact, drew criticism as 'ghettoes' that must be opened up and liberated. The gay liberationists' objective was, rather, to transform the whole of society.

There were differences between movements that primarily sought a kind of cultural transformation (as was the case in America), and those for whom a revolutionary tradition was stronger (as in France and Germany).[35] All shared a fundamental principle, however: 'It's too late for liberalism'[36] — too late, that is, to expect inclusion in society through polite requests for reform.

The liberal, middle-class order thus faced a challenge to one of its most fundamental precepts: the distinction between public and private. The slogan 'the personal is political' expressed faith in the transformative potential of expressing one's private, authentic self in public. For homosexuals, this meant revealing themselves in the open: 'coming out'. For earlier generations, the expression had denoted making oneself recognizable to other homosexuals inside an alternative public sphere;[37] now it encapsulated the need to affirm one's own identity in the *official* public sphere, thereby denying a difference

The Gay Activists' Alliance abandoned the Gay Liberation Front's desire for wholesale political revolution and focused its campaigns solely on the question of equal rights for homosexuals. The GAA knew how to use the media to its advantage: its 'zaps' – speedy confrontations with offending institutions or individuals – ensured that the issue of gay rights was often in the news. This zap was held in New York around 1970; the banner in the background shows the group's emblem, the Greek letter lambda.

between one's public and private roles. 'Closet queenery must end', wrote activist Carl Wittman in his *Gay Manifesto* (1969): the closet was an emblem of oppression, an interiorization of homophobia that could only be overturned by coming out and speaking out.

For the gay liberationists, the sexual act itself was revolutionary: in the view of Guy Hocquenghem, a French philosopher and one of the leaders of FHAR, patriarchy was founded on the contrast between the public power of the phallus and the privatization of the anus. To liberate the anus through male sexuality was therefore to undermine the foundations of patriarchal social relationships.[38] For the Italian writer and activist Mario Mieli, gay men, by cross-dressing and getting screwed, challenged the very notions of hetero-sexuality and masculinity, therefore contributing to the liberation of the human race.[39] For the Australian political scientist Dennis Altman, gay male sexuality offered the potential for new configurations of social relationships.[40] The ideology and style of gay liberation became provocative, demonstrative and sometimes humorous: 'Putting on make-up is a lifestyle', cried the French Gazolines, a situationist group closely tied to FHAR and heirs of the *folles* stigmatized ten years earlier by Baudry and the French homophiles. 'We'll mount the next barricades in evening dress', they added.

The public activities of the gay liberationists were in themselves provocative and constituted a break with past practice. An example was the first significant public outing of the newly formed FUORI, which took place in April 1972 in San Remo, at a conference of the Italian Centre of Sexology devoted to the causes of homosexuality and therapies for overcoming it. Among its illustrious guests was the British psychiatrist Philip Feldmann, a supporter of 'aversion therapy' who advocated electric-shock treatment. Forty demonstrators protested outside, while inside some of the activists asked to address the assembly. In front of the speechless participants, the president of FUORI, Angelo Pezzana, began by declaring, 'I am a homosexual and am happy to be one.'

The heyday of gay liberation movements was over within a few years, as political radicalism began to disappear in the second half of the 1970s. The conviction that revolution was imminent, and that gays and lesbians only had to jump on the bandwagon, became less and less plausible. Gay movements everywhere were facing serious organizational problems and above all stumbled on the issue of a type of politics founded on identity. As a fundamental factor in the workings of oppression and as a basis for collective mobilization, 'identity' for many years widened the range of forces fighting for change. At the same time, however, it also provided an impetus for fragmentation among these uneasy alliances and encouraged the development of ever more particular agendas. This was evident, for example, in the United States, where African-American homosexuals felt that the movement did not offer enough to individuals oppressed not only on the basis of their sexuality, but also because of the colour of their skin. Almost everywhere, lesbians remained dissatisfied, turned away by the majority of feminist groups and disillusioned with a misogynist and centralized gay movement. This discontent gave rise to the need for new theories of lesbianism, the emergence of the feminist lesbian, and even contributed to the idea of lesbian separatism.

The decline of the gay liberation movements led to their break-up into a multiplicity of ideologies, groups and trends. Nonetheless, the liberationists bequeathed a continuing emphasis on 'coming out' and on the destruction of the barrier between private and public self as part of the struggle against homophobia. As such, their legacy reflected general changes that had taken place in gay and lesbian life, changes that ensured that the objectives and methods of the gay liberation movements of the 1970s differed profoundly from those of homophile movements in the 1950s.

Activism

The decline in the enthusiasm for political change that had hitherto characterized gay liberation left the field open for another type of militancy – the so-called 'activist' groups. Already in existence in some places in the heady days of 1970s radicalism, activist groups multiplied considerably in the following years. The most important, the Gay Activists' Alliance, was created when a dissident group split from the Gay Liberation Front. Their political agenda, and that of similar organizations, was for the most part broad: changes in civil rights legislation (including the decriminalization of homosexual acts in countries where they were still illegal) and the promotion of a more sympathetic treatment of homosexuals in the media. They too placed a strong emphasis on coming out and on the language of pride and self-affirmation, and they sometimes involved themselves in defiant and angry protests.

Gay activists differed substantially from the gay liberation movement in at least two respects, however. First, the activists' programme was focused exclusively on gays and lesbians rather than an attempt to provoke wholesale social and political revolution. Second, their organizations were well structured along more traditional lines (rather than being 'fronts', collectives or other vague alliances), and – crucially – they knew how to interact with the political system effectively, setting up pressure groups, lobbying on specific causes, recruiting members and using the media to further their ends. Activist groups also targeted other, non-political institutions, such as professional associations that they believed were implicated in oppression. This tactic was not without significant results: in the United States, for example, activists scored an important victory in 1973 when the American Psychiatric Association eliminated homosexuality from its list of mental diseases, and two years later they were successful in persuading the US Civil Service Commission to remove the ban on gay and lesbian federal employees that had been in place since the 1950s. Activist groups have also negotiated with local authorities and with the police, though sometimes entering into open conflict with them and using their capacity for mobilization when they deemed such tactics necessary.

Persecution by the police had decreased considerably in many cities, however, above all in middle-class neighbourhoods. In the second half of the 1970s, in fact – particularly in the United States, but also in some European capitals and in various Australian and Canadian cities – a transition occurred as gay life moved 'from the bars to the streets, from nightlife to daytime, from "sexual deviance" to an alternative lifestyle'.[41] Homosexuals were increasingly integrated into the mainstream. Among the conditions necessary for this 'normalization' was a critical mass of gay men and lesbians clustered in a particular area, as well as successful lobbying by activist groups. For white middle-class gay men in particular, this shift was accompanied by a redefinition of lifestyle, even if the benefits effected by this move into 'normal' public space did not reach the socially disadvantaged.

The majority of men who take part in the public world of sociability and sexual exchange are not activists. Political associations have gradually lost their appeal, for the reason that their negotiations and political lobbying are almost invisible, and because many of their objectives may appear to have been more or less achieved. In 1974 the recently formed *Spartacus International Gay Guide* commented on this phenomenon; its British editor, having taken part in the battle for civil rights, felt the need to remind his 'consumers' that their new liberties were thanks to those who had fought earlier battles. He took the decision to include 'a lot of information of [about] national gay

The AIDS crisis prompted a level of political mobilization and direct action that had not been witnessed since the early 1970s. Delay and prevarication by government health organizations around the world prompted the establishment of groups that campaigned tirelessly for resources and effective treatment. Perhaps most famous was ACT UP (AIDS Coalition to Unleash Power), which made use of these two campaigns: 'Silence = Death' (1986), a slogan that came to signify AIDS activism for a generation; and 'The Government Has Blood on Its Hands' (1988), which protested graphically against health policy in New York.

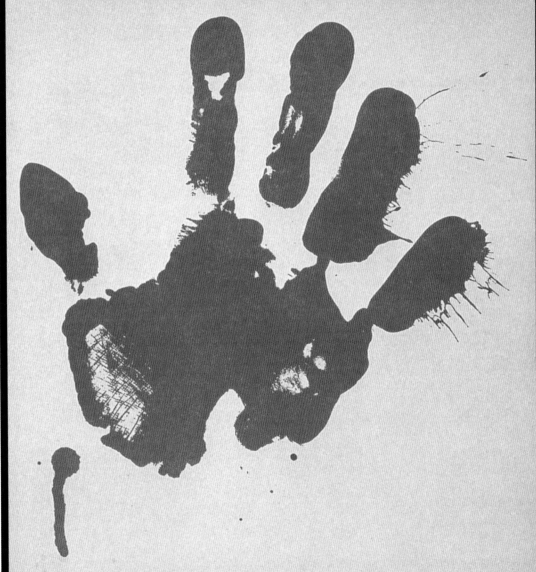

organizations ... to encourage every reader to contact the groups in his country and to support at least one of them'.[42] The very success of the *Spartacus* guide, its lists of gay and lesbian venues expanding in every year's edition, attested to an explosion in both demand for and supply of commercial socializing. The golden age of bars, nightclubs and baths occurred in the late 1970s, when a liberated sexuality seemed to manifest itself in everything from pornography to pop music culture, turning a song like the Village People's 1978 'YMCA' into not only an international hit, but also an anthem for a generation.

In reality, the gap between political movements and the commercial subculture was only bridged by the crisis brought on by AIDS, the virus that struck the gay male community with particular violence from the early 1980s onwards. The imperative of formulating an effective response to the epidemic meant that homosexual organizations reached a level of sophistication, influence and stability that the activists of the 1970s had failed to attain. Many individuals who had never before been militants now began taking a part in political activism, claiming that only homophobia could explain why an epidemic killing tens of thousands of homosexuals initially attracted so little attention from governments and media. More than any other issue, AIDS revealed not only the persistent and systematic character of the oppression of homosexuals, but also its ties to other forms of social injustice. Many claimed that only by viewing the matter from a radical perspective could one explain the delay in public intervention: aside from homosexuals, those struck down by the epidemic in American cities were African Americans and Latinos, many them intravenous drug users.

When it came to establish legal and welfare aid groups, the movement that fought against AIDS and against the inattention of governments and public institutions enjoyed access to new economic resources, great expertise and numerous volunteers. It also benefited from greater involvement in a wider political agenda. There was an upsurge in local activism, with groups forming in places that previously had never experienced any kind of mobilization. The crisis necessitated tactics of direct action and civil disobedience on a scale not seen since the 1970s (witnessed, for example, in the public protests undertaken by ACT UP – AIDS Coalition to Unleash Power – in the late 1980s). Minority ethic groups, such as Latinos and African Americans in the Unites States, North Africans and Turks in Europe, and Asians in Australia, also became involved. One effect of the epidemic on activist organizations was a closing of the gender gap: lesbians assumed positions of responsibility in associations that promoted safer sex, provided care for AIDS sufferers and campaigned for increased funding for AIDS research and treatment. Their involvement was partly a result of lesbian separatism's loss of appeal and partly due to lesbians' increasingly experimental sexual behaviour, which brought them more in line with their male counterparts. In addition, the epidemic promoted a new emphasis on intimacy and on the couple – a cultural reaction to the disease, especially in the context of heated debates on the link between public sex and dangerous sex.[45] In the wider political climate, in which leftist groups were experiencing organizational difficulties and a decline in the number of members, gay associations, by contrast, gained ground in the wake of the AIDS epidemic.

In the decades that separated 1980s activism from the first homophile initiatives of the 1950s, consumer culture seems to have levelled individual differences between homosexuals and heterosexuals. Legal reforms have also lessened the difference between the legal status of homosexuals and that of their heterosexual counterparts. The opportunities for individuals to interact with others on a personal basis or in the wider community have increased and diversified, and they can, if they so choose, claim a social identity founded on their sexual orientation and their particular lifestyles. Even as the goal of equality seems closer and closer, however, in one respect the contemporary Western state continues unchanged: its foundation at a constitutional level on the married heterosexual family as its basic social unit. The conflict between public life and the private sphere endures.

Loving Women in the Modern World
LEILA J. RUPP

What does it mean to be a 'lesbian' in the modern world? In the 21st century it means loving women, desiring women, forming relationships with women, engaging in sexual behaviour with women, claiming an identity as a lesbian, and perhaps forming communities with other lesbians, although not all of these are necessary to the definition. But what do we make of women who loved, desired, formed relationships with and had sex with women before the concept and identity of 'lesbian' were available? What do we make of such women in cultures that have different categories of gender and sexual behaviour? We might call them 'lesbian-like' or talk of same-sex love, desire or sexual acts.[1] What is crucial is that we contemplate, as best we can, the ways in which women in the past and in different parts of the world negotiated and understood their desire, love and self-conceptions.

I explore here different patterns of loving women in various parts of the world, from around the beginning of the 19th century up to the present. It is impossible, of course, to be comprehensive, since research on many societies remains sketchy or is entirely lacking. Nor is there space to do justice to more than a few places. But my aim is to give a sense of women's lives with other women before, during and after the 'discovery', naming and claiming of lesbian identity. Although lesbianism is often dismissed in societies subject to Western imperialism as an imported perversion (and in Western societies traditionally attributed to those of 'other' races, classes or nations), women all around the world have found many ways of loving other women.

The story of loving women in the modern world is a tale of women who dressed and passed as men and who married women, of female husbands and manly women, of romantic friends who made lives together, of trysts in domestic spaces, of secretive and not-so-secretive communities, of sapphists and female inverts and marriage-resisters and bulldaggers and butches and fems and lesbians. Yet it is not simply a tale of women with same-sex desires freeing and naming themselves as the modern world came into being. What history teaches us is how differently sexuality has been conceived and practised in the past and in various societies, and how mistaken we are to think solely in terms of progress. As a way of disrupting a narrative of progress, I have approached the history of loving women thematically, looking first at marrying women, then desiring women, and finally at women claiming diverse identities.

During the 1920s Berlin was home to a vibrant lesbian subculture. An astonishing number of bars, clubs, groups and periodicals catered to women who loved women, and cabaret acts dealt explicitly with the theme of lesbian love. This watercolour by Jeanne Mammen from *c.* 1927 captures something of the androgynous look popular at the time.

Edward De Lacy Evans had left Ireland in 1856 as Ellen Tremaye but once in Australia adopted a male persona. He worked in the gold fields for over twenty years (as illustrated in this engraving of 1879) and married three times, which would suggest a sexual as much as a social or economic reason for his decision to cross the gender line.

Marrying women

One of the most persistent patterns of what may or may not accurately be called female same-sex sexuality is the case of women crossing the gender line to live as men and to marry women. What we do not know in such cases is whether women became men solely for the economic and social freedom that male dress and employment provided, whether a sexual motivation figured in their decisions, or whether they conceived of themselves as something akin to transgendered, even if no such concept existed. We are particularly in the dark about the motives of their wives. What we do know is that such gender-crossing and marriage to women existed in a number of contexts.

Consider the story of Edward De Lacy Evans, born a woman, who lived as a man for twenty-three years in Victoria, Australia.[2] The case came to light in 1879 when he was forcibly stripped for a bath, having just arrived at Kew Asylum in Melbourne. Evans had emigrated to Australia from Ireland in 1856 as Ellen Tremaye, but after working for a short time as a domestic servant began dressing as a man and married one of his shipmates. He went to work as a miner and, when his first wife left him for another man, explaining that Evans was actually a woman, he married a young Irishwoman. When she died, he married a third young woman, who bore a child after being impregnated by her sister's husband. Although Evans claimed the child as his own, it was the birth, it seems, that sent Evans to the asylum.

What grabbed public interest was not the masquerade itself but the three marriages. Newspaper stories reported Evans's interest in women on board ship, and one journalist concluded that 'the woman must have been mad on the subject of sex from the time she left Ireland.'[3] The fact that Evans had been committed may have explained his sexual deviance, but how was one to account for his wives? It was difficult to ignore the fact that his third wife had borne a child, so therefore must have engaged in sexual intercourse with a man. Although she claimed not to know either that Evans was a woman or how she became pregnant, her speculation that Evans had one night substituted a real man for himself suggested that she and Evans did indeed regularly have sex. One newspaper story reported that his wives did not expose him because they were 'nymphomaniacs', suggesting knowledge of the emerging medical literature that linked excessive heterosexual desire and prostitution with female same-sex sexuality. When Evans's wife eventually named her brother-in-law as the father of the child in a bid for support, Evans testified in court that he had witnessed the two in bed together, but that it was so painful he could barely speak of it.

Evans's story, like so many tales of women who became men and married women, leaves us uncertain what to think.[4] Clearly there was more here at stake than occupational mobility. That Evans loved and desired women seems evident, but did he think of himself as male? Did his wives? What was crucial to the public commentary was the insistence that gender transgression was a sign of mental illness, and in fact the doctors proclaimed Evans cured only when he donned female clothing.

In other cultures in other parts of the world, 'manly women' might marry women without the need for deception. The crucial difference was societal acceptance of gender-crossing or the existence of a third (or more) category of gender. In some Native American cultures, what are called 'two-spirit' manly females are conceptualized as a mixture of the masculine and feminine, a gender apart from either women, men or womanly men. The two-spirit role has to do with spirituality, occupation, personality and gender more than sexuality, so when sex does take place between a manly woman and another woman, it may technically be 'same-sex sex' — because the bodies involved are physiologically alike — but in fact the sex is more accurately conceptualized as cross-gender.[5] Among the Mohaves, *hwames* are women who take on male roles and who are able to marry women and serve as fathers of children borne by their wives.

Oral tradition among the Kutenai of British Columbia tells of a female member who married a white fur trader in the early 19th century but returned a year later announcing that her husband had transformed her into a man. She took the name 'Gone-To-The-Spirits' and began to dress and act like a man and to court women. She married a woman who had divorced her husband, and rumour spread that she had made a phallus out of leather with which to pleasure her wife. When her wife left because of Gone-To-The-Spirits' gambling, she pursued a series of women. With one of them she took up the role of guide for white traders, one of whom described them as 'two strange Indians, in the character of man and wife', although he later noted that 'they were in fact both women'.[6] She became known as the 'Manlike Woman' among the white traders.

Native American societies were not the only ones that conceptualized multiple genders and allowed same-sex but cross-gender relationships, nor were they the only social group in which two biological women might marry one another. In more than thirty African groups woman–woman marriage has been, and in some cases still is, a possibility. As among the Mohaves, a female husband could be the father of children born to her wife from a union with a biological male. In that sense, she is a 'social male'. In at least some cases, such a role involved male dress and occupations, as for third-gender Native Americans. In Nigeria in the 1990s, an elderly Ohagia Igbo *dike-nwami* ('brave-woman') by the name of Nne Uko told an ethnographer that she 'was interested in manly activities' and felt that she was 'meant to be a man'.[7] Although she was divorced from a husband, she farmed and hunted, joined men's societies and married two women who gave birth to children biologically fathered by her brother. The fundamental reason for the existence of such marriages is economic and familial: if a woman cannot conceive, she can continue her family line by taking a wife who will bear children. Women might choose a female husband for a number of reasons, including the possibility of greater sexual freedom, more companionship, less quarrelling and physical violence, distaste for men, more input in household decisions or more bridewealth.[8] We know little or nothing about the emotional and sexual aspects of having a female husband, although scholars tend to insist that sex is

Eleanor Butler and Sarah Ponsonby
were Anglo-Irish gentlewomen who
eloped together in 1778 and settled in
Wales. As the 'Ladies of Llangollen' they
came to exemplify the possibility of close
emotional attachments between women.
Famous visitors to their home at Plas
Newydd included the Duke of Wellington,
William Wordsworth, Sir Walter Scott
and the artist Lady Leighton, who
painted this portrait around 1813.

not a part of such marriages. One ethnographer who spent two years studying
the Bangwa of Cameroon in the 1970s suggested the presence of at least an
emotional component when he described his best woman informant's relationship with one of her wives, commenting on 'their obvious satisfaction in each
other's company'.[9]

A quite different kind of marriage from one in which a partner passed as a
man or became a social male developed in the Euro-American world in the late
18th and early 19th centuries. As an ideology of sexual difference between
women and men took hold among the urban middle classes, the phenomenon
known as 'romantic friendship' flourished. Women, assigned the domestic
sphere of the home and assumed to be emotional and asexual, developed
strong and passionate ties to other women that thrived in addition to or alongside marriage to men. When romantic friends in certain privileged
circumstances chose not to marry as expected, they sometimes formed marriage-like relationships that became known in the United States, because of
their prevalence in the north-east, as 'Boston marriages'.

No doubt the most famous marriage between romantic friends was that of
Eleanor Butler and Sarah Ponsonby, who ran away together from their aristocratic Irish homes in 1778 when they were thirty-nine and twenty-three
respectively. Although Butler, the elder of the pair, dressed and behaved in a
masculine manner, they lived respectably, if eccentrically and not without
occasional criticism, in a rural retreat in Wales for fifty-one years. As the
'Ladies of Llangollen' they came to embody romantic friendship and the possibility of marriage, in practice if not in name, between two women. They called
each other 'my Better Half', 'My Sweet Love' and 'my Beloved'.[10] Visitors

flocked to their home, newspaper accounts described their house and garden, and other women who loved women viewed them as icons of female love. Anne Lister, a member of the Yorkshire gentry who was quite forthright about her love and lust for women, visited the Ladies in 1822 and felt a connection. She concluded that the long marriage between the two women must have been held together by 'something more tender still than friendship'.[11] When Butler died, leaving Ponsonby almost penniless, friends managed to arrange for Butler's pension to be paid to her – in effect a recognition that they had been married.

Anne Lister's particular interest in the relationship of the Ladies of Llangollen may be attributable to the fact that she longed to marry her own lover, Mariana Belcombe, who for economic reasons ended up married to a man. Before the wedding, Lister gave Mariana a ring to wear in place of the one she had been given by her husband-to-be, insisting that their marriage was the real one and wanting Mariana to acknowledge her as her 'first husband'.[12] Despite her belief in her marriage to Mariana, however, she agonized over whether they were in fact committing adultery.

In 1824, despite her continued love for Mariana, Lister visited Paris and fell in with a widow, Maria Barlow, who wanted to be Lister's wife but had to settle for the status of 'mistress'. Barlow thought that Lister, with her masculine appearance, could pass as a man and marry her publicly and openly. 'It would have been better had you been brought up as your father's son', Barlow told Lister, but Lister was not keen on the idea of having no access to women's company, since she found so many lovers that way.[13] Instead, Lister recommitted herself to Mariana, exchanging pubic hair to wear in lockets, and Barlow sadly accepted her 'divorce'.[14]

At the end of her life, Lister obtained her wish to marry a woman when she courted Ann Walker, an heiress whose property adjoined hers. At first Walker described their relationship as 'as good as a marriage'; later they exchanged rings, moved in together, rewrote their wills, and in every other way acted as husband and wife.[15] Although Lister was considered odd by her community, she also held economic and social power. Despite gossip and even incidents in which neighbours witnessed Lister and Walker kissing, the two women lived together without censure.

The Ladies of Llangollen and Anne Lister and her wives and mistress lived in societies that did not have a category for women who married women. Their relationships were nonetheless accepted, or at least tolerated, because of class privilege and because of ignorance, wilful or otherwise, that sexual relationships formed part of the arrangements. In 19th-century England and Wales, as throughout Europe and the United States, romantic friendships crossed the boundaries of respectability if there was too much gender transgression or suspicion of sexual activity beyond kissing and cuddling, as we shall see. But by the end of the 19th century, as the science of sexology began to describe and categorize masculine women and women with same-sex desires as 'inverts' or 'perverts', everything began to change.

Consider the case of Alice Mitchell and Freda Ward in late 19th-century Memphis, Tennessee. Mitchell, a middle-class white nineteen-year-old, fell in

Two Danish friends: until the early 20th century romantic friendships were a tolerated, even fashionable, means by which middle- and upper-class women could express love for each other. While an erotic component might or might not have been present, such relationships offer an important picture of female intimacy in a period before self-identification as 'lesbian' was possible.

The story of Billy Tipton shows that, for some women, passing as a man continued to be an option well into the 20th century. Born as Dorothy Tipton in 1914, Billy lived as a man for more than fifty years, partly so that he could pursue a career as a jazz musician. Tipton married several times and adopted children, all of whom were unaware of his true sex until after his death in 1989.

love with her seventeen-year-old friend Freda Ward (known as 'Fred') and hatched a plot to dress as a man, run away with her and marry her. To this point their attachment seemed, to their families, to fit the familiar pattern of romantic friendship. Then Ward's family uncovered the plot and sent back Mitchell's engagement ring and other tokens of their love, forbidding them to see each other. Even worse from Mitchell's perspective, Ward began to be courted by a man. Early on in their plans to run away, Mitchell had said that she would kill Ward if she backed out of her promise to marry her, and she acted on this threat by slashing Ward's throat on the streets of Memphis in 1892. The case attracted attention from doctors and the popular press not only because of its drama, but also because it seemed to fit so perfectly the newly emerging theory of gender inversion and sexual deviance as inextricably linked. That is, Alice Mitchell became the embodiment of the 'invert' or 'lesbian' in American medical and popular discourse.[16] Her family's strategy for the defence was to have her declared insane, and she died in an asylum.

Across the Atlantic, at about the same time, the Hungarian count Sandor Vay was accused by his father-in-law not only of forgery, but also of fraud, since he 'was only a woman, walking around in masculine clothes'.[17] Unlike Mitchell, Vay was a 'passing woman' who was raised as a boy, had affairs with women and worked as a journalist and writer. His father-in-law testified that one could see the shape of (rather large) male equipment between Vay's legs, and Vay's wife reported that she had given herself to him and had had no idea prior to his arrest that he was not biologically a man. Yet other witnesses testified that they knew the count to be a woman. The doctor who reported on the case to the court was himself confused, finding it difficult to deal with the masculine countess as a lady and much 'easier, natural, and more correct' to think of Sandor as 'a jovial, somewhat boyish student'.[18] At this point the medical authorities proceeded from the story of a passing woman to a diagnosis of inversion and mental illness. As in the case of Alice Mitchell, the emerging ideas of the sexologists concerning gender inversion and same-sex sexual desire came to the fore. Sandor Vay was to Hungary, and to Europe more generally, what Alice Mitchell was to the United States: the embodiment of a sexual invert.

Once women who passed as men became defined in Euro-American cultures as sexual inverts and subsequently as mannish lesbians, marriages between women — whether passing women, manly women, social males, female husbands or romantic friends — had the potential to take on an air of sexual deviance. Nevertheless, some women continued to cross the gender line secretly, to live their lives as men and to marry women. Billy Tipton, a US jazz musician, originally invented himself as a man in order to earn a living during the Depression, but in 1989, when he died, his secret was revealed. He had been married several times and had adopted sons, and none of his immediate family — including his wives — knew that he had been born a woman.[19]

In the contemporary world, women in a few places can actually marry. In Belgium, Canada, Denmark, The Netherlands, Sweden and, in the United States, Massachusetts, lesbian marriages are taking place. Even in India, a society that does not condone same-sex relations, the fact that the Hindu Marriage Act allows diverse communities to define marriage means that some same-sex couples are able get married.[20] In the 1990s in a very poor rural region of India, Geeta, a woman from a *dalit* or 'untouchable' family who was married to an abusive husband, met Manju, an older woman whose masculinity had won her a great deal of respect and power in her village. They came to know each other at a residential school run by a women's organization devoted to equality and empowerment, and they fell in love. As Geeta put it, 'I do not know what happened to me when I met Manju but I forgot my man. I forgot that I had been married. We were so attracted to each other that we immediately felt like husband and wife.'[21] Geeta accepted Manju as her husband at a Shiva temple, Manju's family accepted Geeta as a daughter-in-law, and Manju became both a second mother and a father to Geeta's daughter.

Marriage between women, then, has a long and complicated history. Many of the stories of women who married other women involve gender transgression, whether secret or open. Some take place in societies that recognize more than two genders or, for a variety of reasons, accept the idea of women as social males. There are many reasons why women might choose to cross the gender line or identify with a third or fourth gender, sexual desire for other women

Two Chinese women friends, 1914. In early 20th-century China, the traditional phenomenon of 'marriage-resisters' and changing gender roles met the translation of the works of Western sexologists, casting suspicion on such innocent portrayals of friendship but also creating new possibilities for female same-sex love.

being only one. We know even less about why women might choose to marry female husbands. But what is clear is that women in various places in modern history have chosen to live their lives with other women.

Desiring women

What do we know of women's sexual activities with one another, much less of their desires? This is a question not only of evidence, but also of interpretation. What counts as 'sex'? Kissing, hugging, cuddling? And what about acts that seem clearly sexual from a contemporary Western perspective but might have little to do with erotic desire in other contexts? These are tricky questions. What we do know is that, despite all the obstacles, some record of women's same-sex desires has survived.

Let us begin with romantic friendship in the 18th- and 19th-century Western world, since one of the central debates in the history of sexuality hinges on the question of whether or not these passionate, intense, loving and physically affectionate relationships included sex, by which we presumably mean the involvement of genitals and/or sexual desire and/or sexual gratification. Certainly some of what romantic friends wrote to each other sounds like declarations of desire. There is Alice Baldy, a white woman from the US state of Georgia, writing in 1870 to her beloved, Josie Varner: 'Do you know that if you only touch me, or speak to me there is not a nerve or fibre in my body that does not respond with a thrill of delight?'[22] Or 19th-century Czech writer Božena Němcová writing to Sofie Rottová, a fellow author: 'Believe me, sometimes I dream that your eyes are right in front of me, I am drowning in them, and they have the same sweet expression as they did when they used to ask: "Božena, what's wrong? Božena, I love you."'[23] Or African-American poet Angelina Weld Grimké writing in 1896 to her school friend Mamie Burrell:

'Oh Mamie if you only knew how my heart beats when I think of you and it yearns and pants to gaze, if only for one second upon your lovely face.'[24] Are these expressions of physical desire? Formulaic expressions of friendship? Or sometimes the former, sometimes the latter and sometimes both?

One of the cases that most troubles our understanding of the relationship between romantic friendship and sexual desire is that of Scottish schoolteachers Jane Pirie and Marianne Woods. In the early 19th century, Pirie and Woods fulfilled a dream by establishing a school together in Edinburgh. Then their plans all came crashing down one day when one of their students, Jane Cumming, born of a liaison between an Indian woman and an aristocratic Scottish man serving the empire in the East, reported shocking behaviour to her grandmother. According to Jane Cumming, the two teachers visited each other in bed, lay one on top of the other, kissed and shook the bed. Furthermore, Cumming reported that Jane Pirie said one night, 'You are in the wrong place', and Marianne Woods replied 'I know', and asserted that she was doing it 'for fun'. Another night, said Cumming, Pirie had whispered, 'Oh, do it, darling.' And she described a noise she heard as similar to 'putting one's finger into the neck of a wet bottle'.[25]

One can only imagine the reactions of the judges in the case, forced to make an impossible choice between believing that respectable Scottish schoolteachers might engage in sexual behaviour or believing that decent schoolgirls could make up such tales. As one judge put it, making clear the acceptability of normal romantic friendship, 'Are we to say that every woman who has formed an intimate friendship and has slept in the same bed with another is guilty? Where is the innocent woman in Scotland?'[26] Ultimately, they had to decide whether Pirie and Woods kissed, caressed and fondled 'more than could have resulted from ordinary female friendship', suggesting a line between affectionate behaviour and sexuality that could be crossed.[27] The only way out of the dilemma was provided by Jane Cumming's heritage and childhood in India, where surely, many of the judges decided, she must have learned not only about sex, but also about sexual relations between women – something no respectable Scottish schoolgirl would be able to imagine.

That romantic friendship could indeed contain sexual desire and sexual activity is suggested by all-too-rare evidence from outside the walls of a courtroom. Anne Lister left us the most extensive record of her activities as a 'female rake'.[28] In her voluminous diary, some of it kept in code, Lister wrote of her lovemaking with Mariana Belcombe, using 'kiss' to mean 'orgasm': 'From the kiss she gave me it seemed as if she loved me as fondly as ever. By & by, we seemed to drop asleep but, by & by, I perceived she would like another kiss & she whispered, "Come again a bit, Freddy"… . But soon, I got up a second time, again took off, went to her a second time &, in spite of all, she really gave me pleasure, & I told her no one had ever given me kisses like hers.'[29]

And Mariana was not the only lover to enjoy kisses with Lister. Maria Barlow, the widow Lister courted in Paris, came to her room one night and climbed into bed with her. 'I was contented that my naked left thigh should rest upon her naked left thigh and thus she let me grubble her over her petticoats.

Anne Lister, a gentlewoman from Halifax in Yorkshire, left a remarkably frank account of her infatuation and love affairs with other women at the beginning of the 19th century. A series of diaries, kept between 1817 and her death in 1840, both record everyday events and, in coded sections (such as that shown opposite), refer explicitly to her romantic and sexual relationships with various women. Above: a portrait of Lister by Joshua Horner, *c.* 1830.

All the while I was pressing her between my thighs ... . Now and then I held my hand still and felt her pulsation, let her rise towards my hand two or three times and gradually open her thighs, and felt … that she was excited.'[30]

If Lister is exceptional in both the extent of her conquests and her explicit depictions of them, she is not the only 19th-century woman to have left a record of sexual activities. As Brett Genny Beemyn relates in an earlier chapter, two African-American women across the Atlantic, freeborn domestic servant Addie Brown and schoolteacher Rebecca Primus, shared a passionate relationship in Hartford, Connecticut, in the 1860s. Some of their correspondence echoes the expressions of love and longing of other romantic friends: 'Rebecca, when I bid you good by it's seem to me that my very heart broke ... . My Darling Friend I shall never be happy again unless I am near you.'[31] Yet Brown also refers to Primus's caressing of her breasts and compares Rebecca's kisses with those of her male employers, concluding 'No *kisses* is like youres.'[32]

The stories of Addie Brown and Rebecca Primus, Anne Lister, Mariana and Maria, and of Marianne Woods and Jane Pirie complicate the notion that intense and passionate relationships between women found acceptance in the

Western world in the 19th century because no one imagined that women might indulge in sexual behaviour together. These tales do not mean that all romantic friendships involved the caressing of breasts or the exchange of 'kisses'. But they do open up the possibility that more romantic friends than we know of might have acted on their erotic desires, regardless of how they considered such activities.

Romantic friendship attracts so much attention because literate women often left a written record of their love for one another in letters and in diaries. But other kinds of sources allow us a glimpse into the lives of women whose voices do not reach us directly. In 19th-century northern India, for example, Urdu *Rekhti* poetry, written by men but in the personae and language of women, spoke of love between women. A poem might praise the beauty of a woman's female friend and lover: 'Why should my heart not throb in my breast? / Your beauty is like that of gold.'[35] Relationships between women needed to be kept secret, so poems refer to lovers sneaking into each other's rooms and hiding their love behind the screen of friendship. But the poems make clear – as does the vocabulary used to describe love and sex between women – that such relationships were not unknown. Poems describe sexual acts, including tribadism (the mutual rubbing of vulvas), stroking with fingers, and the use of dildoes: 'The way you rub me, ah! It drives my heart wild / Stroke me a little more, my sweet *Dogana* (woman friend).' Verses also compare female same-sex lovemaking favourably with heterosexual intercourse: 'Let her go to men who wants stakes hammered into her / Can she ever get these hours and hours of pleasure?' Says another, 'There's no pleasure in the world like clinging to a woman.'[34]

Although some scholars have dismissed *Rekhti* as pornographic, we should not assume so easily that representations of love and sexual activity between women, even if intended in whole or part to titillate men, bear no relationship to behaviour. The men who wrote *Rekhti* used the language of prostitutes, making it clear that they had contact with courtesans, some of whom at this time were educated and highly accomplished women. Women's quarters and courtesans' households provided the kind of female space in which love between women might be pursued in an otherwise restrictive society. An earlier commentary on the *Kamasutra* made this point: 'Sometimes, in the secret of their inner rooms, with total trust in one another, they [women] lick each other's vulva, just like whores.'[35] This comment suggests both the private spaces in which women's sexual activities took place, meaning that they left little trace in the public record, and a historical connection between female same-sex love and prostitution.

In fact, the assumption that prostitutes made love with each other, and not just for the pleasure of men, is one that crops up in other societies as well. In his 1836 study of prostitution in Paris, pioneering sexologist Alexandre-Jean-Baptiste Parent-Duchâtelet made the connection between commercial sex with men and sex with women.[36] For although, on the surface, women who had sex with men for money might seem to belong to the opposite end of a sexual spectrum from women who preferred to make love with women, both were deemed to suffer from hypersexuality. That the connection was not merely a fantasy of sexologists is suggested by such evidence as Parisian street songs from the late 19th century. One referred to a famous brothel: 'The girls from la Farsy's place / Are lezzies (*gougnottes*), my girlfriends. / Happy the girl to whom God gives / A real tough dyke (*gousse*) from la Farsy's place.' Another referred to women arrested for prostitution: 'You've got to see this at night in the holding cell, / The little women kissing like mad / On the straw. / And when the sun goes down, / They go down too, / Without a fuss. / It's a helluvah lot more fun.'[37] Such sources suggest that, even if sexologists like Parent-Duchâtelet were wrong when they claimed it was 'repugnance for the most disgusting and perverse acts … which men perform on prostitutes' that was responsible for 'driving these unfortunate creatures to lesbian love', we can nevertheless learn something about sex between women from what went on in brothels.[38]

In describing and defining lesbianism, sexologists have left us some of the first detailed and reliable records of female same-sex sexual behaviour. Despite the filter of the doctors' own intentions and interpretations, women's voices do sometimes break through. In one famous US study of 'sex variants' in New York in the 1930s, women described their sex lives and bragged about their ability to satisfy their lovers. Perhaps playing with both traditional notions about lesbians and the experts' belief in the hypersexuality of black women, a number of African-American subjects boasted of their sexual technique: 'I insert my clitoris in the vagina just like the penis of a man ... Women enjoy it so much they leave their husbands.'[39] Far more reliable are oral histories collected by historians sympathetic to their narrators. In the working-class lesbian bar culture of 1940s and 1950s Buffalo, New York, white, black and Native American butches saw their role as pleasuring their fems, primarily through tribadism or what they called 'friction'.[40] Oral sex became more acceptable in the 1950s at the same time that the idea of the 'untouchable' or 'stone butch' – the 'doer' who did not let her lover make love to her – became more firmly entrenched. As one stone butch from the 1950s put it, 'I wanted to satisfy them, and I wanted to make love – I love to make love. I still say that's the greatest thing in the world.'[41]

These varied sources from different places provide evidence of kissing, the caressing of breasts, tribadism, manual stimulation, the use of dildoes, and oral sex. Sex practices change over time and vary in different cultures. But what all this evidence makes clear is that there is a long history of women desiring other women and acting on that desire. How women thought about what they did with each other, both before and after 'lesbian' became a possible identity, we know less about. Yet women who loved women did, in different contexts, come to define identities that were based on their love and desire.

Claiming an identity

The story of the emergence of lesbian identity has both geographical and chronological limitations, but the notion of love, sexual desire or sexual activity making one a kind of person has more fluid boundaries. That is, the term 'lesbian' has a relatively recent origin in Western culture, but there were other words or concepts that women applied to themselves to describe their desires and actions. Before the invention of the term 'homosexuality' in 1869, Anne Lister saw her love and desire for women as a defining characteristic. She knew the term 'Saffic', considered her attraction to women natural, and proclaimed proudly that 'I love, & only love, the fairer sex & thus beloved by them in turn, my heart revolts from any other love than theirs.'[42]

At the same time we need to remember that there have always been, and still are, women who love and desire other women but do not see that as defining their identities in any way. In Lesotho, for example, a small, poor country entirely enclosed by South Africa, women love other women and engage in activities that seem to a modern Western sensibility to be sexual; yet they neither identify as a particular category of 'sexual being' nor even define what they do as 'sex', which in Lesotho requires a penis.[43] As in much of the rest of the world, women must expect to marry and bear children. But boarding-school girls pair up as 'Mummy' and 'Baby' and kiss, rub each others' bodies, sometimes have genital contact, and jealously guard their relationships. Older

Radclyffe Hall (right) and her lover, Una Troubridge, photographed in 1927, a year before the publication of *The Well of Loneliness*. Perhaps the most influential lesbian novel ever written, Hall's book was the subject of an English law suit in 1928 and was eventually banned for obscenity. Yet the trial also represented perhaps the first time that a fully formed image of lesbianism entered the public consciousness.

women greet each other with long 'French' kisses, fondle one another and engage in tribadism and cunnilingus, all of which they describe as 'loving each other', 'staying together nicely', 'holding each other' or 'having a nice time together', but not as sex.[44] And they are not lesbians.

In other cultures, women may engage in actions that provide an identity, but not one that corresponds to the concept 'lesbian'. At the end of the 19th century in Canton, a Chinese silk-producing area, women organized 'sworn sisterhoods' (*zishu*) and identified as 'marriage-resisters' (*dushen zhyyi nüzi*, literally 'women believing in remaining single').[45] Although there were economic and cultural reasons behind their decision, commentators at the time attributed the phenomenon in part to the fact that women 'acquired intimate friends with whom they practiced homosexual love'.[46]

Once the sexologists had undertaken the process of naming and defining the kind of people who loved others of the same sex, what did such definitions mean to women who loved other women? For some, the medicalization of same-sex love brought unwanted attention and shame; for others, self-understanding and an identity. Jeannette Marks, a professor of English at Mount Holyoke College, Massachusetts, who lived in an intimate relationship with Mary Woolley, the college's president from 1901 to 1937, was one who worried that others might see her as a lesbian. In her writing she denounced 'unwise college friendships', such as the one she had shared with Woolley, as 'abnormal', and insisted that the only relationship that could 'fulfill itself and be complete is that between a man and a woman'.[47] Others were less vehement but worked to distinguish themselves from the pathologized subjects described by the sexologists. In a 1930 autobiography, the pseudonymous 'Mary Casal' described her sexual relationship with another woman as 'the very highest type of love' and 'on a much higher plane than those of *the real inverts*'.[48] In the same vein, US prison reformer Miriam Van Waters, in an intimate relationship with her benefactor Geraldine Thompson from the 1920s until Thompson's death in 1967, struggled to differentiate her own 'normality' from the gender inversion and pathology of lesbianism as described in medical literature and attacked in the women's reformatory that she supervised.[49]

On the other hand, the concept of lesbianism as a defining characteristic allowed some women to embrace their own sexuality more fully. British feminist Frances Wilder expressed her gratitude to homosexual sexologist Edward Carpenter, whose work made her realize that she 'was more closely related to the intermediate sex than I had hitherto imagined'.[50] In *The Well of Loneliness*, Radclyffe Hall had her famous character Stephen discover her true nature when she finds a copy of Richard von Krafft-Ebing's monumental work *Psychopathia Sexualis*. Hall hoped that her novel would help young women like herself come to terms with their desires, as well as elicit sympathy from heterosexual readers.[51]

But it would be a mistake to assume that the experts defined lesbian identity independently, leaving women-loving women either to reject or embrace what was offered them. For the sexologists fashioned their analyses from what they saw around them, including the cases of women such as Alice Mitchell

Painter Tamara de Lempicka fled Russia for Paris in 1919 and soon became associated with the sophisticated lesbian circle surrounding Natalie Clifford Barney. Her portrait of the Duchesse de la Salle (opposite), from 1925, captures the emancipation enjoyed by the wealthy Parisian set in the 1920s.

Berlin was home to a large number of lesbian bars, clubs and cabarets during the 1920s and early 1930s. The city's lesbian nightlife even boasted its own guidebook (*Berlin's Lesbian Women*, 1928), which featured a preface by the homosexual sexologist Magnus Hirschfeld. This illustration by Jeanne Mammen of a women's gambling club (right) appeared in Agnes Esterhazy's *The Vices of Women* (1930).

and Sandor Vay. And in the early 20th century a self-fashioning of the modern lesbian was taking place in communities where women with same-sex desires found others like themselves.

In Paris, the salon of the American Natalie Clifford Barney was the heart of one such lesbian community from the 1890s to the 1930s. A wealthy heiress, Barney wasted no time agonizing over the conclusions of the sexologists. Secure in her sexual desire for women, feminine in her self-presentation and protected by class privilege, Barney flourished in an environment in which homosexuality was celebrated among the elite. In her salon, she gathered around her a coterie of writers, artists and lovers whose works celebrated lesbianism. And she eschewed shame: 'Albinos aren't reproached for having pink eyes and whitish hair, why should they [society] hold it against me for being a lesbian? It's a question of nature: my queerness isn't a vice, isn't "deliberate", and harms no one.'[52] Flamboyant and self-confident, Barney had no qualms about flaunting her non-monogamous lesbianism.

Berlin, too, was home in the 1920s to a vibrant lesbian world. Until the Nazi rise to power, an astonishing number of lesbian clubs, bars, balls, groups, circles and publications catered to women who loved women, and cabaret acts openly represented lesbian love.[53] The periodical *Die Freundin* ('The Girlfriend'), published in Berlin from 1924 to 1933, directed its stories and

Erscheint jeden Mittwoch

5. Jahrgang – Nummer 9
28. August 1929

20 Pf.

Die Freundin

**Wochenschrift für ideale Frauenfreundschaft. – Offizielles
Publikationsorgan des „Bund für Menschenrecht, e. V.", Berlin.**

Bezugspreis im geschlossenen Brief monatlich Berlin 1,40 Mark, außerh. 1,80 Mark. Drucksache
Berlin 0,80 Mark, außerh. 1,— Mark. Ausland 2,30 Mark, Drucksache 1,30 Mark
Redaktionsschluß: Montag mittag 1 Uhr, für die kommende Woche. — Geschäftszeit: 8–6 Uhr
Geschäftsstelle: Berlin S 14, Neue Jakobstraße 9 (Untergrundbahn Inselbrücke und Neanderstraße)
Tel.: F. 7. Jannowitz 4545. — Postscheckkonto: Anschrift Friedrich Radszuweit, Berlin Nr. 151 122

Liebelei / *Karola Neumann*

Heut verliebt und — morgen schon
Weiß das Herz nichts mehr davon,
Liebe auf den ersten Blick,
Ist ein seltenes Geschick.

Liebe, die so leicht entsteht,
Schnell oft, wie der Wind verweht,
Und von dem erhofften Glück,
Kaum ein Hauch nur bleibt zurück.

Leicht entzündet sich das Blut; —
Nimm die Sinne denn in Hut,
Prüf', ob Herz zu Herz sich fand,
Knüpfest du der Freundschaft Band!

Melancholie / *Rico*

Leise tönen Akkorde mir im Ohr,
Im harmonischen Reigen sich wiegend,
Als sängen unsichtbare Wesen im
    Chor,
Im Äther schwebend und fliegend.

Es packt ein erhabenes Fühlen mein
    Herz,
Befreit vom irdischen Drange,
Vergißt es den herben Alltags-
    schmerz,
Doch bald wird von neuem ihm bange.

Wer bin ich? Was tue ich, Wie sollte
    es sein?
Von solchen Gedanken gequälet,
So fühl' ich des Lebens trügerisch
    Sein,
Fühle daß Vieles in einem mir fehlt!

Garçonne
Junggesellin

Aus dem Inhalt:

Annette Eick: Tag des Buches
Hildegard G. Fritsch: Die Magie
 der Modenschau.
Herta Laser: Hände
Beba: Es fiel ein Reif in der Frühlings-
 nacht
März-Horoskop

Marga Kurth: Mariedl
Der Transvestit: Transvestitismus von
 Maria Weiß
Femina - Kosmetik, geleitet von
 Franz Scott. Unterredung zwischen
 Dir und mir — Normen weiblicher Schön-
 heit — Die großen Poren

Roman-Beilage: Ruth Marg. Roellig: **Ich klage an . . .**

The relative freedom enjoyed by the press during the Weimar period
enabled the publication of several magazines targeted specifically at
lesbian women. Both examples shown here featured articles, fiction
and photographs; *Die Freundin* (opposite) was particularly successful,
appearing between 1924 and 1933.

A SPOT IN THE VILLAGE

June 6, 1932

BORED MALE: *"I think I'll call Percy and we'll make a party of it."*

A cartoon from 1932 satirizing the unconventional nightlife of New York's Greenwich Village. A bored-looking man, surveying the same-sex couples around him, says: 'I think I'll call Percy and we'll make a party of it.' Sexual fluidity also characterized the nightclubs of Harlem, where entertainers such as Mabel Hampton (below) performed, and where the blues songs often referred explicitly to same-sex love.

articles to women described as 'same-sex loving' (*gleichgeschlechtlichliebend*), 'homosexual' (*homosexuell*), 'homoerotic' (*homoerotisch*) or 'lesbian' (*lesbisch*).[54] The transnational aspects of lesbian culture among elites is evident in the title of another periodical published in Berlin in the 1930s. *Garçonne* (the French for 'boy' with an added feminine ending, meaning also an 'emancipated woman') catered to a lesbian and male transvestite audience.[55] Both periodicals featured photographs and illustrations of a variety of lesbians: some cross-dressed, some in butch–fem couples, some entirely feminine.

New York was also home to commercial and private venues that catered to a crowd with same-sex desires, and not just to elite women. By the 1920s, two neighbourhoods – Greenwich Village and Harlem – had established reputations as welcoming places for lesbians as well as gay men. Like Paris and Berlin, both districts were also artistic and bohemian centres. The Harlem Renaissance in particular spread word of lesbian love through literature, art and the blues. Lucille Bogan, in 'B.D. Women Blues', sang of 'bulldagger' women, and in fact many of the great women blues singers were themselves lesbian or bisexual. Mabel Hampton, a black performer who in her teens lived in Harlem, described private parties where women who desired women might meet: 'The bulldykers used to come and bring their women with them, you know.'[56]

Such vibrant lesbian communities were the exception rather than the rule, however, for in much of the world the idea that women should live independently of men remained unthinkable. But even where the conditions for such lesbian communities were lacking, the language of same-sex love began to enter the vernacular. In Republican China, indigenous developments – such as the emergence of marriage resistance, the widespread existence of same-sex

Butches and fems socializing in the United States, *c.* 1945. Rooted in an urban, working-class lesbian culture, the organizing principle of butch and fem created a world in which women's same-sex sexual desire could be displayed in public. In lesbian bars and on the streets, butches and fems proclaimed their right to love as they chose.

love relations in sex-segregated schools, and changes in gender roles accompanying urbanization – combined with the translation of the work of Western sexologists and drew attention to the new concept of 'same-sex love' (*tongxing ai*) that had migrated from Japan.[57] A number of women writers from the progressive May Fourth movement wrote about love between women, often telling of relationships between women in school. One such author, Lu Yin, in *Lishi's Diary* (1923) tells the story of a woman who does not wish to marry and whose feelings for her school friend Yuanqing change from 'ordinary friendship' to 'same-sex romantic love'. They make plans to live together, and Lishi that night dreams that they are rowing a boat in the moonlight. Then Yuanqing's mother forces her to move away and plans to marry her off to her cousin. Yuanqing writes to Lishi, 'Ah, Lishi! Why didn't you plan ahead! Why didn't you dress up in men's clothes, put on a man's hat, act like a man, and visit my parents to ask for my hand?'[58] In the end, Yuanqing repudiates their dream and Lishi dies of melancholia. Lu Yin herself married twice, but her writings suggest that she struggled with lesbian desire. She described her urge to dress as a man and visit a brothel, although she feared that if anyone found out, they would have 'dreadful suspicions' about her.[59]

In Japan, too, the work of Western sexologists made an impact, and in the early 20th century discussion of lesbians and cross-dressing women came to public attention. By the first years of the 20th century loanwords such as 'homosexual' (*homosekushuaru* or *dōseiai*), 'lesbian' (*rezubian*) and 'garçon' (*garuson*), meaning a masculine woman, had become household words.[60] As Japan undertook a programme of modernization and urban men adopted Western dress, masculine or 'new' women came to be identified with lesbianism and to represent the threat of social disorder. In this context, tales of butch–fem couples attempting suicide out of love captured the public imagination. Such was the case when Saijō Eriko, who played a woman's part in an all-female revue, and Masuda Yasumare, a masculine zealous fan who had taken on a male name, failed to carry out their love pact in 1935. Their story seemed symptomatic of what one account called the 'recent, disturbing increase ... in lesbian affairs between upper-class girls and women'.[61]

The process of building a lesbian community and constructing a lesbian identity required some level of economic independence and the creation of social spaces, things not available to women in all cultures. In much of the world, marriage to men was and remains essential for women, so that even if a society is tolerant of same-sex female relations, they take place at the margins of heterosexual marriage. In most of Latin America, for example, until the 1970s women who loved women had few options besides marriage or the convent, and even women who worked to support themselves and could refrain from marriage had to conduct their relationships with women in a clandestine manner. The same is true in contemporary Egypt, where women with female lovers seem to lead normative heterosexual lives.[62]

In the 1960s and 1970s, in conjunction with movements for social justice that were appearing around the world, women who identified as lesbians began to speak out and organize public protests, even in places where that put them in a great deal of danger. When the United Nations-sponsored first International Women's Year Conference came to Mexico City in 1975, the press attacked the lesbian presence as imported and alien to Mexican culture, but four years later a group of lesbians promoted their cause publicly at the first World Sexology Congress.[63] In South Africa, groups such as Sunday's Women in Durban, the GLOW (Gay and Lesbian Organization of the Witwatersrand), Lesbian Forum in Soweto-Johannesburg, and Lesbians in Love and Compromising Situations (LILACS) in Cape Town emerged during the 1980s.[64] Today, lesbians with sufficient class or organizational privilege connect at international feminist and gay/lesbian conferences such as those sponsored by the International Lesbian and Gay Association. The Asian Lesbian Network brings together lesbians from ten Asian countries and Asian lesbians living outside Asia, and the Encuentros de Lesbianas Feministas are conferences for lesbians in Latin America and the Caribbean.[65]

Claiming an identity – as Saffic or lesbian; as a marriage-resister, a *garçonne* or a bulldagger; as *bombero* (literally 'firefighter', for butch) or *mucama* ('housemaid', for fem) in Argentina, or as *chapatbaz* (women who engage in tribadism) in Urdu – requires one to have a concept of a particular kind of person with which one can relate, a notion that there are others like oneself with whom one might build a community. Although identity is important to the construction of the modern lesbian, we must remember that there are still women all around the globe who are crossing the gender line, loving women and engaging in sexual relations without thinking of themselves as lesbians.

Loving women

What does it mean to love women in the modern world? As all of these manifestations of relationships between women make clear, there are many and various ways in which women love other women. Some cross the gender line to marry their lovers, as did Edward De Lacy Evans, Gone-to-the-Spirits, Sandor Vay and Billy Tipton. Others – with varying degrees of success – form marriage-like relationships, as did Eleanor Butler and Sarah Ponsonby, Anne Lister and Ann Walker, Geeta and Manju. Some, like the *hwame* of the Mohave people and the *garçonnes* of Berlin, embrace gender crossing or blurring, whereas others adopt feminine personae. Some, such as Alice Baldy, Sofie Rottová, Angelina Weld Grimké and the women of *Rekhti* poetry, express their love in passionate language. Some, such as Anne Lister, Addie Brown and Rebecca Primus, the jailed French prostitutes of street songs, the women of the New York sex study, 1950s butches and fems, and Natalie Clifford Barney made love to each other with hands and tongues and vulvas. And others, in different ways, celebrated their love, claimed an identity and joined together to make the world a more hospitable place for loving women.

Discovering Homosexuality: Cross-Cultural Comparison and the History of Sexuality
LEE WALLACE

Sexuality and cultural difference

The relationship between sexuality and cultural difference is far from straightforward, since sexuality has so frequently been invoked to demarcate where civilization begins and ends. If this is true of sexuality in general, then it is doubly true of homosexuality. While European representations of the sexual abandonment of the East are often dismissed as examples of Western imperialism, historians of homosexuality are frequently drawn to this Orientalist archive for its descriptions of same-sex desires that are more commonly absent or erased from the historical record. Thus Richard Burton's treatise on the 'Sotadic Zone', that region of the globe (supposedly encompassing the Mediterranean and Middle East) in which sodomy is allegedly endemic, Lady Mary Wortley Montagu's 18th-century *Turkish Letters*, with their suggestion of tribadic relations among women of the harem, and Gustave Flaubert's Egyptian letters and travel journals that recount his decadent sexual encounters with Arab boys have become crucial texts in an alternative gay canon. Far from being documentary evidence of oriental sexual practices, these literary and artistic representations are important in that they identify the changing terms on which Europeans understood erotic possibilities between men and men, women and women, in the historical periods that precede the emergence of modern homosexual and lesbian identities.

As many of the essays in this volume lay bare, the relationship between historical instances of same-sex behaviour and contemporary gay and lesbian identities cannot be assumed as self-evident. The closer we examine the history of sexuality, the more we are confronted not just by continuities in sexual practices, but also by the differing social or affective significance bestowed on these actions in different historical periods. Considering the same-sex sexual relations contained in the Orientalist archive more specifically, Joseph Boone suggests that the non-correspondence between sexual past and sexual present might be one of the most politically valuable insights generated by the gay inquiry into the antecedents of homosexuality. In an essay representative of the queer, or anti-identitarian, turn taken by the gay historical project since the early 1990s, Boone argues that the homoerotic aspect of Orientalist writing works not to secure Western sexual supremacy over the East but to partially dissolve 'those paradigmatic fictions of otherness that

We'Wha, perhaps the most famous of the berdaches, photographed in 1885. We'Wha was Zuni, one of scores of Native North American tribes who recognized the existence of 'two-spirit' persons. Generally speaking, both male and female berdaches assumed the social role of the opposite gender while remaining sexually oriented towards their own sex. Yet many tribes recognized them as belonging to third, or even third and fourth, genders – a potential pitfall for scholars attempting to apply Western concepts of gender and sexuality and to non-Western peoples.

have made the binarisms of West and East, of heterosexuality and homosexuality, at once powerful and oppressive'.[1] The unravelling of sexuality in the past becomes a means of disputing the inevitability of the opposition between homosexual and heterosexual that has dominated the 20th-century experience of sex, and which has consistently seen homosexual practices morally, psychically and emotionally devalued in comparison with the heterosexual ideal.

A similar insight has been generated by the cross-cultural study of sexual differences, which reveals the manifold varieties of human sexual behaviour. While the sexual customs of traditional societies have always been of anthropological interest, a focus on native same-sex sexual activity also has repercussions for the way we think about modern Western homosexuality. The differences between metropolitan and indigenous sexual practices have the capacity to undo prevailing assumptions about sexual orientation and identity. Indeed, the comparative study of sexuality and cultural difference has contributed greatly to our understanding of both homosexual eroticism and the social forms that develop around sexual preferences and practices.

The resurgence in the 1980s and 1990s of gay academic interest in the anthropological study of same-sex sexual behaviours was linked, however implicitly, to more general – and specifically Western – arguments about the social acceptability of homosexuality and lesbianism. The wide take-up of Gilbert Herdt's research on Sambian male–male insemination practices among a general gay readership, for instance, reflects this political impulse.[2] By demonstrating the importance of homosexual relationships in a particular tribal configuration, Herdt's study challenged the dominant Western position that homosexuality is an aberrant behaviour undeserving of social sanction. Herdt's agenda-setting study of sexual rituals within the Sambia, one of the New Guinea highlander tribes, provided an exemplary account of a masculinist ideology of same-sex conduct, wherein proper male development necessarily involved the sexual induction of boys by older youths. Among the Sambia, Herdt revealed, young boys learn to fellate older bachelors in order to obtain and ingest the semen they require to grow into physically strong, socially mature and reproductively competent men. Living in the tribal men's house, boys commence this secret initiation process at ten years old before graduating, at around fifteen years old, to the role of semen-donor for younger boys. Later still, these young bachelors take up sexual relations with women as part of their socially prescribed way of life. Thus for the Sambians, homosexual relations are not a deviation from the proper course of sexual and social maturation but a compulsory aspect of a rite of passage into an adulthood eventually marked as exclusively heterosexual. No wonder, therefore, that this anthropological account of the ubiquity and centrality afforded to same-sex sexual relations in Sambian culture would excite a gay and lesbian audience wanting to throw off the derogatory status Western culture has uniformly bestowed upon them.

However ethical or progressive its outcomes, this comparative tradition is increasingly complicated by post-colonial critical insights that dispute the political innocence of relativist accounts of culture and also by the global reach of contemporary gay culture, with its capacity to turn ostensibly different sexual cultures into more of the same. Rather than abandoning this comparative method wholesale, or thinking we can step outside these cross-cultural considerations by insisting on the manifest differences between sexual behaviours and identities within historically or geographically distant cultural regimes, we might learn more by taking a closer look at their origin. By concentrating on three separate geographical areas – the pre-Columbian Americas, sub-Saharan Africa and Oceania – in which the encounter between indigenous and alien cultures explicitly involved conflicting sexual systems, we can appreciate not only the historical distance between earlier forms of sexual behaviour and our own, but also the way in which the ideologies that framed those earlier moments continue to shape the sexual possibilities of the present moment. Considering how same-sex sexual relations were viewed in each of these locations will allow me to demonstrate the emergence of benign attitudes towards sexual variation in the modern era. Insofar as these observations of sexual behaviour on the periphery of the colonial world have influenced nascent metropolitan understandings of sexual practices and identities, it can be argued that modern homosexuality has always been configured across cultural lines.

Sexual discovery in the New World

Rather than looking for the homosexual in history, recent queer scholarship has focused on the development of heteronormative frameworks that would, sometime in the 19th century, see sexual possibilities narrowed into the governing binary system of heterosexuality and homosexuality. This shift in focus from the history of homosexuality to the history of heteronormativity can be seen in several important studies of the early modern period. Although the distinction between homosexual and heterosexual does not pertain in the early modern period, the field of sexuality is nonetheless highly contested in ways that are integral to wider cultural politics and ambitions. The essays anthologized in *Queer Iberia*, for instance, establish that the medieval Christian condemnation of same-sex sexual acts – often personified in the sexually voracious Saracen or Moor and the catamites who served him – was a means of establishing the political authority of Christianity, a religion that was itself organized around the adoration of the male body.[3] The volatile distinction between a sanctioned Christian tradition of erotic male martyrdom and Islamic sexual practice considered to defile masculinity was not just a religious matter but crucially important to other cultural phenomena such as nation-building and imperial expansion. That is to say, discourses surrounding sexuality often assist political agendas that would seem to be entirely separate.

Many commentators now agree that the incoherent meanings attached to sodomy in the early modern period assisted rather than inhibited Western cultural and political consolidation, particularly when these sodomitical discourses were deployed against alien peoples as they were in the discovery of the New World.[4] In the classic Foucauldian formulation, sodomy is less a specifiable bodily practice than a rhetorical figure for improper or unnatural

The conquistador Vasco Nuñez de Balboa sets his hunting dogs on forty Panamanian Indians accused of sodomy; an engraving by Théodore de Bry (1590). The discovery of sexual and gender diversity in the New World provided Europeans with moral justification for campaigns of violence and subjugation against native peoples.

relations. As such, sodomy has no immediate relationship with those desires and identities now organized under the modern terms of sexual orientation. Describing the inhabitants of the Americas, the chronicler Bernal Diaz del Castillo identifies as one of the improprieties of native culture the practice of cross-dressing, whereby boys and men would present themselves in the manner and dress of women: 'Most of them moreover were sodomites, especially those who lived in the coastal and warm areas. Boys walked about dressed like women and engaging in this diabolic and abominable activity.'[5]

Sodomy of this kind features in the Spanish texts of discovery, where it was used to license violent pogroms against the inhabitants of the Americas. In 1513, for instance, Vasco Nuñez de Balboa, having defeated the chieftain of Quarequa and many of his warriors, discovered among this people a host of 'younge men in womens apparel, smoth and effeminately decked' and kept for the pleasure of 'preposterous venus'. Accused of the 'most abhominable and unnaturall lechery', forty of these cross-dressed minions were fed to the Spanish attack dogs.[6] Recorded in an engraving by Théodore de Bry, the finding and execution of these young men who dressed as women and sexually serviced other men bestowed moral purpose on the Spanish invasion of the New World, a moral purpose that was amplified in the aftermath of the execution when, according to the account of Peter Martyr, the surviving villagers delivered to Balboa more young men 'infected with that pestilence'.[7] The discovery and eradication of sodomy, Jonathan Goldberg argues, served to divide the native population into noble and ignoble savages, which allowed the Spanish conquest to be framed as a liberating intervention made at the request of those who suffered the 'stinkynge abhomination' practised by their corrupt leaders.[8] Accordingly, sexual difference became the justification of colonial encounter. Moreover, the violence wrought on the bodies of effeminate indigenes inaugurated a larger system of heteronormativity that had implications for both native and imperial subjects and the homosexuals and heterosexuals they would ultimately become. A number of scholars have recently argued, for instance, that the *machismo* associated with Latin-American cultures is the social outcome of the encounter between different sexual regimes brought about by the Spanish conquest. In the culture of *machismo* specific to Latin America, homophobic contempt is reserved for the anally receptive subject, whereas the sexual aggressor in acts of buggery is thereby considered to establish his unimpeachable manliness.[9]

As these example show, it is the effects of power generated by the cross-cultural specification of sexual difference that are of critical interest. Accounts of the sexual diversity of Native American cultures unavoidably become entangled with other cultural narratives. In particular, accounts of the berdache, the gender-liminal figure observed in many tribal structures, repeatedly test our understandings of the appropriate social form sexuality may take. The word 'berdache' derives from the Arabic *berdaj* and suggests the conflation of male social effeminacy with the anally receptive character of the catamite — a figure well known in Old World categorizations of sexual role and social power, which divided, and judged, sexual agents in terms of whether they penetrated others or allowed themselves to be penetrated.[10] Yet travellers' early descriptions of the New World often stress the capacity of the berdache to combine the traits of masculinity and femininity, and so-called active and passive sexual propensities, in lifestyles without European precedent. While Francisco Coreal noted that 'effeminates' who sexually abandoned themselves to men were excluded from male society and employed 'in all the diverse handiworks of women', Cabeza de Vaca attests to their virility and strength in traditional manly occupations: 'They are bowmen and carry great weights ... Their limbs are stronger than those of other men and they are taller also; they support great cargos.'[11] Though apparently at odds with each other, these accounts in fact consistently demonstrate that one of the ways in which the New World berdache departs from the Old World catamite is in being recognized as a member of a socially coherent minority or subclass, whose contribution to the larger culture is not limited to their sexual services.[12]

Indeed, the social significance of the berdache role has tended to dominate 20th-century anthropological inquiry almost to the point of excluding discussion of the berdaches' erotic profile. In Ruth Benedict's *Patterns of Culture* (1959), for instance, the sexual role of the Zuni berdache is largely obscured by a discussion of the spiritual role or social prestige accorded him.[13] More recently, feminist scholarship has had difficulty sustaining discussion of the erotic aspect of the Native American man or woman who elects to take on the social work and dress associated with the opposite gender but maintains a sexual orientation towards their own sex. Harriet Whitehead's influential research considers the berdache as gender-crossers who take on the gender role of the opposite sex, but, as Will Roscoe points out, in Whitehead's analysis 'social gender is based on the "natural facts" of sex; and since there are only two sexes ... there is no possibility that cannot be defined by reference to male or female.' In such a two-gender system, Roscoe concludes, 'there can be only one sexual orientation, the attraction of these opposite sexes, or heterosexuality'.[14] In taking for granted the correspondence between sex and gender, Whitehead's analysis reproduces the very Western sexual hierarchies and categories it might be presumed to challenge.

Roscoe's biography of We'Wha, a Zuni berdache who achieved a high degree of American public attention in the 1880s, and Paula Gunn Allen's discussion of 'women-oriented women' and female–female 'affectional alliances' among the Lakota explicitly challenge this anthropological tradition and the heterosexual presumption that underpins it.[15] Both of these critics argue against the use of two-gender models when considering gender diversity in Native American cultures that do not subscribe to such a binary system or to the compulsory heterosexuality that is its logical outcome. In the case of the Zuni, for instance, a third-gender or two-spirit role, known as *Ihamana*, is acknowledged. We'Wha's inclination to become an *Ihamana* was first demonstrated when as a young boy of three or four he wanted to dress in girls' clothes and take on the domestic chores of women. We'Wha assumed this female role so convincingly that as an adult, in 1886, he was presented to the president of the United States as an 'Indian Princess'. Known as a shrewd and progressive cultural ambassador, We'Wha maintained a position on the highest of the Zuni councils. This high cultural status was not thought inconsistent with We'Wha's feminine presentation, nor with the homoerotic relations he engaged in with boys and men.

Among the Mohave, the spiritual significance of the two-spirit role is inscribed within mythological tradition. The transformative process required to take on this role includes not only the social enactment of gender-specific roles, but also the symbolic enactment of reproductive function. Thus, in addition to performing the household tasks of a woman, the *alyha* or man–woman two-spirit person regularly enacts menstruation by scratching between his/her legs and, like other menstruating women, retires from social life for the duration of the menses. Occasionally, the *alyha* imitates childbirth by self-administering medicines that induce extreme constipation. The sexual pleasure of the *alyha* is specifically linked to being penetrated anally and to achieving ejaculation while a male partner is inside him/her. The *alyha*'s counterpart – the woman–man two-spirit person or *hwame* – engages in homoerotic sex by rubbing her vulva against a female partner who lies beneath her until she/he achieves orgasm. Although these roles have been transformed as a result of colonization, partnerships between two-spirit and ordinary persons were formerly recognized among the Mohave, and these couples could adopt children.[16]

As these possibilities make clear, many Native North American cultures do not recognize strict male/female dualisms but allow for symbolic transitions between sexual roles that are not determined by birth sex. Indeed, the wider significance of the American-Indian two-spirit figure, and multiple-gender paradigms more generally, lies in their ability to unhinge gender and biological sex, thus enabling forms of sexual morphology that do not limit themselves to masculine or feminine identification and object choice as they are thought to do in Western culture.[17] To demonstrate that even in matters of bodily sex not all cultures are the same, Roscoe points out that in traditional Zuni belief 'a series of interventions were considered necessary in order to ensure that a child has a "sex" at all'. Commencing while the child is still a foetus, these interventions continue after birth in order to ensure that physical sex is achieved:

> The midwife massaged and manipulated the infant's face, nose,
> eyes and genitals. If the infant was male, she poured cold water
> over its penis to prevent overdevelopment. If the child was female,
> the midwife split a gourd in half and rubbed it over the vulva
> to enlarge it. In this context, knowing the kind of genitals an
> individual possesses is less important than knowing how bodies are
> culturally constructed and what particular features and processes
> (physiological and/or social) are believed to endow them with sex.[18]

In this Native American example, sexual anatomy is achieved rather than determined at birth, an insight that dislodges the common Western assumption that while gender is social, sex is biological. Of course, this insight also

In 1835, on his journey through the Great Plains, George Catlin witnessed this ceremonial *Dance to the Berdashe* among the Sauk and Fox Indians. The two-spirit person stands on the right, while his fellow tribesmen tease him but also vie for his attention, which is deemed an honour.

has implications for the concept of homosexuality as a process of becoming, a cultural achievement rather than an evolutionary throwback.

Sub-Saharan Africa and 'primitive' homosexuality

If Native American cultures have become almost synonymous with departures from a two-gender sexual system and the alternative sexualities they permit, it is interesting to note how frequently sub-Saharan Africa has been invoked to demonstrate the cultural absence of homosexuality. In the 19th century Edward Gibbon declared that no same-sex sexual practices occurred in the region, a belief upheld by many writers well into the 20th century who argued that there was no indigenous tradition of such behaviour, although sodomy might have been introduced by the early Portuguese colonizers of West and West Central Africa or, in Senegal and the Guinea Coast, by Arabs.[19] In 1899, in a letter to the explorer Oskar Baumann, the folklorist Michael Haberlandt described a highly developed network of male prostitution on the island of Zanzibar, the origins of which he traced to the Arab practice of training black slaves in effeminacy. In this letter Haberlandt also describes 'contrary-sex aligned women' who 'seek sexual satisfaction with other women', engaging in cunnilingus and frottage or availing themselves of an 'Arabic invention' designed for use in the harem – a 'stick of ebony in the shape of a male member ... which one of the women ties around her middle in order to imitate the male act with the other'.[20]

The idea that Africans are not naturally disposed to homosexual activity, turning to it only through cultural corruption or situational necessity, is also manifest in the work of Jacobus X, a French colonial surgeon, who also doubted that masturbation was known among the natives. In *L'Amour aux colonies* (1893), one of several volumes Jacobus published on sexual perversion, he distinguishes between the 'psychical sodomy' diagnosed in his European patients and the opportunistic vice of the native pederast, who 'uses a man when he cannot get a woman, and, when he *can* get a woman, no longer practices the vice. With him it is not a morbid passion ... it is simply a mutual exchange of kindnesses which are quite simple and natural.'[21] Bringing together the discourses of sex and race, medical anthropology of this kind produced a one-dimensional understanding of primitive sexuality untouched by erotic or romantic sophistication.

The belief that indigenous homosexuality did not exist in sub-Saharan Africa is, however, contradicted by a number of 20th-century accounts that attest to the many and diverse same-sex practices evident in different tribal societies, including age-stratified, gender-differentiated and egalitarian patterns of relations. In the 1930s E. E. Evans-Pritchard, the most influential authority on traditional African cultures, conducted fieldwork among the Zande of the northern Congo that established age-stratified sexual practices among warriors and boys, although he suppressed any mention of this in his classic study *Witchcraft, Oracles and Magic among the Azande* (1937). The anthropologist did not publish his findings until two decades later, in an essay that revealed his informants' claims that 'in the past' Zande princely men regularly slept with boys while at court, and that 'some princes may even have

A **prince** of the Zande tribe with his family. Ethnographers working in central Africa in the 20th century gathered information on many types of same-sex practice among traditional cultures. According to the influential anthropologist E. E. Evans-Pritchard, it was regarded 'as very sensible' among the Zande 'for a man to sleep with boys when women are not available or are taboo'; he was also told that some Zande princes preferred boys to women 'just because they like them'.

preferred boys to women, when both were available'. Zande men gave a bride-price for their chosen boys, who were youths anywhere between the age of ten and twenty, so that they could act as their page, and they paid compensation to other men if they had relations with their boy. Evans-Pritchard's male inform-ants also told him of female same-sex practices linked to the monopoly on brides exercised by rich and powerful men. Among the polyandrous Zande, multiple wives were kept in seclusion and carefully watched for adulterous relations with other men. 'Totally deprived of the sex life normal in smaller homes', neglected wives 'would cut a sweet potato or manioc root in the shape of the male organ, or use a banana for the purpose. Two of them would shut themselves in a hut and one would lie on the bed and play the female role while the other, with the artificial organ tied around her stomach, played the male role. They then reversed roles.' Unlike the socially legitimate boy—husband roles, sexual relationships between women were, according to Evans-Pritchard, not approved by the Zande but associated with witchcraft and bad luck, as was 'any unusual action of the female genitalia'.[22]

In his 1928 volume *Dark Rapture: The Sex-life of the African Negro*, Felix Bryk reported lesbian practices among the Nandi tribe of West Kenya, where women 'satisfied each other alternately' with wooden dildoes. Bryk also claimed that in the same region were many non-masculine men who took the passive role in anal intercourse. Among the Bagishu these 'hermaphrodites' were called *mzili*, and among the Margole, *kiziri*. A much later study of these and other Bantu groups of the greater Interlake region reveals that while many tribes have a word for a man who appears effeminate, the Kikuyu also have a name, *onek*, that specifically applies to a man who takes the active role in sex with other men.[23]

Many early 20th-century anthropologists, when describing what they referred to as 'institutionalized homosexuality' among primitive societies,

Eva Meyerowitz, working in the 1920s in what is now Ghana, came across intriguing but uncorroborated reports that female same-sex activity was prevalent among the matrilineal Akan people. The similarly matrilineal structure of Ashanti (Asante) society also allowed for the acceptance of cross-dressing men who had sexual relations with other men. Here, two *Nkotimse* girls, attendants of the queenmother of Ashanti, hold ceremonial pipes.

emphasized the power-, age- and gender-differentials inherent in these acts at the expense of considering their sexual or erotic profile. Contemporary anthropology, however, tends to recognize that in traditional patrilineal African societies it is heterosexuality, not homosexuality, that is institutionalized rather than personalized. Insofar as arranged marriages are a mandatory practice and the union of men and women for reproduction is a compulsory requirement of adulthood, tribal cultures do not need the concept of heterosexual desire or romance. 'Familial intervention and kinship obligations guarantee that marriage will happen', write Stephen O. Murray and Will Roscoe, and in such societies men can pursue homosexual relations 'provided such affairs remain secondary and socially invisible'.[24] Homosexuality is viable, that is, as long as it does not exclude heterosexuality. Desires for other men can be experienced as intrinsic to one's nature, as they are among the Muslim Hausa of Sudanic West Africa, but they do not release a man from the social and sexual responsibilities of patriarchal marriage and parenthood. Among the Hausa, even effeminate men marry women and have children, at the same time maintaining their more covert identity as *masu harka*, or 'those who do the business' with other men. While these relationships between effeminate and masculine men reproduce the strictly gender-delineated roles of Hausa society more generally, other same-sex sexual relationships are transacted between male peers who do not differentiate between themselves in terms of gender or sexual role. According to Rudolf Gaudio's recent research, these egalitarian sexual relationships between Hausa men, whether they are both feminine-identified or masculine-identified, are referred to by the in-group term *kifi*, meaning lesbianism. 'The notion of "lesbian" sex in a male context', writes Gaudio, 'connotes that neither party insists on a particular sexual role; for example, partners are said to *yi canji*, "do an exchange", that is, alternate between insertive and receptive roles. Sexual reciprocity is but one manifestation of … a relationship in which neither partner seeks to exercise a kind of unilateral power over the other by virtue of gender, age, or wealth.'[25]

Working in the Congo River region in the 1930s, Gustave Hulstaert reported that among the Nkundo tribe younger boys took the active sexual role, anally penetrating their older partners, a pattern rarely observed in age-stratified homosexual relationships in Africa or elsewhere.[26] Hulstaert also described lesbian arrangements between Nkundo girls who played 'husband and wife' and between married co-wives. According to his informants, these relationships had their primary motive in 'intimate love between two women' and were only secondarily related to the difficulty of satisfying female desire under polygamous marriage. Among the Nkundo these women are known as *yaikya bonsángo*, or 'a woman who presses against another woman'.[27] A decade earlier, conducting fieldwork among the matrilineal Akan people of present day Ghana, Eva Meyerowitz heard unconfirmed reports that 'lesbian affairs were virtually universal' before marriage and sometimes persisted afterwards, involving 'perhaps half-a-dozen women' in group sex sessions. Meyerowitz also noted that the matrilineal structure of Ashanti society provided a social incentive for men to become women, and that, before missionary intervention,

As part of the circumcision rites of the Ndembu tribe, boys who have just undergone circumcision retire to a lodge (*ng'ula*) such as the one above. Fieldwork undertaken in the 1950s revealed that during their seclusion, the boys mime copulation with one of the tribe's elders.

'men who dressed as women and engaged in homosexual relations with other men were not stigmatized but accepted'.[28]

Many of these reports are tantalizingly brief, but one of the richest accounts of African homosexuality is provided by the German ethnographer Gunther Tessman, who worked among the Bantu-speaking tribes of Central Africa until after the First World War. Tessman reported that reciprocal anal intercourse (*jigele keton*) among boys regarded as too young to have intercourse with females was prevalent among the Bafia peoples of Cameroon. Throughout puberty, and ordinarily until they are eighteen or twenty, boys satisfy their sexual desires with other boys, whom they approach indirectly via the customary enquiry of 'flowers'. They offer their chosen friends plates of fruit and earthnuts, which the chosen boy accepts if he sexually consents. Tessman also observed this same practice of coming to an arrangement among the Baja and Pangwe tribes: 'One of them gathers any sort of debris, dry stalks, dirtclods, etc., from the village square, puts them in a leaf wrapping and gives them to his friend with the words: "Here is the food I cooked for you!" The other takes the bundle, opens it and acts as if he were eating it, if he consents, or, if he doesn't, just throws it away.' The Pangwe attached a further meaning to such relationships, particularly as they persisted into adulthood, when it was thought that sex between males created 'wealth medicine' but also risked bringing down yaws or leprosy.[29] Same-sex relationships were nonetheless common among peers and between adults and youths, the older men disposed to forming such relationships being described as *bian nku'ma*, or having 'a heart for boys'.[30]

While the example of the Pangwe suggests a supernatural punishment for male–male relationships that extend into adulthood, several tribes from the Central Africa region are known to give male–male relations a positive symbolic role. In his study of the Ndembu tribe, which was based on fieldwork undertaken in the 1950s, Victor Turner revealed that as part of the circumcision rites known as the *Mukanda*, the novice male mimed copulation with an adult male's penis. Among other Central Bantu groups, boy initiates go unclothed as they recover from their circumcision in the seclusion of the sex-segregated lodge and are required to manipulate the phalluses of the lodge-keeper, his assistants and any visitors in order to ensure their own own organs will grow large and strong.[31]

If such traditional practices are subject to erasure under the rule of colonialism, it is worth noting that the migratory work patterns that have become customary for many tribes in southern Africa since the 1890s, and the gender-segregated living conditions that accompany this work, particularly mining, have generated new social forms for traditional same-sex arrangements among both peers and men of different ages. Although colonial leaders condemned these 'primitive' relationships, they were forced to recognize that, in recruiting native labour for the mining industry, they encouraged this conduct to thrive. As early as 1907 an official British report lamented that 'It appears to have become a well-recognized custom among the mine natives recruited from the East Coast to select from the youths and younger men what are termed *amankotshane* or *izinkotshane*. An *izinkotshane* may be described as a fag and is utilized for satisfying the passions. Any objections on the part of the youth to becoming an *izinkotshane* are apparently without very much difficulty overcome by lavishing money and presents on him.'[32]

In 1927 Henri Junod, a Swiss missionary, described elaborate ceremonies among Tsonga miners from southern Mozambique in which a *nima*, or husband, took a *nkhonsthana*, or boy-wife, in a wedding feast in which a brideprice was paid to the boy-wife's brother. Domestic and sexual duties were then fulfilled by the boy, who was rewarded with presents and money The sex between husband and wife was restricted to intercrural intercourse, but fidelity was expected and the relationships were marked by intense feeling and jealousy and could be terminated in divorce. Elaborate rules governed the relationships transacted in these ceremonies, rules that in many cases are enforced by black mine authorities in order to ensure the smooth running of the industry. Although most informants describe these relations as situational, that is, dependent on the temporary circumstances in which they arise, at least one Tsonga informant speaking in the late 1980s claimed that the marriages could extend beyond the term of a single work contract and that some boy-wives even accompanied their husbands home, where the relationship would be acknowledged and accepted by the man's other wives and tribal elders. Such relations were not confined to mining settlements. In the 1950s in Mkumbane, an officially segregated settlement near Durban for black workers who pursued wage-labour in the city, similar weddings between men occurred almost every month, with the feast lasting an

Ndembu novices are painted with a decorative disguise before their 'coming out' ritual. The boys' circumcision and seclusion form part of a rite of passage, during which they undergo a symbolic death before emerging as new adult males.

entire weekend. Some boy-brides wore Zulu dress, others the bridal whites dictated by Western tradition.[33]

Judith Gay has investigated the same-sex sexual friendships that develop among the women of Lesotho who remain in their home villages while their men must remove to neighbouring South Africa to work. These friendships, initiated voluntarily on the basis of attraction, are stratified across an average age difference of five years. Known by the English term 'mummy-baby', they provide emotional support for girls prior to marriage but sometimes persist beyond marriage. Although Gay assumes that these lesbian relationships originate in the 1950s when the terms 'mummy' and 'baby' were first used in this context, Murray and Roscoe link them to the traditional female rulers of the Lovedu, who kept a harem of female wives. Similarly, while Gay confines her interpretation of these relationships to preparation for heterosexual relationships or to substitute sexual activity in the absence of a male partner, Murray and Roscoe point out that they may also be motivated by marriage avoidance, since some women remain 'mummies' well into their thirties. What is incontestable is the emotional significance given to these sexual friendships between Lesotho women. This is particularly apparent when the relationships are considered against the still-practised tradition whereby young girls, alone or in small groups, manipulate their own and each other's genitals in order to lengthen their labia minora and so enhance their later experience of sexual pleasure. As Gay acknowledges, these labial manipulations appear to 'provide opportunities for auto-eroticism and mutual stimulation between girls', which establishes that all Lesotho girls are capable of sexual relations with other girls, even if only some of them later fall in love.[34] This Africanist model offers a highly suggestive antidote to Adrienne Rich's influential 'lesbian continuum' model of female desire — which is, after all, a strongly Western concept — whereby all women love other women to a degree, but only some develop sexual desire for other women.

According to Joseph Carrier and Stephen Murray, woman–woman marriage, in which one woman pays brideprice to secure husbandly rights over another, occurs in over thirty African populations, all of which reserve a political role for women.[35] The key factor in these relationships, however, is not sexual desire but the social status of the female husband, who must have the bridewealth to obtain her female partner. Children are conceived within these relationships by the wife having intercourse with a man approved by her female husband. In all cases the female husband, who remains childless, is the social father of her wife's children, who are regarded as being of her lineage. Although anthropologists have consistently claimed that woman–woman marriages do not involve lesbianism, Carrier and Murray argue that erotic desire is no more or less likely to develop within such relationships than in any other arranged alliance transacted for reasons of prestige. As they point out, 'the very possibility of a formal status for female husbands reflects the divergence between gender and sex in African societies', and this fact alone should check the Western tendency to assume that sex is only — or always — the result of interactions across gender.[36]

Sexual encounter in the Pacific

Although the literature on African homosexuality is sparse, there is a comparatively rich archive describing same-sex practices and departures from two-gender social models in Oceania. This is partly because the European discovery of the Pacific was marked by the rationalist concerns of the Enlightenment, which, in comparison with earlier ideologies of conquest, sought to explain, not simply judge, the sexual customs of other cultures. The 18th-century observation of same-sex sexual activity among indigenous peoples made, for the first time in history, the possibility that similar relations might exist among Western subjects reasonable or rational rather than treasonous or offensive.[37]

The many and varied Polynesian sexual practices witnessed by European voyagers, especially those that involved sexual pleasures between men, were the subject of an intense and sustained scrutiny throughout the years of Pacific expansion and colonization. In Tahiti in 1789, William Bligh observed indigenous gender behaviour in some detail:

> On my Visit this Morning to Tynah and his Wife, I found with her a person, who altho I was certain was a Man, had great marks of effeminacy about him and created in me certain notions which

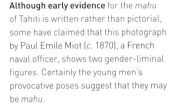

Although early evidence for the *mahu* of Tahiti is written rather than pictorial, some have claimed that this photograph by Paul Emile Miot (*c.* 1870), a French naval officer, shows two gender-liminal figures. Certainly the young men's provocative poses suggest that they may be *mahu*.

During his two trips to Polynesia at the close of the 19th century, Paul Gauguin not only recorded the daily lives and customs of the native peoples, but was also a surprising observer of ambiguous male sexuality. When taken together, these two pictures from 1902 of the same long-haired model – *Marquesan Man in a Red Cape* and *Bathers* – appear to describe the dual (male and female) nature of the *mahu*.

I wished to find out if there were any foundations for. On asking Iddeeah who he was, she without any hesitation told me he was a friend of hers, and of a class of people common in Otaheite called Mahoo [*mahu*]. That the Men had frequent connections with him and that he lived, observed the same ceremonies, and eat as the Women did. The Effeminacy of this persons speech induced me to think he had suffered castration, and that other unnatural and shocking things were done by him, and particularly as I had myself some Idea that it was common in this sea. I was however mistaken in all my conjectures except that things equally disgusting were committed. Determined as I was either to clear these people of such crimes being committed among them, or to prove that they were so, I requested Tynah to inform me, which as soon as I had requested it, a dozen people and even the Person himself answered all my questions without reserve, and gave me this Account of the Mahoos.[38]

The sight of the *mahu* triggers 'certain notions' in Bligh, which suggests that his familiarity with the Pacific has already caused him to speculate about the possibility of male–male sexual activity among the Tahitians. It is these speculations his interrogation is designed to end, and yet, rather than turn up incontestable proof of innocence or guilt of sodomy, Bligh uncovers a phenomenon whose sexual and social meaning exceeds the limits of his experience:

These people, says Tynah, are particularly selected when Boys and kept with the Women solely for the carnesses [*sic*] of the men, here the Young Man took his Hahow or Mantle off which he had about him to show me the connection. He had the appearance of a Woman, his Yard & Testicles being so drawn in under him, having the Art from custom of keeping them in this position; those who are connected with him have their beastly pleasures gratified between his thighs, but are no farther Sodomites as they all positively deny the Crime. On examining his privacies I found them both very small and the Testicles remarkably so, being not larger than a boys of 5 or 6 Years Old, and very soft as if in a State of decay or a total incapacity of being larger, so that in either case he appeared to me [as] effectually a Eunuch as if his stones were away. The Women treat him as one of their Sex, and he observed every restriction that they do, and is equally respected and esteemed.[39]

Bligh's interest in the possibility of sexual relations between men, and in the precise manner in which they are pursued, means that his encounter with this transgressive body, whose masculinity can never finally be erased, however small and ineffectual its 'privacies' are said to be, is shockingly intimate.

Early European records of Pacific encounters likewise describe the gender-liminal figures integral to Samoan, Tongan and Marquesan culture.[40] Like the Tahitian *mahu*, these figures (*fa'afafine*, *fakaleiti* and *mahui*, respectively) have been recognized as comprising a third gender, and their increased prevalence in the post-colonial Pacific is often linked to changes in traditional cross-gender sexual relations, particularly the increased control of female sexuality resulting from Christianization. These effeminate and (to varying degrees) transvestite males sexually service men who identify as masculine, most frequently by fellating them, although these sexual encounters are now publicly denied in ways they were not when Bligh made his enquiry. Since no sexual identity attaches to the non-gender liminal men thus pleasured, the sexual role played by the third-gender figure can be seen to stabilize potentially fraught relations between men and women in a culture where female virginity is highly valued and men's sexual access to women is strictly policed.[41]

The documents relating to James Cook's third Pacific voyage (1776–80) describe the Hawaiian *aikane*, a male figure whose sexual relations with other men carry no suggestion of social effeminacy. Throughout their time in the Sandwich Islands, the expedition's officers encountered socially privileged young men attached to the train of chiefs who served their Hawaiian leaders both politically, acting as their intermediaries in all negotiations with the British, and sexually.[42] This 'Sett of Servants … are called Ikany [*aikane*] and are of superior Rank', wrote David Samwell, surgeon's mate on the *Resolution*, 'and their business is to commit the Sin of Onan upon the old King.'[43] More recent studies of the *aikane* reveal that relations between chief and male favourite do not adhere to an active–passive sexual divide and are socially egalitarian, insofar as distinctions of rank and age between the partners tend to

disappear once the *aikane* relationship is established.[44] *Aikane* are unquestionably men and, moreover, men to be reckoned with. Samwell was particularly fascinated by these intimate practices between men and by the failure of stigma to attach to them: 'This, however strange it may appear, is fact, as we learnt from frequent Enquiries about this curious Custom, and it is an office that is esteemed honourable among them.'[45] Samwell's mention of custom here identifies him as a reflective observer: his inquiries, persistently renewed, are motivated by interest but are morally neutral, as if the actions he observes make no claim upon him. This proto-ethnographic observation is markedly different from his account of the sexual availability of women at Kealakekua Bay, which provokes in him an urbane literary style that draws on conventional tropes of the Orient and places the British subject at the commanding centre of these scenes of sexual provocation, as the presence of a Sultan inflames a harem: 'We live now in the greatest Luxury, and as to the Choice & number of fine women there is hardly one among us that may not vie with the grand Turk himself.'[46] The ease with which Samwell holds one sexual spectacle at arm's length while writing himself into the other is all the more remarkable when he goes on to record how his attempts to discover more about male–male sexual practice were met with a reciprocal question from the Hawaiians, who 'frequently asked us on seeing a handsome young fellow if he was not an Ikany to some'.[47] Samwell's entry for 5 March 1779 goes further, revealing not only that the Hawaiians saw something similar to the *aikane* relationship among the officer elite of the British expedition, but also that they made approaches to these men: Kalanikoa, 'being on board the Resolution to day and seeing a handsome young fellow whose appearance he liked much, offered six large Hogs to the Captain [Charles Clerke] if he would let him stand his Ikany for a little while, such is the strange depravity of these Indians'.[48]

Observations of sexual customs in Australia and Melanesia from the 19th century frequently refer to the institution of pederasty, though they give scant details. At the end of the century, ethnographer R. H. Mathews argued that ritual masturbation and sodomy were endemic to all parts of the Australian continent but more prevalent in the tribes of the Kimberley District and the Central Desert. Among the tribes of Western Australia, Mathews reported that brothers served as sexual surrogates for their sisters until the affianced couple attained marriageable age. Following his circumcision, a young man is 'allotted a boy who has not yet been operated upon. This youth is the brother of the woman whom the man is entitled to claim as his wife. The boy is used for purposes of masturbation and sodomy, and constantly accompanies the man.'[49] Brabazon Purcell studied the role of the boy-wife among the Kimberley District tribes, publishing his findings in 1893: 'They are called Mullawongahs, and are used as follows. The man tickles the boy's penis into an erection, then lapping [*sic*] his mutilated one round the boy's, has an emission.'[50] Purcell also described how, during the male initiation rites, boys were strengthened by drinking semen collected from adult men. These early reports have been confirmed by later and more sustained anthropological fieldwork, which has also provided evidence of a practice among other tribal groups in which a young

A European view of prelapsarian sensuality in F. W. Murnau's film *Tabu*, 1931. The film's opening sequence features an all-male community of Tahitian fishermen, whom Murnau imbues with an almost classical heroism.

man stands as sexual partner to his future father-in-law and, as a reward for taking the passive role in anal intercourse, eventually receives the daughter as his wife.

Although some of these Australian practices demonstrate a continuity with the traditional Melanesian initiation and insemination rites described in Gilbert Herdt's work, they differ insofar as they are not surrounded by secrecy. Whereas the Highland New Guinea tribes maintain the illusion that women are ignorant of all such male practices, indigenous Australian women would openly discuss with outside observers the sexual relations between their brothers and their future husbands. Although early ethnography stressed the ritualized, age-structured and transitional nature of indigenous male sexual customs, native Australian practices also produced a new cultural profile for the European observer. In the Australian and Melanesian reports in particular, same-sex sex acts, rather than pertaining to specified minorities or the members of a 'third sex' (as was the case in Polynesia), relate at least potentially to entire male populations. It is this recognition that male–male sexual relations are a possibility for any man that in many ways continues to energize debates surrounding the distinction between homosexuality and heterosexuality.

As can be seen, Oceanic expansion and the sexual discovery that went with it elicited a new, proto-ethnographic inquiry that respectfully deferred to

traditional practices while at the same time reworking European codes of sexual possibility. The sexual practices uncovered in the indigenous cultures of the Pacific Basin throughout the 18th and 19th centuries were not categorized according to extant models of sexual crime or sexual sin but helped define modern homosexuality as the inherently contradictory thing it remains. D. Michael Quinn points out that while much 20th-century anthropological commentary on Polynesian same-sex customs is indexed, however implicitly, to modern understandings of homosexuality, earlier responses to these traditions were not so consistent.[51] In *Same-Sex Dynamics Among Nineteenth-Century Americans*, he argues that Mormon missionaries working in the Pacific observed the Tahitian *mahu* and Hawaiian *aikane*, and the social networks to which they were integral, and subsequently grafted these models of masculine conduct and same-sex sexual behaviour onto their own highly gendered social forms. For Quinn, the interaction between the American Mormons and the Polynesian cultures among whom they proselytized contributes to Mormonism's singularity as a sect in which homosexual relations are known on terms other than those that circulate in the United States at large. This recognition, as Quinn demonstrates, helps us understand how Mormonism can simultaneously cast out homosexuality and act as its most attentive host: although vehemently anti-homosexual, the Mormon community continues to make a place for intense affective intimacies between men that are devalued in American culture more generally. Although Quinn's research into same-sex experiences among early Mormons has led to his being charged with apostasy and excommunicated from the Church of the Latter Day Saints, this example suggests that the significance of indigenous same-sex sexual practices lies not in their affinity with or departure from Western models, but in the reciprocal evolution of those twin systems.

Cultural difference and sexual convergence

The inconsistency of attitudes towards homosexuality is frequently magnified rather than resolved by cultural difference. Particular sexual meanings coalesce around certain sites; if I have concentrated on forms of sexual encounter in America, Africa and the Pacific, that is not to diminish the importance of other sexual sites in relation to the history of sexuality but merely to insist on the specificity of these three. As case studies they demonstrate that the history of sexual encounter is a history of cultural exchange, whereby different manifestations of erotic desire influence and alter one other. Imperialism has frequently provided the geopolitical context for the meeting between European and indigenous sexual systems; thus, by considering the sexual aspects of conquest, colonization and ethnography, we can trace the transformation of both Western and indigenous regimes of sexuality. These encounters are by no means over, and similar transcultural sexual influences continue to operate in post-colonial spheres around the world, as well as in contemporary gay culture itself, with its increasingly global coordinates.

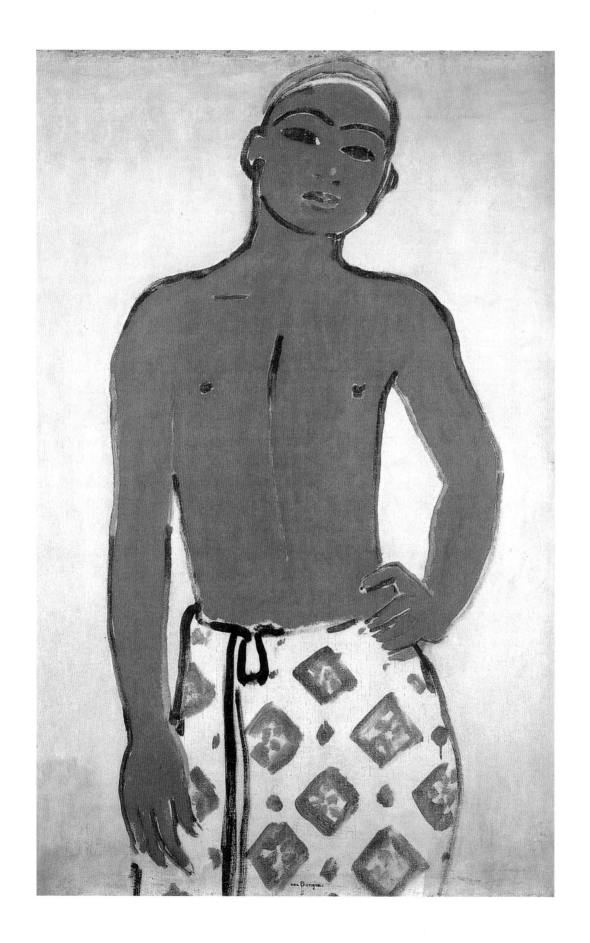

Homosexuality in the Middle East and North Africa
VINCENZO PATANÈ

The Qur'an and homosexuality

The advent of Islam (literally, 'submission') effectively brought about a prohibition on homosexual acts, which seem to have been widely practised in the nomadic and polytheistic societies of the Arabian Peninsula where the teachings of the prophet Muhammad (570–632 CE) developed. The Islamicization of the Middle East and North Africa[1] was as rapid as it was effective and profound, being accomplished in little more than a century after the flight of Muhammad to Medina in 622 CE (the Hegira, the event with which the Islamic calendar begins). Since that time the Qur'an has become the religious, ethical, legal and social point of reference for every Muslim, so much so that it regulates every aspect of public and private life.

As the Divine Word, dictated without human mediation, that which is written (*mektub*) in the sacred Islamic text has an incontrovertible value for Muslims. It condemns homosexuality harshly in a number of places, all of which arise in relation to two principal themes. The first is the story of Lot and the destruction of Sodom and Gomorrah, which the Qur'an shares with the Judaeo-Christian Old Testament; the second involves the prescriptions regulating the sexual life of the believer, which spell out what is permissible and what are considered illicit types of fornication (*zinā*).[2] In all of these cases, male homosexuality (like its female counterpart, which is named only once, in Sura 33:30) is judged to be a base act (*al-fahisha*), to be severely punished. This judgment is confirmed by two of the best-known passages: 'If two men among you are guilty of lewdness, punish them both. If they repent and amend, leave them alone; for God is Oft-returning, Most Merciful' (Sura 4:16); and 'Of all the creatures in the world, will ye approach males / And leave those whom Allah has created for you to be your mates? Nay, ye are a people transgressing (all limits)' (Sura 26:165–66).[3]

Equally severe are the other fundamental texts of Islam, the *hadīth* (sayings attributed to the Prophet, not always reliably): they affirm that 'Whenever a male mounts another male, the throne of God trembles', and that those who commit the same acts as the people of Lot, be they active or passive, should be stoned to death.

Many exegetes maintain that the Qur'an's strong line is justified by the context in which it was written – the Prophet's struggle against the society of

Kees van Dongen's portrait of a young Arab, painted around 1910 while the artist was travelling through Morocco. Like many Western visitors to the Arab world, van Dongen seems to have been attracted by the self-confident sensuality he encountered. Nearly all northern travellers, homosexual and heterosexual, were tempted to project their fantasies of the 'other' onto the cultures of the East.

his time, in which homosexuality acts were used above all as a form of abuse against the weak, such as children, slaves and enemies.[4] One plausible explanation also takes into consideration the difference between the Meccan verses, which tend to be shorter and more forceful, and the later Sura revealed to the Prophet at Medina, by which time Muhammad had already become the indisputable leader of an entirely new society.

The golden age of Islamic civilization: Abū Nuwās

Notwithstanding the Qur'an's condemnation of homosexual acts, homosexuality has at various times played a significant role in Islamic culture, unlike its Christian counterpart. There is evidence that it was particularly appreciated in the courts of many dynasties, including the Spanish Umayyads (756–1031), the Seljuks in Persia (1037–1194), the Mamluks in Egypt (1250–1517) and, to some degree, the Ottomans in Turkey (1300–1923).

The golden age of Islam (*dar al-Islam*) – for which many later intellectuals felt a great deal of nostalgia – comprised the Umayyad dynasty (661–750), based in Damascus, and above all the first period of the Abbasid dynasty in Baghdad (750–1258). The Arab contingent in these cosmopolitan courts played a significant part in political life but were of secondary importance to the Persians, who had a culture of their own and who occupied the key posts of government. This was an urban, mercantile society, lively and opulent, in which every field of Arab culture reached heights of sophistication that would never be repeated. Within this society, homosexuality was a variant of an eroticism celebrated in all its facets; and an adult man might have sex with an adolescent boy, provided that the man took the active role.

During the caliphate of the fabled Hārūn ar-Rashīd (786–809) in Baghdad, the anthology of the *Thousand and One Nights* (*Alf Layla wa-Layla*) – Indian in origin – was further developed and its homoerotic undertones increased. Poets abandoned the usual stereotypes of Bedouin life (notions such as chaste love, valour and courage during war) in order to exalt wine, passion and sensuality in libertine fashion.

Abū Nuwās (757–815), considered one of the leading poets in Arabic literature, moved in this circle, and biographies of his life, which have the flavour of legend, recount his many relationships with boys and women slaves.[5] He lived both the bohemian and courtly life to the full, above all during the four years in which al-Amīn was caliph (809–13), with whom Abū Nuwās shared dissolute sprees. His substantial *Dīwān*, a collection of lyrics, tells of a euphoric thirst for a carnal, secular life experienced fully, one that is satisfied by four things: 'flowing water, gardens, wine and the beautiful face of the beloved'. His most famous poems are the erotic works (the *ghazal*), and the *khamriyyāt*, which praise wine (*khamr* or *rāh*) and revelry.

In his lyrical, if ambiguous, *ghazal*, Abū Nuwās celebrates love for ephebes (*ghulām amrad*) and better yet fifteen-year-olds (*khumāsi*) – although younger or even slightly older boys are not to be disdained, even those who have started to sprout a beard (*muaddir*). His poetry compares boys to pale gazelles, fawns or kid-goats, and his descriptions of the ideal youth conform to

Although representations of homosexual love are rare in Islamic art, a group of miniature painters working in the Persian court in the 16th and 17th centuries produced exquisitely drawn scenes of male seduction. This miniature, drawn by the masterful Mohamed Qāsim Mussavir in 1627, shows the Persian ruler Shah Abbas I embracing a page.

the *topoi* of the age: a supple and slender body, smooth skin, narrow hips, firm buttocks, a face that shines like the moon, hair streaked with ambergris, languid eyes, pink cheeks, pearly lips, a clear voice and musky kisses. The most dramatic situation evoked by Abū Nuwās in his works is the seduction of a Persian cupbearer during a night of debauchery in a tavern. Pages, slaves or the young male prostitutes who spent the night in mosques also suffice: boys, in general Christians or Zoroastrians, won over by the clink of gold coins or with presents. His verses bespeak a burning passion; sometimes the beloved accepts, but at other times he scorns or is scandalized by the poet's intentions. Apart from *ghazal*, Abū Nuwās also wrote more melancholic poems (when a beautiful youth denies him favours, for example), as well as some ironic, licentious and explicit examples (known as *mujūn*).

Homoerotic Islamic literature

Erotic literature, often of a very high standard, flourished throughout the period in which homosexuality played a significant role in Islamic culture. This can in part be explained by the fact that Islam does not recognize the marked separation between spirit and flesh present in Christianity, and in fact values sexual pleasure highly.

In the field of poetry, the Persian Muhammad Ibn Dāwūd (868–909) composed *The Book of the Flower* (*Kitab al-zahara*) at the age of sixteen – an anthology examining the stereotypes of amorous lyric poetry and giving much space to homoerotic verses. The work of the Andalusian Ibn Quzmān (*c.* 1080–1160) is also worthy of note; his 149 *zajal* celebrate a sensual love for boys, expressed in a deliberately popular style and rich with moments of eroticism. Arabo-Sicilian poetry, above all that of Ibn Hamdīs (*c.* 1053–1133), also treated this theme with great beauty and skill.

The subject of homosexuality was still more widespread in narrative prose, particularly the abundant didactic works that dealt with the practical aspects of lovemaking (*bāh*). The most famous Islamic erotic manual is *The Perfumed Garden* (*Ar-rawd al-atir fi nuzhatil khatir*), composed by the Tunisian sheikh Muhammad Ibn Umar al-Nafzāwi probably between 1410 and 1434. Rich with advice on how the believer can experience sex to the full, it does not, however, dedicate much space to homosexuality, although it seems that a chapter on the subject might have been lost. Otherwise, almost every manual discusses the theme. In the Abbasid age, *The Book of the Respective Merits of Maids and Youths* (*Kitab mufaharat al-jawari wa-l-ghilman*), written by Abū Ūthmān al-Jāhiz (777–869), a learned man of Basra, stands out. As the title suggests, the book takes the form of a witty dialogue on the question of whether love for young men or for young women should be preferred. In the end the latter wins out, its case strengthened by the fact that boys – although particularly desirable because 'they do not menstruate and do not become pregnant' – are attractive for only a brief period, until their beards start to grow. Still appreciated today is *The Ring of the Dove* (*Tawq al-Hamāma*): written by the Cordovan jurist Ibn Hazm (994–1064), this treatise discusses the diverse forms love can take, and uses stories, anecdotes and poetic citations to demonstrate the effects of sinful desire, both heterosexual and homosexual, on the individual. *The Meadow of Gazelles: In Praise of Beautiful Youths* (*La prairie des gazelles: Éloge des beaux adolescents*; original Arabic title unknown)[6] by the Egyptian Muhammad al-Nawādji (*c.* 1383–1455) is a collection of poetry that magically blends the erotic and the divine to glorify the beauty of young men, 'the tender gazelles of the frightened eyes'. The most entertaining, however, is without doubt *The Delight of Hearts: or What You Will Not Find in Any Book* (*Nouzhat Al Albab fi ma la youjad fi kitab*), by the Tunisian Ahmad al-Tīfāshī (1184–1253). Written with exceptional liveliness and a sense of humour, it narrates many anecdotes about sex in all its variations.

Although this extraordinary period in Arab literature had reached its peak by the 12th century, the theme of homosexuality continued to be very much present, for example in the poetry of the Ottoman Mehemmed Ghazali (d. 1535), with his particularly daring language, or in the works of the Egyptians Ibn Daniyal (1248–1310) and al-Safadi (d. 1363), who were writing during the Mamluk sultanate.

It is above all in Persian literature, whose classical period began with the Mongol invasion in the early 13th century and ended two hundred years later, that Arab poetry reached its zenith. In particular, we see the emergence of texts related to Sufism, a mystical movement of Islam with ascetic tendencies that did not, however, preclude physical love. In terms that recall the theories of Plato, the Sufis celebrate the love of absolute beauty, which eventually becomes conflated with a love of God and which acts as a form of sublimation to elevate the world of the senses. Although always an indistinct figure, the loved one is recognizable as an ephebe (*shāhid*, or 'witness' of divine beauty), vaunted along with wine as that which makes the pain of living worthwhile.

Particularly important among Persian writers are Omar Khayyām (mid-11th century–1126), whose *Robāiyyāt* expresses a fully epicurean and open sensuality, and Sa'dī of Shiraz (1184–1291), for many the quintessential expression of the Persian spirit, serene and optimistic. In his delicate *ghazal* and the fifth chapter of *The Rose Garden* (*Golestān*), love for ephebes is discussed in spiritual terms, while a sharp, almost pornographic, sensuality pervades his *Jests* (*Motāyebāt*). The *ghazal* composed by Hāfiz (*c.* 1319–*c.* 1390) interweave mysticism with evocations of the perfect beauty of ephebes, which leads to union with the divine. Like the work of Abū Nuwās, Hāfiz's poetry is intoxicated with wine and with love for beautiful cupbearers, who are modelled on the typical Ottoman adolescent: beardless, pale-skinned, with a round face and a slightly pronounced mouth. The greatest of all the mystic poets, however, is considered to be Jalāl ad-Dīn Rūmī (1207–73), who lived mainly in what is now Turkey. His *Dīwān* is dedicated to a wandering dervish, Shams of Tabriz; these intense verses record the unexpected apparition of Shams in the poet's life, their spiritual (perhaps also physical) friendship, and Shams's mysterious disappearance, from which the poet never recovered. In addition to Mansour al-Hallaj (858–922) – a complicated and controversial personality whose works also contain homosexual references –

there is 'Obeid Zakānī (d. 1371), a witty and sarcastic poet known for being nonconformist and foul-mouthed. His work contains many homosexual undertones: *The Book of the Beard* (*Rīsh-nāmè*), for example, plays on the cruelty of the bristles that irrevocably destroy ephebes' faces. He also gives an original rendition, from a gay angle, of the legend of the mythical Persian hero Rostam, who has engages in sexual intercourse with his opponent Human – one of the few examples in Islamic literature of sex between adult males (they also switched sexual roles).

Homosexuality has left a decidedly smaller legacy in Islamic art. Homoerotic scenes are particularly rare, especially since orthodox Islam disapproves of the depiction of human beings. The art of miniature-painting, rather than large-scale works, touched on the subject, most particularly during two specific periods: Persia under the Safavid dynasty (1502–1722) and Turkey between the 16th and the 19th centuries. Working in the Persian court of Shah Abbas the Great (r. 1588–1629) were Mohamed Qāsim Mussavir and Riza-i Abbas, the latter often very explicit in his images, while from 19th-century Turkey comes the *Quintet* (*Khamsa*) by Nevi Zade Atai, which features explicit scenes of penetration. Generally, however, by the time of the later Turkish period depictions of same-sex behaviour are more understated, and Atai makes do with cupbearers in lascivious poses or male bodies sensuously intertwined.

Diversity and common characteristics

Despite the occasional appearance of works of exceptional quality, the 'golden age' of a multicultural and tolerant Arab empire lasted only three centuries, ending with the fall of Baghdad at the hands of the Mongols in 1258. Certain attacks on the artistic and cultural symbols of the old society followed, and the earlier sophistication gave way to different attitudes. An increasing tide of cultural censorship in the Ottoman Empire meant that women were obliged to wear veils, images of human beings were absolutely forbidden and homosexuality was viewed with hostility. According to many scholars, the moralism and hypocrisy of bourgeois Europe (the Victorians in particular) contributed to the homophobia of the Ottomans during 19th century. Only towards the end of the century did any signs of a homosexual culture re-emerge.

In the countries of the former Ottoman Empire, which had been almost entirely Islamic, recent regimes have been incapable either of complete democratic modernization or of reducing social tensions (a situation exacerbated by the Israeli–Palestinian conflict). In all these societies a narrow, bourgeois mentality dominates; inflexible religious institutions and ideas have gained ground, profiting from the indigence of the population (half of whom are under twenty years of age), unemployment and illiteracy (written texts are in the hands of the few).

The situation obviously varies from state to state, because Islam (in which a minority of believers are of Arab heritage) is a body composed of many nations, all with entirely different political and economic situations yet glued together by a shared religion and by the act of belonging to the *Umma*, the universal Islamic brotherhood. In addition, culture and outlook differ widely

Men and boys by a stream: a ceramic panel commissioned by Shah Abbas I for a palace pavilion in Isfahan, 1590. The idyllic setting recalls both the Qur'anic conception of Paradise and the poetry of such figures as Abū Nuwās, who wrote in his *Dīwān* of the satisfaction to be found in 'flowing water, gardens, wine and the face of the beloved'.

between large urban centres and areas of tourism (obviously subject to a greater circulation of ideas), and the countryside (usually somewhat under-developed). There are thus great contrasts within the same country, so much so that it is not unusual to see women with the *chador* and those dressed noncha-lantly in a Western style walking next to each other in the street.

Homosexuality is officially outlawed everywhere in the Islamic world. It is a taboo to which absolute silence is applied, broken only by the voices of authority who flatly deny its existence with harsh, arrogant words broadcast by the mass media.[7] All of this obviously contradicts the reality of everyday life, in which homosexual behaviour is undeniably present, and perhaps widespread.[8]

One can cautiously identify some common characteristics of homosexual-ity in these disparate places. One fundamental observation is that sodomy (*liwat*, a term that derives from Lot) is severely forbidden (*harām*) in every Islamic state, being condemned on all sides: by the Qur'an, the *hadīth*, the *sunna* (traditional rules for correct behaviour), the *fiqh* (jurisprudence) and the *sharī'a* (the law). Homosexuality thus transgresses three codes: nature itself, the Qur'an, and the laws that make it a crime.

Homosexuality is therefore present in the Arab unconscious as a perversion (*sciudud*).[9] In more practical terms, it can act as a disruptive force within mar-riage and can thus upset the established order. In fact, sacred texts locate the only legitimate type of sexual union (*wat*) within marriage (*nikāh*). Sexuality can only be realized through a rigid grid of social and religious rules that lead to the control of desire and sexual drives.[10] Certain fundamental principles (present also in Christianity) must be respected: virginity, sex only between those of different sexes and only within marriage, and intercourse primarily for the purposes of procreation.

Islamic culture is masculinist and strongly hierarchical, with the two sexes living their daily lives in separate worlds, interacting only in certain circum-scribed cases. Everything is played out according to the two opposing but complementary poles of male (*dhakar*) and female (*ountha*). They allow no ambiguity of interpretation: all signs must be unequivocal, beginning with the exterior tokens of gender displayed by the individual (hence the frequent wearing of beards and moustaches). This is fundamental, because from the sphere of the *dhakar* arises the concept of the man (*ragiul*), and all other beings that are 'not-man' are subject to him: women, concubines, boys,[11] slaves, servants, eunuchs, transvestites, hermaphrodites (*khunta*) and even infidels (*kafir*). Love or sentiment do not always accompany acts practised with infe-rior partners, since an emotional detachment is present from the start.[12]

According to this viewpoint, homosexuality acts as a prop to the narcissistic values of virility. In theory, the Islamic man does not have any problems of identity when he has sex with a man, woman or adolescent – provided that he adopts the active role proper to a man. On a physical level, this is sealed by pen-etration, the crucial act around which Arab eroticism revolves. Ejaculation echoes penetration, and the speed at which it is attained is interpreted as a sign of virility (*muruwa*). In the homosexual sphere, intercrural sex and mastur-bation (*kaffat*) are also widespread. Fellatio (*mess el zobe*), however, is not generally valued, principally on account of the belief that the genitals are 'dirty'.[15] Any contact with bodily secretions – obviously including sperm (*mani*) and menstrual blood – leads to impurity (*janāba*), so that after all sexual relations a purifying bath (*ghusl*) is required.

It would be wrong to suggest a general inhibition about identifying as homosexual, inasmuch as no such concept of a 'homosexual identity' exists in Arab culture: instead, the Western polarity of heterosexual/homosexual is replaced by that of active/passive, a distinction based only on the role taken during sexual intercourse. Going to bed with someone of the same sex does not equate with being gay, but merely with engaging in homosexual sex. The act exists only in itself, although it must take place in secret: social visibility (or the lack of it) is of the utmost importance. Homosexuality is expressed therefore only in deed, while every exterior manifestation of it is precluded. Paradoxically, the silence that surrounds the subject heightens the importance of body language and of intriguing glances even further, greatly intensifying desire. This situation gives rise to a most seductive type of eroticism – very different from that of the West, which is as brazen on some occasions as it is disguised by overly sophisticated mechanisms on others. It is not unusual to see two men calmly walking hand-in-hand on the street or, in Tunisia, to see young men wearing bunches of heavily scented jasmine behind their ears as a symbol of virility, although neither gesture necessarily has a homosexual overtone. This eroticism finds its full expression in the *hammam*. Although it is difficult to see completely nude bodies and sex rarely takes place, for some everything in this symbolic space expresses an intense, sensual carnality: the

In the early 20th century a flourishing market for pseudo-ethnographic postcards such as this helped perpetuate the myth of Eastern sensuality and sexual availability to northern Europeans. This postcard of an Arab boy was produced by Lehnert and Landrock around 1910.

labyrinthine form of the *hammam*; its corridors, heat and vapours; sweat, spicy perfumes, mud (*rassoul*) and the masseur (*kessal*).[14]

Homosexual acts are therefore widely practised, albeit completely in secret (like lesbian practices – *musāhaqa* or *sihaq* – which are thought to be widespread, but about which little is known[15]). They manifest themselves above all in certain traditional situations endorsed by society, such as in Qur'anic schools (*m'sid* or *jamā*) where the teacher (*meddeb* or *faqih*) might inflict corporal punishment at will or subject pupils to his own desires. According to Abdelhak Serhane, this 'pure and simple rape in a holy place' is accepted with fatalism by the child's family, who are comforted by the popular belief that 'he who wants to learn must pass beneath the master', and that 'the sperm of the *faqih* includes a dose of intelligence and divine benediction'.[16] Another self-evident situation (a result of the strict segregation of the sexes until marriage) is one in which many teenage boys discover sex with older boys or mature men, who inevitably force them to adopt the passive role. This phenomenon (of which many are aware) is officially condemned by society, perhaps on a moral rather than a legal level. In actual fact, however, this initiation of young boys into sexuality is socially accepted and not considered a tragedy by a culture that sees a manifest expression of superiority in the act of penetration, fully compatible with the different social roles of the adolescent and the adult.

One could maintain, therefore, that relations in some Muslim societies are almost reminiscent of the ancient Greek relationship between the sexually active man (*erastes*) and the passive teenage boy (*eromenos*). (In Classical times – in contrast to Islamic culture – this relationship had a sense of ritual initiation and of the transmission of indispensable values.) The norm is that young boys are used by neighbourhood friends until about the age of sixteen or seventeen, when they are no longer solicited.[17] This behaviour does not stop with adolescence, however: once they are older, many continue to have relationships with younger members of their own sex. If carried out with discretion and with the older man in the active role (*luti* or *louat*), these relationships are tolerated by society, particularly when they occur behind the façade of heterosexual marriage.

Entirely different attitudes, on the other hand, meet those who continue to seek sex exclusively with men (certainly not just a few – numbers may not be dissimilar to those in Western society). Men who manage to avoid marriage (very few in number) are judged severely, since celibacy (*zufri*) is considered an act highly offensive to society. The greatest blame, however, is reserved for adult men who adopt the passive role regardless of who their partners might be, since it is maintained that passivity damages virility irreversibly. All expressions used to define the passive partner – such as *zamel*, *hassass* or *attai*[18] – express strong disdain and describe an inferior completely stripped of the status of 'man'. There being no room for a social identity, passive homosexuals must live out their relationships, whatever they may be, in absolute invisibility. Bound by an iron social control that begins with his neighbours, the *zamel* is forced to live in hiding, with a constant sense of shame (*hchouma*) and guilt (*khata*) exacerbated by the injustices and blackmailing that he experiences. He is thus like a ghostly figure wandering in the margins of society, with no chance of planning a life outside of society's unbreakable laws.

Paradoxically, effeminate homosexuals or transvestites (*mukhannath*), although mocked and harassed by all, in some ways enjoy a greater freedom. In Morocco, for example, popular belief maintains that their effeminacy is due to possession by a feminine spirit (*djinn*); meetings are held in religious sanctuaries in order to chase it away. There, for two weeks, the *mukhannath* may give vent to their feminine side with their family's approval, dressing themselves in *jellaba* and making themselves up with henna and jewels. Practising their sexuality, they enjoy a socially condoned experience that frees them a little from the misery of everyday life.

The Maghreb

The countries of the Maghreb – excluding Algeria, gripped by the aftermath of civil war, and Libya, hampered for decades by a repressive regime – are those in which homosexuality has a margin, albeit a narrow one, in which to express itself.[19] The tourist sex trade is one of the most obvious aspects of this freedom, and it is normal for Western tourists to be accosted on the street by youths who suggest sex. Since the huge demographic explosion and rising unemployment of the last two decades, and as a result of globalization, Maghrebin society has turned a blind eye to the practice whereby many youths exploit their sexual performance (also in the heterosexual arena) in order to earn money[20] and to

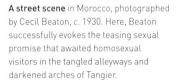

A street scene in Morocco, photographed by Cecil Beaton, *c.* 1930. Here, Beaton successfully evokes the teasing sexual promise that awaited homosexual visitors in the tangled alleyways and darkened arches of Tangier.

obtain a visa, thus freeing themselves from societies that offer an uncertain future to try their fortune in the fascinating and tempting countries of the West. A complex phenomenon, this is the fruit of the 'cultural homogenization' astutely predicted by Pier Paolo Pasolini in the early 1970s. Captivated by the myth of the West, these youths are robbed of their own culture – some believe only superficially in religion, for example – but are excluded from ours, of which they often consume only the most meagre crumbs.

Upon contact with Europeans, the Maghrebin youths begin to change their own customs. Today almost all understand the terms 'homosexual' and 'gay', once unknown within their culture, and they speak naturally about the subject. In addition, they are progressively mastering the rules that govern appearance in the West: they now know how to attract attention by emphasizing their physique and their clothing. At the same time, however, the youths give the impression that they use different criteria to judge physical beauty, and that they are more interested in the spiritual (and economic) qualities of their partner than in his body. Contact with Westerners is also causing them to modify their sexual behaviour, which they change upon request. Young men are in fact more frequently accepting of penetration, albeit after some initial reluctance (perhaps in order to increase the recompense). It is becoming more common to find those who are happy to play both active and passive roles, thus freeing themselves from the perceived shame of offering their 'arses' (*terma* or *zouk*): these are the so-called *nuba*, a word that is used in jargon to indicate versatility in the sexual act. Many, on the other hand, firmly convinced that the European will always be passive, limit themselves to the active role, vigorously refusing to adopt passivity for fear of being seen to lose their virile reputation. Thus relations habitually conclude with the penetration of the Westerner who, while no doubt excited by the supple bodies of the youths, often remains disappointed by the mechanical speed of the act.

The reasons why young men have sex with Europeans are varied: many do it only for money, affirming – like many Western rent boys – that they do not enjoy it and that they are attracted only to women (often the request for money is little more than a means of self-justification); there are those who admit to a certain enjoyment in having sex with men; and there are those who readily declare themselves gay (although they only ever identify the Westerner, *rumi*, as 'homosexual' for the simple reason that he takes the passive role).

On a more general level, traditional customs are being eroded, albeit slowly, by the presence of Westerners and by the process of modernization. In some large cities, such as Casablanca, Rabat or Tunis, and in areas popular with tourists, heterosexual practices formerly inconceivable (like premarital sex or having more than one partner) are beginning to spread. Unprecedented opportunities have also arisen for gay socializing (a prospect that locals obviously approach with caution), which the police periodically try to stifle. There are many meeting places – cafés, bars and nightclubs – that are becoming ever more crowded. There are signs, too, of a burgeoning gay community, with many young men living out their sexuality in an untroubled way and often trying out longterm relationships. This is an absolute novelty, although cases of cohabitation – almost inconceivable in Maghreb society – are still very rare.

The democratic press is also beginning to fall into line. In March 2002 the Moroccan *L'Indépendant Magazine* published a cover story entitled 'Les gays marocains font leur coming-out', outlining how gay Moroccans' way of life is changing thanks to the internet. In 2004 Casablanca's monthly *Tel Quel* published 'Être homosexuel au Maroc', a substantial article that made it clear how difficult it is for homosexuals to live there.[21]

Egypt, Turkey and the Middle East

Egypt and Turkey have always been open to multiple types of eroticism. In Egypt, this attitude is historical: Gustave Flaubert wrote of watching a show put on by transvestite dancers, as well as an act of sodomy in a *hammam*. In Turkey, homosexuality played a fundamental role in the court of the Ottomans, where the sultan and the ruling class (most of whom had originally been Christian slaves, or *kullar*) had pages (*iç oghlanlari*) of great physical ability – also originally foreigners – whom they used for pleasure. There existed a strong tradition of transvestites (called *köçek*), some of whom were seen by Lord Byron and his friend John Cam Hobhouse in 1810, dancing in a tavern in Galata.[22] This easygoing attitude benefited the tourist trade (including the sex trade), which was attracted by two cosmopolitan cities – Constantinople and Alexandria (the city of Constantine Cavafy) – with flourishing cultures and the potential for every type of sensual experience.

As a geographical hinge between the two worlds of the Maghreb and the Middle East (known as the Mashriq), Egypt has for centuries occupied a middle ground. Of late, however, the situation has changed, as was demonstrated dramatically by the arrest in 2001 of fifty-two Egyptians in a gay nightclub, an event that was reported around the world. The defendants were described as 'the shame of the nation', and twenty-three were sentenced to up to five years' hard labour for committing 'sexually deviant acts, shaming the Islamic religion and spreading depraved and obscene ideas'. The trial was followed with great interest by the whole country. In court, the prosecutor exclaimed that 'Egypt will not be used for the defamation of manhood and will not be a hub for gay communities.'[23]

Life for Egyptian homosexuals is now therefore much more difficult. This is partly a result of the ongoing struggle, more political than religious, between the government and followers of Sunni conservatism. (Although Egypt is, in theory, a secular state, very often government policy is dictated by the views of Sunni religious leaders.) The University of Al-Azhar, the most important Sunni religious institution – and among the most conservative – is located in Egypt. It is here that the majority of imams study; they in turn help create a climate favourable to certain political parties through their ever more rigorous *fatwa*: the enormous uproar over adultery and homosexuality is thus a means of reinforcing power and control. In addition, one can read this increasingly repressive stance as an attempt to divert attention from Egypt's economic crisis and as a result of tensions arising from the Israeli–Palestinian conflict.

Turkey is also in a delicate situation. Although secularized by Atatürk's reforms, the country has continued to observe Islamic laws that regard the passive homosexual (*ibne*) with disapproval but are more tolerant towards the active partner (*kulampara*), above all when he is married. These attitudes notwithstanding, homosexual acts are indeed practised among Turks, admittedly with great discretion.[24] In recent years Turkish society, caught in a struggle between secular and fundamentalist groups, is opening up on many fronts. Young Turkish gays are more and more Westernized, and some of the country's most popular singers are also gay. Although persecuted by the police, Lambda (a gay movement founded in 1993) organized a Gay Pride parade in 2003 and was recently invited by the parliament to work on a new law guaranteeing homosexuals minimum rights. At the same time Istanbul, a city that exudes eroticism like few others, continues to be one of the most popular destinations for Western homosexuals – in particular the district of Taksim (which is also the centre of prostitution). Turkey, and Egypt, are thus poised between the denial of homosexuality that stems from fundamentalism and the complete adoption of Western lifestyles. It remains to be seen whether they will become drawn into prolonged conflict with the West or act as a dam against the waves of a new religious obscurantism.

Together with Iraq, Egypt and Turkey are the only states without explicitly anti-homosexual statutes in their law codes. Elsewhere in the Islamic world homosexual acts are subject to severe sentences, generally running from a minimum of six months' to ten years' imprisonment. Within this framework two different approaches can be discerned, however: on the one hand, those states closer to the Mediterranean – Lebanon, Jordan and Syria[25] – enjoy a certain freedom, reasonably comparable with that found in the Maghreb. Palestine is an entirely different story, obviously beset by other problems; in recent times it has become very anti-homosexual, with cases of arrest and torture by the police. On the other hand are those states where *sharī'a* law is in force. In some of these – Saudi Arabia, Yemen, Iran and the United Arab Emirates – the death penalty can be applied for homosexual acts by such means as stoning, decapitation, throat-slitting, burning at the stake, cutting the condemned in two with a scimitar, throwing them off a cliff or crushing them under a toppled wall. If up until some years ago the repression of homosexuality was not particularly common – partly because the school of law used in Saudi Arabia specifies that, in theory, there must be four eyewitnesses to an act of penetration, an improbable circumstance – since the 1990s it has become much more frequent.

Iran has the severest penalties for homosexual acts. Before the Islamic Revolution there existed a tradition of sexual relations between adults and adolescents; and Tehran was perhaps the only Muslim city to boast a gay subculture and some freedom of expression, a situation accepted by the country's liberals. With the rise of fundamentalism, however, everything has changed: the law takes no pity on homosexuals and even mutual masturbation can lead to the death penalty. It is estimated that since 1979 more than 4,000 people have been put to death for homosexuality.[26]

The situation is not much better in the Gulf States. Here, homosexual relations, although widespread, are nevertheless conducted underground or by means of various types of subterfuge.[27] In fact, while the wealthy classes commit every sort of transgression in their princely homes or in luxury hotels overseas, others must live under rigid Qur'anic laws and are punished for homosexuality by death. In Yemen and above all Saudi Arabia decapitations or floggings are numerous. These latter punishments are rather more rare in the other countries of the Arabian Peninsula (where it is nonetheless essential for homosexuals not to cause a scandal): Kuwait, Bahrain, Qatar, the United Arab Emirates and Oman, traditionally the most liberal country.[28]

Iraq and Afghanistan are undergoing a period of transition in the aftermath of strict, totalitarian regimes. While Saddam Hussein's Iraq did not particularly target homosexuals, the Taliban persecuted homosexuality with great force, even instituting a 'Ministry for the Promotion of Virtue and Prevention of Vice'. In Afghan culture men and women have often been highly segregated (partly owing to the harsh terrain and climate of the mountains, where many men spend much of the year), and by the 19th century it had become commonplace for Pashtun tribes to sing love songs about youths. Since the fall of the Taliban, one particular custom has returned – that of young boys (*ashna* or *haliq*) satisfying the sexual appetites of rich Pashtun tribesmen, who are nevertheless almost always married. Predictably, the new government has immediately outlawed sexual relations with minors.

Homosexuality in recent Arab culture

Given the legal situation outlined above, it is not surprising that few Muslims in these countries dare question the status quo; during the last one hundred years homosexuality in Arab countries has only rarely been examined from the inside. Those who have done so have often personally paid a price: the Algerian writer Malek Chebel was greeted with hostility from his government when he produced *L'esprit de sérail* (1988), a work that courageously confronted themes that are considered taboo; and the Moroccan Abdelhak Serhane went into self-imposed exile after his work *L'amour circoncis* (1995) vehemently attacked cultural and religious norms and phobias about sex. He had challenged the untouchable figure of the patriarch: though nothing compared with God, an omnipotent deity to his own family members.

In the 1950s many were taken aback by the Moroccan Driss Chraïbi's celebrated novel *Le passé simple*, which denounced society's skewed value system. While writers like Chraïbi who investigate the theme of homosexuality are rare, the subject nonetheless appears in various forms in the work of several other authors: the Algerians Rachid Boudjedra (*La répudiation*) and Ali Ghanem; the Egyptians Naguib Mahfouz and Albert Cossery; the Tangier writers Mohamed Choukri and Mohamed Mrabet; and the Syrian Ammar Abdulhamid. The verses of Iradj Mirza, who was active in Iran at the beginning of the 20th century, also refer frequently to his attraction to young men.

In the world of cinema, films on the subject of homosexuality are obviously few, although co-productions with European partners – France or Belgium, for example – have made things easier. One such example is the Algerian Abdelkrim Bahloul's *The Assassinated Sun* (*Le soleil assassiné,* 2003), which reconstructs the tragic story of the homosexual Algerian poet Jean Sénac (killed in 1973), who hoped for a new world without cultural or sexual discrimination and who praised the country's youth for their honest and untramelled natures. Otherwise, almost all home-produced films in Arab countries have necessarily limited themselves to veiled hints, in a situation that is somewhat reminiscent of European cinema in the 1950s and 1960s.

The majority of these films come from Egypt: always the cultural beacon of the Arab world, it is known especially for popular music (the extraordinary bisexual singer Umm Kulthūm,[29] for example, not to mention many present-day pop stars) and television (almost all of the TV adaptations shown in Arabic-speaking countries are made in Egypt). Many Egyptian films deal with the theme of transvestism in a way that strips it of some of its seriousness, showing women dressed as men, as in Ahmed Galal's *Daughter of the Pasha in Charge* (*Bint el-bash el-mudir*, 1938), or drag queens, such as the very funny *Miss Hanafi* (*Al Anissa Hanafi*, 1954) directed by Fatin Abdel Wahab. Another genre comprises films on the subject of the *khawalat* – transvestite dancers who until the end of the 1950s worked in brothels as prostitutes' servants or taught belly-dancing. One of the most famous of these films is *Alley of the Pestle* (*Zuqāq al-Midaqq*, 1963) by Hassan Al-Imam – a dim rendering of Naguib Mahfouz's novel of the same name, in which the figure of the *khawal* is viewed with some sympathy.

Among the cinematic works that deal with the subject of homosexuality in the Islamic world, *Man of Ashes* (1986) by Tunisian director Nouri Bouzid is one of the most powerful. The film examines the figure of the powerful father in Arab culture and questions notions of Arab masculinity.

The film that contains the most obviously homoerotic scene is surely Salah Abou Seif's *The Malatily Bath* (*Hammam al-Malatily*, 1973), in which the young protagonist is seduced by an older man he meets in a *hammam*. Gay situations also feature in the work of the veteran filmmaker Youssef Chahine, one of the greatest living directors. *Alexandria ... Why?* (*Iskanderija ... Lih?*, 1979), which opened his *Alexandria Trilogy*, contained subtle references to homosexuality; *An Egyptian Story* (*Hadduta Misrija*, 1982) followed; and the final instalment — the excellent *Alexandria Again and Forever* (*Iskanderija, kaman oue kaman*, 1990) — centres on a director, played by Chahine himself, who is enchanted by a young actor whom he has chosen for the part of Alexander the Great.

Tunisian cinema — where censorship is moderately lenient — is also one of the most sensitive to the theme of homosexuality. The most noteworthy film to treat the subject is probably *Man of Ashes* (*Rih Essed*, 1986) by Nouri Bouzid, which describes the overbearing interference of the father figure in Arab countries. It tells the story of a young man from Sfax who was raped as a teenager, together with a friend, by a man for whom he worked, and who dreams of relationships with people of his own sex. Constrained by society to marry, he rebels against paternal dominance on the very day of his wedding, thus revealing the emptiness hiding behind the arrogance of the Arab patriarch, in reality eaten up with repression and anguish.

Similar to Bouzid's *Man of Ashes* is *The Citadel* (*El Kaala*, 1988), directed by the Algerian Mohamed Chouikh. Here, too, within the setting of an Algerian village, the dominant model of virility is linked to a despotic power, wielded both on a familial and on a wider social level. Thus when the young Kaddour, sensitive and kind, refuses to conform to the views of the village's macho bully, he is labelled a homosexual or 'non-man'. He is punished by his fellow townsfolk with a farcical marriage to a mannequin amid mocking laughter.

This anonymous painting of three male prisoners, probably executed by a French artist around 1930, exemplifies the more lurid Western fantasies of Eastern exoticism, with their overtones of sexual transgression.

Two stills from *Hamam: The Turkish Bath* (1997), by Turkish-Italian director Ferzan Özpetek. Revolving around the relationship between an Italian man and a Turkish youth, the film sites this meeting of two cultures in a *hamam*, a traditional – and much mythologized – environment for male socializing and homoerotic potential.

The view from the West

The problem of discussing homosexuality openly in Islamic societies has meant that almost all recent studies of the subject have come from the West, where many Muslims now live. Numerous articles have been published: most notable are those in 'Les arabes et nous', a celebrated special issue of *Recherches*, the journal edited by the political activist Félix Guattari, that appeared in March 1973. Militants from the French gay group FHAR and many prestigious writers collaborated on the magazine, although all of the articles were carefully kept anonymous. The issue concentrated on homosexuality and Arabs – in particular the *beurs*, French people of Maghrebin origin – and their relationships (almost always for money) with Europeans. The originality of the topic and the frank way in which sex was discussed caused a scandal: almost all copies were immediately confiscated, making it a rarity today.

There are many narrative works on the topic of homosexuality. France produces the majority of these books, thanks to numerous *beur* writers like the Algerian Djallil Djellad, the Tunisian Eyet-Chékib Djaziri, and Rachid O., the Moroccan author of four popular and suggestively homoerotic novels. Among the most notable Western authors with an interest in the subject are the Frenchmen Jean Genet and Tony Duvert, the latter's books infused with a paedophilic eroticism and set in a vague Mediterranean/Maghrebin country, and the Spaniard Juan Goytisolo. In his symbolic and sadomasochistic novels, Goytisolo associates the Maghrebin world with an open and celebratory sexuality, in contrast to Western society, oppressed by heterosexual culture.

Some films have magnified the sensuality of a mythic Orient. Pier Paolo Pasolini's *Arabian Nights* (*Il fiore delle mille e una notte*, 1974) is the most prominent example – a vital celebration of love without boundaries as well as of the pleasures of storytelling. A different but very interesting case is presented by the acclaimed *Pink Narcissus* (1971), whose director long remained anonymous but was later revealed to be James Bidgood (also an accomplished photographer). Here, the beautiful protagonist, a new Narcissus, imagines himself to be a caliph in an oriental palace, for whom a male concubine performs an explicit and highly erotic dance.

There are still many films, however, that deal with today's Islamic world, such as *Fox and His Friends* (*Faustrecht der Freiheit*, 1974) by Rainer Werner Fassbinder; Stephen Frear's *Prick Up Your Ears* (1987); *Savage Nights* (*Les nuits fauves*, 1992) and the short film *Algiers the White* (*Alger la Blanche*, 1985), both directed by Cyril Collard; and *Hamam: The Turkish Bath* (*Hamam: Il bagno turco*, 1997). This last film, by the Turkish-Italian director Ferzan Özpetek, depicts the relationship between an Italian and a young Turk, lyrically contrasting the flavours and atmosphere of a seductive Istanbul with a materialistic and fatuous Western society. Apart from the works of Cyril Collard, many other French films treat the subject: those by Sébastien Lifshitz and Gaël Morel, for instance, or films that feature *beur* protagonists in homoerotic situations (often tied to prostitution) or are made by *beur* directors. Not to be overlooked are the pornographic films of Jean-Daniel Cadinot, such as *Harem* (1984) and *Chaleurs* (1987), now considered classics of their genre. *The*

Perfumed Garden (*Le jardin parfumé*, 2000) is also of interest: an examination of the myth of Arab sensuality by the French-Algerian director Yamina Benguigui, which includes a transgressive interview with Abdelhak Serhane.

Although significant, these works of Western culture offer only limited insights, even when the figurative and photographic arts are included. With the exception of academic essays, they are rarely useful for illuminating how homosexuality is lived in Islamic countries. In fact, they often focus more on the problematic relationship between immigrants and their adopted society, or they limit themselves to tropes of the gay erotic imagination, in line with ideas Europe has held about the 'Orient' for at least three centuries.

The myth of the Orient and Orientalism

The Orient – a term that traditionally encompasses North Africa and the countries of the Middle East – occupies a unique place in the Western imagination, straight and gay. The Western concept of the Orient originated with the translation of the *Thousand and One Nights* by the Frenchman Antoine Galland at the beginning of the 18th century. The story's characters – Scheherazade, the king Shahryar, Aladdin, Sinbad, Ali Baba and the caliph Harun ar-Rashid – quickly became symbols of a seductive world that drove all of Europe mad. Thus everything that seemed oriental – harems and odalisques, eunuchs and slaves, minarets and hookahs – exuded a magical, sensual appeal.

For about one hundred years, northern Europeans with the economic means chose to immerse themselves in the dazzling sun of the Mediterranean. On the Grand Tour, aristocrats and intellectuals from the North journeyed through the southern countries (Italy in particular) in order to learn about the art and culture of antiquity and the Renaissance. They were above all attracted by the idea of the South's unspoilt nature, and by the conviction that in these civilizations, thought to be more genuine and instinctual than their own, people were more open to every type of sexual experience. In effect, the Grand Tour became a way for many, particularly the English, finally to experience the sex denied them in their homeland.[30]

From the second half of the 18th century the myth of the Orient joined that of the Mediterranean and gradually began to supplant it. The most significant places in this romanticized view of the East were the Maghreb, Constantinople (rich with history and monuments) and Egypt (above all in the years following Napoleon's Egyptian campaign) – areas that often became conflated in the Western imagination, even though in reality they varied widely. In the 19th century Orientalism (the word 'orientalist' had first appeared in the English language in 1779) became a discourse in its own right in the literary and artistic culture of the West, complete with a public keen to consume its products. It offered European civilization – gripped by an identity crisis that brought into question values previously considered unassailable – a powerful safety valve for its imagination, of which Orientalism was itself perhaps the result, as Edward Said maintained: 'The Orient was almost a European invention, and had been since antiquity a place of romance, exotic beings, haunted memories and landscapes, remarkable experiences.'[31]

The Orient thus became an intoxicating place for the soul, a fabulous territory in which dreams of sensual, transgressive sex could be satisfied. Right from the start, in fact, nearly all Orientalist works, whether literary or artistic, contained a strongly erotic element that was often explicit and which sprang from the belief that in oriental lands mores were markedly more relaxed than their harsher European counterparts.

In reality, however, the Orient continued to be off limits, which served only to increase its sense of mystery. Only a few subjected themselves to the long and perilous journey – often on camels – from which one could not be entirely sure of returning. Those who did have the courage to reach their destination at the beginning of the 19th century helped light the fire of Orientalism. In the literary sphere a major proponent was Lord Byron, who after a journey to Constantinople wrote several very successful stories praising the romance of these exotic worlds. In the field of art, Orientalism's most important figures were Jean-Étienne Liotard, who spent four years in Constantinople; Jean-Auguste-Dominique Ingres; and above all Eugène Delacroix, who introduced Europeans to an environment imbued with exoticism that he had experienced during his 1832 journey to Algeria and Morocco. Throughout the 19th century, as interest in these mysterious lands grew still further, many others produced suggestive accounts of their trips: painters such as Jean-Léon Gérôme, Eugène Fromentin, Théodore Chassériau and David Roberts; writers including Théophile Gautier, René de Chateaubriand and Gérard de Nerval; scholars such as Edward William Lane; and the trend continued into the early 20th century with adventurers like Lawrence of Arabia.

A better knowledge of these cultures did not diminish their erotic fascination – on the contrary. Further works of Arab and Persian erotic literature were discovered, such as *The Perfumed Garden* or the poetry of Abū Nuwās; in addition, anthropological and ethnographic essays shed light on the freedom with which sexuality was experienced. The greatest contribution to this genre is that of Sir Richard Francis Burton. The first Westerner successfully to enter Mecca (dressed in disguise), Burton notes in his account of the pilgrimage a 'voluptuousness unknown to northern regions', 'the savouring of animal existence; the passive enjoyment of mere sense; the pleasant languor, the dreamy tranquillity, the airy castle-building, which in Asia stand in lieu of the vigorous, intensive, passionate life of Europe'.[32] In his 'Terminal Essay' (which concludes his celebrated translation of the *Thousand and One Nights* of 1885–88), Burton hypothesized about the existence of a 'Sotadic Zone' (named after the Greek poet Sotades) – an area naturally comprising the Mediterranean and the Near East in which homosexual relations, facilitated by a tropical or semitropical climate, were commonly accepted. The anthropologists Edward Westermarck and Carleton S. Coon followed up this line of discussion in the late 1920s and early 1930s,[33] underlining how in Maghrebin societies sexual relations between active adult men and young passive males were not seen in a negative light.

Towards the end of the 19th century the vogue for Orientalist painting had began to decline and ceded its place to photography, which continued to

In the 19th century European artists took up the vogue for orientalizing works of art and produced luxurious, exotic representations of a mysterious world. Jean-Léon Gérôme's image of a naked snake-charmer (c. 1870) hints at the spectators' 'forbidden' desires through their expressions and the symbolism of pipe, sword hilt and rifle barrels.

Moorish women in Algeria: an anonymous photograph from the early 20th century. Such photographs of innocent nudity habitually found their way onto colonial postcards, which to Western viewers were powerfully suggestive.

promote the idea of an idealized Orient. Its chief proponents were the Bohemian Rudolf Lehnert and the Saxon Ernst Landrock, who together founded a studio in Tunis in 1904 and went on to live in Egypt, Palestine, Lebanon and Morocco for long periods. It was due to them that for many years Europe was flooded with photographs and postcards of exotic panoramas and scantily dressed youngsters of both sexes, who to Western eyes exuded a powerful sensuality.

Among the other photographers visiting Islamic countries at this time were the Italian Vincenzo Galdi and the Germans Wilhelm von Plüschow and Wilhelm von Gloeden. Around 1890 von Gloeden, like Galdi, visited Tunisia, where he took many photos of the countryside and its youths. These images never attain the erotic force of those taken in Taormina – perhaps because during his African stay he did not have access to his own studio, or perhaps because the models were less amenable than Sicilian youths to the idea of nude or lascivious poses. More recently, Orion Delain, too, has immortalized youngsters of the Maghreb in extremely suggestive poses; and the work of the celebrated Frenchmen Pierre et Gilles, whose seductive world and enamelled colours verge on the kitsch, harks back to James Bidgood's visions of Eastern licence.

Sex tourism

Gay tourism in the Middle East and the Maghreb goes back to the end of the 19th century, part of the larger phenomenon of intellectuals travelling there in search of powerful sensations. Among the first to make such a journey was

Western views of the East as an erotic utopia are often little more than fantasy. *The Pipe-Smoker – Aziz* (1996) by Pierre et Gilles is a typically languorous image, in which their trademark theatricality serves to highlight the superficiality of certain Western stereotypes concerning the East.

André Gide. In 1893 the writer, then twenty-four years old, arrived in Tunisia, where a relationship with a teenage boy revealed his sexuality to him (Gide had marked tendency towards paedophilia). Two years later, in the Algerian town of Blidah, he met Oscar Wilde and Lord Alfred Douglas, who were fleeing from their European misfortunes. Thanks to the Irish writer, Gide worked up the courage to have other relationships without compunction. Wilde arranged for him to meet a youth one evening, a formative experience of which Gide wrote many years later: 'whenever I have sought pleasure, it is the memory of that night which I have pursued.' Gide returned on other occasions to Tunisia and Algeria – countries that for him came to represent an ideal of sexual freedom, as he recounted in *The Immoralist* (*L'immoraliste*, 1902) and the autobiographical *If It Die* (*Si le grain ne meurt*, 1926). As a result of Gide's writings, from the first half of the 20th century a certain tourist traffic began to grow, with a considerable number of travellers, almost always rich, in search of youths; this led to the story of the Englishmen who would ask their hotel directly for a 'bed and boy'. The preferred destinations of this tourist elite were Constantinople, Egypt and the Maghreb, easily reached and reassuring for those whose palates sought somewhere different but not fundamentally dangerous.

Among the other travellers who thus satisfied the desires that they could not fulfil at home were many famous men. Pierre Loti was one: at Eyüp, near Constantinople, he had many adventures. These are recounted in his semi-autobiographical novel *Aziyadé* (1879), whose eponymous heroine was quite possibly a boy. Another was the French writer Henry de Montherlant, who

An anonymous photograph of an Algerian youth entitled *Le Nègre à l'éventail*, c. 1900. The image is entirely aimed at Western consumption.

Pierre Loti, one of the most prominent French novelists of the late 19th century. *Aziyadé* (1879), the first of several exotic novels written by the author, would seem to be a fictionalized account of Loti's own encounter with the Islamic world; described by Roland Barthes as 'a little Sodomitic epic', it has a clearly homosexual subtext. Here, Loti poses in Eastern garb in the 'mosque' of his home at Rochefort. Photograph by Dornac, 1895.

Cecil Beaton's photograph of an Arab legionnaire from 1943 (above), taken while he was working as a portraitist for the Allied effort in the North African campaign.

A self-confessed 'terrible homosexualist', Beaton returned to North Africa several times and was an astute chronicler of bohemian expatriate society. The photograph opposite, taken in Tangier in 1949, shows Jane Bowles, Paul Bowles (second from right) and Truman Capote (far right).

travelled in Algeria and Tunisia in the 1930s, dreamily maintaining that 'Paradises still exist.' E. M. Forster, already thirty-nine years old, finally managed to have full sexual relations with a young man he met in Alexandria in 1916.

The appeal of the East for tourists acquired even more explicit tones in the 1950s, by which time it had become commonly recognized as a place where homosexuality could be practised more easily. People flocked in particular to Tangier, which during these years was at its peak as a crossroads for all types of traffic and commerce. The city was invaded by an eclectic band of millionaires, smugglers, diplomats, spies and intellectuals from every part of the world. Its lively and cosmopolitan atmosphere seemed likely to offer every kind of freedom, and it attracted many gay men. At the vanguard of gay visitors was Paul Bowles, who first arrived in 1931 and returned periodically, eventually settling there. Bowles — who in 1938 wed the lesbian writer Jane Auer in a marriage of convenience — took full advantage of the sexual liberty offered by the city, finding love with the sixteen-year-old Ahmed Yacoubi. The American writer's experiences — and his fascinating, evocative novel *The Sheltering Sky* (1949) — encouraged the arrival of other intellectuals, such as the photographer Cecil Beaton, the writers Rupert Croft-Cooke, Truman Capote and Gore Vidal, and then, gradually, all the key figures of the Beat Generation, including Allen Ginsberg, William Burroughs and Tennessee Williams. In short, the city was monopolized by waves of Americans, who fought over the favours of local boys to the sound of money changing hands.

The myth of Tangier ended abruptly in 1956, when the city was reincorporated into Morocco, which itself became the destination of choice for rich and famous homosexuals — figures including Roland Barthes, Julian Beck, Joe Orton, Michel Foucault, Francis Bacon, Yves Saint Laurent and Jean Genet (buried, in accordance with his will, on the Atlantic coast at Larache). Orton in particular left a lively account of the adventures he had with his longtime companion Kenneth Halliwell; having visited Libya, where he was disappointed by the lack of available local youths, he went on to Morocco, of which he wrote: 'Daily I have the company of beautiful fifteen-year-old boys who find (for a small fee) fucking with me a delightful sensation.'[34]

Within a few years, the Maghreb and Egypt began to witness not only mass tourism (and, in Morocco, a hippie invasion[35]), but also a specifically gay type of tourism. A number of homosexuals established themselves there permanently, and meeting places began to appear. In short, these countries assumed the position previously occupied by their counterparts in Southern Europe; they even gave visitors the impression of stepping back in time, so much were they reminiscent of places like Sicily or Andalusia with their Arab-influenced culture.

On account of this influx, parts of the Maghreb and Egypt are now much like anywhere else and are losing their distinctive character. The stream of visitors does not seem to have abated, because for many the Maghreb still means readily available sex. The search for intense emotions is still strong, as is the hope of having sex with young men in exciting surroundings — in oases lush with palm trees or on sand dunes that stretch as far as the eye can see, amid

Tangier was colonized by a stream of homosexual artists and intellectuals, attracted by its reputation for sexual liberty. This photograph, of the main figures of the Beat Generation, was taken in Tangier in 1961: sitting in front are Peter Orlovsky (left) and Paul Bowles (right), while behind them, from left to right, stand William Burroughs, Allen Ginsberg, Alan Ansen, Gregory Corso and Ian Sommerville.

the perfume of coriander and cumin. These are not impossible scenarios but they are improbable, tied as they are to stereotyped fantasies and a long way from reality. Many end up disappointed by what they find.[36] Nevertheless, the fascination exerted by these countries remains intact, and there is an undeniable availability of young men who are more eager than ever to meet Westerners. For the most part, these relationships last for one night only, or at least only for the duration of the foreigner's stay. When they go on for longer, relations — especially if conducted over long distances — are generally cut off by the Westerner, who might be used to changing partners frequently and have little interest in a fixed relationship with the same boy, who has perhaps become less attractive as he has grown older. Not infrequently the youth has tired the other with ever more pressing economic demands or with his insistent jealousy.

There are also rare cases of long and stable relationships, marked by frequent exchanges of letters and full of love on both sides. On occasion these lead to happy cohabitation in Europe (perhaps following a successful visa application) or, more rarely, in the youth's country of origin. These are obviously exceptions; more common is the unhappy situation in which the young man, having reached Europe, quickly becomes ungrateful and shows that his only interest in the relationship was in obtaining the longed-for chance to emigrate.

Immigration and the internet

Once living in the West, many Muslims who engaged in homosexual acts in their native countries search them out no longer. But there are also situations in which those who are not fully integrated into their new environments end up in prostitution or transvestism; and there are those who, finally able to live in complete freedom, look for new relationships or live openly with the men who helped them escape the restrictions of their own countries.

Even overseas, it is rare for Muslims to declare themselves gay publicly. There are, however, increasing numbers in Europe and America who do come out. They have quite a challenge ahead of them: to create a new figure, the faithful Muslim who is also homosexual. There have been some successes, such the establishment of organizations – the first was the US-based GLAS (Gay and Lesbian Arab Society) in 1988 – that actively fight against discrimination in Arab countries.

The internet is crucial to the work of these organizations: alongside the satellite dish, it has enabled many Arabs who identify as homosexual to realize that they are not alone and has helped them to find models in other, non-homophobic societies. It gives gay Muslims who have emigrated to the West an opportunity to communicate their way of life, at the same time as allowing us to understand previously unknown aspects of how homosexuality is lived in Arab societies.

The most important internet sites are those connected to organizations whose aim is to support gay Muslims, which continue to grow in size and usefulness. In Europe, the Dutch group Yoesuf and the French Kelma, Filoumektoub and Bab Al Hourria are particularly noteworthy. The two best-known groups, however, are the Al-Fatiha Foundation and Queer Jihad. The former, boasting about three hundred members in twenty-five different countries, was set up in America in 1997 by Faisal Alam, who is Pakistani in origin. The latter – an active and enterprising website, consulted by many gay people, Muslims and non-Muslims – was the creation of Sulayman X, an American journalist and convert to Islam.

The anonymity of almost all who work on or are connected with these websites – from fear of being publicly outed, not to mention the fact that many sites unexpectedly 'disappear' – is a sign of just how taboo the subject of homosexuality is in Islamic culture. To speak of gay rights or the public visibility of gays in Islamic countries might thus seem inappropriate, especially when an upswing in fundamentalism is all that is needed to change a country's characteristics (what has happened in Algeria is proof enough). Something is changing, however, albeit slowly. The current struggle between West and East will continue until, with luck, it resolves itself into a peaceful meeting of two civilizations. Even if they subscribe to different – even antithetical – world views, they must continue to strive for a happy coexistence founded on mutual respect. If this were to happen, it would be a good thing for gay people living in North Africa and the Middle East; we can only hope it does.

Desire and Same-Sex Intimacies in Asia
ADRIAN CARTON

The diaries and memoirs of early European travellers to Asia often contain fleeting references to the moral outrage they experienced upon viewing homosexual practices in places like China.[1] To the European gaze, a cultural landscape in which homosexuality was open rather than repressed caused bewilderment and repulsion. Outside the Judaeo-Christian world view, the meaning of homosexuality is irreducibly different. Very much a product of the 19th-century Western imagination, the term 'homosexuality' has little cultural resonance in Asian societies where (before widespread Western influence) same-sex love did not attract the same degree of culturally conditioned or socially sanctioned scorn that it did in Christian Europe.

'Asia' comprises a huge area and a multiplicity of cultures and traditions. This chapter will confine itself to the three most influential cultural traditions in Asia: those of China, Japan and India. An exploration of political treatises, military histories, philosophical tracts, artistic representations and poetic works will reveal that ideas of love, romance, friendship, virtue and chivalry combined with expressions of homosexuality in different ways, but that they always formed an integral part of the way in which notions of masculinity and femininity were articulated and understood in prevailing religious traditions.

China
Literary metaphors and imperial favours
Sources from the Zhou dynasty (1122–256 BCE) reveal that by the 8th and 7th centuries BCE male same-sex intimacy was inextricably associated with imperial courtly life. Early literary representations of homosexual intimacy were shaped in a rarefied environment, reflecting both the genteel world of the ruling culture and the scholarly virtues that legitimized male affection within a framework of hierarchical relationships based on respect.

In early literature various metaphors emerged that hinted at male same-sex intimacy within the established codes of elite male bonding. With scholar–pupil, father–son and elder brother–younger brother relationships of absolutely central importance to the Confucian world view, patterns of male attachment occurred along both generational and class lines. Stories tell of homosexual love between rulers and their favourites, for instance, or between older and younger noblemen — relationships framed by strong emotional bonds and deep attachments based on filial loyalty. The best known of these

Same-sex love in Asia – where attitudes were remarkably different from Western concepts of sin – has a long and well-documented history. This woodcut by Hokusai in the erotic *shunga* style, made in 1821, possibly depicts a scene in a brothel.

metaphors are the stories of the 'half-bitten peach', 'Long Yang and the fish' and 'the cut sleeve' – all codes for homosexual intimacy that were understood throughout Chinese history.

The most famous story from the Zhou period is found in chapter twelve of the legalistic philosophical writings of Han Fei Zi (d. 233 BCE). The politics of personal favouritism are explored through the infatuation of Wei, Duke Ling (534–493 BCE), for the court official Mizi Xia. At the imperial court, making use of the ruler's carriage for personal errands was deemed a serious offence, attracting the penalty of foot amputation. When his mother fell ill, Mizi Xia used the carriage in order to visit her; instead of punishing him, the duke praised his protégé's filial duty and respect. Another scene depicts Mizi Xia and the duke walking through an orchard; the favoured official gives the ruler a half-eaten peach to eat, inspiring the duke to contemplate Mizi's sense of devotion and self-sacrifice. Such was the influence of this fable that the name 'Mizi Xia' and the metaphor of the 'love of the shared peach' (*fen tao zhi ai*) evoked the phenomenon of homosexual intimacy for generations to come.[2]

A second literary metaphor from the 3rd century BCE also illustrates well the position of favourites within the setting of the Zhou court. In this tale, the king of Wei and his court favourite, Lord Long Yang, share a boat while fishing. Visibly distressed, with his eyes full of tears, Long Yang explains to the king that he was pleased with the first fish that he had caught. 'But afterward I caught a larger fish, so I wanted to throw back the first fish I had caught. Because of this evil act, I will be expelled from your bed!'[3] Revealing the insecurity that resulted from robust competition among favourites, this anecdote confirms the extent of homosexual intimacy among the elite, also securing the name of *long yang* as a synonym for a homosexual lover.

The more reliable records of the Han dynasty (202 BCE – 220 CE) confirm that homosexuality could exist alongside the conventions of heterosexual marriage. Perhaps the most significant evidence comes from Sima Qian's *Memoirs of the Historian* (*Shi ji*) and Ban Gu's *Records of the Han* (*Han shu*) – histories that chart the private lives of the Han emperors, ten of them openly bisexual, and their involvement with male favourites. According to Sima Qian, 'It is not women alone who can use their looks to attract the eyes of the ruler; courtiers and eunuchs can play at that game as well. Many were the men of ancient times who gained favour this way.'[4] Male favourites could include astrologers, musicians and generals or, indeed, illiterate boys or eunuchs from lowly origins. Through their intimacy with the emperor they could rise to positions of great power, influencing future appointments and determining access to the royal person. With homosexuality and heterosexuality both present in society, moreover, patriarchal privilege allowed men of high status to have sexual relations with whomever of a lower social status they chose.

The ambiguous term *chong*, referring to love, patronage, favour or respect, was applied to heterosexual relationships and platonic friendships in general. The Chinese tradition also recognized a greater variety of male same-sex relationships as part of the cosmology of devotion and affection, an attitude that stands in stark contrast to the repression of overt male intimacy in Christian

Known as the 'love of the cut sleeve', male homosexuality first appears in China in anecdotes concerning the love lives of earlier rulers that date from the 3rd century BCE. For the Chinese, morality was based not on religion but on such concepts as temperance, wisdom, justice and duty. Scroll painting by Wang Sheng from the late Ming period (early 17th century).

By the end of the 18th century, homosexuality and the exclusively male world of the Chinese theatre had become closely associated. *Sheng* actors played the men's parts, while the female roles were taken by *tan* actors, who frequently attracted a great deal of attention from admiring patrons. This scroll from the Qing dynasty (1644–1911) depicts two actors from the Peking opera, recognizable by their elaborate costumes and distinctive headdresses.

Europe. The works of Sima Qian and Ban Gu show a more varied vocabulary for describing the dynamics of male same-sex intimacy in the Han era than previously existed, with both authors using the term *ning xing* – those who obtained love and favour (*xing*) through flattery (*ning*) – to refer to imperial favourites.[5] *Ai ren* ('beloved', 'partner' or 'spouse') is also used in Han texts. Such terms do not refer directly to homosexual practices or identities, or even to a separate treatment of male same-sex intimacy. Sexuality was not considered a sphere of existence removed from social relations at large.[6]

Ban Gu supplies perhaps the most famous example of male intimacy, which became a synonym for homosexual desire in China. The tale of Emperor Ai and his favourite, Dong Xian, speaks of an affectionate tenderness that seems universal. The couple were sleeping, with Dong Xian stretched out across the sleeve of the emperor. Not wanting to disturb his companion, the ruler cut off the sleeve of his own robe so that he could rise and resume his duties. The metaphor of the 'cut sleeve' (*duan xiu*) thus became a recognized euphemism for homosexuality;[7] it reflected the extent to which homosexual intimacy had permeated the culture of upper-class Chinese life, but it also conveyed enduring noble qualities of loyalty, respect and filial attachment intrinsic to the moral fabric of the Confucian universe.

Same-sex intimacy

The gender ambiguity of classical Chinese nouns often makes it impossible to distinguish between heterosexual and homosexual love, but references to strong emotional bonds between men have been noted by scholars.[8] The disintegration of the Han dynasty after 220 CE saw the arrival of a broader range of cultural artefacts exploring homosexual love: popular poetry, theatre, opera and works of art, as well as humour and pornography. Whereas the elite constructions of romantic love were written in classical Chinese, out of the reach of ordinary people, an increased circulation of writings in the vernacular, as well as of non-written representations of desire, revealed the attitudes of a broader section of society.

During the Jin dynasty (265–420), much poetry reflected a growing awareness of male prostitution and of sexual love between men that took place outside their social milieux. Zhang Hanbian wrote a complimentary tribute to the fifteen-year-old prostitute Zhou Xiaoshi, exploring the connection between prostitution and acting in the tendency of performers to wear cosmetics and dress extravagantly. The representation of male prostitution in literature continued into the Song dynasty (960–1280), when the practice itself had become notoriously widespread and, by the early 12th century, the object of restrictive legal codes. Male prostitution flourished also during the Ming period (1368–1644): according to Shen Defu (1578–1642), officials displayed a preference for young men after the emperor had ordered them to refrain from sleeping with courtesans. Known as *xiaochang*, these male prostitutes had become a prominent part of Chinese life by the 17th century.[9]

Since the stage was an exclusively male domain (men played both male and female roles), the association between homosexuality and the theatre was

A scene of lovemaking between a young actor and a young scholar: a scroll painting from the end of the Qing period.

strong. The *tan* actors who played female roles had a subordinate status, while the *sheng* actors playing male roles were considered superior. These gendered roles were often acted out in the context of same-sex relationships off-stage as well as in the theatre. Several prominent *tan* actors became famous for homosexual affairs with the scholar-officials who patronized them. This phenomenon continued throughout Chinese history, reaching a peak with the idealization of *tan* actors in the Peking Opera of the 18th and 19th centuries.[10]

By the time of the Ming dynasty, the representation of homosexual love had reached an apogee thanks to increased literacy, enhancements in printing technology, and growing mass demand for inexpensive and popular literature with sexual themes. The erotic novel *The Golden Lotus* (*Jin ping mei, c.* 1610) – which also tells of affairs between men – reflects the popular taste for explicit and entertaining descriptions of sexual conduct in the vernacular. However, interest in the history of same-sex relationships undoubtedly culminated with a 17th-century compilation of homoerotic writings known collectively as *Records of the Cut Sleeve* (*Duan xiu pian*).[11] The dissemination of erotic homosexual prints mirrored the public interest in sex that could also be witnessed in scholarly jottings, plays and novels. Of particular note was the emergence of a specific pornographic genre in Ming fiction, which began at the end of the 16th century and peaked in the first half of the 17th century.[12]

A change in the terms used to label male same-sex love indicates that cultural emphasis was shifting from the social relations of intimacy to the erotic act itself. The expression *nanfeng* referred to the 'male custom' or 'male practice', but since the word for 'south' was pronounced as *nan*, too, the term could also be translated as the 'southern custom' or 'south wind' – a clever homophone playing on the belief that homosexuality was more common in the southern provinces of Fujian and Zhejiang.[13] Shen Defu explained how male couples in Fujian frequently lived together in a type of same-sex marriage occasionally lasting as long as twenty years, in which one partner was 'the bond elder brother' (*qixiong*) and the other 'the bond younger brother' (*qidi*). Shen Defu also remarked that the prevalence of same-sex intimacy in Fujian may have derived from the influence of pirate culture, in which homosexuality was encouraged.[14] In any case, government officials attempted to suppress a sodomitical cult there in the 18th century.[15]

Not until the Qing dynasty (1644–1911) did legal intervention attempt to regulate the sexual lives of ordinary Chinese citizens. Laws prohibiting sodomy, such as statues from 1690 and 1740, were directed particularly at preventing acts of sexual violence and strengthening the ideology of the family.[16] Representations and practices of same-sex love continued to be tolerated, despite this codification and the Qing dynasty's increasing social conservatism.

Hierarchies and cosmologies of desire

Whereas the rejection of same-sex intimacy in the West derived from a negative interpretation of Judaeo-Christian texts, attitudes towards sexuality in China have come from interpretations of desire that are very different. Taoism, China's oldest religion, is based on a concept of life that rejects

Taoism's concept of social equilibrium and wellbeing was based on the balance of opposite forces – *yin* and *yang*. This system governed all aspects of life, including sexual behaviour, in which it was desirable above all to preserve one's supply of *chi'i*, the circulating life-force. This illustration from a medical work of 1622 shows a Taoist adept balancing the male and female principles.

essentialism or innate qualities that develop independently of their context. Social equilibrium is maintained through the correlative interaction of two forces: *yin* and *yang*. Although *yin* is associated with qualities of femininity and passivity, and *yang* with masculinity and activity, neither exists without the other.

Within Taoism, this balance is attained through the proper exchange of *chi'*, or life energy, which is contained in either semen (*yang*) or vaginal secretions (*yin*). Sexual activity was viewed as beneficial to one's longevity and health as long as *chi'i* was not lost or wasted. According to this theory, men were thought to have a limited supply of *chi'i*, which could be replenished by absorbing the unlimited supply of *chi'i* in women. As a consequence male masturbation and celibacy were culturally frowned upon, while the ultimate state of harmony was achieved through sexual intercourse if the man brought the woman to climax without ejaculating. Within the Taoist universe same-sex sexual relations were not treated as a separate phenomenon; for men, they merely involved an exchange of *yang chi'i*, in which the losses and gains of feminine and masculine energies could cancel each other out, thus leaving one's life energies unaffected.[17] Neither did sexual acts between women cause any disruption to the exchange of energy, since women had an inexhaustible supply of *yin chi'i*.[18]

Confucianism was the dominant ideology in China for over two thousand years. Whereas Taoism was concerned with spiritual harmony, Confucian thought placed a strong emphasis on social order. All social behaviour – including sexual activities – was regulated by the 'five relationships', by means of which all human interactions were arranged hierarchically. From the Han dynasty (202 BCE – 220 CE) onwards, the notion of hierarchy was assimilated into popular cosmological theories of *yin* and *yang*: the harmony of the universe was thus understood in terms of dominance and subordination. The notions of respect, duty and submission became intrinsic to social relations and underpinned a hierarchy of fathers over sons, husbands over wives, elder brothers over younger brothers, and masters over pupils. Confucian cosmology gave moral legitimacy to natural inequality.

In addition, Confucianism promoted the idea of the *guojia* or state-family: the social hierarchies outlined above were extended to include the sphere of state governance, so that political submission was regarded as a social duty. This system assumed the submission of

A young woman uses a dildo to pleasure her lover. In China sexual acts between women did not attract opprobrium; this was not on account of tolerant attitudes towards lesbianism, but because sex between women neither transgressed the male-centred Taoist principles of sexuality nor was visible within China's patriarchal society. This illustration dates from the late Ming period (1628–44).

women to men in both social and political contexts, relegating them to a lower status and encouraging their seclusion from public life.[19] In parallel, the promotion of male privilege through primogeniture, the prestige accorded to male friendships and the importance of hierarchical patterns of male mentorship led to the establishment of institutions in which men were more likely to spend time with fellow men rather than with women.[20] Such patterns of male bonding may have facilitated same-sex sexual behaviour, which was acceptable as long as it did not disrupt hierarchical relations.[21] As long as the rules governing social relations between classes and genders went unchallenged, it appears that homosexuality was not viewed as dangerous. The increasing attempts in the Qing period to control anal intercourse were directed not at homosexuality *per se*, but at those who were penetrated, since they transgressed their gender role within the family order.[22]

The situation surrounding lesbianism is also significant, since women were perceived to have no sexuality outside of the traditional patriarchal hierarchies.[23] Literary representations of lesbian love are rare; the most famous is perhaps the play *Pitying the Perfumed Companion* (*Lianxiang ban*) by Li Yu (1611–80), which depicts the devotion between two women in a Buddhist convent. Such works as *Feng Sanniang*, by Pu Songling (1640–1715), also explore intimacies between women. Today's scholars have noted the scarcity of works on female sexuality: it seems that male writers employed certain rhetorical strategies to keep love between women trivialized and contained within patriarchal parameters.[24] Female same-sex love was subject to the general Confucian perception of women as submissive to men, and thus, in a social system where all female sexuality was closely policed, it became 'invisible'.

The formulation of the Qing law code of 1740 was an attempt to curb the widespread practice of selling children into prostitution or concubinage. It was thus more concerned with family values and the protection of children than with the policing of same-sex adult love. However, the modernization of China along Western lines in the 20th century ushered in a new era for homosexuality. Centuries of tolerance were abandoned for an attitude of open hostility and punitive measures. Sex became detached from its cosmological context. Western scientific models of sexuality, which pathologized same-sex love as 'unnatural', were adopted after 1949 as part of a modernization project, and from then onwards homosexuals were viewed as decadent, morally dangerous and antithetical to the aims of the new proletarian society. In more recent years, as the Chinese state has become more liberal and pluralistic, gay subcultures have emerged in the largest cities, reflecting the modern Western idea that identity is inextricably linked to sexual orientation – a far cry from the poetic metaphors of the 'half-bitten peach' and the 'cut sleeve'.

A youth spies on two others making love. This scroll painting dates from the
late Qing dynasty (1644–1911) – a period when Chinese authorities sought to
impose a 'return to order'. They attempted to regulate sodomy and other sexual
behaviour that was seen as threatening the gender status quo.

Japan
Nanshoku: a convergence of traditions

Reverence for the superior culture of the Middle Kingdom, with its established tradition of male same-sex desire, had a direct influence in Japan. Alongside Chinese philosophy, language, art, literature and calligraphy, Japanese culture absorbed Confucian precepts about the importance of social order, Taoist ideas about sexuality, and masculinist presuppositions about the nature of desire.

Unlike in the situation in China, where there are reliable historical records, there is little direct evidence of a flourishing tradition of *nanshoku* ('love of males') within the early Japanese court. The diaries of several aristocrats from the Heian period (794–1185), however, provide more explicit stories of homosexual encounters between emperors or aristocrats and dancers, servants, actors and handsome youths.[25] These court diaries also recount examples of transvestism and comment on the fact that gender identity was malleable and performative. Ultimately, however, these colourful portrayals of courtly life are rare morsels, and there are very few accounts of same-sex desire in elite circles before the 11th century, leading commentators to conclude that the ruling culture did not foster the same homoerotic sensibilities as it did in China.

According to legend, Kūkai (also known as Kōbō Daishi, 'the Great Teacher'; 774–835), founder of the Shingon sect of Buddhism, was responsible for the introduction of homosexuality into Japan and the establishment of the *nanshoku* tradition. The monk returned from China in 806 after two years of studying under the master Hui-kuo and became one of Japan's most revered cultural figures, going on to found the famous monastery at Mount Kōya and (it is said) to invent the Japanese syllabary. The idea that same-sex love was 'imported' from China or the proposition that homosexuality did not exist in Japan before Kūkai's return seem highly improbable, but the legend did serve to establish the legitimacy of *nanshoku* in Japan. If anything, the association of Kōbō Daishi, the Shingon (or 'True Way') sect of Buddhism and *nanshoku* gave male same-sex love a sacred, otherworldly status drawn upon in later, secular portrayals of homosexual desire.[26]

It is Buddhist culture rather than the imperial court that provides us with written evidence of a tradition of male–male intimacy in Japan. A collection of stories called *Tales Gleaned From Uji* (1212–21) describes same-sex relationships between monks; and from the beginning of the 14th century appeared novels (called *chigo monogatari* or '*chigo* stories') depicting monastic homosexuality. The love affairs that they recount, between elder monks and younger companions, often end with the tragic death of one of the lovers, leaving the surviving partner to a life of asceticism and mourning.[27] In theory, Buddhist monks were denied sexual relations with the opposite sex, yet Buddhist monasteries housed young male acolytes (*chigo*), who, in addition to performing temple duties and household chores, also provided companionship and sexual gratification for older monks. Relationships between monks and boys were accepted since they accorded with the concept of *nanshoku* as a spiritual cult. While the boys could be objects of sexual love, they were also objects of worship, devotion and spiritual admiration – to the point that a beautiful *chigo* could be considered the incarnation of a *bodhisattva*.[28] From the European perspective, such spiritual attachments were considered abominable vices. Upon learning of the relationship between Buddhism and same-sex love, the first missionaries to reach Japan, in the 1540s, quickly denounced the religion as idolatrous and immoral, reaching the verdict that Sodom on earth had been discovered in the Far East. In his *Historia del principio y progresso de la Companía de Jesús en las Indias Orientales* (1542–64), the Jesuit Alessandro Valignano comments on the relationships between monks and the *chigo*, who are guilty of 'the sin that does not bear mentioning'.[29]

The association of homosexuality with the Buddhist establishment in Japan seems at odds with the ascetic traditions of Chinese Buddhism and its emphasis on abstention and sexual neutrality. However, Shingon Buddhism and other sects developed in isolation from the main centres of Buddhist culture in Asia, and after the 9th century the direct influence of Chinese mainland spirituality on Japan waned considerably. More significantly, Japanese Buddhism developed close symbiotic relationships with other spiritual traditions – Shintoism, Taoism and Confucianism – producing a culturally unique and hybrid moral world view different from that found in China. Shinto tradition in particular, with its lack of moral restrictions and its promotion of sex as a healthy outlet, tended to eroticize spirituality. Phallus worship and the cult of phallic shrines were evidence of an explicit adoration of the male sexual organ, which fuelled a more physically charged homoeroticism than in China.

Furthermore, *nanshoku* was closely associated with Zen Buddhism. Introduced into Japan in 1236 from China, where it had developed into an austere, disciplined and devotional cult with an emphasis on masculine bonding and group loyalty, Zen Buddhism influenced Japanese art, poetry, literature, gardening and such social rituals as the tea ceremony. Zen monks made the subject of same-sex love integral to their cultural view of the universe through literary works that circulated widely during the Muromachi period of the Ashikaga Shogunate (1338–1573).[30] This combination of Buddhist spirituality, disciplined social outlook and homoeroticism would find a niche among a new, more powerful political class.

Warriors and wakashudō: rituals of masculine bonding

The convergence of the traditions of Zen Buddhism with an existing mythology of *nanshoku* and a cult of homoeroticism was to find full political expression within Japan's feudal warrior society. As the authority of the Heian emperors eroded and local administrative structures disintegrated, the country was left with a power vacuum that local lords were quick to fill. The Hōgen Rebellion of 1156, a civil war over imperial succession, was followed by the more decisive Heiji Rebellion in 1159, in which rival subjects of Emperor Go-Shirakawa struggled for power. The warlord Minamoto Yorimoto emerged triumphant, and Go-Shirakawa named him shogun, or supreme military commander. A military capital was established at Kamakura, far from the influence of the imperial court, and the country was governed by military rule.

The age of the shoguns lasted over six hundred years, and its influence has been well mythologized in the popular imagination. It was, however, in the rituals of the samurai class who rose to political prominence during the 12th century that the tradition of *nanshoku*, which drew legitimacy from Zen Buddhism, found new expression. Historians have recently argued that homo-eroticism was at the core of samurai culture, which welded male same-sex practices to the state in a way unthinkable in contemporary Europe.[31] Echoing both the Confucian master–pupil relationship and the Buddhist monk–*chigo* bond in a new eroticized framework, the samurai model of male same-sex relations had become intextricably interwoven into the political system by the 15th and 16th centuries.

The samurai model typically consisted of a pederastic relationship between an older *nenja*, the active partner and protector, and a younger *chigo*, the object of desire and affection.[32] A military environment, from which women were excluded, provided the ideal homosocial space in which such relationships could flourish. Samurai relationships were valorized by notions of honour, respect, mutual obligation and loyalty within a robust, aggressive and often

A **samurai warrior** and his *wakashu* (pupil), a rare photograph from the second half of the 19th century. In Japanese feudal society, earlier traditions of homosexuality culminated in the institution of *wakashudō* ('the way of youths'). Adolescent pupils were mentored by older, more experienced samurai, who would teach them political strategy and the art of warfare within the context of an intimate sexual relationship.

violent environment. The young apprentice warriors who learnt warfare and political strategy from their mentors were referred to in samurai texts as *wakashu*, and the love of the *wakashu* was known as *wakashudō* ('the way of youths'). This is often abbreviated simply to *shudō*, although Japanese texts also refer to it as *bidō* ('the beautiful way').

The end of the Minamoto shogunate in 1333 led to a short-lived imperial restoration; this, in turn, gave way to the shogunate of the Muromachi clan, under whom male same-sex love continued. The lover of Yoshimochi (1368–1427), the fourth shogun, was a younger samurai called Akamatsu Mochisada; the father of seven children, he was granted three provinces by his powerful admirer. Yoshimochi's brother, Yoshinori, who became the sixth shogun, had been the *chigo* of a Buddhist monk from the age of ten. When he acceded to the position of supreme military commander, he made favourites of his vassals' sons and did not hide his love for the young actors whom he enter-tained within the palace walls: his favourite was the young Akamatsu

Ashikaga Yoshimochi, the fourth shogun of the Muromachi period, painted before 1414. Yoshimacha took a fellow samurai, Akamatsu Mochisada, as his lover and bestowed upon him three whole provinces – an act of generosity that infuriated Mochisada's political rivals and precipitated the samurai's suicide.

Sadamura, whom he promoted to great political power. The lovers of both Yoshimochi and Yoshinori were murdered by the same lord, Akamatsu Mitsusuke — their political sway, gained through the control of land, sent danger signals to other clans about the exercise of power through sexual favours.[33]

Wakashudō permeated the consciousness of the samurai ranks and became the most important type of relationship — one through which a sense of loyalty could be maintained. Most shoguns and warlords are thought to have engaged in the practice of having sex with boys, most especially in times of war. Ōta Kinjō noted in 1813 that, in wartime, '*nanshoku* became prevalent, and many strong and courageous warriors emerged from among the warriors' male same-sex partners'.[34] Indeed, over half of the shoguns who ruled Japan between 1338 and 1837 had same-sex affairs.[35]

As with male—male relationships in China, the love of samurai for younger apprentices gained social legitimacy. *Wakashudō* also respected hierarchies of age, rank and status. The object of desire was an adolescent, who became an acolyte or pupil under the mentorship of an older, more experienced warrior. This balance of power was reflected during the sexual act, with the passive role of the *wakashu* accentuating the virility and strength of the older warrior. This relationship did not prevent either partner from engaging in sexual activity with women, however. On the contrary, both heterosexual and homosexual relationships could coexist, and bisexuality rather than exclusive homosexuality seems to have been the norm.

In the martial and overtly homosocial world of the samurai, women were not only excluded and desexualized, but also perceived — with profound misogyny — as a threat to good governance, social cohesion and political unity. For example, the writer and poet Urushiya Ensai describes one samurai who would not eat a particular type of rice dumpling because it was associated with a female festival. Another text cites a Shinto belief concerning the dangers of menstrual pollution that was widely held among samurai and which provided a justification for avoiding social contact with women.[36]

Mirrors of 'the beautiful way'

The traditions of *nanshoku* and *wakashudō* in Japanese society originated in the monastery, the imperial court and the military camp — all fields in which male same-sex relationships flourished and which provided the context for the stories that entered poetic legend. However, these monastic and military forms of homoeroticism began to express themselves in new, more popular guises as Japanese society underwent rapid transformation. Between 1568 and 1603, political power was centralized and disparate feudal territories were reunified. Society became increasingly urbanized and a money-based economy emerged, creating a nascent bourgeoisie. One result was that the older traditions of *nanshoku* began to give way to expressions of same-sex male intimacy based on commercial transactions.

Perhaps the most visible sign of this shift in the homosexual tradition was the growth of prostitution. Since its origins in the 14th century, the boy actors of Nō theatre had been greatly admired by male aristocratic patrons for their

Courtesans, visitors and clients stroll beneath the cherry trees in the Yoshiwara brothel district of Edo. With Japan's rapid urbanization and a new and affluent middle class, sexual behaviour became increasingly commercialized. Districts such as Yoshiwara and Yokohama offered numerous theatres, tea houses and brothels, both male and female. Woodcut by Utagawa Hiroshige, *c.* 1834–35.

depiction of female roles and their transvestism. During the Tokugawa period (1603–1868), the association of prostitution with kabuki theatre was even more explicit. Originally established as women's theatre, in which females performed erotic dances and advertised 'after hours' services, the kabuki style was a great hit in the early 17th century, although it was banned in 1629 because of violent quarrels among potential suitors and paying customers.[37] Kabuki was made an all-male affair, and the young actors who played female roles often continued their interpretations off-stage in order to perfect their femininity. More significantly, kabuki theatres in large cities such as Edo (modern Tokyo) were often adjacent to the so-called *nanshoku* tea houses, male brothels where actor-prostitutes met patrons.

The commodification of same-sex practices saw *nanshoku* depart from its monastic and samurai traditions to become a practice available to those who could pay for it. The typical patron was the new urban bourgeois man with cash to spend. Indeed, although they were patronized by clients from a wide range of social backgrounds,[38] the rise of the tea houses represented the pinnacle of bourgeois prosperity in early modern Tokugawa Japan, which saw one of the most tolerant cultures for homosexuality in world history. The *nanshoku* tradition fostered the idea that sexual practices were divorced from personal

In kabuki theatre boy actors who played female roles with great conviction were greatly admired. They would also moonlight as prostitutes, entertaining clients in full female character. Right: a young male prostitute at night, holding a lantern (*c.* 1745). Far right: a portrait of the famous actor Segawa Kikunojo III, whose femininity was considered so beguiling that it was even imitated by geishas (*c.* 1785).

Japanese art of the Tokugawa period reflected Edo's thriving sex industry, and there are numerous prints that show exquisitely dressed actor-prostitutes entertaining clients in tea houses. Although samurai and monks continued in their patronage of the *nanshoku* tradition, most of the prostitutes' clients came from a prosperous middle class of merchants and artisans. In this woodcut by Kitagawa Utamaro (c. 1790) a client prepares a male prostitute for sexual intercourse.

identity, and in society at large there was no moral taboo against 'sodomy'. Male same-sex subcultures blossomed – a situation reflected in the art and literature of the period, where the *nanshoku* tradition assumed new and popular forms.

One of these forms was erotic art. Depictions of male same-sex intimacy proliferated at the height of Tokugawa rule: many were graphic images of anal intercourse between men, usually with prostitutes in tea houses or in threesomes with a female partner. These finely detailed and colourful images typically show the actor-prostitute, dressed in a female kimono, engaging in sexual acts with patrons, samurai or monks in a realistic setting. This public demand for *nanshoku* in visual form was accompanied by an appetite for erotic literature. Some of the first illustrated books produced for the mass market in Japan feature same-sex love, and *The Tale of a Boor* (*Denbu monogatari*), written around 1640, was the first significant work to discuss homosexuality.[39] In 1676 Kitamura Kigin completed the manuscript of *Wild Azaleas* (*Iwatsutsuji*), an illustrated anthology of male homoerotic poetry finally published in 1713. Here, as a reaction against the urban commercialization of *nanshoku*, Kigin attempts to present love between males as a tradition available to a wider audience by giving it both a cultural context and a history.[40] Literature featuring homoerotic themes reached its apogee with the forty short stories on same-sex love by Ihara Saikaku. Published in 1687, *The Great Mirror of Male Love* (*Nanshoku Ōkagami*), as the collection is known, depicts same-sex love not as an aberration but as a theme integral to the broader history of Japan.[41]

The opening of ports to Western trade in 1859 broke Japan's long period of relative isolation and signalled the beginning of the end for centuries of toleration. Following the Meiji Restoration and the return of imperial control in 1868, Japan's modernization along Western models was infused with clear overtones of Christian morality. Shinto phallic shrines; the monastic love of boys; male relationships among the samurai; the popularity of actor-prostitutes; and erotic art that attested to male same-sex practices: all were denounced as decadent remnants of a feudal past to be overcome. In 1873 Japan made homosexual relations between men a crime, although the law was repealed ten years later and never re-enacted. As Japan transformed itself into a successful capitalist economy with close political and commercial ties with the West, homosexuality was forced underground. Although male same-sex practices never attracted the degree of spiritual and moral condemnation in Japan that they did in the Christian West, ultimately the lack of social taboo did not result in the preservation of a rich and important cultural tradition. In recent years, however, a newly politicized gay subculture in Japan is attempting to reconcile the 'beautiful way' of the past with the demands of a globalized queer future. Voices from behind the cloak of conformity are once again singing songs of *nanshoku*.

The humorous short stories of Ihara Saikaku frequently include aspects of *nanshoku* culture; indeed, he is famous for devoting an entire collection to male same-sex love. This woodcut illustrates a scene from Saikaku's *Life of an Amorous Man* (1682), in which the hero visits a male house of entertainment.

India
Vedic legacies

Much less is known of the historical situation in India than in Japan or China. Whether this is due to lack of a reliable historical records or to a general social taboo remains unclear, but until very recently there prevailed a moral and a cultural silence on the subject of same-sex desire in India on account of a commonly held belief that homosexuality was a foreign import. Homosexuality did not enjoy the privilege of being incorporated into a recognized historical tradition in India until very recently.

This seems surprising when one considers that questions of sexuality are integral to India's ancient religious cultures, with early Hindu sacred texts and art heavily charged with an erotic sensibility.[42] Sexual desire, intimate friendship and gender ambiguity are issues central to ancient understandings of human relationships and the way in which they relate to the universe. Significantly, recent scholarship on sexuality has alerted us to religious texts in south Asian languages that reveal ample evidence of same-sex relations. According to the *Rg-Veda* (c. 1500 BCE), a collection of sacred hymns in Sanskrit charting the beginnings of the universe, desire is at the heart of creation.[43] What we actually desire as human beings is an aspect of otherworldly forces rather than an aspect of physical allure. For example, intimate friendships between women or men are regarded in the *Rg-Veda* as a highly spiritual bonding of souls leading to harmony with the universe. In the Vedic creation myths, of which this text is the best known, the parents who bring the universe into being need not necessarily be of opposite sexes. On the contrary, Agni — one of the most significant deities in the *Rg-Veda* — is often described as the 'child of two mothers' (*dvi-matri*), who is also nurtured by a group of mothers. Likewise, the text idealizes various members of the same sex as paired deities (*jamitva*) to be worshipped, such as twin brother-gods the Asvins.[44] Although these references do not specifically mention homosexuality, they do point to the ancient belief that same-sex intimacy was connected to notions of the divine.

The same concept reappears in the *Mahabharata* epic (c. 200 BCE – 200 CE), which charts the cosmic friendship between Krishna and Arjuna and presents it as a force that leads towards immortality and perfect bliss. Perhaps the most famous male friendship in any ancient Indian text, the relationship between Krishna and Arjuna reaches its climax in the section of the epic known as the *Bhagvad-gita*. The central proposition is that, like the human and the divine, the two characters are really one — loving reflections of each other.

Within Hindu mythology, love, sex and desire are of divine origin and do not correspond to modern understandings of a fixed sexual identity. Largely cosmic in nature, these concepts are linked to the idea that humans are mirrors of the universe. Many divine entities represent both sexes in unison, such as the hermaphroditic representations of Shiva in sculpture and painting (female on the left and male on the right) or the famous and popular deities who change gender, such as Ardharnarisvara and Sikandin. Krishna's son, Samba, was known for his love of cross-dressing, and Arjuna is described in the *Mahabharata* as dressing as a woman in order to teach music and singing at the court of King Virata.[45] In one of his many incarnations Vishnu manifested himself as a beautiful woman and together with Shiva produced a dual-gendered god called Ayyappa. In his pure Vedic form, Shiva is both male and female and encompasses the sum total of all consciousness, which has no gender. Ganesh, the elephant-headed god of wisdom and son of Shiva and Parvati, displays qualities of simultaneous force and kindness, thus representing the perfect equilibrium of male and female energies. Both Shiva and Ganesh are represented in popular Hindu iconography in an androgynous form. The message at the heart of these epics and images is that all humans are essentially a combination of masculine and feminine qualities, a belief that expresses itself most explicitly in the teachings of Tantric Hinduism, in which the Supreme Being is held to be one unified body containing both male and female sexual organs.[46]

Practices now regarded as 'homosexual' were linked in the Hindu imagination to the idea of a 'third sex' and given etymological significance through Sanskrit terms such as *napumsaka*, which means 'lacking maleness' or 'not masculine or feminine'.[47] This idea of a 'third sex' encompassed different subcategories of cross-gender individuals: ancient words such as *kliba* and *pandakas* were used to describe impotent, longhaired dancers, while *hijra* (a later Urdu term) referred to eunuchs, but also to transvestites and effeminate homosexual men. The acceptance of a 'third sex' category reflects the Hindu notion that sexual ambiguity can be cosmic. Eunuchs are an integral part of ancient Hindu tradition – references can be found as far back as the *Vedas*, in which they were charged with guarding the women's quarters or acted as singers, dancers and prostitutes.

Representations of female same-sex relations are also present in the ancient Indian tradition. A pertinent tale from the *Ramayana* epic (3rd century BCE) tells how the monkey god Hanuman spotted two women lying in each other's arms in the manner of lovers. An ancient ayurvedic surgery text, the *Sushruta Samhita* (*c.* 800–600 BCE), notes that two virile women could have intercourse with each other; if their secretions should mix in the womb of one of them, conception would occur but the child would be born without bones.[48] Female eroticism has also found its way into examples of Indian sculpture, such as the depiction of sexual interaction between women found in the Shiva temple at Ambernath (constructed in 1060 CE) and the representation of women engaged in mutual cunnilingus at a temple in Bhuveshar, in Orissa, dating from the 10th or 11th century CE.

In Hindu mythology the fusion of genders symbolizes the cosmic powers of the universe and the dual nature of creation. Here, in an 11th-century bronze statue from Tamil Nadu, Shiva is shown in his androgynous aspect as Ardharnarisvara: half of his body is male, and half recognizably female.

Two women enjoying sexual intercourse: a panel
from the Surya (Sun) temple at Konarak, *c.* 1238–58.
Temples in the Orissa district of northeastern India
are known for their exuberant and erotic sculptures,
which celebrate sexuality in all its forms. Such
buildings can be interpreted as symbolic of the
union between the earthly and the divine.

The *hijra* in India represent the existence of a third gender role. While some are transvestites and others are eunuchs, all are believed to possess the ability to bring good luck or to cast curses. For this reason they are regarded with a mixture of reverence and suspicion. Traditionally, they earn a living by blessing newborn males, performing at weddings or working as servants or prostitutes.

The *Kamasutra*, composed sometime between the fourth and sixth centuries CE, includes representations of same-sex sexual acts that are diverse, explicit and revelatory. All types of sexual intercourse between men and women, and between men and men, are described in great detail, as are female same-sex acts, sadomasochism, bestiality and group sex. Of particular note are the vivid descriptions of female same-sex intimacy. Liberated and independent women who refused marriage (*svairini*) appear in scenes where they use dildoes for 'virile copulation' with other women. Ancient Indian literature and culture indeed contained numerous references suggesting that women had their own social worlds where desire was not structured in patriarchal terms.[49]

The *Kamasutra* also provides practical advice for eunuchs in the art of 'mouth congress', carefully explaining the manual and oral techniques that stimulate the *lingam*, or penis. Unlike Chinese and Japanese representations of male-to-male sex, which emphasize anal sex – and the roles of 'inserter' and 'insertee' that mirror the heterosexual act – as the standard mode of intimacy between men, most ancient Indian texts focus on oral stimulation.[50] Moreover,

The Ishwara *lingam*, or *lingam-yoni* (below), is a popular fertility symbol and a common object of veneration (opposite). Comprising a phallic emblem (the *lingam*) set in an ovoid base (the *yoni*, or vulva), it represents the union of Shiva with his perennial consort, Parvati – together India's most revered cosmic parents.

veneration of the penis has a broader, spiritual aspect. In fact, both the male and the female organs appear in art and sculpture in their cosmic forms, and the *lingam* (the penis) and the *yoni* (the vagina) are worshipped as symbols of fertility. The *lingam* is associated especially with the cosmic powers of Shiva's manhood: in the earliest Hindu temples at Ellora in Maharashtra, rock carvings dating from the mid-6th century are dedicated to Shiva in the form of shrines to the phallic symbol. The popular Ishwara *lingam* symbolizes the union of *yoni* and *lingam*, and thus of Shiva and Uma (another name for Parvati), and is worshipped as a cosmic manifestation of fertility.[51]

Yet there exists a central contradiction in ancient Indian accounts of same-sex intimacy. While representations of sex speak of desire as something closely connected to a notion of divine bisexuality, religious texts dealing with matters of law and conduct discussed homosexuality in terms of social taboo or ritual pollution. For example, the *Manusmriti* (or *Laws of Manu*, compiled *c.* 1500 BCE) state: 'A twice-born man who commits an unnatural offence with a male, or has intercourse with a female in a cart drawn by oxen, in water, or in

the daytime, shall bathe, dressed in his clothes.' This represents another significant departure from the attitude in China, where same-sex sexuality was not subject to moral regulation, and from the Japanese Buddhist situation, where *nanshoku* enhanced one's spiritual status. The moral prescriptions of Hindu law were often at odds with the divine culture of sexual transgression.

Diverse landscapes

The Buddhist tradition in India, components of which were exported across Southeast Asia during the first five centuries CE, taught that all social behaviour must be regulated according to five moral precepts, of which the third governed sexual conduct. Same-sex sexuality is rarely singled out for special attention in the Buddhist canon, and the teachings of the Buddha himself do not bring it up as a topic separate from the broader concerns of correct conduct. Under the third precept, it is important for believers to observe principles of mutual consent, honesty and restraint, making adultery (which relies on deceitful behaviour) and sexual relations with those lacking free choice (such as girls and prisoners) particularly undesirable. That Japanese Buddhism should be intimately associated with male same-sex relations appears to be a unique phenomenon. Generally speaking, the *Vinaya* – the code of discipline that directs monastic life – requires monks to be celibate and prohibits them from engaging in any sexual activity in which the sexual member enters any orifice of the body.

Despite the lack of condemnation of homosexuality in the Buddhist canon itself, other Buddhist texts paint a less straightforward picture. This ambiguity can be seen clearly by comparing Buddhist texts that extol the virtues of same-sex intimacy with writings that abhor the physical act of same-sex relations. In the *Jatakas*, for example – ancient Indian folktales narrating the previous lives of the Buddha – the virtues of heterosexual love and marriage are not applicable to those living a monastic existence, but intimacy and love between two monks is held to enhance a sense of moral obligation and spiritual duty. The *Jatakas* tell of how the *bodhisattva* (the Buddha himself before he attained supreme enlightenment) was attended by a beautiful and devoted disciple, Ananda, who was his constant companion on the road to perfection and nirvana.[52] Yet the *Vinaya* condemns the explicit desire for same-sex activity as an example of uncontrollable lust. The text here uses the term *pandaka*, which literally means 'eunuch' but also encompasses men who engage in passive anal or oral intercourse (thus losing their maleness) – effectively transvestites and passive homosexuals banned from entering monastic life.[53] In the broader scheme of Buddhist cosmology, however, moral disapproval of the *pandaka* derives from the view that abstinence is to be preferred to sex, and that all intercourse undertaken for the sake of pleasure, whether between men and women or between men and men, hinders one's spiritual progress towards nirvana.

The case of Islam in India is particularly poignant. The historical record speaks of a relatively tolerant attitude towards same-sex love in Muslim India in tandem with a new appreciation for male beauty in literary and artistic representations. The long Islamic conquest of India from the seventh to the twelfth centuries started to establish new modes of artistic expression that

This Mughal miniature from the 18th century shows a remarkably natural and relaxed view of female–female intimacy. The gradual Islamic conquest of India brought with it not only new artistic styles, but also new attitudes towards same-sex relations; and the stringent segregation of the sexes must also have facilitated opportunities for same-sex relationships.

formed the foundation for the hybrid traditions of the later Delhi Sultanate and Mughal dynasties. With them came a different set of social attitudes towards same-sex relations in the Muslim courts. While orthodox interpretations of the Qur'an point to moral prohibitions against homosexuality, everyday practices were different. For example, harems of young boys were kept by Muslim *nawabs* for their pleasure. *Hijra* occupied a revered social position as guardians of female chastity and propriety in the Mughal courts, often having relationships with their noble Muslim masters. The Samarkand poet-scholar Mutribi Samarqandi travelled to India during the reign of Jahangir (1605–27), and his Persian-language *The Fair and the Dark Boys* tells of the mesmerizing effect that handsome slaves had on the Mughal court. Through the literary tropes of the *ghazal* and the *masnavi*, Sufi poetry in particular can be interpreted as an evocation of male same-sex love, albeit through the lens of the power relations (age, status and so on) inherent in a patriarchalist environment.[54] The emerging genre of Urdu poetry also provided opportunities for the articulation of same-sex desire: of particular note are the products of 19th-century *Rekhti* poetry, whose little-known representations of female same-sex intimacy provide an alternative to the more common depictions of male same-sex love that existed in the elite Persian tradition.[55]

Although most evidence of same-sex love in Indian contexts has come down to us through the northern Hindu, Buddhist and Muslim traditions, the Dravidian cultures of southern India offer yet another landscape of diversity where notions of desire and intimacy between people of the same sex were integrated into local traditions. In particular, the matrilineal and matrifocal culture of the Tamil-speaking regions provides a literary tradition that focuses on the intimate and supportive friendships of women and ignores the conventions of heterosexual marriage. The Tamil epic *Manimekhalai*, from the 3rd century CE, tells the story of a woman who refuses to marry the prince Udayakumara and is protected by her female relatives and close companions in her quest of independence – she even turns into a man in order to study ancient texts. Folk literature outside the ambit of the great historical epics testifies to the popularity of female bonding as a theme. One Tamil folk tale, *Alliyarasanimalai* (also from the 3rd century CE), speaks of the legendary Queen Alli and her pursuit of an all-female kingdom with the aid of martial women with whom she develops close relationships. This legend remains popular in the Tamil region, where it is recited, sung as a ballad or performed on stage.[56] Although not concerned with female homoeroticism per se, the Tamil tradition of representing female friendships offers a distinct perspective on same-sex intimacy.

In India, same-sex relations and intimate friendships were facilitated by strict gender roles, sex segregation and the exclusion of women from the public sphere. Opting out of marriage to form permanent partnerships, however, was not feasible. Same-sex relations, whether physical or simply homoerotic, coincided with the general expectation that one would marry and reproduce according to cultural tradition. The colonial era ushered in a new set of moral regulations, in particular the introduction of Section 377 of the

Two examples of temple sculpture that provide us with a rare glimpse of medieval Indian attitudes to same-sex intimacy. In the group shown above, from the Temple of Visvanatha, Khajuraho (10th century), a monk caresses a layman; while the panel illustrated opposite, from a 12th-century temple in Chhapri, shows a monk performing *auparashtika* (oral sex) on a high-caste visitor.

Indian Penal Code in 1860, which made 'sodomy' a criminal offence, thus transferring the Christian model of 'unnatural acts' to the Indian cultural landscape.[57] This law remains in effect in India to this day, and, despite recent campaigns to have it abolished by a new generation who identify on the basis of same-sex desire, religious fundamentalism and those who claim to defend 'family values' have obstructed decriminalization.[58] The recent growth of gay and lesbian organizations, especially in Mumbai, nonetheless reveals how same-sex desire has become a focus for identity, despite the enormous pressure in society at large to marry and uphold conventional gender roles.

Close examination of the historical evidence for categories of sexuality and their meaning for cultures of the past allows a rich tapestry of same-sex love in China, Japan and India to emerge. While the Judaeo-Christian tradition of moral revulsion and social taboo forms the backdrop to many conventional histories of the Western experience of same-sex love, a different trajectory emerges in Asia. Beyond the Western world view, there is a story of same-sex desire that can be detached both from the moral censure shaped by Christian notions of sodomy and the idea that every individual possesses an irreducible personal identity based on the preferred object of their sexual desire.

Poster sponsored in part by
HX FOR HER NEW YORK CITY
ANOTHER PUBLIC ART PROJECT BROUGHT TO YOU BY
DAM!
DYKE ACTION MACHINE
dam@echonyc.com
Not what I had in mind!
Is it worth being
Boring
for a Blender?
GAY MARRIAGE
You might as well be straight.

The Gay World: 1980 to the Present
GERT HEKMA

A world of pleasure

Berlin had a rich and varied homosexual subculture in the 'roaring twenties', and during the 1950s gay life in Paris, Copenhagen and Amsterdam really took off.[1] But since the late 1960s and the so-called sexual revolution, a public gay culture has developed in an ever greater number of cities. The raid on the Stonewall Inn in New York's Christopher Street in 1969 and the rebellion that followed are often seen as a watershed in the United States, and in fact the resistance of these homosexual and transgendered men and women assumed international significance. The day of the uprising, 27 June, is now commemorated with Stonewall parades and Christopher Street Days.[2]

Queer bars had existed before, but they were mostly mixed (patronized by gays and straights), and the police often raided or closed down places where 'unwelcome elements' such as homosexuals congregated. This world was unstable and faced interventions by state authorities and the straight public. Its shifting nature was also a result of the different types of sexual object sought by homosexuals. 'Queens' and 'sissies', who often loved straight men, or 'trade' — sailors, soldiers, working-class youths — did not necessarily depend on bars to meet their love objects, finding the streets more worthwhile.[3] Later, gay men increasingly sought sex with their equals — clones, machos and leather men — and they ventured into a world of bars with darkrooms and saunas. From northwestern Europe and from the east and west coasts of the United States, this new arena of gay sex and love spread all over the globe.

The gay world of the 1960s and 1970s became more exclusively gay. Bars and bathhouses had historically served both 'queens' (self-identified homosexuals) and 'trade', while venues in post-Stonewall times catered almost entirely to gay men; straight men who continued to frequent them would now be classified as bisexuals or 'closet cases'. This world also became increasingly specialized, with particular venues appealing to particular groups: gay activists, for example, or men in leather, drag artists, or younger or older men. While drinking and drunkenness had always been a part of the gay social sphere, the discos of the 1970s and 1980s saw the use of drugs as well. The old-style dance parlour turned into a discotheque: whereas the preferred accompaniment had been folk or French *chansons*, pop and disco music — the soundtrack to the sexual revolution — took over; and the elegant waltzing of

Although gay marriage is one of the most debated topics of recent years, not everyone aspires to an image of wedded bliss. For some, marriage represents a heterosexual institution that has no relevance to the way they live their lives. This poster, by Dyke Action Machine, was fly-posted around New York City in 1997.

By the late 1970s bars and clubs had become central to gay urban culture. They were both more visible than before and more specialized, with particular venues reflecting specific tastes in sexual object. Here is the Cuckoo's Nest, a leather bar in Amsterdam, providing a place for socializing for one of the most recognizable gay subcultures.

couples was replaced by clones in tight blue jeans, t-shirts and work boots dancing wildly. (These masculine men often rejected the effeminacy of the queens and pumped their bodies in gyms — which by the 1990s had become, in some places, more important for same-sex sociability than bars and discos.) The most important change of the 1970s, however, was the intense sexualization of gay culture. When bars and discos did not offer the possibility of instant and anonymous sex on the premises, gay men could go elsewhere, to their bedrooms, a quiet spot in an alley, a sauna, a cruisy park or a public toilet. The men who enjoyed 'homosex' had more of it in this short period before the advent of AIDS, with fewer qualms about family or police, and when venereal diseases could be cured with a shot of penicillin, than they had ever done in the past.

This new homosexual culture gave rise to a patchwork of sexual relations, romantic relationships and acquaintances. Some one-night stands developed into grand passions and love affairs, while others became lasting friendships. Homosexuals had traditionally felt threatened by family, friends, neighbours, state institutions and even sexual partners and lovers, but in gay 'ghettos' the pressures of the outside world became less insistent. Here they created places

Before the arrival of AIDS, gay life for many men had come to mean the ever-present promise of sex and the chance of instant gratification. Photographer Alvin Baltrop recorded the cruising scene around the derelict West Side piers in New York during the mid-1970s; it was an era of almost unparalleled sexual liberation, although few who were a part of it remain. This work, entitled *Don't Let Them See You*, dates from 1977.

in which to live together and invented multiple forms of sociability. While the straight world saw a growing dichotomy between singles and couples, the gay world found many ways to bridge the rift between the two. The main reason for this was that most homosexuals felt able to separate love and sex; and they no longer believed in monogamy, but in experiencing love and sex in a whole range of different relationships. Edmund White has sung the praises of this vibrant world in his writing, while Patrick Moore has suggested reviving it.[4]

The growth of this new gay culture was nevertheless uneven. In The Netherlands and Denmark (that is to say, in Amsterdam and Copenhagen), it developed during the 1960s, appearing in cities on the east and west coasts of North America, in Britain and in Germany in the 1970s. Spain had to wait for the death of Franco in 1975 before Madrid and Barcelona blossomed in the 1980s; and at the same time Paris closed down its old mafia-controlled bars. Milan and Sydney were next in line, followed by non-Western cities such as Rio de Janeiro, Tokyo, Bangkok and Manila. After the fall of the Iron Curtain in 1989, gay culture established itself in Eastern Europe. So it was that the gay world in cities around the globe became a community, with both a sense of

A male brothel in Amsterdam. We may often view prostitution as a form of oppression, but these young men, and their smiling madam, seem quite happy to be working in that particular service industry.

identity — of belonging — and of space. Homosexuals started to live near gay-owned bars and businesses (especially in North America), and thus the gay world began to spread to whole neighbourhoods. Political, social and sports organizations flourished, and gay districts became destinations for gay tourists and immigrants.

Yet alongside the global spread of a gay community a serious problem was emerging. The arrival of AIDS in the early 1980s almost halted the spread of a gay scene and effectively ended the reigning culture of sexual pleasure. The effects of the epidemic were most devastating in the United States, where it had begun. The government reacted with repressive measures, and all over the country police and health officials shut down places of sexual pleasure such as saunas and backrooms. Owing to the close involvement of gay political movements in AIDS prevention, however, countries in northwestern Europe decided not to close sex venues — it was better, they argued, to use such settings to give out information on AIDS and safer sex than drive gay men underground, where they would probably continue unsafe practices. The countries that were less restrictive in their response to the AIDS crisis did indeed prove more successful in preventing the disease. Much depended on the timing of the epidemic; the attitudes of the gay movement, entrepreneurs (bar owners, for example, were among the first to provide condoms) and the public; and on the speed with which individual countries realized the gravity of the situation (the French gay press, for instance, initially denied the severity of AIDS). But by the end of the 1980s, no gay man in the Western world could convincingly say that he did not know what AIDS and safe sex were, although debates concerning precise definitions of safe and unsafe sex would continue.[5]

In the 1990s the gay community started to grow again and once more sexual pleasure became an important part of gay social life, although homosexuals were now more aware of what constituted safer sex. The subculture expanded and, on account of AIDS, it also moved above ground. Media attention surrounding the epidemic had sparked a general interest in gay men and venues, while the politics of safe sex had brought previously covert terminology out into the open. The gay world became differentiated internally even as it became more homogenized on a global scale. Lesbians, drag queens, transgenders and bisexuals played a greater role than before, now establishing their own events and organizations, and minorities of African, Asian and Arab origin set their own agendas. Information networks such as Minitel in France, sex phonelines and the internet made it possible for those with all kinds of sexual interests to make contact. Thus the 'kinky' scene in particular underwent great diversification: fans of rubber and sports clothing appeared alongside established leather and S&M groups, while bears, skinheads, and lovers of army and police uniforms created their own meeting places for sex and sociability.

While the bigger cities saw a proliferation of venues designed for sexual pleasure, smaller tourist destinations, often beach resorts, joined the list: Mykonos, Sitges and Ibiza in Europe, and Fire Island, Provincetown, Miami's South Beach, Palm Springs and Russian River in the United States. Weekend trips to urban destinations combined the consumption of 'high culture' with opportunities for sex and sociability. In the past, only a few cities had a specific attraction for homosexuals looking for a short holiday; nowadays, any major Western city is a possible gay destination, as are such non-Western places as Marrakech, Cairo, Manila, Bali and Bangkok. Many cities in Latin America and South and East Asia now harbour lively local gay scenes. Guidebooks have opened up a global gay sphere that is quite recognizable for a Western tourist, although the Arab world, China, India, Japan and Thailand in particular continue to host same-sex sexual practices and venues that are utterly peculiar to their own cultures – not gay in a Western sense – and often difficult for outsiders to access.

Gay life has always been largely urban because a city's communities made identification along homosexual lines easier. In a highly suburbanized country such as The Netherlands, a gay venue is never further than 30 miles (50 km) away – a big difference from the situation in a larger country like the United States, where people may live many hours from the closest bar or club. Gays in remote places had little chance of finding sex and love, and straight people would not have come across homosexuality. Nowadays, however, the internet brings the gay world into one's home, and email and similar programs make communication possible over long distances. While it may remain difficult for

Frustrated by the failure of government agencies to subsidize research into HIV/AIDS or provide adequate healthcare, groups such as ACT UP organized campaigns of civil disobedience reminiscent of the heydays of gay activism. This newspaper clipping from 1988 reports a 'die-in' staged by ACT UP at the offices of the Food and Drug Administration in Rockville, Maryland. More than one thousand people took part in the nine-hour protest.

overleaf
A powerful visual symbol of the terrible toll taken by the AIDS epidemic in the United States. Started in 1987, the AIDS Memorial Quilt is composed of blocks that typically contain eight panels, each of which represents a life lost to AIDS. This public display in 1992 in front of the Washington Memorial included 20,000 quilts; the panels are now so numerous that it is no longer possible to show them together in a single space.

those who live in the countryside to find physical proximity with other gay men or women, cheap airfares allow others to participate in city-hopping and party-going, to join demonstrations or to visit friends and lovers.

AIDS

The segregated homosexual world of the 1970s appears to have been the ideal breeding ground for venereal disease (VD). Most sexually transmitted diseases could be cured with simple treatment, and gays could even meet partners in VD clinics and joke about the risks of sex. New diseases that appeared at the end of the 1970s and in the early 1980s were not so easy to cure or make fun of. First there appeared various types of hepatitis and chlamydia. Then, in the early 1980s, homosexuals began to come down with diseases atypical for their generation and profile, such as Kaposi's sarcoma and lung diseases. In June 1981, the US Centers for Disease Control (CDC) issued its first report on an unknown syndrome that affected younger gay men, and the mysterious disease claimed its first victims. Most people showing symptoms of the illness died very quickly, and gay organizations and health authorities worried that a new and fatal epidemic was on its way. Doctors first called it Gay-Related Immune Deficiency (GRID), about a year later changing its name to Acquired Immune Deficiency Syndrome (AIDS). The symptomatic diseases were explained as a breakdown of the immune system in those who were affected. Homosexuals feared that the AIDS epidemic would be a major setback for gay life and the gay movement, while Christian crusaders saw it as a punishment for sin. It was a disaster for the gay world, and tens of thousands died of AIDS in the following decades, especially in the United States.

Most governments nevertheless reacted very slowly to the epidemic, since it was thought to affect only homosexuals — a position that created despair and anger among the gay community. It soon became clear that AIDS was also affecting other, non-gay groups, the famous 'four Hs': homosexuals, heroin addicts, haemophiliacs and Haitians. The second and third groups became infected through unclean needles used to inject drugs and through blood transfusions, while it seemed that the epidemic had apparently begun in Haiti at the same time as in the United States. Like a true plague, the disease soon spread beyond these four groups to what was termed the 'general population'. Such terminology was extremely offensive to homosexuals, since it implied that they were a category apart; furthermore, it seemed that worries about the disease exploded only once heterosexuals, and not just marginal groups, began to contract AIDS.

French scientists in 1984 isolated the cause of AIDS — later named the Human Immunodeficiency Virus (HIV) — although they bickered with colleagues at the American CDC who claimed to be the first to have discovered it. Once the agent was known, testing became possible. This raised the question of whether patients who might have been infected should be tested: there was no therapeutic medicine available, and the knowledge of having been infected could create psychological problems and social difficulties, for example with insurance companies and mortgage lenders. In some countries people were initially advised against taking the test. When effective medication was developed, however, that advice was reversed. Before the exact method of transmission was discovered, many myths circulated: that it was possible to catch the disease by sharing glasses, toilets or toothbrushes with infected persons, for instance, or through insect bites or even by shaking hands. Scientists eventually discovered that the virus was spread by blood, sperm and other bodily fluids, and that it could not survive for long outside the body. This made it possible for doctors to recommend 'safe sex' – no anal sex without a condom. (To what extent oral sex is unsafe has remained a topic of debate.)

At the beginning of the epidemic, alliances between health authorities and gay political movements were difficult to establish, but individual physicians and gay health groups helped to bridge the gap. Particularly important were organizations that delivered health care and mental and social support to patients, such as the Gay Men's Health Crisis, founded in 1982 in New York; the San Francisco AIDS Foundation; the Terrence Higgins Trust in London; and AIDES, established by Daniel Defert in Paris after the death of his lover, Michel Foucault. Because medical and political authorities were slow to react to the epidemic, patients and gay men became radicalized. First in the United States, and subsequently in other Western countries, the failure of the state to pay for research and provide good healthcare angered the gay community. Radical queer groups attacked social and medical policies: the most prominent was ACT UP (AIDS Coalition to Unleash Power), who coined the slogan SILENCE = DEATH and used aggressive methods of protest. Meanwhile artists and advertising specialists were contributing to the success and visibility of radical groups, and gay writing, too – which had come of age during the 1970s – drew attention to the epidemic.

AIDS organizations were successful in several innovative ways. They came up with the idea of 'buddies' – volunteers who helped patients with daily chores. Since AIDS victims and their friends included many well-educated and self-aware young men, groups were articulate and confident enough to be able to criticize and ultimately change the medical system. The most important contribution of ACT UP, the most active of these organizations, was to democratize and critically examine the medical system, suggesting alternative methods of care and research; the trial of new treatments was speeded up on their insistence. Some groups started to import promising medicines illegally, while others created consumers' organizations and provided information on the disease and reputed cures. They lobbied for more money for research. Patients with other diseases picked up on such innovations and started organizing themselves proactively. Even the funeral industry changed through AIDS, as gays created new forms of burial and remembrance ceremonies.

In some countries the government, health authorities and the gay movement worked together to combat the epidemic and to help its victims. This model of cooperation had begun in Scandinavia and The Netherlands, where it proved successful, and was taken up in other locations. Its achievements were the end of discrimination in visiting rights, social security and health care; the wide dissemination of information on AIDS and safer sex; and

The ever-expanding Memorial Quilt, decorated with names, items of clothing, messages and mementos, is at once both a personal and public memorial to the victims of AIDS. Although prompted by a disastrous epidemic, such projects played an important role in once more politicizing the gay community against ignorance and discrimination.

the provision of clean needles for drug addicts. Hospitals created special wards for AIDS patients, and mental care was made available.

Around 1990, antiviral medicines such as AZT were introduced that prolonged the lives of the patients, but which nevertheless had negative side effects and did not prevent patients from dying. In 1996 a new cocktail of different medicines became available that for most patients made AIDS a chronic disease rather than a fatal illness, since it extended life expectancy by many years. Although the cocktail did not restore full health, it made a more or less normal life possible. One unexpected drawback of this success was that some people paid less attention to safer sex, a few even going as far as to run the risk of contracting HIV by engaging in risky behaviour ('barebacking', or practising anal sex without a condom). Yet warnings made at the beginning of the epidemic have largely been heeded, producing a slowdown in the rate of infection, at least in Western countries. Homosexuals in particular have taken safer sex campaigns seriously and changed their sexual practices radically. Such high levels of acceptance of health advice is rare in disease prevention, and the gay world has done an exemplary job in changing behaviour and preventing further spread of the disease.

Although AIDS has been a disaster, there have been a few beneficial results. The rise of a concerned and self-conscious 'client group' is one such development. It has also become possible to speak in clearer language about sex. The crisis fostered a stronger cooperation between gays and lesbians. Loving relationships received more attention: whereas previously it had been

difficult for gays to share lives with each other because of the interference of families, neighbours and institutions, with AIDS it became clear that such intimate relationships were essential. Gays were not merely sexual beings, but also people who maintained loving partnerships. AIDS also pointed up such issues for patients and their partners as hospital visiting rights, housing, insurance, pensions, and wills and bequests. The particular needs of same-sex couples became a political issue, which in turn opened a debate on the subject of same-sex marriage.[6]

Homophobia and heteronormativity

Despite its successes during the 1960s and 1970s — at least in some countries — the gay rights movement has not ended anti-homosexual discrimination or modified the dominant straight culture. In all countries, changes in civil and criminal law may have led to less official discrimination, but social discrimination continues. Criminal laws that targeted male homosexuals have been abolished in Britain, Germany, The Netherlands, France, Spain and many other European states since the late 1960s; and the European Union has outlawed anti-homosexual legislation and endorses anti-discrimination policies in the workplace.[7] But even in The Netherlands, considered by many one of the most tolerant societies, anti-homosexual attitudes and homophobic violence remain widespread. Notwithstanding the fact that a new generation has grown up in a culture where homo- and heterosexuality are regarded as equal, many youngsters (mainly young men) still harbour a prejudice against homosexuals and act upon their sentiments. Discrimination ranges from murder to more covert forms of harassment, for example in political and intellectual circles. About twice a year, for instance, a male prostitute kills a gay man in Amsterdam — a crime police do not take very seriously, either because the perpetrators are often arrested soon after or because officers see it as a minor form of robbery or as a fight between lovers. Although authorities have stopped considering the murderers as the victims, they continue to blame homosexuals as somehow responsible for their fate.[8]

Homosexuals face abuse not only in the world of prostitution, but also in cruising areas, bars and discos, in workplaces and at home;[9] the mutilation in early 2004 of a gay man in his own garden by young men made headlines in France and clarified how equal rights, such as marriage, were needed to end anti-homosexual discrimination. Anti-gay slang words are common in school playgrounds, and discrimination, either explicit or implied, exists in families, workplaces, and in the fields of health care and recreation. Promotions are refused and lovers are rejected or neglected, while many regulations regarding housing, health care, insurance and pensions do not cover homosexuals or same-sex couples. In employment, there is a 'glass ceiling' for homosexuals similar to that experienced by women, and the heterosexist assumptions of society at large — gays and lesbians are seen as straight until the opposite is proven — pose a continuing problem. Although there is no reliable data covering cases of discrimination and violence, the information available indicates that gay men face high levels of verbal and physical abuse. To make the situation worse, gays and straights are both inclined to deny or neglect anti-homosexual

The relationship between homosexuals and organized religion has seldom been an easy one. But non-conformist churches have sprung up in recent decades to minister to the spiritual needs of gay men and women who have often felt excluded from religious worship. The photograph above was taken at Washington National Cathedral, DC, during an investiture held by the Metropolitan Community Church, the largest and most influential of the gay churches.

violence and abuse, sometimes with the argument of 'that's the way life is'.

Since the 1960s European countries have gradually decriminalized homosexuality, and there is now no European state in which homosexuality is specifically prohibited. Decriminalization has also occurred in such countries as Australia and South Africa. In 1989 the US Supreme Court upheld sodomy laws, leading to a major protest; in 2003 it overturned the earlier decision in a landmark ruling that named specific criminalization of homosexual acts as unconstitutional. Homosexuality's status as pathology has become highly contested, and few psychiatrists in Western Europe now hold homosexuality *per se* to be a psychiatric illness, although many continue to view homosexuality negatively. This change of position followed the removal of homosexuality from the US list of psychiatric disorders in 1973 and from a similar list kept by the World Health Organization in 1992.[10] Beyond the Western world, homosexuality is nevertheless still widely seen as a vice.

For the most part, negative attitudes derive from a past in which homosexuality was considered a sin, a crime and a disease. The oldest and strongest source for the rejection of homosexuality, at least in countries that have a predominantly Judaeo-Christian tradition, is religion. Although some Protestant denominations have changed their position since the sexual revolution of the 1960s, the conversion has been only partial. The Danish Lutheran church successfully opposed the possibility of church ceremonies for same-sex partnerships when the government granted them legal status in 1989. Anti-homosexual statements have come from recent popes and from Roman Catholic clergy, from mainstream Protestant and evangelical leaders, and from Jewish rabbis. When they discuss the topic publicly, Eastern Orthodox clergy and Muslim imams are negative about homosexual sex and gay people almost without exception, and they have spoken out against homosexual rights. Some religious groups began to accept the sinner but not the sin, exhorting their gay members to remain chaste; thus the Catholic Church maintains that the problem lies not in being homosexual, but in homosexual sex. Such positions have led gays and lesbians to create their own churches, the most important being the Metropolitan Community Church, which was founded in California in 1968. Despite their rejection of homosexuality, most churches count significant numbers of clerics with queer desires — a fact that became public knowledge with the various paedophile scandals involving priests in the United States and Europe, although their erotic interests are not usually focused on underage boys.[11] Notwithstanding the anti-gay and pro-reproductive stances of most religions, the relationship between homosexuality and religious desire remains strong — partly on account of the frequently recognized link between femininity, spirituality and homosexuality,[12] and partly because religious communities are often homosocial environments.

Anti-homosexual sentiments vary according to ethnicity as much as religion. In many European countries, complaints are raised against male youths from ethnic minority backgrounds who behave violently against homosexuals. Their families often come from Muslim countries where homosexual practices, despite being widespread, are considered to be sinful. Muslim leaders

For all the progress of recent years against prejudice and discrimination, it sometimes feels as if there is an awfully long way to go. While almost all countries still battle against anti-homosexual sentiment, the situation in the United States has been exacerbated by a rise in religious conservatism. Above: A Baptist minister holds two signs reading 'God Hates Fags' at an anti-gay demonstration in Columbia, Missouri, 1998. Opposite: An issue of *Time* magazine from 26 October 1998, entitled 'The War Over Gays'. It appeared a few weeks after the brutal homophobic murder of 21-year-old Matthew Shepard in Laramie, Wyoming.

have repeatedly maintained that, according to Islamic holy scripture, homosexual acts deserve the death penalty.[13] There are no answers to the many questions this argument raises, nor are there statistics to prove that youths from ethnic minorities account for a greater number of homophobic crimes, or whether they are influenced by their cultural or religious heritage. Often the youths subject gays to verbal abuse in order to test the limits of tolerance, and anti-gay attitudes are facilitated by authorities who are afraid of engaging in discussions on homosexuality.[14] Meanwhile, gay youngsters from ethnic minorities themselves have to face serious conflicts. Their families often say they have become too Western by choosing partners of the same sex, while the gay world stereotypes them as unreliable hustlers, queerbashers or pickpockets. Some have created their own groups and spaces for socializing. London has Chinese and Indian groups; gay Turks have established organizations in Germany; Arabs are able to join Kelma in Paris or the Habibi-Ana in Amsterdam; and the Yoesuf Foundation tries to create a bridge between Islam and homosexuality in The Netherlands. The Parisian 'Beur-Black-Blanc' tea dances cater to Arabs, blacks and whites, while in many cities Long Yang clubs attract Asians and Europeans with mutual erotic interests.

There are, of course, many positive stories of gays who are embraced by their families, friends or work colleagues. There are indeed certain workplaces that prefer men without children to heterosexuals who take time off for childcare. There are also professions that are largely beyond homosexual discrimination, such as the worlds of fashion and art. The token gay in the straight world or the token black in the gay world are sometimes welcomed as expressions of political correctness.

The United States and Europe offer similar pictures of contemporary gay life, but the situation in the United States is generally worse. In world surveys, Americans express anti-homosexual sentiments more often than Europeans, and violence targeted explicitly against gay people is also more common in the United States (where the general level of violence is also higher), while the researcher Luiz Mott has suggested that the number of victims of anti-gay violence are higher still in Brazil.[15] Some US cities and states accord equal rights to homosexuals, but in most places legal, civil and social discrimination still rules.[16] Notwithstanding positive changes, verbal and physical violence continues everywhere and is nowhere a high priority of the police or courts.

With homosexuality growing in visibility, in many places homophobic violence is also on the rise, especially where homosexuality is considered a Western disease, as in Zimbabwe, the Arab world or in India. There have recently been anti-gay laws and raids, for instance, in Egypt, the United Arab Emirates, Tanzania, Nepal and Malaysia. In Zimbabwe, former president Canaan Banana was convicted for sodomy in 1998, and in Malaysia the deputy prime minister, Anwar Ibrahim, was convicted of the same offence in 1999 (this ruling was overturned in 2004). Both convictions created scandal because they combined sexual repression with political corruption. On the other hand, gay cultures and political movements have come into open existence in most countries, including the non-Western world. They are sometimes very successful in their aims, as is the case in South Africa, where homosexual rights are now enshrined in the post-apartheid constitution.

The main problem for gays and lesbians everywhere is that society remains largely defined by heterosexuality and excludes or marginalizes other choices; it is for this reason that the queer movement has wanted to defy heteronormativity and create a 'queer public culture'. Even in tolerant societies, such as The Netherlands or Scandinavia, public life remains straight: heterosexuality is the norm and homosexuality is viewed as a second-class option. Heteronormativity gives rise to a dichotomy between public and private, in which 'public' equals 'heterosexual', and 'homosexual' is reduced to a personal and private affair. This creates a strange Catch-22 situation, in that gays are supposed to come out, but if they do so, others complain that their sexual preference does not matter in public. Homosexuals are thus forced to search for an impossible balance between being silent and loudly proclaiming their sexual interests. At the same time, they have to suffer others' endless and very public small talk of heterosexual 'private matters'. This straight norm indicates that discrimination against homosexuality has not disappeared; indeed, it shows that, following the gay struggle for legal equality, there is a difficult battle for social emancipation still to be fought — difficult because its targets are harder to define, and because various subgroups sometimes have opposing interests.

The media

Since the 1970s newspapers and television news programmes have begun to pay more attention to gay issues, covering such topics as legal struggles for equality, gay pride marches, debates surrounding a 'gay gene' and same-sex marriage — in fact, the entertainment industry and media in general cannot stop talking about what was once unmentionable. This radical change was partly a result of the AIDS epidemic, which forced health and public authorities to speak publicly and explicitly in a way impossible in earlier times. By the 1990s the media had become eloquent and verbose concerning what had been unspeakable.

There are great differences among various countries, however. In Northern Europe media attention is generally friendly, but some places do prefer the scandal-mongering typical of the sensationalist tabloid press. Germans, and even more so the British, are obsessed with the sexual transgressions of famous people. Major scandals surrounded British Liberal Party leader Jeremy Thorpe in 1976 and the German NATO deputy supreme commander in Europe, General Gunter Kiessling, in 1984. Politicians in the past were forced to resign because of gay or kinky interests, but even Britain nowadays can have an openly gay political leader (although more closeted cases remain the norm). Gay celebrities have also attracted greater attention, not always voluntarily: George Michael, for instance, was a victim of unwelcome attention after police arrested him for having sex in a public place. Now that more homosexuals in high places have come out, scandal is beginning to appear outdated. Many who work in the theatre, the arts and in politics are openly gay and often receive respectful media coverage. Soaps, sitcoms and talk shows have increasing numbers of gay characters; Hollywood makes mainstream movies with gay storylines, such as *Philadelphia* (1994), *Gods and Monsters* (1998) and *Brokeback Mountain* (2005); and the British series *Queer as Folk* (1999) has enjoyed global success. There is now a set of gay icons representing high and low culture, from science to comedy: Oscar Wilde, Marcel Proust, Rock Hudson, Pier Paolo Pasolini, Pedro Almodóvar, Alan Turing, Michel Foucault, Andy Warhol, and many playwrights, actors and fashion designers. Their lives, their work (which has illustrated a variety of gay themes) and their status have contributed greatly to gay visibility, showing queer life in all its diversity. To the list also belong 'dangerous' figures such as serial killers and the Nazi leader Ernst Röhm. It has even been claimed recently that Adolf Hitler was homosexual.[17] A younger gay crowd — frequently pop stars, fashion designers and actors — have joined the gay icons of earlier days, although few sports figures and businessmen appear on the lists.

In most countries it has thus become virtually impossible not to come across gay imagery or at least public discussion of homosexuality, though it may not always be favourable. This exposure has had both beneficial and dangerous consequences. The increased visibility of homosexuals is a positive step, while the gap that exists between their exposure in the media and their everyday lives has not been bridged. In some places, the prominence of news relating to the issue of homosexuality in Western media has led to claims that it is a Western import that should be combated or eradicated. The tables have turned: while in the past the West attributed vice to the inhabitants of Africa and the Orient, nowadays some in Africa and Asia locate the origin of the homosexual 'disease' in the Occident. This has led to widespread anti-homosexual sentiment.

The newest addition to the media, the internet, has made it possible for gays and lesbians in parts of the world where any kind of public visibility is well-nigh absent, such as China and the Arab world, to communicate via their computers. In the West, it has allowed those who have difficulty in finding or fitting in with gay life, including young people and those who live outside large towns, to access it. The variety of ways in which people can meet on the internet, and discuss political issues in chat rooms and on discussion lists, is a challenge with which businesses and political institutions are constantly trying to keep up. In addition to chat and discussion forums, the web is an amazingly rich source of information, hosting everything from academic texts to kinky pornography. The abstraction of the internet provides an interesting contrast with the physicality of the gay scene.

The Gay and Lesbian Movement

The continuing homophobia of state and society on the one hand, and the openings promised by the 1960s and 1970s on the other, gave the gay and lesbian movement a new impetus during the 1970s. It became more radical and achieved undeniable results: the abolition of the most repressive legislation; the removal of homosexuality from lists of psychiatric disorders; and a greater visibility for homosexuals in the media and in the streets, partly through political demonstrations.[18] These results nevertheless varied greatly among different countries.

Two satirical views of the United States' 'gays in the military' debate. In 1993 Bill Clinton, attempting to end a ban on homosexuals serving in the armed forces, devised the policy known as 'Don't Ask, Don't Tell'. In the event, this legislation has not only failed to end discrimination, but actually seems to have increased it. Despite all appearances, the poster opposite claims the army to be 'Certified 100% Homo-Free'. The cartoon on the right, however, shows a soldier breaking the news to his sergeant. 'Sir, I'm gay, sir', he says, while his superior is trying hard not to hear him.

The issues that have mobilized the gay rights movement have included equality in criminal, civil and labour laws, sex education, housing, social security, pensions and taxes; combatting violence and prejudice; immigration laws and political asylum; equal rights and anti-discrimination legislation; laws against abuse and vilification; claims on gay spaces; and same-sex marriage. In most places, even such respectable goals have not been reached. The more radical aims of the 1960s, such as the abolition of sexual and gender dichotomies, were soon forgotten.

After the radicalism of the early 1970s, the gay liberation movement became less revolutionary, in part because activists had already paved the way for those more mainstream gays and lesbians who wanted respectability and toleration. The movement showed its strength in annual parades: starting as small-scale demonstrations that put forward political demands, they became massive celebratory events more in the spirit of community days or weekend festivals. Commercial institutions played a growing role and political leaders now took the front row. The marches that had started in New York in 1970 with the first anniversary of the Stonewall Riots spread over the United States, Europe and Australia, and are now being taken up in various non-Western countries. Demonstrations in Belgrade in 2001 and Zagreb in 2002 – the first to be held in their respective countries – and marches in Krakow and Poznań in 2004 sparked ferocious attacks by hooligans and right-wing nationalists. (Even in the Amsterdam Gay Pride parade of 2004, troublemakers amused themselves by throwing revellers into the canals.) In 1981 activists in Sydney moved their celebrations commemorating Stonewall from June to February to coincide with the southern summer, thus creating the Mardi Gras, now the world's largest gay event. German cities developed a programme of parades that followed one after another during weekends in June and July. In the United States, massive marches were organized in Washington, DC, in 1979, 1987, 1993 and 2000, where politics once again took centre stage; but the high hopes that had followed the Supreme Court's repeal of sodomy laws in 2003 and the

AUGUST 28 - SEPTEMBER 5 · KE

Sport – often considered the last true bastion of heterosexist attitudes – is enjoying increasing popularity among gay men and women. Since the establishment of the Gay Games in San Francisco in 1982, gays and lesbians have enjoyed the chance to compete on an international level.

PIC GAMES

R STADIUM · SAN FRANCISCO

quick spread of recognized same-sex marriages in 2004 were disappointed by the re-election of President George W. Bush.

In the 1980s and 1990s increasingly conservative gay leaders came forward. In the United States, several authors defined the aim of gay emancipation as 'getting a place at the table'[19] — principally same-sex marriage and the right to serve in the armed forces. Yet such activists also wanted to get rid of those at the margins of the gay world — in the first place paedophiles, but also drag and leather queens, and men who cruise for sex in public places — because they spoiled the image of homosexuals. These conservatives also believed in a 'gay gene', in the innateness of homosexuality. They were opposed by some who believed that the struggle should not stop with equality for homosexuals, but should bring about sexual freedom for all: for them, the question of whether or not sexual preference was biologically determined was irrelevant. Notwithstanding a massive turnout of gays and lesbians at marches and parades, and intense debate surrounding gay issues, even the most generally shared aims of the gay rights movement in the United States have not been reached. The American military remain closed to homosexuals despite the implementation of Bill Clinton's policy of 'Don't Ask, Don't Tell', since when more homosexuals have been discharged from the army than ever before.[20] A more conservative turn has also become visible in the gay movements of other countries. Integration into the political machine often means compromising the aims of gay equality: even several leaders of right-wing parties have been openly gay — the neo-Nazi Michael Kühnen in Germany, for instance, who died of AIDS in 1991, and Pim Fortuyn in The Netherlands, who was murdered in 2002.

Apart from issues of criminal law, AIDS, the armed forces and marriage, the gay rights movement also deals with questions of housing, health care, social security, partner benefits and inheritance. In the late 1980s, in the wake of the AIDS crisis, the success of ACT UP led to the establishment of Queer Nation, a group that wanted to re-energize the gay movement by making queerness visible in the straight world and by queering heteronormative society. Queer Nation, which operated mainly in the United States, espoused queer theory, which emphasized that concepts of identity and community were unstable.[21] Since the recent conservative turn in US politics, however, Queer Nation's goals seem postponed to a distant future. Similar confrontational politics became the trademark of the London-based OutRage!, whose leading voice was Peter Tatchell. Among other examples of discrimination, they fought against the Thatcher-era Clause 28, which forbade what the Conservative government saw as the 'promotion' of homosexuality. 'Queer', once an insult, became a popular word in the 1990s, for some indicating rage and a radical struggle against straight norms and gay conservatism, for others suggesting a way to remain closeted; in Croatia, 'queer' means simply 'gay' and expresses the desire of young men to live happily together. In English-speaking countries the term has become outdated and no new terminology has yet taken its place.

The proliferation of gay groups with various agendas has led to the creation of local and international networks that have contributed greatly to emancipation. Many groups focus on local issues, for example organizations that represent businesses and help to combat discrimination against bars, promote the local scene or organize events. Sex Panic, a radical queer group in New York, lost its struggle against the 'cleaning up' of Times Square and against the city's zoning policy, which forced most sex venues to close down.[22] An Amsterdam group was more successful, keeping a local park (a popular cruising ground) available for homosexuals. Other organizations offer safe sex venues or establish facilities for increasingly popular gay and lesbian sports activities; since 1982, the Gay Games have offered an international platform for gay and lesbian athletes.

Openly homosexual politicians have been another major force for gay and lesbian emancipation. Some came out after being elected, but others won an election victory after making their homosexuality public. In 1977 the flamboyant Harvey Milk became a supervisor (councillor) in San Francisco but was murdered a year later by a former colleague. Gerry Studds in 1983 and Barney Frank in 1987 were the first openly gay US congressmen, and, in 1988, Svend Robinson was the first Canadian MP to come out. Many European countries have openly gay MPs: Chris Smith, for example, who came out in 1984 in the UK. The first male-to-female transsexual to become an MP was New Zealand's Georgina Beyer in 1999. In The Netherlands, openly gay men and lesbians made up seven per cent of the members of parliament in 2001. The socialist mayors Bertrand Delanoë of Paris (once severely wounded by a homophobic attacker) and Klaus Wowereit of Berlin both came out before being elected in 2001.

In countries where the legal aims of gay activists have been achieved, the movement is almost moribund. In Scandinavia and The Netherlands, for example, interest in gay organizations has declined dramatically. In these cases, equality under the law has been realized, even if social discrimination has not ended. Gay rights movements have not been as successful in changing the focus from legal to social issues, in part because social discrimination is more difficult to pinpoint. Often they now target external goals instead, addressing problems of discrimination in other countries. Since 1978, the whole gay rights movements has been organized under the banner of the International Lesbian and Gay Association (ILGA), but results have been limited. The United Nations has frequently refused to give the ILGA observer status, and indeed the UN Human Rights Commission in 2004 postponed a discussion on human rights protection for sexual orientation. The ILGA nevertheless has stimulated gay movements to look beyond national boundaries, to learn from each other and to support sister organizations. Other institutions, including the European Union and Amnesty International, have extended human rights definitions to include homosexuals, and the United Nations accords partnership benefits to employees from countries where their relationships are legally recognized.

Boy-love

In the 1970s, in the wake of the gay liberation movement, paedophile groups came into existence with the hope that they, too, could benefit from emancipation, reasoning that the gay movement had often been supportive of intergenerational sex (sometimes referred to as 'boy-love'). For a long time the gay world had viewed the boy as a sexual ideal alongside masculine adults, and until the 1950s homosexual imagery focused on adolescents and teenagers, as can be seen in the works of such photographers as Wilhelm von Gloeden. The Radical Fairies group of the early 1970s supported transvestism, sadomasochism, public sex and also paedophilia, although this alliance of interests proved short-lived. In The Netherlands, the psychiatrist who had done most to depathologize homosexuality suggested in a 1976 report for the National Centre for Mental Health that the same should be done for paedophilia. The head of the Rotterdam vice squad voiced support, as did health workers, scholars and paedophile apologists. Their efforts were met with interest, but the times were changing. Around 1980, feminists started to battle against the sexual abuse of women by men, and of daughters by fathers, and shifted the focus from the medical topic of abuse of children by their parents to the gendered problem of the sexual abuse of girls perpetrated by men. While the discussion had initially concentrated on the issue of violence in the family, it soon widened to take in the risks presented by unknown outsiders. The abusers remained men, but the victims now included both genders. The United States witnessed a long series of scandals, ranging from serial killings and satanic rituals to the abuse of boys and young men by Catholic priests. Today, most people in the West find relations between minors and adults unacceptable, although research has indicated that in general young people suffer no negative consequences from intergenerational sex unless it happens inside the family or unless violence is used against them.[23] Western societies have seen a major change in that sexual desire, once based on differences of gender, age and class, is now founded on equality and symmetry. Power relations have become unacceptable, and this is especially true for intergenerational contact.

New laws were passed to counter the 'paedophile menace'.[24] In 1996 the United States enacted the Child Pornography Prevention Act, broadening the definition of child pornography to include computer-morphed imagery, but the Supreme Court declared the law unconstitutional in 2002. Meanwhile, the European Union obliged member states to draft similar laws and, under outside pressure, Japan did the same in 1999, raising the age of consent from 13 to 18 years. In the past, the production and sale of intergenerational erotic material was forbidden only because it resulted from the sexual abuse of children. Nowadays, however, the possession of such material is forbidden because it is also seen as promoting abusive relations. The United States and the European Union have set up vice squads that monitor internet material. Undercover officers in the United States have even enticed people into buying child pornography or meeting youngsters for sex.[25] Other laws have required authorities to notify the public of released 'sex criminals' in the vicinities where they live. These laws target not only child abusers, but also homosexuals convicted of public sex. Irate neighbours have attacked and even murdered some of these men and other innocent people 'recognized' from pictures on the internet or in newspapers.[26] In the few places where they still exist, paedophile movements such as the North American Man/Boy Love Association (NAMBLA) and Dutch Vereniging Martijn were kicked out of gay and lesbian parades in the 1990s. In 1994, under

Gay and lesbian culture is now a global phenomenon. Politically and culturally, the gay community has benefited greatly from a worldwide network of support and cooperation. Yet it has also undoubtedly become more homogenized: the rainbow flag, for instance – an internationally recognized symbol of gay diversity – can now be seen fluttering over shops, bars and other businesses everywhere from San Francisco to Manila. Here, two women celebrate Gay Pride in Brasilia, 2005.

pressure from the Clinton government, paedophile groups were expelled from the ILGA. Nevertheless, men have been coming out at increasingly younger ages,[27] while higher ages of consent inhibit their access to the gay world. This poses the problem of how to incorporate youngsters into gay society.

Globalization and differentiation

A global culture in which men and women identified as homosexual developed from the late 19th century onwards and spread quickly in the years following the Second World War.[28] For a long period attitudes had been exported around the world by means of colonization, with overseas possessions absorbing the opinions of imperial powers through laws, religion, culture, social work and academic writing. Although some such influences have continued into the post-colonial period, views in the West have now changed. Homosexuality is no longer a crime in most Western states, fewer physicians consider it a disease, and some religious groups have stopped viewing it as a sin. Yet at the same time evangelical groups are once more exporting anti-homosexual attitudes to poor countries, and the US government has stopped giving aid to organizations that provide abortion or (safer) sex education while not also preaching pre-marital chastity. Aside from culture and religion, the media play a huge role in the process of globalization, whose ever more frequent reports on gay issues now reach even the deepest hinterlands. Medical and social sciences contribute to

an international homogenization through their findings and activities, particularly with regard to AIDS and 'men who have sex with men'. Gay tourism, too, has promoted a standard conception of what it means to be gay, although most cities continue to display their own local specialities and particularities. Nowadays 'gay' often equals young, masculine, affluent, good-looking, fashionable and ready for sex – a stereotype that represents only a minority of homosexuals and excludes others who might wish to participate.

The gay world may have become more homogenized as a result of globalization, but it has also become more fragmented. In some countries the common aims of the past – primarily the struggle to end legal discrimination – have been achieved, and no new widely shared goals have emerged. On the contrary, some journalists have defined new aims that contradict the desires of many: no drag, intergenerational sex or flaunting of S&M; no public cruising or promiscuity.[29] At the same time, the gay world has broken down into many subgroups. There are suburban lesbians interested in bringing up children and in education; urban queers who need space for sexual experimentation; homosexuals from ethnic minority backgrounds who are trying to combat the prejudices both of racist gay men and of homophobic ethnic groups; transgenders who want to pass and queens who want to be outrageous; young men and women who long to be part of gay culture; corporate gays who have difficulty coming out of their closets; and queers who like public sex and need recreational venues. Gays can be right-wing or left-wing, out or closeted, black or white, poor or rich, old or young, well educated or poorly educated, masculine or unmasculine, into sex of many and various kinds and into relationships, keen on sports or interested in religion. There are very many different ways to relate to this gay world. Many men more or less live in gay bars or chat rooms, while others hate the scene because it flaunts promiscuity, is too queeny or, inversely, too macho. Others do not feel at home because they are bisexual, too old, or because they do not correspond to its ideals of beauty and fashion. Some men like gay sex but would rather have love affairs with women. These many conscious and unconscious exclusions create conflicts over the aims of the movement.

Same-sex marriage

Notwithstanding the gay world's diversity, political and religious debates on homosexuality have recently focused on same-sex marriage above all other issues. In the past, the social control exerted by family, neighbours and others made it well-nigh impossible for two men (or, to a lesser extent, two women) to live together as a couple. Marriage was an unassailable institution and fundamentally heterosexist. Before the sexual revolution, homosexuals were often advised to marry to rid themselves of unacceptable desires; yet after psychiatrists had discovered that it was impossible to change someone's sexual orientation, gays were advised against marriage since it would make themselves, their wives and their children unhappy. The institution of marriage also changed, from being an arrangement between two families designed to encourage reproduction and to safeguard economic security to a relationship based on love between two individuals. These shifts in the purpose of marriage

In 1989 Danish partners Axel and Eigil Axgil were the first gay couple to enter a civil partnership anywhere in the world (opposite). By the time of the ceremony they had been together for nearly forty years; the photograph above was taken in 1950, the year that they met. Axel had founded the Danish gay rights movement in 1948, and both were imprisoned for gay rights activism during the 1950s. In 1957 they combined their first names into a new surname to express their union publicly.

and in attitudes towards homosexuality – as well as the climate created by the AIDS epidemic – made marriage more attractive to gays and lesbians not only as as a symbol of commitment, but also as a form of contract that systemizes social and financial affairs between partners and with the world at large. Depending on national laws, a marital contract brings with it a whole range of consequences and responsibilities covering all aspects of one's interaction with society. Another reason to demand the right to marry is for the legal recognition of children (perhaps from a previous marriage) and the possibility of adoption.

Denmark was the first country to legalize same-sex relationships, in 1989, but its special legal partnership excluded the right to bring up children or to have a religious ceremony; although it was a step forward, it did not guarantee the full privileges of marriage. Other Scandinavian countries followed the Danish example with legislation allowing civil partnerships. The Dutch and French opposed any special arrangements for gays and lesbians on account of their *universaliste* ideologies, reasoning that all people should be equal under the law regardless of sexuality. The Dutch 'Registered Partnership' and French 'PACS' (Pact of Civil Solidarity) were therefore non-specific and could also be entered into also by heterosexual couples. In 2001 The Netherlands became the first country to give the full rights of marriage to same-sex couples, followed by Belgium in 2003, the US state of Massachusetts in 2004, Spain and Canada in 2005, and South Africa in 2006. Despite the provisions made by their government, marriage is not popular among Dutch gays and lesbians; only about five per cent of same-sex couples have taken advantage of the marriage legislation. In the United States, same-sex marriage became a major topic of domestic politics in the presidential elections of 2004, with George W. Bush promising to reintroduce a nationwide law forbidding same-sex marriages that had recently been defeated. Although opposition meant that this move did not happen, legislation outlawing same-sex marriage was introduced in both Australia (2004) and Uganda (2005). Debate, particularly in the United States and in France, has been ferocious, and clerics, politicians, family organizations and psychiatrists have spoken out against it in the strongest terms. (Nevertheless, in July 2004 a French court judged that two lesbians could together be legally responsible for their children.) Because of strong opposition, legislation allowing same-sex partnerships has been retracted or defeated in, among other places, Hawaii, Vermont and San Francisco. At some point in the future resistance may disappear, as it did in Europe and in Canada, while marriage itself will undergo a further evolution.

Alongside the issue of same-sex marriage is that of gay and lesbian partners who wish to bring up a child. Studies in the San Francisco Bay Area have suggested that such households often function in quite traditional ways, with one partner acting as the chief wage-earner and the other looking after domestic arrangements.[30] British researchers, on the other hand, have underlined the transgressive nature of such families, in which relationships tend to be more open than among heterosexual marriages. Parents share childcare with others, living arrangements often go beyond those of the traditional nuclear family, and monogamy is not necessarily the norm.[31] The main question for the future will be not whether marriage is extended to same-sex couples, but how homosexuals organize their social and sexual lives. Many gays and lesbians are very happy with the security offered by the nuclear family – with its established roles, its domesticity and the chance it offers to integrate into the local community – and enjoy the pleasures of monogamy. Others would rather return to the open relations of the 1970s, when homosexuals constructed a web of relationships based on sex, love and friendship.

Towards the future

The sexual revolution of the 1960s brought with it great changes for gays and lesbians. The freedoms they attained did not undermine the basic structure of Western sexual ideology that had emerged during the Enlightenment. This ideology stresses the biological side of sexuality, and today includes discussion of sex drives, genes and hormones: sex should come naturally and need no cultivation. The distinctions drawn between men and women have not changed greatly since the 18th century, despite the recent re-examination of traditional gender roles. Dichotomies of sex and gender, so criticized during the sexual revolution, have remained largely unaffected by transgender and queer alternatives. For some, the rise of same-sex marriages and monogamy denies a rich gay culture, in which love and sex were both combined and successfully kept apart. The desire to come out of the closet and occupy the streets has not put an end to the straight norms of public life: sex remains a private affair, and the political consequences of the sexual aspects of citizenship are not taken seriously.[32] The world has changed, but the dominant heterosexist ideology has not. Gay space remains limited to bedrooms, bars and the media.

The situation is ambiguous. On the one hand, a lively gay scene has developed in many major cities around the world, and the gay movement, founded on the notion of identity, has had some success, more so in Western Europe and South Africa than in other places. On the other hand, there are strong anti-homosexual trends in various parts of the world, especially in Muslim countries and where various Christian denominations are vocal in their condemnation of homosexuality. The persecution of gays and lesbians continues, sometimes by state institutions and often by private parties. Although it seems that the balance is tilting in favour of further rights for homosexuals, even some of the more positive developments of recent years are open to debate: the fact that same-sex couples in some parts of the world can now marry, for instance, may mean that alternative forms of relationship and sexual behaviour become less tolerated. The future is open, and the direction in which emancipation will lead us remains unclear.

NOTES AND BIBLIOGRAPHIES

CHAPTER 1

ROBERT ALDRICH

is Professor of European History at the University of Sydney. He is the author of *The Seduction of the Mediterranean: Writing, Art and Homosexual Fantasy* and *Colonialism and Homosexuality*. With Garry Wotherspoon, he edited *Who's Who in Gay and Lesbian History: From Antiquity to World War II* and *Who's Who in Contemporary Gay and Lesbian History: From World War II to the Present Day*, as well as several volumes of essays on Australian gay and lesbian studies.

Notes

1   See David M. Halperin, 'Heroes and Their Pals', in *One Hundred Years of Homosexuality and Other Essays on Greek Love* (New York 1990), pp. 75–87.
2   See the chapter by Adrian Carton in the present volume.
3   Stephen Garton, *Histories of Sexuality* (London 2004).
4   Robert Aldrich, *The Seduction of the Mediterranean: Writing, Art and Homosexual Fantasy* (London 1993).
5   Robert Aldrich, *Colonialism and Homosexuality* (London 2003).
6   Jonathan Ned Katz (ed.), *Gay American History* (New York 1976).
7   Kenneth Dover, *Greek Homosexuality* (London 1978); John Boswell, *Christianity, Social Tolerance, and Homosexuality: Gay People in Western Europe from the Beginning of the Christian Era to the Fourteenth Century* (Chicago 1980).
8   Alan Bray, *Homosexuality in Renaissance England* (London 1982).
9   Lillian Faderman, *Surpassing the Love of Men: Romantic Friendship and Love between Women from the Renaissance to the Present* (New York 1981), followed by her *Odd Girls and Lesbians: A History of Lesbian Life in Twentieth-Century America* (New York 1991).
10 Michael Rocke, *Forbidden Friendships: Homosexuality and Male Culture in Renaissance Florence* (Oxford 1996); George Chauncey, *Gay New York: Gender, Urban Culture, and the Making of the Gay Male World, 1890–1944* (New York 1994).
11 Louis Crompton, *Homosexuality and Civilization* (Cambridge, MA 2003).
12 Notably David Halperin, *How to do the History of Homosexuality* (Chicago 2002).
13 Jonathan Ned Katz, *Love Stories: Sex Between Men Before Homosexuality* (Chicago 2001); Martha Vicinus, *Intimate Friends: Women Who Loved Women, 1778–1928* (Chicago 2004).
14 Gays and Lesbians Aboriginal Alliance, 'Peopling the Empty Mirror: The Prospects for Lesbian and Gay Aboriginal History', in Robert Aldrich (ed.), *Gay Perspectives II: More Essays in Australian Gay Culture* (Sydney 1994), pp. 1–62.
15 Material on Australia taken from Garry Wotherspoon (ed.), *Being Different: Nine Gay Men Remember* (Sydney 1986); Garry Wotherspoon, *City of the Plain: History of a Gay Sub-Culture* (Sydney 1991); Robert French, *Camping by a Billabong: Gay and Lesbian Stories from Australian History* (Sydney 1993); Dino Hodge, *Did You Meet Any Malagas? A Homosexual History of Australia's Tropical Capital* (Nightcliff, NT 1993); Clive Moore and Kay Saunders (eds), *Australian Masculinities: Men and Their Histories*, special issue of the *Journal of Australian Studies*, no. 56 (1998); Clive Moore, *Sunshine and Rainbows: The Development of Gay and Lesbian Culture in Queensland* (St Lucia, Qld. 2001); David Coad, *Gender Trouble Down Under: Australian Masculinities* (Valenciennes 2002); the essays in Robert Aldrich and Garry Wotherspoon (eds), *Gay Perspectives: Essays in Australian Gay Culture* (Sydney 1992); Aldrich, *Gay Perpectives II*; Garry Wotherspoon (ed.), *Gay and Lesbian Perspectives III: Essays in Australian Culture* (Sydney 1996); Robert Aldrich and Garry Wotherspoon (eds), *Gay Perspectives IV: Studies in Australian Culture* (Sydney 1998); David L. Phillips and Graham Willet (eds), *Australia's Homosexual Histories* (Sydney 2000).
16 See Catie Gilchrist, 'Space, Sexuality and Convict Resistance in Van Diemen's Land: The Limits of Repression', *Eras*, no. 6 (November 2004).
17 Garry Wotherspoon, 'Moonlight and … romance? The death-cell letters of Captain Moonlight and some of their implications', *Journal of the Royal Australian Historical Society*, vol. 78, no. 3–4 (1992), pp. 76–91.
18 Clive Faro (with Garry Wotherspoon), *Street Seen: A History of Oxford Street* (Melbourne 2000).
19 Ruth Ford, Lyned Isaac and Rebecca Jones, *Forbidden Love – Bold Passion: Lesbian Stories 1900s–1990s* (North Fitzroy, Vic. 1996).
20 See Smart's autobiography, *Not Quite Straight* (Port Melbourne, Vic. 1996), and Donald Friend's diaries, the first four volumes of which have been published: Anne Gray (ed.), *The Diaries of Donald Friend* (Canberra 2001–6).
21 Dennis Altman, *Homosexual: Oppression and Liberation* (Ringwood, Vic. 1971).
22 Graham Willett, *Living Out Loud: A History of Gay and Lesbian Activism in Australia* (St Leonards, NSW 2000); Robert Reynolds, *From Camp to Queer: Re-making the Australian Homosexual* (Carlton South, Vic. 2002); Graham Carbery, *A History of the Sydney Gay and Lesbian Mardi Gras* (Port Melbourne, Vic. 1995).
23 G. W. Dowsett, *Practicing Desire: Homosexual Sex in the Era of AIDS* (Stanford, CA 1996).
24 Gays and Lesbians Aboriginal Alliance, 'Peopling the Empty Mirror'; Peter A. Jackson and Gerard Sullivan (eds), *Multicultural Queer: Australian Narratives* (New York 1999).

CHAPTER 2

CHARLES HUPPERTS

teaches Classics and ancient philosophy at the University of Amsterdam. He is the author of a two-volume doctoral thesis, *Eros dikaios*, on homosexuality in Classical Athens, and he has published a number of books on various topics related to ancient civilization. He has also published a dictionary of the Greek language, and has translated such ancient texts as Aristotle's *Nicomachean Ethics*.

Bibliography

Eva Cantarella, *Bisexuality in the Ancient World*, trans. C. O. Cuilleanáin (New Haven 1992)
John Boswell, *Christianity, Social Tolerance, and Homosexuality: Gay People in Western Europe from the Beginning of the Christian Era to the Fourteenth Century* (Chicago 1980)
Félix Buffière, *Eros adolescent. La pédérastie dans la Grèce antique* (Paris 1980)
Paul Cartledge, 'The Politics of Spartan Pederasty', *Proceedings of the Cambridge Philological Society*, no. 27 (1981), pp. 17–36
John R. Clarke, *Looking at Lovemaking: Constructions of Sexuality in Roman Art, 100 B.C.–A.D. 250* (Berkeley, CA 1998)
David Cohen, *Law, Sexuality, and Society: The Enforcement of Morals in Classical Athens* (Cambridge 1991)
Angelika Dierichs, *Erotik in der Kunst Griechenlands* (Mainz 1993)
Kenneth Dover, *Greek Homosexuality* (London 1978)
Maud W. Gleason, *Making Men: Sophists and Self-Presentation in Ancient Rome* (Princeton 1995)
David M. Halperin, *One Hundred Years of Homosexuality* (New York 1990)
David M. Halperin, John J. Winkler and Froma I. Zeitlin (eds). *Before Sexuality: The Construction of Erotic Experience in the Ancient Greek World* (Princeton 1990)
Jeffrey Henderson, *The Maculate Muse: Obscene Language in Attic Comedy* (New York 1991)
Lex Hermans, *Bewust van andere lusten. Homoseksualiteit in het Romeinse keizerrijk* (Amsterdam 1995)
Charles Hupperts, *Eros dikaios* (Amsterdam 2000)
Charles Hupperts, *De macht van Eros. Plato Symposium* (Amsterdam 2002)
Eva C. Keuls, *The Reign of the Phallus: Sexual Politics in Ancient Athens* (New York 1985)
Martin F. Kilmer, *Greek Erotica* (London 1993)
Gundel Koch-Harnack, *Knabenliebe und Tiergeschenke. Ihre Bedeutung im päderastischen Erziehungssystem Athens* (Berlin 1983)
Wilhelm Kroll, 'Kinaidos', *Real-Encyclopädie*, vol. 11 (Stuttgart 1921), pp. 459–62
Wilhelm Kroll, 'Knabenliebe', *Real-Encyclopädie*, vol. 11 (Stuttgart 1921), pp. 897–906
Hans Licht, *Sittengeschichte Griechenlands* (Dresden 1925–28)
Hans Licht, *Sexual Life in Ancient Greece*, trans. J. H. Freese (London 1932)
Saara Lilja, *Homosexuality in Republican and Augustan Rome* (Helsinki 1983)
Martha C. Nussbaum, *The Fragility of Goodness: Luck and Ethics in Greek Tragedy and Philosophy* (Cambridge 1986)
Martha C. Nussbaum and Juha Sihvola (eds), *The Sleep of Reason* (Chicago 2002)
Harald Patzer, *Die griechische Knabenliebe (Sitzungsberichte der Wissenschaftlichen Gesellschaft an der Johann Wolfgang Goethe-Universität Frankfurt am Main*, vol. 19, no. 1) (Wiesbaden 1982)
William Armstrong Percy, *Pederasty and Pedagogy in Archaic Greece* (Urbana, IL 1996)
Sarah B. Pomeroy, *Goddesses, Whores, Wives and Slaves: Women in Classical Antiquity* (London, 2nd edn 1994)
Carola Reinsberg, *Ehe, Hetärentum und Knabenliebe im antiken Griechenland* (Munich 1989)
Amy Richlin (ed.), *Pornography and Representation in Greece and Rome* (New York 1992)
Amy Richlin, 'Not Before Homosexuality: The Materiality of the *Cinaedus* and the Roman Law against Love between Men', *Journal of the History of Sexuality*, vol. 3 (1993), pp. 523–73
Aline Rousselle, *Porneia: On Desire and the Body in Antiquity*, trans. F. Pheasant (Oxford 1988)
Bernard Sergent, *L'homosexualité dans la mythologie grecque* (Paris 1984)

Bernard Sergent, *L'homosexualité initiatique dans l'Europe ancienne* (Paris 1986)

Beert C. Verstraete, 'Slavery and the Social Dynamics of Homosexual Relations in Ancient Rome', *Journal of Homosexuality*, vol. 5 (1980), pp. 227–36

Craig A. Williams, *Roman Homosexuality* (New York 1999)

John J. Winkler, *The Constraints of Desire: The Anthropology of Sex and Gender in Ancient Greece* (New York 1990)

CHAPTER 3
BERND-ULRICH HERGEMÖLLER

is Professor of Medieval History at the University of Hamburg, where he teaches political, social and constitutional history, as well as the history of sexuality. He is the author of *Krötenkuß und schwarzer Kater: Ketzerei, Götzendienst und Unzucht in der inquisitorischen Phantasie des 13. Jahrhunderts, Chorknaben und Bäckerknechte: Homosexuelle Kleriker im spätmittelalterlichen Basel* and *Sodom and Gomorrah: On the Everyday Reality and Persecution of Homosexuals in the Middle Ages.*

Bibliography

Bérinus, *Roman en prose du XIVe siècle*, ed. Robert Bossuat, 2 vols (Paris 1931–33) (Société des Anciens Textes Français, 77.I.II)

Marc Boone, '"Le tres fort, vilain et detestable criesme et pechié de zodomie": Homosexualité et répression à Bruges pendant la période bourguignonne (fin 14e – début 16e siècle)', in Hugo Soly and René Vermeir (eds), *Beleid en Bestuur in de Oude Nederlanden. Liber Amicorum Prof. Dr. M[ichel] Baelde* (Ghent 1993), pp. 1–18

John Boswell, *Christianity, Social Tolerance, and Homosexuality: Gay People in Western Europe from the Beginning of the Christian Era to the Fourteenth Century* (Chicago 1980)

John Boswell, *Same-Sex Unions in Premodern Europe* (New York 1994)

Bernd-Ulrich Hergemöller, *Krötenkuß und schwarzer Kater: Ketzerei, Götzendienst und Unzucht in der inquisitorischen Phantasie des 13. Jahrhunderts* (Warendorf 1996)

Bernd-Ulrich Hergemöller, *Männer, 'die mit Männern handeln', in der Augsburger Reformationszeit*, Forum Homosexualität und Geschichte München (Munich 2000)

Bernd-Ulrich Hergemöller, *Sodom und Gomorrha: Zur Alltagswirklichkeit und Verfolgung Homosexueller im Mittelalter* (Hamburg, 2nd edn 2000). English edition: *Sodom and Gomorrah: On the Everyday Reality and Persecution of Homosexuals in the Middle Ages*, trans. John Phillips (London 2001)

Bernd-Ulrich Hergemöller, *Chorknaben und Bäckerknechte: Homosexuelle Kleriker im spätmittelalterlichen Basel* (Hamburg 2004)

Harry Kuster, *Eros in het Avondland. Werkelijkheid van gelijkgeslachtlijke liefde. Een Bibliografie* (Veenendaal 1999)

Peter von Moos, *Hildebert von Lavardin 1056–1133. Humanitas an der Schwelle des höfischen Zeitalters* (Stuttgart 1965) (Pariser Historische Studien, vol. 3)

Helmut Puff (ed.), *Lust, Angst und Provokation. Homosexualität in der Gesellschaft* (Göttingen 1993)

Helmut Puff, 'Die Sünde und ihre Metaphern. zum "Liber Gomorrhianus" des Petrus Damiani',

Forum: Homosexualität und Literatur, no. 21 (1994), pp. 45–77

Helmut Puff, 'Localizing Sodomy: The "Priest and Sodomite" in Pre-Reformation Germany and Switzerland', *Journal of History of Sexuality*, vol. 8 (1997), pp. 165–95

Christine Reinle, 'Zur Rechtspraxis gegenüber Homosexuellen. Eine Fallstudie aus dem Regensburg des 15. Jahrhunderts', *Zeitschrift für Geschichtswissenschaft*, vol. 44 (1996), pp. 307–26

Christine Reinle, 'Konflikte und Konfliktstrategien eines elsässischen Adeligen. Der Fall des Richard Puller von Hohenburg (+ 1482)', in Kurt Andermann (ed.), *'Raubritter' oder 'Rechtschaffene vom Adel'? Aspekte von Politik, Friede und Recht im späten Mittelalter* (Sigmaringen 1997), pp. 89–113

Michael J. Rocke, 'Male Homosexuality and its Regulation in Late-Medieval Florence' (PhD thesis, State University of New York at Binghamton, 1989)

Richard Trexler, 'La prostitution florentine aux XVe siècle. Patronage et clientèle', *Annales. Economies, Sociétés, Civilisations*, no. 6 (1981), pp. 983–1015

CHAPTER 4
HELMUT PUFF

is Associate Professor in the Department of History and the Department of German Studies at the University of Michigan in Ann Arbor. His research focuses on the history, literature and culture of the early modern German-speaking lands. He is the author of *Sodomy in Reformation Germany and Switzerland, 1400–1600* and is co-editor of the journal *Gender & History*.

Notes

1 See Yvonne Ivory, *Inverting the Renaissance, Fashioning the Self: Thomas Mann, Oscar Wilde, and Fin-de-Siècle Sexual Dissidence* (PhD thesis, University of California at Los Angeles, 2001). This highly erotic gaze on the Renaissance holds true even for Jacob Burckhardt, despite the fact that he only alludes to this theme in his seminal *The Civilization of the Renaissance in Italy* (1860). I would like to express my gratitude to Kathryn Babayan, Kerry Boeye and Jakob Michelsen for having commented on earlier drafts of this chapter.

2 Leonard of Udine, *Quadragesimale de legibus* (Lyon 1494), T2v.

3 Michael J. Rocke, 'Sodomites in Fifteenth-Century Tuscany: The Views of Bernardino of Siena', in Kent Gerard and Gert Hekma (eds), *The Pursuit of Sodomy* (London 1989), pp. 7–31; Franco Mormando, *The Preacher's Demons: Bernardino of Siena and the Social Underworld of Early Renaissance Italy* (Chicago 1999). On caution in the confessional, see, for instance, Jean Gerson, 'De confessione mollitiei', in *Oeuvres complètes*, vol. 8 (Paris 1971), pp. 71–75.

4 *Sandro Botticelli: The Drawings for Dante's Divine Comedy*, exh. cat. by Hein-Th. Schulze Altcappenberg (London 2000), pp. 74–75. What the passage in Dante refers to has been a matter of debate for Dante scholars since, typically, the sin is not explicitly named. See Richard Kay, 'The Sin(s) of Brunetto Latini', *Dante Studies*, vol. 112 (1994), pp. 19–31; John Boswell, 'Dante and the Sodomites', *Dante Studies*, vol. 112 (1994), pp. 33–51 (with more bibliographical references).

5 Michael Goodich, 'Sodomy in Medieval Secular Law', *Journal of Homosexuality*, vol. 1 (1976), pp. 295–302; David F. Greenberg, *The Construction of Homosexuality* (Chicago 1988), pp. 279–323.

6 Helmut Puff, *Sodomy in Reformation Germany and Switzerland, 1400–1600* (Chicago 2003), pp. 29–30.

7 Bruce R. Smith, *Homosexual Desire in Shakespeare's England: A Cultural Poetics* (Chicago 1991), pp. 43–47.

8 Michael J. Rocke, *Forbidden Friendships: Homosexuality and Male Culture in Renaissance Florence* (New York 1996).

9 Guido Ruggiero, *The Boundaries of Eros: Sex, Crime and Sexuality in Renaissance Venice* (New York 1985); Patricia H. Labalme, 'Sodomy and Venetian Justice in the Renaissance', *Tijdschrift voor Rechtsgeschiedenis*, vol. 52 (1984), pp. 217–55; Bernd-Ulrich Hergemöller, 'Das "Collegium contra sodomitas" im spätmittelalterlichen Venedig', in Bernd-Ulrich Hergemöller (ed.), *Sodom und Gomorrha: Zur Alltagswirklichkeit und Verfolgung Homosexueller im Mittelalter* (Hamburg, 2nd edn 2000), pp. 141–58; N. S. Davidson, 'Sodomy in Early Modern Venice', in Tom Betteridge (ed.), *Sodomy in Early Modern Europe* (Manchester 2002), pp. 65–81.

10 Eve Levin, *Sex and Society in the World of the Orthodox Slavs, 900–1700* (Ithaca, NY 1989).

11 Peter Kunz, letter to Joachim Watt, in Emil Arbenz (ed.), *Vadianische Briefsammlung*, vol. 5 (St Gallen 1903), p. 526.

12 Marc Boone, 'State Power and Illicit Sexuality: The Persecution of Sodomy in Late Medieval Bruges', *Journal of Medieval History*, vol. 22 (1996), pp. 142–47.

13 Jeffrey Richards, *Sex, Dissidence and Damnation: Minority Groups in the Middle Ages* (London 1990), p. 148.

14 Maria R. Boes, 'On trial for sodomy in early modern Germany', in Betteridge, *Sodomy in Early Modern Europe*, pp. 27–45.

15 Rocke, *Forbidden Friendships*.

16 Bernd-Ulrich Hergemöller, 'Die "unsprechliche stumme Sünde" in Köln am Ende des 15. Jahrhunderts', in Hergemöller, *Sodom und Gomorrha*, pp. 97–140.

17 Luiz Mott, 'Love's Labors Lost: Five Letters from a Seventeenth-Century Portuguese Sodomite', in Gerard and Hekma, *The Pursuit of Sodomy*, p. 99.

18 Mary Elizabeth Perry, 'The "Nefarious Sin" in Early Modern Seville', in ibid., pp. 67–89.

19 Federico Garza Carvajal, *Butterflies Will Burn: Prosecuting Sodomites in Early Modern Spain and Mexico* (Austin, TX 2002), p. 77. See also Rafael Carrasco, *Inquisición y represión en Valencia: Historia de los sodomitas (1565–1785)* (Barcelona 1985); Mary Elizabeth Perry, *Crime and Society in Early Modern Seville* (Hanover, NH 1980), p. 124.

20 Philippe Reliquet, *Le Moyen Age: Gilles de Rais, maréchal, monstre et martyr* (Paris 1982).

21 Puff, *Sodomy in Reformation Germany*, pp. 45–48.

22 Cynthia B. Herrup, *A House in Gross Disorder: Sex, Law, and the 2nd Earl of Castlehaven* (Oxford 1999).

23 Helmut Puff, 'The Sodomite's Clothes: Gift-Giving and Sexual Excess in Early Modern Germany and Switzerland', in Karen Encarnacion and Anne McClanan (eds), *Personal Objects, Social Subjects: The Material Culture of Sex, Procreation, and Marriage in Pre-Modern Europe* (New York

2002), pp. 251–72. See also Joan Cadden, *Meanings of Sexual Difference in the Middle Ages: Medicine, Science, and Culture* (Cambridge 1993).

24 Sodomites were at times isolated from other prisoners. See Perry, *Crime and Society*, pp. 123–24.

25 Bernd-Ulrich Hergemöller, 'Das Verhör des "Sodomiticus" Franz von Alsten (1536/37): Ein Kriminalfall aus dem nachtäuferischen Münster', *Westfälische Zeitschrift*, vol. 140 (1990), pp. 31–47.

26 Bernd-Ulrich Hergemöller, *Männer, 'die mit Männer handeln', in der Augsburger Reformationszeit* (Munich 2000).

27 See Richard Trexler, *Public Life in Renaissance Florence* (Ithaca, NY 1991).

28 StAZ, Ratsbuch B VI.209, 193r–195v (Staatsarchiv Zürich, Switzerland).

29 StAZ, A 27.10 (Kundschaften und Nachgänge *c*. 1530–70) (1541); Puff, *Sodomy in Reformation Germany*, pp. 97–100.

30 Augustin Güntzer, *Kleines Biechlin von meinem gantzen Leben: Die Autobiographie eines Elsässer Kannengießers aus dem 17. Jahrhundert* [1618], ed. Fabian Brändle and Dominik Sieber (Cologne 2002), p. 139.

31 StALU A1 F6 SCH 826, 1629 (Staatsarchiv Luzern, Switzerland).

32 Helmut Puff, 'Localizing Sodomy: The "Priest and Sodomite" in Pre-Reformation Germany and Switzerland', *The Journal of the History of Sexuality*, vol. 8 (1997), pp. 165–95.

33 Alan Bray, 'Homosexuality and the Signs of Male Friendship in Elizabethan England', in Jonathan Goldberg (ed.), *Queering the Renaissance* (Durham 1994), pp. 40–61.

34 Michel de Montaigne, *The Complete Essays*, ed. M. A. Screech (London 1991), p. 209. Screech chose to translate the essay's title as 'On affectionate relationships'.

35 Ibid., p. 210. See also Marc Schachter, '"That Friendship Which Possesses the Soul": Montaigne Loves La Boétie', *Journal of Homosexuality*, vol. 41, no. 3/4 (2001), pp. 5–21.

36 Alan Bray, *The Friend* (Chicago 2003), p. 7.

37 Bernd-Ulrich Hergemöller, 'Homosexuelle als spätmittelalterliche Randgrupp', *Forum: Homosexualität und Literatur*, no. 13 (1987), pp. 61–63.

38 Katherine B. Crawford, 'Love, Sodomy, and Scandal: Controlling the Sexual Reputation of Henry III', *Journal of the History of Sexuality*, vol. 12 (2003), pp. 513–42.

39 Bray, *The Friend*, p. 96. Cf. Michael B. Young, *King James and the History of Homosexuality* (New York 2000).

40 Dirk J. Noordam, *Riskante relaties: Vijf eeuwen homoseksualiteit in Nederland, 1233–1733* (Hilversum 1995), p. 109.

41 Helmut Puff, 'Sodomie und Herrschaft: Eine Problemskizze', in Ingrid Bauer, Christa Ehrmann-Hämmerle and Gabriella Hauch (eds), *Liebe und Widerstand: Ambivalenzen historischer Geschlechterbeziehungen* (Vienna 2005), pp. 139–57.

42 Alan Bray, *Homosexuality in Renaissance England* (London 1982), pp. 20–21, 63–65.

43 Robert W. Scribner, 'Vom Sakralbild zur sinnlichen Schau: Sinnliche Wahrnehmung und das Visuelle bei der Objektivierung des Frauenkörpers in Deutschland im 16. Jahrhundert', in Klaus Schreiner and Norbert Schnitzler (eds), *Gepeinigt, begehrt vergessen* (Munich 1992), pp. 309–36.

44 *Ovide moralisé en prose (Texte du quinzième siècle)*, ed. C. de Boer (Amsterdam 1954) (= Verhandelingen der Koninklijke Nederlandse Akademie van Wetenschapen, Afd. Letterkunde, n.s., part 61, no. 2), pp. 257–58. See also Helmut Puff, 'Orpheus after Eurydice (according to Albrecht Dürer)', in Basil Dufallo and Pegg McCracken (eds), *Dead Lovers* (Ann Arbor 2006).

45 On homoeroticism in Italian Renaissance art, see James M. Saslow, *Ganymede in the Renaissance: Homosexuality in Art and Society* (New Haven 1986); Andreas Sternweiler, *Die Lust der Götter: Homosexualität in der italienischen Kunst: Von Donatello zu Caravaggio* (Berlin 1993); James M. Saslow, *Pictures and Passions: A History of Homosexuality in the Visual Arts* (New York 1999), pp. 79–124.

46 Bette Talvacchia, *Taking Positions: On the Erotic in Renaissance Culture* (Princeton 1999).

47 Antonio Beccadelli, *Hermaphroditus: Lateinisch und Deutsch* (Leipzig 1991).

48 Herwarth Röttgen, *Caravaggio: Der irdische Amor oder Der Sieg der fleischlichen Liebe* (Frankfurt am Main 1992).

49 Patricia Simons, 'European Art: Renaissance', in Claude J. Summers (ed.), *The Queer Encyclopedia of the Visual Arts* (San Francisco 2004), pp. 134–36. Simons challenges us to pay more attention to women as potential viewers of art that could be understood as homoerotic.

50 Louis Crompton, *Homosexuality and Civilization* (Cambridge, MA 2003), pp. 278–81.

51 Leonard Barkan, *Transuming Passion: Ganymede and the Erotics of Humanism* (Stanford, CA 1991).

52 Margaret A. Gallucci, *Benvenuto Cellini: Sexuality, Masculinity, and Artistic Identity in Renaissance Italy* (New York 2003), p. 23.

53 Benvenuto Cellini, *My Life*, trans. Julia Conaway Bondanella and Peter Bondanella (Oxford 2002), p. 321.

54 Sven Limbeck, 'Plautus in der Knabenschule: Zur Eleminierung homosexueller Inhalte in deutschen Plautusübersetzungen der frühen Neuzeit', in Dirck Linck, Wolfgang Popp and Annette Runte (eds), *Erinnern und Wiederdecken: Tabuisierung und Enttabuisierung der männlichen und weiblichen Homosexualität* (Berlin 1999), pp. 15–67.

55 Martin Luther, 'Wider das Papsttum zu Rom, vom Teufel gestiftet', in *Werke: Kritische Gesamtausgabe*, vol. 54 (Weimar 1928), pp. 222–23.

56 Winfried Schleiner, 'Linguistic "Xenohomophobia" in Sixteenth-Century France: The Case of Henri Estienne', in *The Sixteenth Century Journal*, vol. 34 (2003), pp. 747–60.

57 Anette Kruszynski, *Der Ganymed-Mythos in Emblematik und mythographischer Literatur des 16. Jahrhunderts* (Worms 1985); R. Po-Chia Hsia, *The World of Catholic Renewal, 1540–1770* (Cambridge 1998), pp. 152–64.

58 Joan DeJean, *The Reinvention of Obscenity: Sex, Lies, and Tabloids in Early Modern France* (Chicago 2002), pp. 29–53.

59 Jonas Liliequist, 'State Policy, Popular Discourse, and the Silence on Homosexual Acts in Early Modern Sweden', *Journal of Homosexuality*, vol. 35 (1998), p. 18.

60 *A Woman's Life in the Court of the Sun King: Letters of Liselotte von der Pfalz*, trans. and ed. Elborg Forster (Baltimore 1984), p. 87. See also Jeffrey Merrick and Bryant T. Ragan, Jr. (eds),

Homosexuality in Early Modern France: A Documentary Collection (New York 2001), pp. 124–26.

CHAPTER 5
MICHAEL SIBALIS

is Associate Professor of History at Wilfred Laurier University in Waterloo, Ontario. With Jeffrey Merrick, he has co-edited *Homosexuality in French History and Culture*. Other recent publications include 'Urban Space and Homosexuality: The Example of the Marais, Paris' "Gay Ghetto"' in vol. 41 of *Urban Studies*, and 'Homophobia, Vichy France, and the "Crime of Homosexuality": The Origins of the Ordinance of 6 August 1942', in vol. 8 of *GLQ: A Journal of Gay and Lesbian Studies*.

Notes

1 Quoted in Nicholas Davidson, 'Theology, Nature and the Law: Sexual Sin and Sexual Crime in Italy from the Fourteenth to the Seventeenth Century', in Trevor Dean and K. J. P. Lowe (eds), *Crime, Society and the Law in Renaissance Italy* (Cambridge 1994), p. 75 n.

2 Quoted in Peter Wagner, *Eros Revived: Erotica of the Enlightenment in England and America* (London 1988), p. 39.

3 Theo van der Meer, 'Sodomy and the Pursuit of a Third Sex in the Early Modern Period', in Gilbert Herdt (ed.), *Third Sex, Third Gender: Beyond Sexual Dimorphism in Culture and History* (New York 1994), p. 171.

4 Cristian Berco, 'Uncovering the Unmentionable Vice: Male Homosexuality, Race, and Class in Spain's Golden Age' (unpublished PhD thesis, University of Arizona, 2002), p. 99.

5 Gordon N. Ray, *Thackeray* (New York, 2 vols, 1955–58), vol. 1, p. 452, n. 39; *The Memoirs of John Addington Symonds*, ed. Phyllis Grosskurth (London 1984), p. 94.

6 Robert Oresko, 'Homosexuality and the Court Elites of Early Modern France: Some Problems, Some Suggestions and an Example'; James D. Steakley, 'Sodomy in Enlightenment Prussia: From Execution to Suicide'; and Dennis Rubini, 'Sexuality and Augustan England: Sodomy, Politics, Elite Circles, and Society', in Kent Gerard and Gert Hekma (eds), *The Pursuit of Sodomy: Male Homosexuality in Renaissance and Enlightenment Europe* (New York 1988), pp. 105–28, 163–75, 349–81 respectively; Johann Rosell, 'Gustav III', in Robert Aldrich and Garry Wotherspoon (eds), *Who's Who in Gay and Lesbian History: From Antiquity to World War II* (London 2001), p. 194.

7 Quoted in Richard Davenport-Hines, *Sex, Death and Punishment: Attitudes to Sex and Sexuality in Britain since the Renaissance* (London 1990), p. 55.

8 Louis Petit de Bachaumont, *Mémoires secrets pour servir à l'histoire de la République des lettres de France* (London, 36 vols, 1777–89), vol. 23 (13 October 1783).

9 Rictor Norton, *The Myth of the Modern Homosexual: Queer History and the Search for Cultural Unity* (London 1997), pp. 245 ff.

10 Maurice Lever, *Les bûchers de Sodome: Histoire des 'infâmes'* (Paris 1985); Michel Rey, 'Police and Sodomy in Eighteenth-Century Paris: From Sin to Disorder', in Gerard and Hekma, *The Pursuit of Sodomy*, pp. 129–46; and Michel Rey, '1700–1750, Les Sodomites parisiens créent un mode de vie', in *Cahiers Gai Kitsch Camp*, no. 24

(Lille 1994), pp. xi–xxxiii, revised version of 'Parisian Homosexuals Create a Lifestyle, 1700–1750s', in R. P. Maccubbin (ed.), *'Tis Nature's Fault: Unauthorized Sexuality During the Enlightenment* (New York 1987), pp. 179–91.

11 Edward J. Bristow, *Vice and Vigilance: Purity Movements in Britain since 1700* (Bristol 1977), pp. 11–51; Robert B. Shoemaker, 'Reforming the City: The Reformation of Manners Campaign in London, 1690–1738', in Lee Davison *et al.* (eds), *Stilling the Grumbling Hive: Response to Social and Economic Problems in England, 1689–1750* (New York 1992), pp. 99–120; Rictor Norton, *Mother Clap's Molly House: The Gay Subculture in England 1700–1830* (London 1992), p. 49 (for quotation).

12 Simon Schama, *The Embarrassment of Riches: An Interpretation of Dutch Culture in the Golden Age* (New York 1987), pp. 601–6; Louis Crompton, 'Gay Genocide from Leviticus to Hitler', in Louie Crew (ed.), *The Gay Academic* (Palm Springs, CA 1978), pp. 67–91.

13 Gert Hekma, 'Amsterdam', in David Higgs (ed.), *Queer Sites: Gay Urban Histories since 1600* (London 1999), pp. 65–67; Van der Meer, 'Sodomy and the Pursuit of a Third Sex', pp. 151–53; Dirk Japp Noordam, 'Sodomy in the Dutch Republic, 1600–1725', in Gerard and Hekma, *The Pursuit of Sodomy*, pp. 214–18.

14 Norton, *Mother Clap's*, *passim* (p. 55 for quotation).

15 Quoted in Rey, 'Parisian Homosexuals', pp. 187–88.

16 Van der Meer, 'The Persecution of Sodomy', pp. 290–91; Randolph Trumbach, 'London', in Higgs, *Queer Sites*, p. 99; Norton, *Mother Clap's*, pp. 107–8; Rey, 'Parisian Homosexuals', pp. 183–84; Jakob Michelsen, 'Gleichgeschlechtliche Sexualität im frühneuzeitlichen Hamburg: Lebensrealitäten, Wahrnehmungen und Verfolgung' (unpublished Master's thesis, University of Hamburg, 2003), *passim*.

17 Davenport-Hines, *Sex, Death and Punishment*, p. 79; Van der Meer, 'Sodomy and the Pursuit of a Third Sex', pp. 160–62.

18 *La Cauchoise* (Paris 1784), p. 453. Quoted in Kathryn Norberg, 'The Libertine Whore: Prostitution in French Pornography from Margot to Juliette', in Lynn Hunt (ed.), *The Invention of Pornography: Obscenity and the Origins of Modernity, 1500–1800* (New York 1996), pp. 239–40.

19 Steakley, 'Sodomy in Enlightenment Prussia', pp. 170–71.

20 Michelsen, 'Gleichgeschlechtliche Sexualität', pp. 67, 95, 121.

21 Robert Holloway, *The Phoenix of Sodom, or the Vere Street Coterie* (London 1813), pp. 12–13.

22 Quoted in Rey, '1700–1750', p. xxix.

23 Norton, *Mother Clap's*, p. 104.

24 Theo van der Meer, 'Private Acts, Public Space: Defining Boundaries in Nineteenth-Century Holland', in William Leap (ed.), *Public Sex/Gay Space* (New York 1999), p. 236.

25 Archives Nationales, Paris, Y 13408 and Y 11725, police reports for 11 April 1781 and 13 May 1785.

26 See the following by Randolph Trumbach: 'Gender and the Homosexual Role in Modern Western Culture: The 18th and 19th Centuries Compared', in Dennis Altman *et al.* (eds), *Homosexuality, Which Homosexuality? International Conference on Gay and Lesbian Studies* (London 1989), pp. 149–69; 'The Birth

of the Queen: Sodomy and the Emergence of Gender Equality in Modern Culture, 1660–1750', in Martin Bauml Duberman, Martha Vicinus and George Chauncey (eds), *Hidden from History: Reclaiming the Gay and Lesbian Past* (New York 1989), pp. 129–40; 'London's Sodomites: Homosexual Behaviour and Western Culture in the 18th Century', *Journal of Social History*, vol. 11 (1977–78), pp. 1–33.

27 Norton, *The Myth of the Modern Homosexual*, *passim*; Gert Hekma, 'Same-sex Relations among Men in Europe, 1700–1990', in Franz X. Eder, Lesley A. Hall and G. Hekma (eds), *Sexual Cultures in Europe* (Manchester 1999), p. 80; David M. Halperin, *How to do the History of Homosexuality* (Chicago 2002), *passim*.

28 Quoted in Dirk van der Cruysse, *Madame Palatine, princesse européene* (Paris 1988), p. 181.

29 Van der Meer, 'Sodomy and the Pursuit of a Third Sex', pp. 190–92.

30 Antoine Bruneau, *Observations et maximes sur les matières criminelles* (Paris 1715), p. 403; William Blackstone, *Commentaries on the Laws of England* (Oxford, 4 vols, 1769), vol. 4, pp. 215–16.

31 Quoted in Wilhelm von Rosen, 'Sodomy in Early Modern Denmark: A Crime Without Victims', in Gerard and Hekma, *The Pursuit of Sodomy*, pp. 190–91.

32 Richard J. Evans, *Rituals of Retribution: Capital Punishment in Germany 1600–1987* (Oxford 1996), pp. 118, 122; James D. Steakley, *The Homosexual Emancipation Movement in Germany* (New York 1975), pp. 10, 21; Steakley, 'Sodomy in Enlightenment Prussia', p. 166 (quotation).

33 Barbara Fröhlich, 'Austria: Brief Historical Overview', International Gay and Lesbian Human Rights Commission (2003), http://www.iglhrc.org/files/iglhrc/reports/4UR _Austria.pdf (accessed 16 Sept. 2005).

34 Michelsen, 'Gleichgeschlechtliche Sexualität', pp. 24–25, 94–95, 104–5, 127.

35 Karl Wegert, *Popular Culture, Crime and Social Control in 18th-Century Württemberg* (Stuttgart 1994), pp. 189–90.

36 Margaret C. Jacob, 'The Materialist World of Pornography', in Hunt, *Invention of Pornography*, pp. 190, 372 n. 43.

37 Lever, *Les bûchers de Sodome*; Jeffrey Merrick and Bryant T. Ragan, Jr. (eds), *Homosexuality in Early Modern France: A Documentary Collection* (New York 2001), pp. 77–79.

38 Henry Charles Lea, *A History of the Inquisition of Spain* (New York, 4 vols, 1906–7; reprinted 1966), vol. 4, pp. 361–71; Stephen Haliczer, *Inquisition and Society in the Kingdom of Valencia, 1478–1834* (Berkeley, CA 1990), pp. 302–3, 311; Berco, 'Uncovering the Unmentionable Vice', p. 104.

39 Luiz Mott, '*Justitia et Misericordia*: A Inquisição portuguesa e a repressão ao nefando pecado de sodomia', in Anita Novinsky and Maria Luiza Tucci Carneiro (eds), *Inquisição: Ensaios sobre mentalidade, heresias e arte* (São Paolo 1992), pp. 703–38; Luiz Mott, 'Le pouvoir inquisitorial et la répression de l'abominable péché de sodomie dans le monde luso-brésilien', in Gabriel Audisio (ed.), *Inquisition et pouvoir* (Aix 2004), pp. 203–18.

40 Rosen, 'Sodomy in Early Modern Denmark', pp. 177–204.

41 Jonas Liliequist, 'State Policy, Popular Discourse, and the Silence on Homosexual Acts in Early

Modern Sweden', *Journal of Homosexuality*, vol. 35 (1998), pp. 15–52.

42 Eve Levin, *Sex and Society in the World of the Orthodox Slavs, 900–1700* (Ithaca, NY 1989), pp. 199–204; Laura Engelstein, *The Keys to Happiness: Sex and the Search for Modernity in Fin-de-Siècle Russia* (Ithaca, NY 1992), pp. 57–60.

43 Jan Löfström, 'A Pre-Modern Legacy: The "Easy" Criminalization of Homosexual Acts Between Women in the Finnish Penal Code of 1889', in Jan Löfström (ed.), *Scandinavian Homosexualities: Essays on Gay and Lesbian Studies* (New York 1998), pp. 53–79.

44 'The Women-Hater's Lamentation', in Gerard and Hekma, *The Pursuit of Sodomy*, pp. 379–80.

45 Davenport-Hines, *Sex, Death and Punishment*, pp. 59–93; Arthur N. Gilbert, 'Buggery and the British Navy, 1700–1861', *Journal of Social History*, vol. 10 (1976–77), pp. 72–98.

46 Netta Murray Goldsmith, *The Worst of Crimes: Homosexuality and the Law in Eighteenth-Century London* (Aldershot 1998), p. 44; Crompton, *Byron and Greek Love: Homophobia in Nineteenth-Century England* (Berkeley, CA), pp. 21–22; Don Herzog, *Poisoning the Minds of the Lower Orders* (Princeton 1998), p. 408.

47 Crompton, *Byron*, pp. 32–33.

48 Van der Meer, 'Sodomy and the Pursuit of a Third Sex', pp. 139–41, 144, 146, 154; and 'The Persecutions of Sodomites in Eighteenth-Century Amsterdam', in Gerard and Hekma, *The Pursuit of Sodomy*, pp. 263–307; L. S. A. M. von Roemer, *Uranism in the Netherlands till the Nineteenth Century, with Special Emphasis on the Numerous Persecutions of Uranians in 1730*, trans. Michael A. Lombardi (Los Angeles 1978); Arend H. Huussen, Jr., 'Sodomy in the Dutch Republic during the Eighteenth Century', in Maccubbin, *'Tis Nature's Fault*, p. 173; Hekma, 'Same-sex Relations', pp. 79–82.

49 Quoted in Darrin M. McMahon, *Enemies of the Enlightenment: The French Counter-Enlightenment and the Making of Modernity* (Oxford 2001), p. 37.

50 Pierre Peyronnet, 'Le péché philosophique', in Paul Viallaneix and Jean Ehrard (eds), *Aimer en France 1760–1860* (Clermont-Ferrand, 2 vols, 1980), vol. 2, pp. 471–78.

51 Jacob Stockinger, 'Homosexuality and the French Enlightenment', in George Stambolian and Elaine Marks (eds), *Homosexualities and French Literature* (Ithaca, NY 1979), pp. 161–85; D. A. Coward, 'Attitudes to Homosexuality in Eighteenth-Century France', *Journal of European Studies*, vol. 10 (1980), pp. 231–55; Bryant T. Ragan, Jr., 'The Enlightenment Confronts Homosexuality', in Jeffrey Merrick and Bryant T. Ragan (eds), *Homosexuality in Modern France* (New York 1996), pp. 8–29; Michel Delon, 'The Priest, the Philosopher and Homosexuality in Enlightenment France', in Maccubbin, *'Tis Nature's Fault*, pp. 122–31.

52 See the following by Théodore Tarczylo: '"Prêtons la main à la nature": L' "Onanisme" de Tissot', *Dix-huitième siècle*, vol. 12 (1980), pp. 79–96; *Sexe et liberté au siècle des Lumières* (Paris 1983).

53 Immanuel Kant, *Lectures on Ethics*, trans. Louis Infield (New York 1963), pp. 169–71.

54 Quoted in Robert Tobin, *Warm Brothers: Queer Theory and the Age of Goethe* (Philadelphia 2000), p. 98.

55 Voltaire, *Dictionnaire philosophique* (Paris 1961), pp. 18–21.

56 Denis Diderot, 'Pensées détachées', *Oeuvres complètes: Édition chronologique*, (Paris, 15 vols, 1969–73), vol. 10, p. 86; Delon, 'The Priest, the Philosopher and Homosexuality', pp. 126–29.

57 Donatien de Sade, *La Philosophie dans le boudoir*, in *Oeuvres complètes du Marquis de Sade: Edition définitive* (Paris, 16 vols, 1973), vol. 3, p. 460.

58 Cesare Beccaria, *On Crimes and Punishments*, trans. Henry Paolucci (Englewood Cliffs, NY 1963), pp. 4, 83–86. Beccaria echoed the arguments of Montesquieu (1689–1755), who stated in 1750 that if the social conditions encouraging sodomy were eliminated 'one will immediately see nature either defend her rights or take them back'. See *Montesquieu: The Spirit of the Laws*, trans. and ed. Anne M. Cohler *et al.* (Cambridge 1989), pp. 195–94.

59 Quoted in Merrick and Ragan, *Homosexuality in Early Modern France*, pp. 160–61.

60 In Merrick and Ragan, *Homosexuality in Early Modern France*, pp. 192–98.

61 Mark Blasius and Shane Pelan (eds), *We Are Everywhere: A Historical Sourcebook of Gay and Lesbian Politics* (New York 1997), p. 35.

62 Michael Sibalis, 'The Regulation of Male Homosexuality in Revolutionary and Napoleonic France, 1789–1815', in Merrick and Ragan, *Homosexuality in Modern France*, pp. 80–84.

63 Van der Meer, 'Private Acts, Public Space', pp. 223–45.

64 Nicolás Pérez Cánovas, *Homosexualidad, homosexuales y uniones homosexuales en el derecho español* (Granada 1996), p. 13.

65 Giovanni Dall'Orto, 'La "Tolleranza Repressiva" dell'Omosessualità' (1987), http://www.giovannidallorto.com/saggistoria/tollera/tolle2.html (accessed 10 April 2006); and 'Codici penali italiani preunitari e omosessualità', http://www.giovannidallorto.com/saggistoria/tollera/codici.html (accessed 10 April 2006).

66 Karl Heinrich Ulrichs, *The Riddle of 'Man-Manly' Love*, trans. Michael A. Lombardi-Nash (Buffalo, NY, 2 vols, 1994), vol. 2, pp. 616–18.

67 Quoted in Isabel V. Hull, *Sexuality, State, and Civil Society in Germany, 1700–1815* (Ithaca, NY 1996), p. 357.

68 Hull, *Sexuality, State, and Civil Society*, pp. 340–50, 357–58; Florence Tamagne, 'Allemagne', in Louis-Georges Tin (ed.), *Dictionnaire de l'homophobie* (Paris 2003), p. 16.

69 Steakley, *The Homosexual Emancipation Movement*, pp. 10, 21; Steakley, 'Sodomy in Enlightenment Prussia', p. 171; H. G. Stümke, *Homosexuelle in Deutschland: Ein politische Gesichte* (Munich 1989).

70 Fröhlich, 'Austria'.

71 Dan Healey, *Homosexual Desire in Revolutionary Russia: The Regulation of Sexual and Gender Dissent* (Chicago 2001), pp. 80–81.

72 Davenport-Hines, *Sex, Death and Punishment*, pp. 59–93; A. D. Harvey, 'Prosecutions for Sodomy in England at the Beginning of the Nineteenth Century', *The Historical Journal*, vol. 21 (1978), pp. 939–48; H. Montgomery Hyde, *The Love That Dared Not Speak Its Name: A Candid History of Homosexuality in Britain* (Boston, MA 1970), pp. 36–40, 92–93.

73 Graham Robb, *Strangers: Homosexual Love in the Nineteenth Century* (New York 2004), p. 30.

74 Quoted in Herzog, *Poisoning the Minds*, p. 410.

75 Montgomery Hyde, *The Love That Dared Not Speak Its Name*, pp. 83–86.

76 H. Montgomery Hyde, *The Strange Death of Lord Castlereagh* (London 1959).

77 Julien-Frédéric Tarn, *Le Marquis de Custine* (Paris 1985), p. 69.

78 Angus McLaren, *Sexual Blackmail: A Modern History* (Cambridge, MA 2002), pp. 10–29.

79 Jean Tulard, *Joseph Fiévée, conseiller secret de Napoléon* (Paris 1985).

80 Quoted in Norton, *Mother Clap's*, p. 58.

81 Archives Nationales, Paris, Y 11725, police report, 25 May 1785.

82 Van der Meer, 'Private Acts, Public Space', p. 237.

83 See the following by Louis Crompton: *Byron*, pp. 19–62; *Homosexuality and Civilization* (Cambridge, MA 2003), pp. 530–33; 'Jeremy Bentham's Essay on "Paederasty"', *Journal of Homosexuality*, vol. 3 (1977–78), pp. 383–87, and vol. 4 (1978–79), pp. 91–107.

84 Quoted in Crompton, *Byron*, pp. 42, 27 respectively.

85 James A. Notopoulos, *The Platonism of Shelley* (Durham, NC 1949), pp. 404–13.

86 Wilhelm von Rosen, 'Hössli, Heinrich', in Aldrich and Wotherspoon, *Who's Who in Gay & Lesbian History*, pp. 214–16.

87 Robert A. Nye, 'Sex Difference and Male Homosexuality in French Medical Discourse, 1830–1930', *Bulletin of the History of Medicine*, vol. 63 (1989), pp. 32–51; Ivan Dalley Crozier, 'The Medical Construction of Homosexuality and its Relation to the Law in Nineteenth-Century England', *Medical History*, vol. 45 (2001), pp. 61–82; Jörg Hutter, 'The Social Construction of Homosexuals in the Nineteenth Century: The Shift from the Sin to the Influence of Medicine on Criminalizing Sodomy in Germany', *Journal of Homosexuality*, vol. 24 (1992–93), pp. 73–93.

88 Auguste-Ambroise Tardieu, *Une étude médico-légale sur les attentats aux moeurs* (Paris 1857).

89 Hekma, 'Same-sex Relations', p. 84.

90 Quoted in Sibalis, 'Paris', p. 18.

91 Quoted in Davenport-Hines, *Sex, Death and Punishment*, pp. 107–8.

92 Matt Cook, *London and the Culture of Homosexuality, 1885–1914* (Cambridge 2003), pp. 13–14; Sibalis, 'Paris', pp. 19–21, 23; Hekma, 'Amsterdam', p. 72; Trumbach, 'London', pp. 103–4.

CHAPTER 6
LAURA GOWING

is Reader in Early Modern History at King's College London. She has written extensively on women's history in early modern England. Her most recent book is *Common Bodies: Women, Touch and Power in Seventeenth-Century England.*

Notes

1 See the Introduction in Valerie Traub, *The Renaissance of Lesbianism in Early Modern England* (Cambridge 2002).

2 Judith M. Bennett, '"Lesbian-Like" and the Social History of Lesbianisms', *Journal of the History of Sexuality*, vol. 9, no. 1–2 (2000), p. 1.

3 Ibid.

4 See for example Traub, *Renaissance of Lesbianism*; Harriette Andreadis, *Sappho in Early Modern England: Female Same-Sex Literary Erotics, 1550–1714* (Chicago 2001); Emma

Donoghue, *Passions Between Women: British Lesbian Culture 1668–1801* (London 1993); Elizabeth Susan Wahl, *Invisible Relations: Representations of Female Intimacy in the Age of Enlightenment* (Stanford, CA 1999).

5 Traub, *Renaissance of Lesbianism*, chapter 6; see also Patricia Simons, 'Lesbian (In)visibility in Italian Renaissance Culture: Diana and other cases of *donna con donna*', *Journal of Homosexuality*, vol. 27 (1994), pp. 81–122.

6 Father Poussin, *Pretty Doings in a Protestant Nation* (London 1734), pp. 23–24; the passage was repeated in *Satan's Harvest Home* (London 1749), p. 18. The mention of Twickenham refers to Lady Mary Wortley Montagu, who lived there.

7 Donoghue, *Passions Between Women*, chapter 6.

8 Jane Sharp, *The Midwives Book* [1671], ed. Elaine Hobby (Oxford 1999), p. 40.

9 Katharine Park, 'The Rediscovery of the Clitoris: French Medicine and the Tribade', in David Hillman and Carla Mazzio (eds), *The Body in Parts* (London 1997), pp. 175–77.

10 See for example Donoghue, *Passions Between Women*, p. 37.

11 Park, 'Rediscovery of the Clitoris', p. 171.

12 Lorraine Daston and Katharine Park, 'The Hermaphrodite and the Orders of Nature: Sexual Ambiguity in Early Modern France', *GLQ: A Journal of Lesbian and Gay Studies*, vol. 1, no. 4 (1995), p. 427.

13 Israel Burshatin, 'Written on the Body: Slave or Hermaphrodite in Sixteenth-Century Spain', in Josiah Blackmore and Gregory Hutcheson (eds), *Queer Iberia: Sexualities, Cultures, and Crossings from the Middle Ages to the Renaissance* (Durham, NC 1999), pp. 420–56.

14 *Onania* (17th edition [with supplement], London c. 1725), pp. 319–30.

15 Patricia Crawford and Laura Gowing, *Women's Worlds in Seventeenth-Century England: A Sourcebook* (London 2000), p. 149.

16 Wahl, *Invisible Relations*, p. 22, quoting Jacques Duval, *Traité des Hermaphrodites* (Rouen 1612), p. 263.

17 Louis Crompton, 'The Myth of Lesbian Impunity: Capital Laws from 1270 to 1791', *Journal of Homosexuality* , vol. 6, no. 1–2 (1980), pp. 13, 18.

18 Traub, *Renaissance of Lesbianism*, pp. 276–77.

19 Park, 'Rediscovery of the Clitoris', p. 185.

20 Helmut Puff, 'Female Sodomy: The Trial of Katherina Hetzeldorfer (1477)', *Journal of Medieval and Early Modern Studies*, vol. 30, no. 1 (2000), pp. 41–61.

21 Brigitte Eriksson, 'A Lesbian Execution in Germany, 1721: The Trial Records', *Journal of Homosexuality*, vol. 6, no. 1–2 (1980), p. 31.

22 Ibid., p. 33.

23 Donoghue, *Passions Between Women*, p. 75; Rudolf M. Dekker and Lotte C. van de Pol, *The Tradition of Female Transvestism in Early Modern Europe* (Basingstoke 1989).

24 Michele Stepto and Gabriel Stepto (eds), *Lieutenant Nun: Memoir of a Basque Transvestite in the New World* (Boston, MA 1996), p. 17.

25 Patricia Crawford and Sara Mendelson, 'Sexual Identities in Early Modern England: The Marriage of Two Women', *Gender and History*, vol. 7, no. 3 (1995), quotations from p. 365; Giovanni Bianchi, *The True History and Adventures of Catharine Vizzani*, trans. John Cleland (London 1755), p. 60.

26 Dekker and van de Pol, *Tradition of Female Transvestism*, pp. 52–53.

27 Bianchi, *True History*, pp. 1–5. For further discussion of Vizzani see Donoghue, *Passions Between Women*, pp. 80–85.

28 Judith Halberstam, *Female Masculinity* (Durham, NC 1998), chapter 2.

29 On this monument see Alan Bray, *The Friend* (Chicago 2003), pp. 228–29.

30 Mary Turner, 'Two Entries from the Marriage Register of Taxal, Cheshire', *Local Population Studies*, vol. 21 (1978), p. 64.

31 Crawford and Gowing, *Women's Worlds*, pp. 236–38.

32 Lillian Faderman, *Surpassing the Love of Men: Romantic Friendship and Love Between Women from the Renaissance to the Present* (London 1985).

33 Traub, *Renaissance of Lesbianism*, chapters 6–7.

34 Donoghue, *Passions Between Women*, p. 162; see also Rachel Weil, *Political Passions: Gender, the Family and Political Argument in England, 1680–1714* (Manchester 1999), chapters 7–8.

35 Donoghue, *Passions Between Women*, p. 146.

36 Margaret R. Hunt, 'English Lesbians in the Long Eighteenth Century', in Judith M. Bennett and Amy M. Froide (eds), *Singlewomen in the European Past, 1250–1800* (Philadelphia 1999), p. 287.

37 Tim Hitchcock, *English Sexualities 1700–1800* (Basingstoke 1997), p. 86.

38 Rictor Norton, *Mother Clap's Molly House: The Gay Subculture in England 1700–1830* (London 1992), chapter 15; Randolph Trumbach, 'London's Sapphists: From Three Sexes to Four Genders in the Making of Modern Culture', in Julia Epstein and Kristina Straub (eds), *Body Guards: The Cultural Politics of Gender Ambiguity* (London 1991).

39 Theo van der Meer, 'Tribades on Trial: Female Same-Sex Offenders in Late Eighteenth-Century Amsterdam', in John C. Fout (ed.), *Forbidden History: The State, Society and the Regulation of Sexuality in Modern Europe* (Chicago 1992), p. 197.

40 Jeffrey Merrick and Bryant T. Ragan, Jr. (eds), *Homosexuality in Early Modern France: A Documentary Collection* (Oxford 2001), pp. 74–75.

41 Mary Elizabeth Perry, *Crime and Society in Early Modern Seville* (Hanover, NH 1980), p. 84.

42 Judith C. Brown, *Immodest Acts: The Life of a Lesbian Nun in Renaissance Italy* (Oxford 1986), p. 117.

43 The Quakers Katherine Evans and Sarah Cheevers, for example. See Elspeth Graham *et al.* (eds), *Her Own Life: Autobiographical Writings by Seventeenth-Century Englishwomen* (London 1989), pp. 116–30.

44 For 'bosom sex', see Karen V. Hansen, '"No Kisses is Like Youres": An Erotic Friendship between Two African-American Women during the Mid-Nineteenth Century", *Gender and History*, vol. 7, no. 2 (1995), pp. 153–82.

45 Eriksson, 'Lesbian Execution', p. 33.

46 Lister's diaries are published in two volumes edited by Helena Whitbread: *I Know My Own Heart: The Diaries of Anne Lister 1791–1840* (London 1988) and *No Priest But Love: The Journals of Anne Lister from 1824–1826* (Otley, Yorks. 1992). On Lister, see in particular Bray, *The Friend* (especially p. 271) and Anna Clark, 'Anne Lister's Construction of Lesbian Identity', *Journal of the History of Sexuality*, vol. 7, no. 1 (1996), pp. 23–50.

CHAPTER 7
BRETT GENNY BEEMYN

is Director of the Stonewall Center at the University of Massachusetts, Amherst. He has edited or co-edited five books, including *Creating a Place for Ourselves: Lesbian, Gay, and Bisexual Community History*, *Queer Studies: A Lesbian, Gay, Bisexual, and Transgender Anthology*, and a special issue of the *Journal of Gay and Lesbian Issues in Education* on 'Trans Youth'.

Notes

1 Clark L. Taylor, 'Legends, Syncretism, and Continuing Echoes of Homosexuality from Pre-Columbian and Colonial Mexico', in Stephen O. Murray (ed.), *Latin American Male Homosexualities* (Albuquerque 1995), p. 84; Rudi C. Bleys, *The Geography of Perversion: Male-to-Male Sexual Behavior Outside the West and the Ethnographic Imagination, 1750–1918* (New York 1995), pp. 23–24.

2 Taylor, 'Legends, Syncretism', p. 84.

3 Bleys, *The Geography of Perversion*, pp. 25–26; David Higgs, 'Rio de Janeiro', in David Higgs (ed.), *Queer Sites: Gay Urban Histories since 1600* (New York 1999), p. 138.

4 Stephen O. Murray, 'South American West Coast Indigenous Homosexualities', in Murray, *Latin American Male Homosexualities*, p. 279; Ward Stavig, 'Political "Abomination" and Private Reservation: The Nefarious Sin, Homosexuality, and Cultural Values in Colonial Peru', in Pete Sigal (ed.), *Infamous Desire: Male Homosexuality in Colonial Latin America* (Chicago 2003), p. 138.

5 Jonathan Katz, *Gay American History: Lesbians and Gay Men in the USA* (New York 1976), p. 285; Sabine Lang, *Men as Women, Women as Men: Changing Gender in Native American Cultures* (Austin, TX 1998), pp. 17, 66–67; Walter L. Williams, *The Spirit and the Flesh: Sexual Diversity in American Indian Culture* (Boston, MA 1986), pp. 67–68.

6 Katz, *Gay American History*, pp. 285–86; Will Roscoe, *Changed Ones: Third and Fourth Genders in Native North America* (New York 1998), p. 12.

7 James M. Saslow, *Pictures and Passions: A History of Homosexuality in the Visual Arts* (New York 1999), p. 110.

8 Sabine Lang, 'Lesbians, Men-Women and Two-Spirits: Homosexuality and Gender in Native American Cultures', in Evelyn Blackwood and Saskia E. Wieringa (eds), *Female Desires: Same-Sex Relations and Transgender Practices Across Cultures* (New York 1999), p. 92; Lang, *Men as Women, Women as Men*, p. 6; Williams, *The Spirit and the Flesh*, p. 83.

9 Leila Rupp, *A Desired Past: A Short History of Same-Sex Love in America* (Chicago 1999), p. 24; Bleys, *The Geography of Perversion*, p. 35; Stephen O. Murray and Will Roscoe (eds), *Boy-Wives and Female Husbands: Studies of African Homosexualities* (New York 1988), p. 9.

10 Higgs, 'Rio de Janeiro'; Bleys, *The Geography of Perversion*, p. 34; João S. Trevisan, *Perverts in Paradise* (London 1986), pp. 42, 53.

11 Trevisan, *Perverts in Paradise*, pp. 66–67.

12 Taylor, 'Legends, Syncretism', p. 88.

13 Jonathan Ned Katz, *Gay/Lesbian Almanac* (New York 1983), p. 663; John D'Emilio and Estelle B. Freedman, *Intimate Matters: A History of Sexuality in America* (Chicago 1997), p. 30.

14 Katz, *Gay/Lesbian Almanac*, p. 90.

15 Collin L. Talley, 'Gender and Male Same-Sex Erotic Behavior in British North America in the Seventeenth Century', *Journal of the History of Sexuality*, vol. 6, no. 3 (1996), pp. 396–97.

16 Katz, *Gay/Lesbian Almanac*, p. 75, and Richard Godbeer, *Sexual Revolution in Early America* (Baltimore 2002), pp. 113–14.

17 Gary Kinsman, *The Regulation of Desire: Homo and Hetero Sexualities* (Montreal, 2nd edn 1996), p. 98.

18 Talley, 'Gender and Male Same-Sex Erotic Behavior', p. 401; Robert Oaks, '"Things Fearful to Name": Sodomy and Buggery in Seventeenth-Century New England', *Journal of Social History*, vol. 12 (1978), p. 269.

19 Godbeer, *Sexual Revolution in Early America*, pp. 44–50; Katz, *Gay/Lesbian Almanac*, pp. 111–18; Rupp, *A Desired Past*, pp. 31–32.

20 Katz, *Gay/Lesbian Almanac*, pp. 85–86, 92–93; Rupp, *A Desired Past*, p. 28.

21 The History Project, *Improper Bostonians: Lesbian and Gay History from the Puritans to Playland* (Boston, MA 1998), p. 17.

22 Rupp, *A Desired Past*, pp. 33–35; Kathleen M. Brown, '"Changed … into the Fashion of Man": The Politics of Sexual Difference in a Seventeenth-Century Anglo-American Settlement', *Journal of the History of Sexuality*, vol. 6, no. 2 (1995), pp. 188–89.

23 Rupp, *A Desired Past*, p. 35.

24 Oaks, 'Things Fearful to Name', p. 278; Richard Godbeer, 'Colonial America', in Marc Stein (ed.), *Encyclopedia of Lesbian, Gay, Bisexual, and Transgender History in America*, vol. 1 (New York 2004), p. 240.

25 George Painter, 'The Sensibilities of Our Forefathers: The History of Sodomy Laws in the United States', *Sodomy Laws Around the World* (2003), http://www.sodomylaws.orgsensibilities/introduction.htm (accessed 30 Sept. 2005); Jonathan Ned Katz, *Love Stories: Sex Between Men Before Homosexuality* (Chicago 2001), p. 63.

26 Painter, 'The Sensibilities of Our Forefathers'.

27 Carroll Smith-Rosenberg, 'The Female World of Love and Ritual: Relations Between Women in Nineteenth-Century America', *Signs*, vol. 1 (1975), pp. 1–29. Cited here is the version of the article that appeared in Carroll Smith-Rosenberg, *Disorderly Conduct: Visions of Gender in Victorian America* (New York 1985), pp. 53–76.

28 Smith-Rosenberg, 'The Female World of Love and Ritual', pp. 55–56.

29 Rupp, *A Desired Past*, p. 38; Godbeer, 'Colonial America', p. 240; Smith-Rosenberg, 'The Female World of Love and Ritual', pp. 54–55; Karen V. Hansen, '"No Kisses Like Youres": An Erotic Friendship Between Two African American Women During the Mid-Nineteenth Century', *Gender and History*, vol. 7 (August 1995), pp. 153–82.

30 Rupp, *A Desired Past*, p. 48.

31 Hansen, '"No Kisses Like Youres"', p. 160.

32 Ibid., p. 164.

33 Ibid., pp. 168–69.

34 E. Anthony Rotundo, 'Romantic Friendship: Male Intimacy and Middle-Class Youth in the Northern United States, 1800–1900', *Journal of Social History*, vol. 23 (1989), pp. 1–25.

35 Martin Duberman, '"Writhing Bedfellows" in Antebellum South Carolina: Historical Interpretation and the Politics of Evidence', in John Howard (ed.), *Carryin' On in the Lesbian and Gay South* (New York 1997), pp. 17, 18.

36 Rotundo, 'Romantic Friendship', p. 18.

37 Byrne R. S. Fone (ed.), *The Columbia Anthology of Gay Literature: Readings from Western Antiquity to the Present Day* (New York 1998), p. 560.

38 Katz, *Gay American History*, pp. 338–39.

39 Charley Shively, *Calamus Lovers: Walt Whitman's Working-Class Camerados* (San Francisco 1987), p. 17.

40 Ibid., p. 67.

41 Ibid., p. 71.

42 John Donald Gustav-Wrathall, *Take the Young Stranger by the Hand: Same-Sex Relations and the YMCA* (Chicago 1998), pp. 45–46.

43 Ibid., pp. 3, 46.

44 Williams, *The Spirit and the Flesh*, pp. 152–64.

45 Ibid., pp. 154–56; B. R. Burg, *Sodomy and the Perception of Evil: English Sea Rovers in the Seventeenth Century Caribbean* (New York 1983), pp. 130–31.

46 Williams, *The Spirit and the Flesh*, p. 159.

47 Les Wright, 'San Francisco', in Higgs, *Queer Sites*, pp. 165, 167; Nan Alamilla Boyd, *Wide-Open Town: A History of Queer San Francisco to 1965* (Berkeley, CA 2003), pp. 2–3.

48 Terry L. Chapman, '"An Oscar Wilde Type": "The Abominable Crime of Buggery" in Western Canada, 1890–1920', *Criminal Justice History*, vol. 4 (1983), p. 107.

49 Kinsman, *The Regulation of Desire*, pp. 101–4.

50 Rupp, *A Desired Past*, p. 59.

51 Katy Coyle and Nadiene Van Dyke, 'Sex, Smashing, and Storyville in Turn-of-the-Century New Orleans: Reexamining the Continuum of Lesbian Sexuality', in Howard, *Carryin' On in the Lesbian and Gay South*, p. 65.

52 Ibid., pp. 55–63.

53 Nancy Sahli, 'Smashing: Women's Relationships Before the Fall', *Chrysalis*, vol. 8 (1979), p. 22.

54 Ibid., p. 22; Rupp, *A Desired Past*, p. 90; Jeanne Boydston, 'Smashes and Chumming', in Stein, *Encyclopedia of Lesbian, Gay, Bisexual, and Transgender History in America*, vol. 3, pp. 126–27; Caryn E. Neumann, 'Jane Addams', in *Encyclopedia of Lesbian, Gay, Bisexual, and Transgender History in America*, vol. 1, pp. 5–6; Gustav-Wrathall, *Take the Young Stranger by the Hand*, p. 3.

55 Katz, *Gay/Lesbian Almanac*, p. 213.

56 Rupp, *A Desired Past*, pp. 79–80.

57 Katz, *Gay American History*, p. 52.

58 Rupp, *A Desired Past*, p. 78; Katz, *Gay/Lesbian Almanac*, p. 219.

59 Brett Beemyn, 'The Geography of Same-Sex Desire: Cruising Men in Washington, DC in the Late Nineteenth and Early Twentieth Centuries', *Left History*, vol. 9, no. 2 (2004), pp. 144, 149–50.

60 Steven Maynard, 'Through a Hole in the Lavatory Wall: Homosexual Subcultures, Police Surveillance, and the Dialectics of Discovery, Toronto, 1890–1930', *Journal of the History of Sexuality*, vol. 5, no. 2 (1994), pp. 207–42; Robert McKee Irwin, Edward J. McCaughan, and Michelle Rocío Nasser (eds) *The Famous 41: Sexuality and Social Control in Mexico, c. 1901* (New York 2003); Oscar Montero, 'Julián del Casal and the Queers of Havana', in Emilie L. Bergmann and Paul Julian Smith (eds), *¿Entiendes?: Queer Readings, Hispanic Writings* (Durham, NC 1995), pp. 92–112; Jorge Salessi, 'Argentine Dissemination of Homosexuality, 1890–1914', in *¿Entiendes?*, pp. 49–91; Trevisan, *Perverts in Paradise*; Daniel Bao, 'Invertidos Sexuales, Tortilleras, and Maricas Machos: The Construction of Homosexuality in Buenos Aires, Argentina, 1900–1950', in John P. DeCecco and John P. Elia (eds) *If You Seduce a Straight Person, Can You Make Them Gay?: Issues in Biological Essentialism Versus Social Constructionism in Gay and Lesbian Identities* (New York 1993), pp. 183–219; James N. Green, *Beyond Carnival: Male Homosexuality in Twentieth-Century Brazil* (Chicago 1999); Higgs, 'Rio De Janeiro'.

61 Bao, 'Invertidos Sexuales', p. 216, n. 53; Salessi, 'Argentine Dissemination of Homosexuality', p. 80.

62 Green, *Beyond Carnival*, pp. 42–43.

63 Carlos Monsiváis, 'The 41 and the *Gran Redada*', trans. Aaron Walker, in Irwin, McCaughan and Nasser, *The Famous 41*, pp. 139–67; Robert McKee Irwin, 'The Famous 41: The Scandalous Birth of Modern Mexican Homosexuality', *GLQ: A Journal of Lesbian and Gay Studies*, vol. 6 (2000), pp. 353–76.

64 Rupp, *A Desired Past*, p. 79.

CHAPTER 8
FLORENCE TAMAGNE

is a senior lecturer at the University of Lille III. She is the author of *A History of Homosexuality in Europe, Vol. 1: Berlin, London, Paris, 1919–1939* and *Mauvais genre? Une histoire des représentations de l'homosexualité*. She has also contributed to Louis-Georges Tin (ed.), *Dictionnaire de l'homophobie*, and Didier Eribon (ed.), *Dictionnaire des cultures gays et lesbiennes*.

Notes

1 Karl Heinrich Ulrichs (1825–95) was a homosexual German lawyer who between 1864 and 1879 published some twelve books on the subject of homosexuality under the pseudonym of Numa Numantius. In describing his theory of the 'third sex', he created the term 'Urning' to denote homosexuals who could, according to him, only be attracted by heterosexual men ('Dionings'). Although his attempts to have anti-homosexual laws abolished proved fruitless (he was so discouraged that he left Germany for Italy in 1880), he was nonetheless highly influential, and there are echoes of his analyses to be found in the work of many doctors, psychiatrists and militants during the first half of the 20th century.

2 'Les types sexuels intermédiaires' (1910), in Magnus Hirschfeld, *Les Homosexuels de Berlin* (Lille 2001), pp. 91–108.

3 Sigmund Freud, *Trois Essais sur la théorie sexuelle* [1905] (Paris 1987), p. 47.

4 Walter Pater, *Studies in the History of the Renaissance* (London 1873); John Addington Symonds, *A Problem in Greek Ethics* (London 1883).

5 See Michael Roper and John Tosh, *Manful Assertions: Masculinities in Britain Since 1800* (London 1991).

6 See Frederick S. Roden, *Same-Sex Desire in Victorian Religious Culture* (London 2002), and Ed Madden, 'The Well of Loneliness, or the Gospel According to Radclyffe Hall', in *Journal of Homosexuality*, vol. 33, no. 3/4, 1997, pp. 163–86. A number of lesbian writers converted to Catholicism at the beginning of the century: Radclyffe Hall in 1912, and also Una Troubridge, Renée Vivien, Tony Atwood and Christopher St John.

7 On the role of the press, see Judith Walkowitz, *City of Dreadful Delight: Narratives of Sexual Danger in Late Victorian London* (London 1992).

8 See especially Charles Upchurch, 'Forgetting the Unthinkable: Cross-Dressers and British Society in the Case of the Queen vs. Boulton and Others', in *Gender and History*, vol. 12, no. 1 (2000), pp. 127–57.

9 See Jeffrey Weeks, 'Inverts, Perverts, and Mary-Annes: Male Prostitution and the Regulation of Homosexuality in England in the Nineteenth and Early Twentieth Century', in Salvatore J. Licata and Robert P. Petersen (eds), *Historical Perspectives on Homosexuality* (New York 1981), pp. 113–34.

10 See Morris B. Kaplan, 'Did "My Lord Gomorrah" Smile? Homosexuality, Class and Prostitution in the Cleveland Street Affair', in George Robb and Nancy Erber (eds), *Disorder in the Court: Trials and Sexual Conflict at the Turn of the Century* (London 1999), pp. 78–99.

11 They were even accused of Satanism. See Nancy Erber, 'Queer Follies: Effeminacy and Aestheticism in Fin-de-Siècle France: The Case of Baron d'Adelswärd-Fersen and Count de Warren', in Robb and Erber, *Disorder in the Court*, pp. 186–208. See also the Dublin Castle affair (1884), which involved various officials; and there was the arrest in France in 1876 of the Count de Germiny for public indecency, following his soliciting of a young workman in a public toilet near the Champs-Elysées. See William Peniston, 'A Public Offense Against Decency: The Trial of the Count de Germiny and the "Moral Order" of the Third Republic', in Robb and Erber, *Disorder in the Court*, pp. 12–32.

12 See Richard Ellmann, *Oscar Wilde* (London 1987).

13 Alan Sinfield, *The Wilde Century: Effeminacy, Oscar Wilde, and the Queer Movement* (New York 1994), pp. 11–12. See also Christopher Breward, *The Hidden Consumer: Masculinities, Fashion and City Life 1860–1914* (Manchester 1999).

14 The eponymous hero of Forster's novel *Maurice* defines himself as 'an unspeakable of the Oscar Wilde sort'.

15 See Michael de Cossart, *The Food of Love: Princesse Edmonde de Polignac (1865–1943) and her Salon* (London 1978).

16 John Grand-Carteret, *Derrière 'Lui': L'homosexualité en Allemagne* (Lille 1992); and James D. Steakley, 'Iconography of a Scandal: Political Cartoons and the Eulenburg Affair in Wilhelmin Germany', in Martin Bauml Duberman, Martha Vicinus and George Chauncey (eds), *Hidden from History: Reclaiming the Gay and Lesbian Past* (New York 1989).

17 Quoted in Susan Kingsley Kent, *Making Peace: The Reconstruction of Gender in Interwar Britain* (Princeton 1993), p. 42.

18 In England during the First World War, 22 officers and 270 soldiers were found guilty of homosexuality, according to Samuel Hynes, *A War Imagined: The First World War and English Culture* (New York 1991).

19 Paul Fussell, *The Great War and Modern Memory* (New York 1975).

20 See Adrian Caesar, *'Taking it Like a Man': Suffering, Sexuality and the War Poets: Brooke, Sassoon, Owen, Graves* (Manchester 1993).

21 Joanna Bourke, *Dismembering the Male: Men's Bodies, Britain and the Great War* (London 1996), p. 136.

22 See Florence Tamagne, *A History of Homosexuality in Europe, Vol. 1: Berlin, London, Paris, 1919–1939* (New York 2004); and *Goodbye*

to Berlin? 100 Jahre Schwulenbewegung (Berlin 1997).

23 In Switzerland a homosexual magazine called *Schweizerisches Freundschafts-Banner* was founded in 1932, following the German model. In 1943 it was renamed *Der Kreis* and continued to be published until 1967.

24 In France the law of 29 July 1881 concerning freedom of the press allowed prosecution for a public offence against decency, punishable by two years' imprisonment and a fine of 2000 francs. Its application remained problematical, however, particularly in the case of literary works, and the main focus seems to have been on ensuring that certain types of depiction remained unseen. In the case of *Inversions*, which contained no texts or photographs that were pornographic or explicit, it would seem to have been the presentation of a positive view of homosexuality that led to the ban.

25 See Jeffrey Weeks, *Coming Out: Homosexual Politics in Britain from the Nineteenth Century to the Present* (London 1979). At the beginning of the 1890s, George Ives founded the Order of the Chaeronea, a secret society for homosexuals.

26 See Alan Kidd and David Nicholls, *Gender, Civic Culture and Consumerism: Middle-Class Identity in Britain 1800–1940* (Manchester 1999).

27 See Jonathan Gathorne-Hardy, *The Public School Phenomenon 597–1977* (London 1977).

28 Noël Annan, *Our Age: English Intellectuals Between the Wars: A Group Portrait* (New York 1991).

29 Regarding sexual geographies, see especially Simon Gunn and Robert J. Morris, *Identities in Space: Contested Terrains in the Western City since 1850* (Aldershot 2001); David Higgs (ed.), *Queer Sites: Gay Urban Histories since 1600* (London 1999).

30 On the role of dress in the lesbian subculture, see Laura Doan, *Fashioning Sapphism: The Origins of a Modern English Lesbian Culture* (New York 2001).

31 On London, see especially Matt Cook, *London and the Culture of Homosexuality 1885–1914* (Cambridge 2003).

32 See Seth Koven, 'From Rough Lads to Hooligans: Boy Life, National Culture and Social Reform', in Andrew Parker, Mary Russo, Doris Summer and Patricia Yarger (eds), *Nationalisms and Sexualities* (New York 1992).

33 See, for example, Matt Houlbrook, '"Lady Austin's Camp Boys": Constituting the Queer Subject in 1930s London', in *Gender & History*, vol. 14, no. 1 (April 2002), pp. 31–61.

34 See Magnus Hirschfeld, *Les homosexuels de Berlin* [1908] (Paris 1993), and Ruth Margarete Roellig, *Les lesbiennes de Berlin* [1928] (Paris 1992).

35 See Timothy d'Arch Smith, *Love in Earnest: Some Notes on the Lives and Writings of English 'Uranian' Poets from 1889 to 1930* (London 1970).

36 See Robert Aldrich, *The Seduction of the Mediterranean: Writing, Art and Homosexual Fantasy* (London 1993).

37 See Robert Aldrich, *Colonialism and Homosexuality* (London 2003), and Ronald Hyam, *Empire and Sexuality: The British Experience* (Manchester 1990).

38 This was the case in France, where the 'damned women' so dear to Baudelaire and Balzac (*La Fille aux yeux d'or*, 1835) were a commonplace of decadence, and also in Austria: see Neda Bei, Wolfgang Förster, Hanna Hacker and Manfred

Lang (eds), *Das Lila Wien um 1900: Zur Ästhetik der Homosexualitäten* (Vienna 1986).

39 See Shari Benstock, *Women of the Left Bank: Paris 1900–1940* (Austin, TX 1986).

40 See Flora Leroy-Forgeot, *Histoire juridique de l'homosexualité en Europe* (Paris 1997).

41 In spite of the vagueness of this expression, jurisprudence chose to interpret it in a restricted manner, since only 'acts similar to coitus' were punishable by law, which notably excluded male masturbation. To compensate for the lack of clarity in this definition, the testimony of a medical expert at a trial could prove decisive.

42 Male soliciting was dealt with in a magistrate's court and was punishable by one month's imprisonment or six months in the case of a previous offender.

43 Exceptions were Austria (1852), Sweden (1864), Finland (1889) and some Swiss cantons.

44 Jan Löfström, 'A Premodern Legacy: The "Easy" Criminalization of Homosexual Acts in the Finnish Penal Code of 1889', in 'Scandinavian Homosexualities: Essays on Gay and Lesbian Studies', *Journal of Homosexuality*, vol. 35, no. 3/4 (1998).

45 The legal repression of homosexuality in Finland remained limited, although this did not prevent the exercise of strict social control. In the absence of any really large city (Helsinki had only 90,000 inhabitants in 1900), a specifically gay and lesbian culture could develop only on a small scale. The fact that women could not go into bars without a male escort also reduced the chances of an autonomous subculture developing.

46 H. G. Cocks, *Nameless Offences: Homosexual Desire in the Nineteenth Century* (London 2003).

47 In certain cases, the financial situation of the accused could also provide a means of escape, either by obtaining the services of a renowned lawyer skilled in manipulating proceedings, or by the appointment of a special jury. See Cocks, *Nameless Offences*.

48 See Régis Revenin, *Homosexualité et prostitution masculines à Paris (1870–1918)* (Paris 2005).

49 See Tamagne, *A History of Homosexuality in Europe*.

50 See Michael Baker, *Our Three Selves: A Life of Radclyffe Hall* (London 1985).

51 This view explains why, especially in detective fiction at the end of the 19th century, the character of the private detective is often – though rarely explicitly – intermingled with that of the homosexual (Edgar Allan Poe's Dupin, Conan Doyle's Sherlock Holmes). Both share a capacity for breaking class barriers and penetrating the secrets of the human mind. See Graham Robb, *Strangers: Homosexual Love in the Nineteenth Century* (New York 2004).

52 Florence Tamagne, 'Caricatures homophobes et stéréotypes de genre en France et en Allemagne: la presse satirique de 1900 au milieu des années 30', *Le temps des médias*, no. 1, autumn 2003.

53 The expression was coined by Cyril Connolly and Maurice Bowra.

54 On this subject see especially Rüdiger Lautmann, *Seminar: Gesellschaft und Homosexualität* (Frankfurt am Main 1977); Heinz-Dieter Schilling, *Schwule und Faschismus* (Berlin 1983); Burckardt Jellonek, *Homosexuelle unter dem Hakenkreuz* (Paderborn 1990); and Günther Grau, *Hidden Holocaust? Gay and Lesbian Persecution in Germany 1933–1945* (London 1993).

55 Heinrich Himmler, *Discours secrets* (Paris 1978).

56 Claudia Schoppmann, *Nationalsozialistische Sozialpolitik und weibliche Homosexualität* (Berlin 1991).

57 The expression was used by Maxim Gorky in an article published in *Pravda* on 23 May 1934.

58 On this subject see Klaus Theweleit, *Männerphantasien* (Frankfurt am Main 1979); and Melanie Hawthorne and Richard J. Colsan, *Gender and Fascism in Modern France* (Hanover, NH 1997).

59 See Simon Karlisky, 'Russia's Gay Literature and Culture: The Impact of the October Revolution', in Martin Bauml Duberman, Martha Vicinus and George Chauncey (eds), *Hidden from History* (London 1991), and Laura Engelstein, *The Keys to Happiness: Sex and the Search for Modernity in Fin-de-Siècle Russia* (Ithaca, NY 1992).

60 See Laurie Essig, *Queer in Russia: A Story of Sex, Self and the Other* (Durham 1999).

61 Anthony Copley, *Sexual Moralities in France, 1780–1980: New Ideas on the Family, Divorce and Homosexuality: An Essay on Moral Change* (London 1989); Jean Danet, *Discours juridique et perversions sexuelles (XIXe–XXe siècle)* (Nantes 1977).

62 Michael J. Sibalis, 'Homophobia, Vichy France, and the "Crime of Homosexuality": The Origins of the Ordinance of 6 August 1942', in *GLQ*, vol. 8, no. 3 (2002), pp. 301–18.

63 See Pierre Seel (in collaboration with Jean Le Bitoux), *Moi Pierre Seel, déporté homosexuel* (Paris 1994; English translation by Joachim Neugroschel, *Liberation Was for Others: Memoirs of a Gay Survivor of the Nazi Holocaust*, New York 1997). A historical commission on homosexual deportation was established in 2001 to investigate this little-known aspect of French gay history. More than 200 cases have so far been documented.

64 See George Chauncey, *Gay New York: Gender, Urban Culture and the Making of the Gay Male World 1890–1940* (New York 1994).

CHAPTER 9
DOMENICO RIZZO

is a researcher in late modern history and gender at the University of Naples 'L'Orientale'. Recent publications include *Gli spazi della morale: buon costume e ordine delle famiglie in Italia in età liberale*, and a chapter on 'Marriage on Trial: Adultery in Nineteenth-Century Rome', in P. Wilson's collection *Gender, Family and Sexuality: The Private Sphere in Italy, 1860–1945*. He is also editorial secretary of the journal *Quaderni storici*.

Notes

1 See Eric J. Hobsbawm, *Age of Extremes: The Short Twentieth Century (1914–1991)* (New York 1994), in particular the volume's second section.

2 See Hubert Kennedy, *Der Kreis – Le Cercle – The Circle: Eine Zeitschrift und ihr Programm* (Berlin 1999), published in English as *The Ideal Gay Man: The Story of* Der Kreis (New York 1999).

3 Aversion therapy was developed in the early 1940s by Sandor Rado and was still widely practised in the 1970s. See Henry L. Minton, *Departing from Deviance: A History of Homosexual Rights and Emancipatory Science in America* (Chicago 2002). Another useful source is Ronald Bayer, *Homosexuality and American Psychiatry: The Politics of Diagnosis* (New York 1981).

4 'Es wäre wunderbar, wenn unsere Lebensqual durch eine vollkommene Heilung ein Ende finden würde'. *Der Kreis/Le Cercle*, vol. 11, no. 11 (1943), p. 2.

5 Ibid. Significantly, the man writes not that he 'desires to find', but that he is led 'to desire and to find' ('zu wünschen und zu finden'): it is an act of will and self-constraint.

6 Ibid., p. 3.

7 Ibid., p. 4.

8 George Chauncey, 'Après Stonewall, le déplacement de la frontière entre le "soi" public et le "soi" privé', in *Histoire & sociétés*, vol. 3 (2002), pp. 45–49. There is still much research to do on the subject: we do not know, for example, the extent to which such networks in the middle of the century were self-sufficient, nor do we know in what way sexual orientation informed social and economic practices.

9 Henning Bech, 'A Short History of Gay Denmark 1613–1989: The Rise and the Possibly Happy End of the Danish Homosexual', in *Nordisk Sexologi*, vol. 12 (1994), pp. 125–136.

10 On this construction of the public sphere in Italy, and also for a comparative European perspective, see Domenico Rizzo, *Gli spazi della morale: buon costume e ordine delle famiglie in Italia in età liberale* (Rome 2004).

11 Lawrence v. Texas, 123 Sect. 2472 (2003), an important case because the Supreme Court of the United States established for the first time that it is unconstitutional to use sodomy laws to punish consensual acts between adults carried out in private. On the earlier role of jurisprudence, see Patricia A. Cain, *Rainbow Rights: The Role of Lawyers and Courts in the Lesbian and Gay Civil Rights Movement* (Boulder, CO 2000).

12 Alfred C. Kinsey, *Sexual Behavior in the Human Male* (Philadelphia 1948). Julia A. Erickson devotes much space to it in *Kiss and Tell: Surveying Sex in the Twentieth Century* (Cambridge, MA 1999).

13 *Report of the Committee on Homosexual Offences and Prostitution* (London 1957). Neil A. Radford, 'Wolfenden, John Frederick', in Robert Aldrich and Garry Wotherspoon (eds), *Who's Who in Contemporary Gay and Lesbian History: From World War II to the Present Day* (London 2001), pp. 454–56. On the general context, see also Patrick Higgins, *Heterosexual Dictatorship: Male Homosexuality in Postwar Britain* (London 1996).

14 Dan Healey, *Homosexual Desire in Revolutionary Russia: The Regulation of Sexual and Gender Dissent* (Chicago 2001).

15 See David K. Johnson, *The Lavender Scare: The Cold War Persecution of Gays and Lesbians in the Federal Government* (Chicago 2004).

16 The two homosexual spies were Guy Burgess and Donald Maclean. On the first, in particular, see Tom Driberg, *Guy Burgess: A Portrait with Background* (London 1956); Driberg interviewed Burgess in Moscow. Several works were inspired by the figure of Burgess, including the film *Another Country* (1984, dir. Marek Kanievska), which was based on the play of the same name by Julian Mitchell (1981).

17 See Janine Mossuz-Lavau, *Le Lois de l'amour: les politiques de la sexualité en France de 1950 à nos jours* (Paris 1991).

18 See Higgins, *Heterosexual Dictatorship*.

19 John D'Emilio, 'Dream Deferred: The Birth and Betrayal of America's First Gay Liberation Movement', in *Making Trouble: Essays on Gay History, Politics and the University* (New York 1992), pp. 17–56.

20 Cited in D'Emilio, 'Dream Deferred', p. 46.

21 *ONE Magazine*, vol. 1, no. 1 (January 1953).

22 See Gert Hekma, 'The Amsterdam Bar Culture and Changing Gay/Lesbian Identities', Gay and Lesbian Studies at the University of Amsterdam, http://www2.fmg.uva.nl/gl/gaybar.html (accessed 17 December 2005).

23 For example, the *Guide des établissements homosexuels masculins et féminins*, published by *Der Neue Ring* in December 1958, provides a list of approximately 125 pubs run and/or frequented by homosexuals in the main European cities and in New York.

24 André Baudry, 'Notre responsabilité', in *Arcadie*, November 1961, p. 554. See also G. Sidéris, 'Des folles de Saint-Germain-des-Prés au fléau sociale: le discours homophile contre l'efféminement dans les années 50: une expression de la haine de soi?', in J. C. Benbassa (ed.), *Haine de soi: difficiles indentités* (Brussels 2000).

25 Sidéris, 'Des folles de Saint-Germain-des-Prés'.

26 Charles Welti in *Der Kreis/Le Cercle/The Circle*, vol. 8 (1967), pp. 29–30.

27 Martin Duberman, *Stonewall* (New York 1994).

28 Craig A. Rimmerman, *From Identity to Politics: The Lesbian and Gay Movements in the United States* (Philadelphia 2002).

29 Lisa Power, *No Bath But Plenty of Bubbles: An Oral History of the Gay Liberation Front, 1970–1973* (London 1995), pp. 4–5.

30 Florence Tamagne, *A History of Homosexuality in Europe, Vol. 1: Berlin, London, Paris, 1919–1939* (New York 2004).

31 See Hans-George Stümke, *Homosexuelle in Deutschland: Eine Politische Geschichte* (Munich 1989).

32 See Gianni Rossi Barilli, *Il movimento gay in Italia* (Milan 1999).

33 See Bruce Ryan, 'Rosa von Praunheim in Theory and Practice', in *CineAction!*, vol. 9 (summer 1987), pp. 25–31.

34 Paul A. Robinson, *The Freudian Left: Wilhelm Reich, Geza Roheim, Herbert Marcuse* (New York 1969); David Allyn, *Make Love, Not War: The Sexual Revolution, An Unfettered History* (Boston, MA 2000); Jeffrey Escoffier (ed.), *Sexual Revolution* (New York 2003).

35 Toby Marotta, *The Politics of Homosexuality* (Boston, MA 1981).

36 Martha Shelley, 'Gay is Good', in M. Blasius and S. Phelan (eds), *We Are Everywhere: A Historical Sourcebook for Gay and Lesbian Politics* (New York 1997), p. 391.

37 Chauncey, 'Après Stonewall'.

38 Guy Hocquenghem, *Homosexual Desire*, trans. Danielle Dangoor (London 1978).

39 See Mario Mieli, *Homosexuality and Liberation: Elements of a Gay Critique*, trans. David Fernbach (London 1980).

40 Dennis Altman, 'Sex: The New Front Line for Gay Politics', in *Socialist Review*, vol. 65 (1982), reprinted in Blasius and Phelan, *We Are Everywhere*, pp. 529–34.

41 Manuel Castells, *The City and the Grassroots: A Cross-Cultural Theory of Urban Social Movements* (Berkeley, CA 1983), p. 141.

42 John D. Stamford, preface to *Spartacus International Gay Guide*, 4th edn (1974) pp. 3–4.

43 See Dangerous Bedfellows (eds), *Policing Public Sex: Queer Politics and the Future of AIDS Activism* (Boston, MA 1996); *Private Acts, Social Consequences: AIDS and the Politics of Public Health* (New York 1989).

CHAPTER 10
LEILA J. RUPP

is Professor and Chair of Women's Studies at the University of California, Santa Barbara. She is co-author, with Verta Taylor, of *Drag Queens at the 801 Cabaret* and *Survival in the Doldrums: The American Women's Rights Movement, 1945 to the 1960s*, and is author of *A Desired Past: A Short History of Same-Sex Sexuality in America*, *Worlds of Women: The Making of an International Women's Movement* and *Mobilizing Women for War: German and American Propaganda, 1939–1945*.

Bibliographic essay

Compared to the literature on male same-sex sexuality, coverage on women who loved women is thin. Stephen O. Murray includes information on female same-sex sexuality in his sweeping global survey *Homosexualities* (Chicago 2000). Other, more focused syntheses include Colin Spencer, *Homosexuality in History* (New York 1995), which begins in prehistory and covers the Western world; Neil Miller, *Out of the Past: Gay and Lesbian History from 1869 to the Present* (New York 1995), which covers Europe and the United States; and Leila J. Rupp, *A Desired Past: A Short History of Same-Sex Love in America* (Chicago 1999). *Hidden From History: Reclaiming the Gay and Lesbian Past* (New York 1989), edited by Martin Bauml Duberman, Martha Vicinus and George Chauncey, includes articles on a wide variety of places and time periods. *Lesbian Histories and Cultures*, edited by Bonnie Zimmerman (New York 2000), is similarly broad in its coverage.

A number of books and anthologies on gender-crossing and third-gender people include articles on biological females. These include *The Spirit and the Flesh: Sexual Diversity in American Indian Culture* (Boston, MA 1986); *Two-Spirit People*, edited by Sue-Ellen Jacobs, Wesley Thomas and Sabine Lang (Urbana, IL 1997); and *Third Sex, Third Gender: Beyond Sexual Dimorphism in Culture and History*, edited by Gilbert Herdt (New York 1996). *Boy-Wives and Female Husbands: Studies in African Homosexualities*, edited by Stephen O. Murray and Will Roscoe (New York 1998), contains some material on female same-sex sexuality in Africa.

Martha Vicinus, *Intimate Friends: Women Who Loved Women, 1778–1928* (Chicago 2004) is an essential source on a wide variety of women's relationships in England and the United States. The classic work on women's relationships is Lillian Faderman, *Surpassing the Love of Men: Romantic Friendship and Love Between Women from the Renaissance to the Present* (New York 1981). See also her account of the Pirie–Woods case in *Scotch Verdict* (New York 1983) and her surveys of US lesbian history in *Odd Girls and Twilight Lovers: A History of Lesbian Life in Twentieth-Century America* (New York 1991) and *To Believe in Women: What Lesbians Have Done for America – A History* (Boston, MA 1999). Karin Lützen, *Was das Herz begehrt: Liebe und Freundschaft zwischen Frauen* (Hamburg 1990), a translation from Danish, deals with evidence of love between women from throughout Europe. See also Marie-Jo Bonnet, *Les Deux Amies: Les relations amoureuses entre les femmes du XVIe au XXe siècle* (Paris 1995). Tze-lan D. Sang, *The Emerging Lesbian:*

Female Same-Sex Desire in Modern China (Chicago 2003) provides valuable information on the emergence of the concept of lesbianism and the development of lesbian identities in China from the Republican period to the present.

On lesbian cultures in the 20th century, see Shari Benstock, *Women of the Left Bank: Paris, 1900–1940* (Austin, TX 1986); *Eldorado: Homosexuelle Frauen und Männer in Berlin 1850–1950* (Berlin 1984), an exhibition catalogue with articles and illustrations; and Elizabeth Lapovsky Kennedy and Madeline D. Davis, *Boots of Leather, Slippers of Gold: The History of a Lesbian Community* (New York 1993), on working-class butch–fem bar culture in Buffalo, New York, in the 1940s and 1950s.

Notes

1 Judith M. Bennett, '"Lesbian-Like" and the Social History of Lesbianisms', *Journal of the History of Sexuality*, vol. 9, no. 1–2 (2000), pp. 1–24; Leila J. Rupp, 'Toward a Global History of Same-Sex Sexuality', *Journal of the History of Sexuality*, vol. 10, no. 2 (2001), pp. 287–302.
2 Lucy Chesser, '"A Woman Who Married Three Wives": Management of Disruptive Knowledge in the 1879 Australian Case of Edward De Lacy Evans', *Journal of Women's History*, vol. 9, no. 4 (1998), pp. 53–77.
3 Ibid., p. 60.
4 See Rudolf Dekker and Lott van de Pol, *The Tradition of Female Transvestism in Early Modern Europe* (London 1989), and Julie Wheelwright, *Amazons and Military Maids: Women Who Dressed as Men in Pursuit of Life, Liberty and Happiness* (London 1989).
5 See Sabine Lang, 'Various Kinds of Two-Spirit People: Gender Variance and Homosexuality in Native American Communities', in Sue-Ellen Jacobs, Wesley Thomas and Sabine Lang (eds), *Two-Spirit People* (Urbana, IL 1997), pp. 100–118; and Walter L. Williams, *The Spirit and the Flesh: Sexual Diversity in American Indian Culture* (Boston, MA 1986).
6 Quoted in Williams, *The Spirit and the Flesh*, p. 237.
7 Quoted in Joseph M. Carrier and Stephen O. Murray, 'Woman–Woman Marriage in Africa', in Stephen O. Murray and Will Roscoe (eds), *Boy-Wives and Female Husbands: Studies in African Homosexualities* (New York 1998), p. 259.
8 See Carrier and Murray, *Boy-Wives*.
9 Quoted in Carrier and Murray, *Boy-Wives*, p. 263.
10 Quoted in Martha Vicinus, *Intimate Friends: Women Who Loved Women, 1778–1928* (Chicago 2004), p. 9.
11 Ibid., p. 45.
12 Ibid., p. 20.
13 Ibid., p. 22.
14 Ibid., p. 23.
15 Ibid., p. 26.
16 See Lisa Duggan, *Sapphic Slashers: Sex, Violence, and American Modernity* (Durham, NC 2000).
17 Quoted in Geertje Mak, 'Sandor/Sarolta Vay: From Passing Woman to Invert', *Journal of Women's History*, vol. 16, no. 1 (2004), p. 54.
18 Ibid., p. 61.
19 See Diane Wood Middlebrook, *Suits Me: The Double Life of Billy Tipton* (New York 1998).
20 Ruth Vanita, 'CLAGS Reports', *Centre for Lesbian and Gay Studies News*, vol. 14, no. 2 (2004), p. 14.
21 Quoted in Amanda Lock Swarr and Richa Nagar, 'Dismantling Assumptions: Interrogating "Lesbian" Struggles for Identity and Survival in India and South Africa', *Signs: Journal of Women in Culture and Society*, vol. 29 (2004), p. 500.
22 Quoted in Elizabeth W. Knowlton, '"Only a Woman Like Yourself": Rebecca Alice Baldy, Dutiful Daughter, Stalwart Sister, and Lesbian Lover of Nineteenth-Century Georgia', in John Howard (ed.), *Carryin' on in the Lesbian and Gay South* (New York 1997), p. 48.
23 Quoted in Dasa Francikova, 'Female Friends in Nineteenth-Century Bohemia: Troubles with Affectionate Writing and "Patriotic Relationships"', *Journal of Women's History*, vol. 12, no. 3 (2000), pp. 23–28, quotation on p. 24.
24 Quoted in Gloria T. Hull, *Color, Sex, and Poetry: Three Women Writers of the Harlem Renaissance* (Bloomington, IN 1987), p. 139.
25 Quoted in Lillian Faderman, *Scotch Verdict* (New York 1983), p. 147.
26 Ibid., p. 281.
27 Ibid., p. 82.
28 'Female rake' is the term used by Vicinus in *Intimate Friends*. She provides an extensive analysis of Lister.
29 Anne Lister, *I Know My Own Heart: The Diaries of Anne Lister (1791–1840)*, ed. Helena Whitbread (London 1988), p. 104.
30 Anne Lister, *No Priest But Love: The Journals of Anne Lister from 1824–1826*, ed. Helena Whitbread (New York 1992), p. 65.
31 Quoted in Karen V. Hansen, '"No Kisses Is Like Youres": An Erotic Friendship between Two African-American Women during the Mid-Nineteenth Century', *Gender and History*, vol. 7 (August), p. 159, 160.
32 Ibid., p. 162.
33 Quoted in Ruth Vanita, '"Married Among Their Companions": Female Homoerotic Relations in Nineteenth-Century Urdu *Rekhti* Poetry in India', *Journal of Women's History*, vol. 16, no. 1 (2004), p. 22.
34 Ibid., p. 28.
35 Ibid., p. 34.
36 See Heather Lee Miller, 'Sexologists Examine Lesbians and Prostitutes in the United States, 1840–1940', *NWSA Journal*, vol. 12, no. 3 (2000), pp. 67–91.
37 Quoted in Francesca Canadé Sautman, 'Invisible Women: Lesbian Working-Class Culture in France, 1880–1930', in Jeffrey Merrick and Bryant T. Ragan, Jr. (eds), *Homosexuality in Modern France* (New York 1996), pp. 191–92.
38 Quoted in Miller, 'Sexologists Examine Lesbians and Prostitutes', p. 70.
39 Quoted in Jennifer Terry, *An American Obsession: Science, Medicine, and Homosexuality in Modern Society* (Chicago 1999), p. 242.
40 See Elizabeth Lapovsky Kennedy and Madeline D. Davis, *Boots of Leather, Slippers of Gold: The History of a Lesbian Community* (New York 1993).
41 Ibid., p. 204.
42 Lister, *I Know My Own Heart*, p. 145.
43 Kendall, '"When a Woman Loves a Woman" in Lesotho: Love, Sex, and the (Western) Construction of Homophobia', in Stephen O. Murray and Will Roscoe (eds), *Boy-Wives and Female Husbands: Studies in African Homosexualities* (New York 1998), pp. 223–41.
44 Ibid., p. 233. On boarding-school relationships, Kendall cites Judith Gay, 'Mummies and Babies and Friends and Lovers in Lesotho', *Journal of Homosexuality*, vol. 11, no. 3–4 (1985), pp. 97–116.
45 See Tze-lan D. Sang, *The Emerging Lesbian: Female Same-Sex Desire in Modern China* (Chicago 2003), pp. 52, 377.
46 Ibid., p. 52.
47 Quoted in Lillian Faderman, *Odd Girls and Twilight Lovers: A History of Lesbian Life in Twentieth-Century America* (New York 1991), p. 53.
48 Ibid., p. 54.
49 See Estelle B. Freedman, *Maternal Justice: Miriam Van Waters and the Female Reform Tradition* (Chicago 1996).
50 Quoted in Carroll Smith-Rosenberg, 'Discourses of Sexuality and Subjectivity: The New Woman, 1870–1936', in Martin Bauml Duberman, Martha Vicinus and George Chauncey (eds), *Hidden From History: Reclaiming the Gay and Lesbian Past* (New York 1989), p. 275.
51 See Vicinus, *Intimate Friends*, p. 217.
52 Ibid., pp. 189–90.
53 See the articles in *Eldorado: Homosexuelle Frauen und Männer in Berlin 1850–1950*, exh. cat., Berlin, Schwules Museum (Berlin 1984).
54 Katharine Vogel, 'Zum Selbstverständnis lesbischer Frauen in der Weimarer Republik', in *Eldorado*, pp. 162–68.
55 Quoted in Petra Schlierkamp, 'Die Garçonne', in *Eldorado*, p. 173.
56 Joan Nestle, 'Excerpts from the Oral History of Mabel Hampton', *Signs: Journal of Women in Culture and Society*, vol. 18 (1993), p. 933.
57 See Sang, *The Emerging Lesbian*.
58 Ibid., p. 139.
59 Ibid., p. 144.
60 See Jennifer Robertson, 'Dying to Tell: Sexuality and Suicide in Imperial Japan', *Signs: Journal of Women in Culture and Society*, vol. 25 (1999), pp. 1–35.
61 Ibid., p. 16.
62 Didi Khayatt, 'Egypt', in Bonnie Zimmerman (ed.), *Lesbian Histories and Cultures* (New York 2000), pp. 257–58.
63 Claudia Hinojosa, 'Mexico', in Zimmerman, *Lesbian Histories and Cultures*, pp. 494–96.
64 Ian Barnard, 'South Africa', in Zimmerman, *Lesbian Histories and Cultures*, pp. 721–22.
65 Julie Dorf, 'International Organizations', in Zimmerman, *Lesbian Histories and Cultures*, pp. 398–400.

CHAPTER 11
LEE WALLACE

is Senior Lecturer in the Department of English at the University of Auckland. She is the author of *Sexual Encounters: Pacific Texts, Modern Sexualities*. Her current research project concerns the representation of lesbianism in cinematic space.

Further Reading

Peter A. Jackson and Gerard Sullivan (eds), *Lady Boys, Tom Boys, Rent Boys: Male and Female Homosexualities in Contemporary Thailand* (Binghamton, NY 1999)

Gregory M. Pflugfelder, *Cartographies of Desire: Male–Male Sexuality in Japanese Discourse, 1600–1950* (Berkeley, CA 1999)

Leila J. Rupp, 'Toward a Global History of Same-Sex Sexuality', *Journal of the History of Sexuality*, vol. 10, no. 2 (2001), pp. 287–302

John Whittier Treat, *Great Mirrors Shattered: Homosexuality, Orientalism, and Japan* (Oxford 1999)

Chou Wah-shan, *Tongzhi: Politics of Same-Sex Eroticism in Chinese Societies* (Binghamton, NY 2000)

Notes

1   Joseph Boone, 'Vacation Cruises; or, The Homoerotics of Orientalism', in John C. Hawley (ed.), *Postcolonial, Queer: Theoretical Intersections* (Albany, NY 2001), p. 46.

2   Gilbert Herdt, *Guardians of the Flutes: Idioms of Masculinity, with a New Preface* (Chicago 1994); *The Sambia: Ritual and Gender in New Guinea* (New York 1987). Cultural commentators engaged in contemporary debates for and against same-sex civil unions (the 'gay marriage' debate) have similarly fallen on John Boswell's research on religious ceremonies celebrating the wedlock-like connection of male partners and female partners in the early Eastern and Catholic Churches in the hope of shifting arguments, particularly those invoking Christian precepts of sexual morality. John Boswell, *Same-Sex Unions in Premodern Europe* (New York 1994).

3   Josiah Blackmore and Gregory S. Hutcheson (eds), *Queer Iberia: Sexualities, Cultures, and Crossings from the Middle Ages to the Renaissance* (Durham, NC 1999).

4   See in particular Jonathan Goldberg, *Sodometries: Renaissance Texts, Modern Sexualities* (Stanford, CA 1992), pp. 179–222, and Rudi C. Bleys, *The Geography of Perversion: Male-to-Male Sexual Behavior Outside the West and the Ethnographic Imagination, 1750–1918* (New York 1995), pp. 22–28.

5   Bleys, *The Geography of Perversion*, p. 24. Bleys is translating from the 1605 edition of Bernal Diaz del Castillo's *Historia verdadera de la conquista de la Nueva España*.

6   Goldberg, *Sodometries*, p. 180. Goldberg is citing Peter Martyr's *Decades of the Newe Worlde* in its English translation of 1555.

7   Martyr, *Decades*, quoted in Goldberg, p. 182.

8   Ibid.

9   See Michael Hardin, 'Altering Masculinities: The Spanish Conquest and the Evolution of the Latin American Machismo', *International Journal of Sexuality and Gender Studies*, vol. 7, no. 2 (2002), pp. 1–22. For a more specialized discussion of the colonization of Mayan erotic desire and its bisexual component, see Pete Sigal, *From Moon Goddesses to Virgins: The Colonization of Yucatecan Maya Sexual Desire* (Austin, TX 2000).

10 For discussion of the derivation of the term 'berdache', see Claude Courouve, 'The Word "Bardache"', *Gay Books Bulletin*, no. 8 (1982), pp. 18–19.

11 Francisco Coreal, *Voyages de François Coreal aux Indes Occidentales* (1722), quoted and translated by Will Roscoe in 'How to Become a Berdache: Toward a Unified Analysis of Gender Diversity', in Gilbert Herdt (ed.), *Third Sex, Third Gender: Beyond Dimorphism in Culture and History* (New York 1993), p. 329. Cabeza de Vaca's account, which includes his observation of a marriage ceremony between an effeminate and a non-effeminate man, is cited and translated by Bleys in *The Geography of Perversion*, p. 42.

12 For an overview of the berdaches that locates them in the context of a specifically gay social history, see Jonathan Katz, *Gay American History: Lesbians and Gay Men in the U.S.A.* (New York 1976), pp. 423–39.

13 Ruth Benedict, *Patterns of Culture* (Boston, MA 1959), pp. 262–65.

14 Will Roscoe, *Changing Ones: Third and Fourth Genders in Native North America* (New York 1998), p. 124. See also Harriet Whitehead, 'The Bow and the Burden Strap: A New Look at Institutionalized Homosexuality in Native North America', in Sherry B. Ortner and Harriet Whitehead (eds), *Sexual Meanings: The Cultural Construction of Gender and Sexuality* (Cambridge 1981), pp. 80–115.

15 Will Roscoe, *The Zuni Man-Woman* (Albuquerque, NM 1991); Paula Gunn Allen, 'Lesbians in American Indian Cultures', in Martin Bauml Duberman, Martha Vicinus and George Chauncey (eds), *Hidden From History: Reclaiming the Gay and Lesbian Past* (Harmondsworth 1991), p. 107.

16 Gilbert Herdt, *Same Sex, Different Cultures: Exploring Gay and Lesbian Lives* (Boulder, CO 1998), pp. 92–94.

17 Roscoe, 'How to Become a Berdache', pp. 329–72, and *Changing Ones: Third and Fourth Genders*. See also Sabine Lang, 'There is More Than Just Women and Men: Gender Variance in North American Indian Culture', in Sabina Ramet (ed.), *Gender Reversals and Gender Cultures: Anthropological and Historical Perspectives* (New York 1996), pp. 183–96.

18 Roscoe, 'How to Become a Berdache', pp. 342–43.

19 Bleys, *The Geography of Perversion*, p. 166.

20 Michael Haberlandt, 'Occurrences of Contrary-Sex Among the Negro Population of Zanzibar', translated by Bradley Rose, in Stephen O. Murray and Will Roscoe (eds), *Boy-Wives and Female Husbands: Studies of African Homosexualities* (New York 1998), p. 64.

21 Jacobus X [as 'A French Army-Surgeon'], *Untrodden Fields of Anthropology, Observations of the Esoteric Manners and Customs of Semi-Civilised Peoples; Being a Record of Thirty Years' Experience in Asia, Africa, America and Oceania*, 2 vols (Paris 1898), vol. 2, pp. 280–81.

22 Quoted in Murray and Roscoe, *Boy-Wives*, pp. 26–30.

23 Quoted in ibid., pp. 36–37.

24 Ibid., p. 98.

25 Rudolf P. Gaudio, 'Male Lesbians and Other Queer Notions in Hausa', in Murray and Roscoe, *Boy-Wives*, p. 124.

26 Murray and Roscoe, *Boy-Wives*, p. 142.

27 Quoted in ibid., p. 148.

28 Quoted in ibid., pp. 105–6.

29 Gunther Tessman, 'Homosexuality among the Negroes of Cameroon and a Pangwe Tale', translated by Bradley Rose, in Murray and Roscoe, *Boy-Wives*, pp. 155–56.

30 Murray and Roscoe, *Boy-Wives*, p. 142.

31 Ibid., p. 143.

32 Taberer Report, quoted in ibid., p. 178.

33 Ibid., pp. 178–82.

34 Quoted in ibid., p. 184.

35 See Joseph M. Carrier and Stephen O. Murray, 'Woman–Woman Marriage in Africa', in Murray and Roscoe, *Boy-Wives*, pp. 255–66.

36 Ibid., p. 259.

37 In this section I am compressing the argument I make at greater length in *Sexual Encounters: Pacific Texts, Modern Sexualities* (Ithaca, NY 2003). A longer discussion of William Bligh's involvement in male–male sexual discourse can be found on pp. 13–16.

38 William Bligh, *The Log of the Bounty*, ed. Owen Rutter, 2 vols (London 1937), vol. 2, pp. 16–17.

39 Ibid., p. 17. The second set of square brackets is the editor's.

40 See Niko Besnier, 'Polynesian Gender Liminality Through Space and Time', in Herdt, *Third Sex, Third Gender*, pp. 285–328.

41 For a brief survey of Polynesian gender-defined homosexual roles, see Stephen O. Murray, *Homosexualities* (Chicago 2000), pp. 280–93.

42 This discussion of *aikane* is taken almost verbatim from Wallace, *Sexual Encounters*, pp. 45–47.

43 David Samwell, *Some Account of A Voyage to South Seas in 1776–1777–1778*, in *The Voyage of the Resolution and Discovery, 1776–1780*, vol. 3 of *The Journals of Captain James Cook on His Voyages of Discovery*, ed. J. C. Beaglehole (London 1967), p. 1171.

44 See Robert J. Morris, '*Aikane*: Accounts of Hawaiian Same-Sex Relationships in the Journals of Captain Cook's Third Voyage (1776–80)', *Journal of Homosexuality*, vol. 19 (1990), pp. 21–54, and 'Same-Sex Friendships in Hawaiian Lore: Constructing the Canon', in Stephen O. Murray (ed.), *Oceanic Homosexualities* (New York 1992), pp. 71–102.

45 Samwell, *Some Account of A Voyage*, vol. 3, p. 1171.

46 Ibid., p. 1159.

47 Ibid., pp. 1171–72.

48 Ibid., p. 1226.

49 Quoted in Murray, *Homosexualities*, p. 25.

50 Quoted in ibid., p. 26.

51 D. Michael Quinn, *Same-Sex Dynamics Among Nineteenth-Century Americans: A Mormon Example* (Urbana, IL 1996).

CHAPTER 12
VINCENZO PATANÈ

teaches history of art in Venice. He is the author of *Ebano Nudo*, *Cinema & Pittura*, *Derek Jarman*, *Shakespeare al cinema*, *Arabi e noi: Amori gay nel Maghreb*, and, most recently, *L'altra metà dell'amore: Dieci anni di cinema omosessuale* – a study of gay cinema of the last decade. He also writes for the Italian gay magazines *Babilonia* and *Pride*. A documentary film was made from his book *A qualcuno piace gay*, a study of Italian films with gay and lesbian themes.

Bibliography

Abū Nuwās, *Le Vin, le vent, la vie*, translation into French by Vincent Mansour Monteil (Paris 1979)

Robert Aldrich, *The Seduction of the Mediterranean: Writing, Art and Homosexual Fantasy* (London 1993)

'Les arabes et nous', in *Trois milliards de pervers: Grande Encyclopédie des Homosexualités*, a special issue of *Recherches* (March 1973), pp. 9–63

Abdelwahab Bouhdiba, *La sexualité en Islam* (Paris 1975)

Malek Chebel, *L'esprit de sérail: Perversion et marginalités sexuelles au Maghreb* (Paris 1988)

Malek Chebel, *Encyclopédie de l'amour en Islam* (Paris 1995)

Marc Daniel, 'Arab Civilization and Male Love', *Gay Sunshine*, no. 32 (spring 1977), reprinted in Winston Leyland (ed.), *An Anthology of Gay History, Politics, Sex, and Culture* (San Francisco 1991), pp. 33–75

Kieron Devlin, 'Islamic Art', in Claude J. Summers (ed.), *An Encyclopedia of Gay, Lesbian, Bisexual, Transgender, & Queer Culture*, http://www.glbtq.com/arts/islamic_art.html (accessed 23 January 2006)

Dominique Fernandez, *A Hidden Love: Art and Homosexuality* (Munich 2001)

Ian Littlewood, *Sultry Climates: Travel and Sex Since the Grand Tour* (London 2001)

Stephen O. Murray and Will Roscoe (eds), *Islamic Homosexualities: Culture, History, and Literature* (New York 1997)

Vincenzo Patanè, *Arabi e noi: Amori gay nel Maghreb* (Rome 2002)

Christine Peltre, *Dictionnaire culturel de l'Orientalisme* (Paris 2003)

Maxime Rodinson, *La fascination de l'Islam* (Paris 1980)

Everett K. Rowson and J. W. Wright (eds), *Homoeroticism in Classical Arabic Literature* (New York 1997)

Everett K. Rowson, 'Middle Eastern Literature: Arabic', in Claude J. Summers (ed.), *An Encyclopedia of Gay, Lesbian, Bisexual, Transgender, & Queer Culture*, http://www.glbtq.com/literature/mid_e_lit_arabic,5.html (accessed 23 January 2006)

Edward W. Said, *Orientalism* (New York 1978)

Arno Schmitt and Jehoeda Sofer (eds), *Sexuality and Eroticism among Males in Moslem Societies* (Binghamton, NY 1992)

Abdelhak Serhane, *L'amour circoncis* (Casablanca 1995)

Prods Oktor Skjærvø, 'Middle Eastern Literature: Persian', in Claude J. Summers (ed.), *An Encyclopedia of Gay, Lesbian, Bisexual, Transgender, & Queer Culture*, http://www.glbtq.com/literature/mid_e_lit_persian.html (accessed 23 January 2006)

Notes

1   This chapter is concerned particularly with these countries, which even today are central to a religion that over the course of centuries has encompassed many other nations on several continents.

2   For the most important terms relating to Islamic sexuality the corresponding word in Arabic word is given. It should be noted, however, that despite the existence of an official system of transliteration, an individual word may have numerous variants, depending on regional differences and local languages. That said, I have preferred to present these terms (as with original titles of books in Arabic) in their most commonly used form.

3   There are many translations of the Qur'an in current use, all of which represent only an interpretation of holy Islamic scripture. The quotations used here were taken from Abdullah Yusuf Ali's *The Holy Qur'an: Text, Translation and Commentary* (Lahore 1934–37).

4   There are, of course, a few exegetes who interpret the Qur'an in a way that is much more understanding of homosexuality, and certainly one cannot help but feel perplexed when one reads of the pleasures awaiting the holy in Paradise – not only virgins (*houri*), but also young men (*ghilmān*): 'Round about them will serve, (devoted) to them, young male servants (handsome) as Pearls well-guarded' (Sura 52:24); 'Round about them will (serve) youths of perpetual (freshness), with goblets, (shining) beakers, and cups (filled) out of clear-flowing fountains' (Sura 56:17–18); and 'And round about them will (serve) youths of perpetual (freshness): If thou seest them, thou wouldst think them scattered Pearls' (Sura 76:19) (translations by Yusuf Ali).

5   The name of Abū Nuwās has been traditionally linked to homosexuality, so much so that in some areas of the Maghreb homosexuals are still called *nuwāsī*.

6   The book was rediscovered by René R. Khawam in the form of French edition and published in 1989; the original edition did not include the title in Arabic.

7   One such voice is Sheik Abd al-Azim al-Mitaani, a professor in Cairo, who said some years ago that homosexuality is 'a natural secretion of materialistic Western society' and that 'the true catastrophe is the insistence with which these perverts continue to practise these unclean acts and to demand that they be recognized as legitimate.'

8   The two most useful sources are Stephen O. Murray and Will Roscoe (eds), *Islamic Homosexualities: Culture, History, and Literature* (New York 1997), and above all Arno Schmitt and Jehoeda Sofer (eds), *Sexuality and Eroticism Among Males in Moslem Societies* (Binghamton, NY 1992).

9   The presence of homosexual urges in the Arab unconscious can already be found in the famous *Dreams and Interpretations* (*Muntahab al-Kalām fī Tafsīr al-Ahlām*) by Muhammad Ibn Sīrīn (653–728), of which one section is dedicated to dreams of sexual relations between men. Even though he maintains that male homosexuality is the greatest possible peversion, the author dwells upon these dreams at length, explaining them in different ways depending on the age of the partner involved in the dream.

10   According to Abdelwahab Bouhdiba, *La sexualité en Islam* (Paris 1975), p. 227, these social and religious norms are symbolically sealed through the circumcision of the young boy and the young girl's loss of virginity. These two events share elements of celebration, violence, blood, physical suffering and exhibitionism.

11   The Arabic term *ghulam*, 'boy', has two other meanings: slave and homosexual. The Turkish term *oğlan* means 'boy', but also 'one who is screwed'.

12   The word *habibi*, 'love', thus seems paradoxical. Despite the emotional detachment that often accompanies any type of sexual intimacy, the term *habibi* forms the basis of many expressions in Arabic and is a favourite subject of literature and songs; and in Arabic there are around sixty words to define love in all its variations. See *Qantara*, the journal of the Institut du Monde Arabe, no. 18 (1996), pp. 18–53.

13   The anus, however, is considered to be clean because custom dictates that it should be washed after defecation. See Bouhdiba, *La sexualité en Islam*, pp. 62–73.

14   Even if its erotic import is perhaps overemphasized, the *hammam* continues to inspire a mythic fascination; see Abdelhak Serhane, *L'amour circoncis* (Casablanca 1995), pp. 159–66, and Bouhdiba, *La sexualité en Islam*, pp. 197–213. The latter defines it as a 'hot uterine place', a suggestion based on the dichotomy between hot/cold, hard/soft, feminine/masculine, clean/dirty, pure/impure, internal/external etc.

15   There are few papers on the subject of lesbianism, although Stephen O. Murray's essay 'Woman–Woman Love in Islamic Societies', in Murray and Roscoe (eds), *Islamic Homosexualities*, pp. 97–104, is worthy of note. A 9th-century Andalusian treatise on lesbianism called the *Kitab al-Sahhakat* – probably the very first on the topic – seems to have been lost.

16   See *L'amour circoncis*, pp. 36–51, in which Serhane maintains that the ultimate purpose of this custom is to protect the virginity of young girls. The rape of teenagers in Qur'anic schools is dramatically recounted by Driss Chraïbi in the novel *Le passé simple* and by Rachid Boudjedra in *La répudiation*.

17   See 'Moroccan Boys and Sex' by the Dutch psychologist Andreas Eppink, in Schmitt and Sofer, *Sexuality and Eroticism*, pp. 33–39; and Tony Duvert's *Journal d'un innocent* (Paris 1976) p. 77.

18   Among the many other synonyms for those who 'are affected by perversion' (*ubnah*), I would note *mabun, manyuk, hulāq* or the Syrian *hauel*. The Islamic world's extraordinary variety of words designating the passive role is treated in Stephen O. Murray's exhaustive 'Role Labels', in Murray and Roscoe, *Islamic Homosexualities*, pp. 28–32.

19   For a more complete examination of homosexuality in the Maghreb see Vincenzo Patanè, *Arabi e noi: Amori gay nel Maghreb* (Rome 2002), which also includes interviews with thirteen young Maghrebins who discuss their sexual behaviour with both fellow Arabs and Westerners.

20   There is much historical evidence to suggest that male prostitution, while less obvious than female prostitution (*bighā*), has been widespread in Arab countries for a long time. Since organized prostitution does not exist (with the exception of men who serve an exclusively well-to-do domestic clientele), male prostitution is conducted in a very underground way – so much so that there is no precise term to describe young male prostitutes. On prostitution in general, see 'Une sexualité payante: le travail sexuel' in Abdessamad Dialmy, *Jeunesse, Sida et Islam au Maroc* (Casablanca 2000), pp. 110–12.

21   The situation seems to be changing, however. Many newspapers are taking an interest, such as the French magazine *Têtu*, which included an article on homosexuality in its January 2006 issue. Since 2004, in both Tunisia and Morocco the law has been used more than in the past, and there have been swoops and arrests by the police. In Marrakesh in particular, a popular destination for Western travellers, gay venues have been closed down and areas frequented by gay people have been placed under surveillance.

22   A letter of 1810 Byron claimed that: 'In England the vices in fashion are whoring & drinking, in Turkey, Sodomy & smoking, we prefer a girl and a bottle, they a pipe and a pathic'; and in 1819 he described the Turkish bath as 'a marble palace of sherbet and sodomy'. During his first journey to the region (1809–11), in which he would have been in his early twenties, Byron probably had same-sex relations in Islamic Albania as well as with youths in Greece. Having been asked to repay his bodyguards 'not in money, but in nature', Byron also received the attentions of Ali Pasha and his son Veli Pasha, both notorious pederasts. On Albania, see Stephen O. Murray's 'Male Homosexuality in Ottoman Albania', in Murray and Roscoe, *Islamic Homosexualities*, pp. 187–96.

23 These words, spoken by the prosecutor Ashraf Hilal during the trial, were reported by sources around the world, including *The Times* and the *Washington Post* (both 15 November 2001).

24 Homosexuality and transvestism, which have been part of Turkish society for centuries, have finally found a space for expression: Istanbul currently has over twenty commerical venues for gay and transsexual clients, including an exclusively gay sauna.

25 Beirut in particular is home to a lively gay scene. On Syria, see Gary B. MacDonald, 'Among Syrian Men', in Schmitt and Sofer, *Sexuality and Eroticism*, pp. 43–54.

26 This is the figure given by Homan, a group of Iranian homosexual activists now in exile; it is, however, difficult to give a reliable estimate of the true number of executions that have been carried out since 1979, the year of the Islamic Revolution. What is sure is that since 1990 there has been an increase in the number of cases, with numerous executions. In the most recent example, which took place in 2005 in Mashad, in the north-east of the country, two homosexual boys of sixteen and eighteen years of age were hanged; the official reason for the punishment was that they had raped a thirteen-year-old. The news provoked protests all over the world.

27 Some of these inventive strategems are recounted by Dominique Fernandez in *A Hidden Love: Art and Homosexuality* (Munich 2001), pp. 9–10, who has experienced them firsthand in the United Arab Emirates and other countries of the Arabian Peninsula.

28 On the intriguing phenomenon of the *khanith* in the city of Sohar, Oman (who share some characteristics with the *hijra* of India), see Stephen O. Murray's essay 'The Sohari Khanith', in Murray and Roscoe, *Islamic Homosexualities*, pp. 244–55. The article deals with a specific type of transgender, and the country's inhabitants even maintain that there are three sexes: male, female and *khanith*.

29 This aspect of the singer's life is discussed in the biography *Oum* by Sélim Nassib (Paris 1994).

30 According to the English writer William Beckford, the Mediterranean became 'the place for sinners of a particular species'. See Robert Aldrich, *The Seduction of the Mediterranean: Writing, Art and Homosexual Fantasy* (London 1993), and Ian Littlewood, *Sultry Climates: Travel and Sex Since the Grand Tour* (London 2001).

31 Edward W. Said, *Orientalism* (New York 1978), p. 1.

32 Richard Francis Burton, *Personal Narrative of a Pilgrimage to Al-Madinah and Meccah (1855–1856)* (London 1893).

33 Edward Westermarck, *Ritual and Belief in Morocco* (London 1926); Carleton S. Coon, *Tribes of the Rif* (Cambridge, MA 1931).

34 John Lahr (ed.), *The Orton Diaries* (London 1986), p. 186.

35 *Race d'Ep! Un siècle d'images de l'homosexualité* (1979), a documentary film by Guy Hocquenghem and Lionel Soukaz exploring gay history, provides an excellent account of the transgressive sexual behaviour of the Flower Children.

36 The French writer Roger Peyrefitte once said: 'African loves are easy but mediocre. There is a certain abdication of the Western man when he crosses the Mediterranean in search of homosexual love.'

CHAPTER 13
ADRIAN CARTON
is a lecturer in modern history at Macquarie University, Sydney. He has published work on Asian migration, Eurasian identity in India and cross-cultural sexuality. He is currently completing a book entitled *Destabilizing Anglo-India*, which examines the contested landscapes of hybrid identity in British and French colonial spaces.

Notes

1 I wish to thank Lisa Featherstone for her able and sensitive research assistance, and Robert Aldrich, Michelle Arrow, Romit Dasgupta, Mary Spongberg, Hsu-Ming Teo and Angela Woollacott for their comments and suggestions on earlier drafts.

2 Bret Hinsch, *Passions of the Cut Sleeve: The Male Homosexual Tradition in China* (Berkeley, CA 1990), pp. 20–21.

3 Ibid., p. 32.

4 Ibid., p. 36, and Louis Crompton, *Homosexuality and Civilization* (Cambridge, MA 2003), p. 218.

5 Hinsch, *Passions of the Cut Sleeve*, p. 41.

6 Chou Wah-Shan, *Tongzhi: Politics of Same-Sex Eroticism in Chinese Societies* (New York 2000), p. 13.

7 Robert van Gulik, *Sexual Life in Ancient China* (Leiden 1964), p. 63.

8 Fang-Fu Ruan and Yung-Mei Tsai, 'Male Homosexuality in the Traditional Chinese Literature', *Journal of Homosexuality*, vol. 14, no. 3–4 (1987), pp. 21–33.

9 Vivien Ng, 'Homosexuality and the State in Late Imperial China', in Martin Bauml Duberman, Martha Vicinus and George Chauncey (eds), *Hidden from History: Reclaiming the Gay and Lesbian Past* (New York 1989), p. 78.

10 Crompton, *Homosexuality and Civilization*, pp. 240–43, and Colin Mackerras, *The Rise of the Peking Opera, 1770–1870* (Oxford 1972).

11 Giovanni Vitiello, 'The Dragon's Whim: Ming and Qing Homoerotic Tales from *The Cut Sleeve*', *T'oung Pao: Revue internationale de sinologie*, vol. 78 (1992), pp. 344–45. The *Records* were republished in 1910 by a scholar named Chong Tianzi.

12 Giovanni Vitiello, 'The Fantastic Journey of an Ugly Boy: Homosexuality and Salvation in Late Ming Pornography', *Positions: East Asia Cultures Critique*, vol. 4, no. 2 (1996), p. 295.

13 Vitiello, 'The Dragon's Whim', p. 348.

14 See Dian Murray, 'The Practice of Homosexuality Among the Pirates of Late 18th and Early 19th Century China', *International Journal of Maritime History*, vol. 4, no. 1 (1992), pp. 121–30.

15 See Michael Szonyi, 'The Cult of *Hu Tianbao* and the Eighteenth-Century Discourse of Homosexuality', *Late Imperial China*, vol. 19, no. 1 (1998), pp. 1–25.

16 Vivien Ng, 'Ideology and Sexuality: Rape Laws in Qing China', *Journal of Asian Studies*, vol. 46, no. 1 (1987), pp. 57, 67.

17 van Gulik, *Sexual Life in Ancient China*, p. 48.

18 Paul Rakita Goldin, *The Culture of Sex in Ancient China* (Honolulu 1992), p. 7.

19 Patricia Ebrey, *The Inner Quarters: Marriage and the Lives of Chinese Women in the Song Period* (Berkeley, CA 1993).

20 Susan Mann, 'The Male Bond in Chinese History and Culture', *American Historical Review*, vol. 5, no. 5 (2000), p. 1603.

21 Norman Kutcher, 'The Fifth Relationship: Dangerous Friendships in the Confucian Context', *American Historical Review*, vol. 5, no. 5 (2000), p. 1623.

22 Matthew Sommer, *Sex, Law and Society in Late Imperial China* (Stanford, CA 2000), pp. 148–49.

23 See Tze-Lan D. Sang, *The Emerging Lesbian: Female Same-Sex Desire in Modern China* (Chicago 2003).

24 See H. Laura Wu, 'Through the Prism of Male Writing: Representation of Lesbian Love in Ming-Qing Literature', in *Nannü: Men, Women and Gender in Early and Imperial China*, vol. 4, no. 1 (2002), pp. 1–34.

25 Gary Leupp, *Male Colours: The Construction of Homosexuality in Tokugawa Japan* (Berkeley, CA 1995), pp. 28–29.

26 See Paul Schalow, 'Kukai and the Tradition of Male Love in Japanese Buddhism', in José Ignacio Cabezón (ed.), *Buddhism, Sexuality, and Gender* (Albany, NY 1992), pp. 215–16.

27 José Ignacio Cabezón, 'Homosexuality and Buddhism', in Arlene Swidler (ed.), *Homosexuality and World Religions* (Valley Forge, PA 1993), p. 91.

28 Tsuneo Watanabe and Jun'ichi Iwata, *The Love of the Samurai: A Thousand Years of Japanese Homosexuality* (London 1989), p. 38.

29 Leupp, *Male Colours*, p. 42.

30 Crompton, *Homosexuality and Civilization*, p. 417.

31 See Eiko Ikegami, *The Taming of the Samurai: Honorific Individualism and the Making of Modern Japan* (Cambridge, MA 1995), p. 210.

32 See Furukawa Makato, 'The Changing Nature of Sexuality: The Three Codes Framing Homosexuality in Modern Japan', *US–Japan Women's Journal*, vol. 7 (1994), p. 100.

33 Watanabe and Iwata, *The Love of the Samurai*, pp. 49–51.

34 Leupp, *Male Colours*, p. 52.

35 Crompton, *Homosexuality and Civilization*, p. 422, and Leupp, *Male Colours*, pp. 53–55.

36 Gregory M. Pflugfelder, *Cartographies of Desire: Male–Male Sexuality in Japanese Discourse, 1600–1950* (Berkeley, CA 1999), p. 73.

37 James Brandon, *Kabuki: Five Classic Plays* (Cambridge, MA 1975), p. 2.

38 Leupp, *Male Colours*, p. 77.

39 Ibid., pp. 79–84.

40 Paul Schalow, 'The Invention of a Literary Tradition of Male Love: Kitamura Kigin's *Iwatsutsuji*', *Monumenta Nipponica*, vol. 48, no. 1 (1993), pp. 1–31.

41 Introduction to Paul Schalow (ed.), *The Great Mirror of Male Love* (Stanford, CA 1990), p. 6.

42 See the forum on 'Tracking "Same-Sex Love" from Antiquity to the Present in South Asia', in *Gender and History*, vol. 14, no. 1 (2002), pp. 7–30.

43 *Rg-Veda*, Hymn 10:129.

44 Ruth Vanita and Saleem Kidwai (eds), *Same-Sex Love in India* (London 2001), pp. 14, 15, 17.

45 Vern Bullough, 'Sex in the Indian Subcontinent', in *Sexual Variance in Society and History* (Chicago 1976), p. 267.

46 Serenda Nanda, *Neither Man nor Woman: The Hijras of India* (Belmont, CA 1999), p. 21.

47 Michael Sweet and Leonard Zwilling, '"Like a City Ablaze": The Third Sex and the Creation of Sexuality in Jain Religious Literature', *Journal of the History of Sexuality*, vol. 6, no. 3 (1996), pp. 359–84.

48 Vanita and Kidwai, *Same-Sex Love in India*, p. 26.

49 See Walter Penrose, 'Hidden in History: Female Homoeroticism and Women of a "Third Nature" in the South Asian Past', *Journal of the History of Sexuality*, vol. 10, no. 1 (2001), pp. 3–38; and Gita Thadani, 'The Politics of Identities and Languages: Lesbian Desire in Ancient and Modern India', in *Female Desires: Same-Sex Relations and Transgender Practices Across Cultures* (New York 1999), pp. 67–90.

50 See Bullough, *Sexual Variance*, p. 262.

51 Alain Daniélou, *Gods of Love and Ecstasy* (Rochester, VT 1992).

52 John Garrett Jones, *Tales and Teachings of the Buddha: The Jataka Stories in Relation to the Pali Canon* (London 1979), pp. 105–15.

53 Leonard Zwilling, 'Homosexuality as Seen in Indian Buddhist Texts', in Cabezón, *Buddhism, Sexuality, and Gender*, p. 209.

54 Vanita and Kidwai, *Same-Sex Love in India*, pp. 143–90.

55 Ruth Vanita, '"Married Among Their Companions": Female Homoerotic Relations in Nineteenth-Century Urdu *Rekhti* Poetry in India', *Journal of Women's History*, vol. 16, no. 4 (2004), pp. 12–52. For an alternative interpretation of the female voice in *Rekhti* poetry, see Carla Petievich, 'Rekhti: Impersonating the Feminine in Urdu Poetry', in Sanjay Srivastava (ed.), *Sexual Sites, Seminal Attitudes: Sexualities, Masculinities and Culture in South Asia* (New Delhi 2004), pp. 123–46.

56 Kanchana Natarajan, 'Interfeminine Bonding: Reading Carroll Smith-Rosenberg from a Southern Indian Perspective', *Journal of Women's History*, vol. 12, no. 3 (2000), pp. 13–22.

57 See Suparna Bhaskaran, 'The Politics of Penetration: Section 377 of the Indian Penal Code', in Ruth Vanita (ed.), *Queering India: Same-Sex Love and Eroticism in Indian Culture and Society* (London 2002), pp. 15–29.

58 Ruth Vanita, *Love's Rite: Same-Sex Marriage in India and the West* (New Delhi 2005), pp. 38–41.

CHAPTER 14

GERT HEKMA

teaches gay and lesbian studies in the Department of Sociology and Anthropology at the University of Amsterdam. He has published widely on the sociology and history of (homo)sexuality; his most recent book is *Homoseksualiteit in Nederland van 1730 tot de moderne tijd*. With Kent Gerard he edited *The Pursuit of Sodomy: Male Homosexuality in Renaissance and Enlightenment Europe*; with James D. Steakley and Harry Oosterhuis, *Gay Men and the Sexual History of the Political Left*; and, with Franz Eder and Les Hall, two volumes on *Sexual Cultures in Europe*.

Notes

1 I would to thank Robert Aldrich for his critical comments. Many of the people and events cited in this chapter can be found easily on the internet, and I would refer readers to this source in the first instance; at the same time I have suggested books and articles when they offer a broader perspective on particular issues. General works are Robert Aldrich and Garry Wotherspoon (eds), *Who's Who in Contemporary Gay and Lesbian History: From World War II to the Present Day* (London 2001); Didier Eribon (ed.), *Dictionnaire des cultures gays et lesbiennes* (Paris 2003); George E. Haggerty (ed.), *Gay Histories and Cultures* (New York 2000); David Higgs (ed.), *Queer Sites: Gay Urban Histories since 1600* (New York 1999); Timothy Murphy (ed.), *Reader's Guide to Lesbian and Gay Studies* (Chicago 2000); Louis-Georges Tin (ed.), *Dictionnaire de l'homophobie* (Paris 2003); and www.glbtq.com.

2 Martin Duberman, *Stonewall* (New York 1993); David Carter, *Stonewall: The Riots that Sparked the Gay Revolution* (New York 2004).

3 For the older homosexual bar culture, see Gert Hekma, *De roze rand van donker Amsterdam: De opkomst van een homoseksuele kroegcultuur 1930–1970* (Amsterdam 1992); George Chauncey, *Gay New York: Gender, Urban Culture, and the Making of the Gay Male World, 1890–1944* (New York 1994); and Matt Houlbrook, *Queer London: Perils and Pleasures in the Sexual Metropolis, 1918–1957* (Chicago 2005).

4 Edmund White, *The Farewell Symphony* (London 1997) and *The Burning Library* (London 1994); Patrick Moore, *Beyond Shame: Reclaiming the Abandoned History of Radical Gay History* (Boston, MA 2004).

5 Ronald Bayer and Gerald M. Oppenheimer, *AIDS: Voices from the Epidemic Doctors* (New York 2000).

6 General overviews include Steven Epstein, *Impure Science: AIDS, Activism, and the Politics of Knowledge* (Berkeley, CA 1996) and Douglas Crimp, *Melancholia and Moralism: Essays on AIDS and Queer Politics* (Cambridge, MA 2002).

7 Barry D. Adam, Jan Willem Duyvendak and André Krouwel (eds), *The Global Emergence of Gay and Lesbian Politics* (Philadelphia 1999); Peter Drucker (ed.), *Different Rainbows* (London 2000); Mark Blasius (ed.), *Sexual Identities, Queer Politics* (Princeton 2001); and for national histories, among other works, Frédéric Martel, *The Pink and the Black: Homosexuals in France Since 1968* (Stanford, CA 1999); David Rayside, *On the Fringe: Gays and Lesbians in Politics* (Ithaca, NY 1998), which discusses Britain, Canada and the US; John D'Emilio, William B. Turner and Urvashi Vaid (eds), *Creating Change: Sexuality, Public Policy, and Civil Rights* (New York 2000); and Graham Willett, *Living Out Loud: A History of Gay and Lesbian Activism in Australia* (St Leonards, NSW 2000).

8 Frank van Gemert, 'Chicken Kills Hawk: Gay Murders During the Eighties in Amsterdam', *Journal of Homosexuality*, vol. 26, no. 4 (1999), pp. 149–74.

9 Gary D. Comstock, *Violence Against Lesbians and Gay Men* (New York 1991); Gregory M. Herek and Kevin Berrill (eds), *Hate Crimes: Confronting Violence Against Lesbians and Gay Men* (London 1992).

10 Ronald Bayer, *Homosexuality and American Psychiatry: The Politics of Diagnosis* (New York 1981).

11 Mark Jordan, *The Silence of Sodom: Homosexuality in Modern Catholicism* (Chicago 2000).

12 Randy P. Conner with David Haffield Sparks, *Queering Creole Spiritual Traditions* (New York 2004).

13 For a more positive interpretation of the Qur'an, see Omar Nahas, *Islam en homoseksualiteit* (Amsterdam 2001).

14 See my 'A Dutch Concert. Sex Education in Multicultural Schools', in: *Thamyris*, vol. 7, no. 1–2 (2000), pp. 249–60, and 'Imams and Homosexuality: A Post-Gay Debate in The Netherlands', *Sexualities*, vol. 5, no. 2 (2002), pp. 269–80.

15 Luiz R. Mott, *Epidemic of Hate: Violations of the Human Rights of Gay Men, Lesbians, and Transvestites in Brazil* (Salvador, Bahia, 1996).

16 See among others Michael Bronski, *The Pleasure Principle: Sex, Backlash, and the Struggle for Gay Freedom* (New York 1998); Rayside, *On the Fringe*; and D'Emilio, Turner and Vaid, *Creating Change*.

17 See Lothar Machtan's controversial *The Hidden Hitler* (New York 2001).

18 See the Adam, Duyvendak and Krouwel, *The Global Emergence of Gay and Lesbian Politics*; Martel, *The Pink and the Black*; Rayside, *On the Fringe*; D'Emilio, Turner and Vaid, *Creating Change*; and the various anthologies listed in Note 1.

19 Bruce Bawer, *A Place at the Table: The Gay Individual in American Society* (New York 1993); Paul Robinson, *Queer Wars: The New Gay Right and Its Critics* (Chicago 2005).

20 Craig A. Rimmerman (ed.), *Gay Rights, Military Wrongs: Political Perspectives on Lesbians and Gay in the Military* (New York 1996).

21 Annemarie Jagose, *Queer Theory: An Introduction* (New York 1996); Steven Seidman, *Difference Troubles: Queering Social Theory and Sexual Politics* (Cambridge 1997).

22 Dangerous Bedfellows (eds), *Policing Public Sex: Queer Politics and the Future of Aids Activism* (Boston, MA 1996); Samuel R. Delany, *Times Square Red, Times Square Blue* (New York 1999).

23 Bruce Rind, Philip Tromovitch and Robert Bauserman, 'A Meta-Analytic Examination of Assumed Properties of Child Sexual Abuse Using College Samples', in *Psychological Bulletin*, vol. 124, no. 1 (1998), pp 22–53.

24 Philip Jenkins, *Moral Panic: Changing Concepts of the Child Molester in Modern America* (New Haven 1998).

25 Judith Levine, *Harmful to Minors: The Perils of Protecting Children from Sex* (Minneapolis, MN 2002).

26 See, for example, Paul Luttikhuis, 'Engeland: sociale zuivering', *NRC-Handelsblad*, 10 August 2000, p. 5.

27 Gilbert Herdt and Andrew Boxer, *Children of Horizons: How Gay and Lesbian Teens Are Leading a New Way Out of the Closet* (Boston, MA 1993), p. 6.

28 Dennis Altman, *Global Sex* (Chicago 2001); Arnaldo Cruz-Malavé and Martin F. Manalansan IV (eds), *Queer Globalizations: Citizenship and the Aftermath of Colonialism* (New York 2002).

29 Marshall Kirk and Hunter Madsen, *After the Ball: How America Will Conquer its Fear and Hatred of Gays in the 90s* (New York 1989).

30 Christopher Carrington, *No Place Like Home: Relationships and Family Life Among Lesbians and Gay Men* (Chicago 1999).

31 Jeffrey Weeks, Brian Heaphy and Catherine Donovan, *Same-Sex Intimacies: Families of Choice and Other Life Experiments* (London 2001).

32 David Bell and John Binnie, *The Sexual Citizen: Queer Politics and Beyond* (Cambridge 2000); Ken Plummer, *Intimate Citizenship: Private Decisions and Public Dialogues* (Seattle 2003).

ACKNOWLEDGMENTS FOR ILLUSTRATIONS

p. 1 Brassaï, *Homosexual Couples at the Bal de la Montagne Sainte-Geneviève*, c. 1932. Private collection © Estate Brassaï – RMN, Paris **p. 2** Photo akg images, London. © Viola Roehr, Alvensleben, Munich **p. 6** Staatliche Museen Preussischer Kulturbesitz, Berlin **p. 9** Tate, London Purchased 1980 **p. 10** Dome of Monreale Cathedral, Sicily **p. 11** from Magnus Hirschfeld, *Geschlechtskunde* 4 1930 **p. 12** V & A, London **p. 13** Photo Martin Hürlimann **pp. 14–15** Alinari, Florence **p. 15** Photo T. E. Lawrence **p. 16** Berlinische Galerie, Berlin A 1927.2. Otto Dix © DACS 2006 **p. 17** Private collection **p. 20** National Gallery of Victoria, Melbourne, Felton Bequest, 1932 **p. 21(l)** Police Museum, Melbourne **p. 21(r)** *Australian Sketcher*, 22 November 1879 **p. 24** National Archives of Australia, Canberra, A6135 K13/12/73/3 **p. 25** Rex Features, London, Photo James D. Morgan **p. 28** British Museum, London. GR 1999.4-26.1 **p. 30** Archaeological Museum, Olympia **p. 32** Christina Gascoigne **p. 34** National Archaeological Museum, Naples **p. 35** Museum of Fine Arts, Boston **pp. 36–37** National Archaeological Museum, Athens **p. 38** Photo RMN – © Gérard Blot **p. 39** British Museum, London. B 153 (1836.2-24.46) **p. 40** Staatliche Museen Preussischer Kulturbesitz, Antikenmuseum, Berlin **p. 41** British Museum, London. W39 1865.11-18.39 **p. 42** bpk/Antikensammlung, Staatliche Museen zu Berlin/Johannes Laurentius **p. 43** Musée du Louvre, Paris **p. 44** FRR, Paris **p. 47** Museo Archaeologico, Tarquinia **p. 48** The House of the Vettii, Pompeii **p. 50** Archaeological Museum, Delphi **p. 51** Tunis Museum, Tunis **p. 54** Photo akg-images, London/Pirozzi **p. 56** Kupferstichkabinett, Berlin **p. 58** Codex Vindobonensis 2554, Österreichische Nationalbibliothek, Vienna **p. 60** Musée du Louvre, Paris **p. 62** Photo akg-images, London/British Library **p. 64** Österreichische Nationalbibliothek, Vienna **p. 65(l)** Pierpont Morgan Library, New York **p. 65(r)** Bibliothèque Municipale, Besançon, France **p. 66** Museo Civico Medievale, Bologna **p. 67(tl)** Woodmansterne Publications Ltd **p. 67(tr)** Bibliothèque Nationale, France. FR 2643 **p. 67** from James Dalloway, *Inquiries into the Origin and Progress of the Science of Heraldry in England* (1793) **p. 68** Prado, Madrid **p. 69** from Giovanni Sercambi, *Le Chroniche di Giovanni Sercambi Lucchese* (Lucca 1892) **p. 72** from Edward Fuchs, *Illustrierte Sittengeschichte Ergänzungsband Renaissance* (1909) **p. 74** Fondation des Archives de l'ancien Évêché de Bâle, Porrentruy AAEB. A85/83 **p. 75** Zentralbibliothek, Zurich MS A 5 S. 994 **p. 76** Rijksmuseum, Amsterdam **p. 78** Bridgeman Art Library, London **p 80(t)** Private collection **p. 80(b)** Staatsbibliothek zu Berlin **p. 81** Biblioteca Apostolica Vaticana, Rome, Codex Reg. Lat 1896, fol. 99r **pp. 82–83** Private collection **p. 84** from *The Arraignment and Conviction of Mervin Lord Audley, Earle of Castlehaven* (1642) **p. 85** Metropolitan Museum of Art, New York. Rogers and Gwynne Andrews Funds, 1935 (35.121) **p. 86** Private collection **p. 88** Fondazione Giorgio Cini, Galleria di Palazzo Cini, Venice. No 40025 **p. 89** Photo akg-images, London/Rabatti-Domingie **p. 90** Cabinet des Estampes, Bibliothèque Nationale, Paris. Rés. Na 22 **p. 91** Cabinet des Estampes, Bibliothèque Nationale, Paris **p. 92** Collection Kasteel Amerongen **p. 93** Photo akg-images, London **p. 94(t)** from Boccaccio, *De la genealogie des dieux* (1531) **p. 94(b)** Bargello, Florence **p. 95** Istituto Nazionale per la Grafica, Rome. FC 5947 **p. 96** Gemäldegalerie, Berlin **p. 97** Gemäldegalerie, Berlin **p. 98** Photo akg-images, London/Rabatti-Domingie **p. 100** Prado, Madrid **p. 102** Private collection **p. 104** from William C. B., *Les Bigarrures* (1799) **p. 105** Photo RMN – © Gérard Blot **p. 106(l)** Bibliothèque Nationale, Paris **p. 106(r)** Bibliothèque Nationale, Paris **p. 108** National Portrait Gallery, London **p. 109** Courtesy of Gert Hekma **p. 110(l)** Private collection of Louis Godbout, Montreal **p. 110(r)** Private collection of Louis Godbout, Montreal **p. 111** Guildhall Library, London **pp. 112–13** from Rudolph Ackermann, *Microcosm of London* (1808) **p. 114** Rijksprentenkabinet, Rijksmuseum, Amsterdam **p. 115** *Jahrbuch für sexuelle Zwischenstufen* 8, 1907 **p. 116** Bibliothèque Nationale, Paris **p. 117** Private collection of Michael Sibalis **p. 118** Private collection **p. 120** Bearsted Collection, Upton House, National Trust. © NTPL/John Hammond **p. 121** British Library, London **pp. 122–23** Cabinet des Estampes, Bibliothèque Nationale, Paris **p. 124** Nelson-Atkins Museum of Art, Kansas City, MO. Nelson Fund 32-39 **p. 127** British Library, London **p. 128** from Ambroise Paré, *Of Monsters and Marvels* **p. 129** Wellcome Institute, London **p. 131** Science Museum/Science & Society Picture Library **p. 132** from J. M. de Ferrer, *Historia de la monja alférez, Dona Catalina de Erauso* (Paris 1829) **p. 133** from Giovanni Bianchi, *The True History and Adventures of Catharine Vizzani* (1755) **p. 134** from Daniel Defoe, *A General History of the Robberies and Murders of the Most Notorious Pyrates* (1724) **p. 135** Collections/Malcolm Crowthers **p. 137** Private collection **p. 138** Christie's Images, London **p. 139** Prado, Madrid **p. 140** from John Cleland, *Memoirs of a Woman of Pleasure* (1766) **p. 142** Rijksmuseum, Amsterdam **p. 144** Hulton Archive/Getty Images **pp. 146–47** from Théodore de Bry, *America* (1590) **p. 147** National Museum of the American Indian, Smithsonian Institution, Washington, DC. 21/6905 Photo Carmelo Guadagno **p. 148** National Museum of the American Indian, Smithsonian Institution, Washington, DC. N34256 Photo C. H. Asbury **pp. 154–55** Purchased by the Friends of Art, Fort Worth Art Association, 1925; acquired by the Amon Carter Museum, 1990, from the Modern Art Museum of Fort Worth through grants and donations from the Amon G. Carter Foundation, the Sid W. Richardson Foundation, the Anne Burnett and Charles Tandy Foundation, Capital Cities/ABC Foundation, Fort Worth Star-Telegram, the R. D. and Joan Dale Hubbard Foundation and the people of Fort Worth **p. 156** Library of Congress. LC-USZ62-79930 **p. 158** Private collection **p. 159** Library of Congress. 1169 LC-USZC4-5250 **p. 160** New Orleans Museum of Art **p. 161** from Julia Frotscher Koch scrapbook, Newcomb College Archives, New Orleans **p. 162** Rhode Island Historical Society. Rhi X3 2513 **p. 163** Collection of the New York Historical Society, negative number 40697 **p. 164** Private collection **p. 165** Courtesy Donna Mussenden VanDerZee **p. 166** Musée National d'Art Moderne, Centre Georges Pompidou, Paris. Otto Dix © DACS 2006 **p. 169** Fonds Littéraire Jacques Doucet **p. 170** Essex Record Office, Chelmsford **p. 171** Private collection **p. 172** Photographer unknown **p. 173** Musée d'Orsay, Paris. Given to the Musée du Jeu de Paume in 1922 by Henri Pinard **p. 174(l)** *Der Wahre Jacob* (Stuttgart), no. 447, 26 November 1907 **p. 174(r)** *Die Muskete* (Vienna) vol. 5, no. 111, 14 November 1907 **p. 175** Photo akg-images, London **p. 176** *Die Freundschaft*, no. 8, 1924 **p. 177** (© reserved): collection National Portrait Gallery, London **p. 178(l)** MacFarlane's sanitary appliances catalogue, c. 1870 **p. 178(r)** George Sims (ed.), *Living London*, vol. 2 (London 1906) **p. 179** Private collection, Berlin **p. 180** Brassaï, *Mardi Gras at the Bal de la Montagne Sainte-Geneviève*, c. 1932 © Estate Brassaï – RMN, Paris **p. 182(t)** Ullstein Bild, Berlin **p. 182(b)** ADN Bildarchiv, Berlin **p. 183** Ullstein Bild, Berlin **p. 184** Chateau-Musée, Cagnes. Tamara de Lempicka © ADAGP, Paris and DACS, London 2006 **p. 185(l)** Ronald Grant Archive, London **p. 185(r)** Ronald Grant Archive, London **p. 186** National Gallery of Art, Washington, DC **p. 189** Private collection **p. 190** British Library, London **p. 191** Akademie der Künste, Berlin **p. 192** Artothek, Weilheim **p. 193** Private collection, Berlin **p. 194** Central State Archive of Film, Photographic & Sound Documents of St Petersburg **p. 195** Imperial War Museum, London **p. 196** *Confidential*, October 1965 **p. 198** *Der Kreis/Le Cercle/The Circle*, no. 9, 1957 **p. 199** Medcraft Electronic Corporation **p. 200** Schwules Museum (Gay Museum), Berlin **p. 202** Ronald Grant Archive, London **p. 203** Ronald Grant Archive, London **p. 204** Senate Historical Office, Washington, DC **p. 207** International Gay Information Center Archives, Manuscripts and Archives Division, The New York Public Library. Astor, Lenox and Tilden Foundations **p. 208(l)** Private collection **p. 208(r)** *The Ladder*, October 1957 **p. 209(l)** *Die Insel*, September 1931 **p. 209(r)** *Arcadie*, January 1954 **p. 210** Photo Collection Jan Carel Warffemius **p. 211** Courtesy Gay, Lesbian, Bisexual, Transgender Historical Society of Northern California, San Francisco **p. 213** Private collection **p. 214** The *New York Times* **p. 215** UPI/Bettmann **p. 218** Private collection **p. 219** Private collection **p. 222** Private collection, Jeanne Mammen © DACS 2006 **p. 224** State Library of Victoria, Melbourne. Accession no IAN01/10/79/149 **p. 225** fromT. D. Bonner (ed.), *The Life and Adventures of James P. Beckwourth* (New York 1856) **p. 227** Courtesy Denbighshire Council **p. 228** KVINFO: Danske Kvinders Fotoarchiv, Copenhagen **p. 230** Private collection **p. 232** *Meiyuu*, no. 1, 1914 **p. 234** Kindly lent by Calderdale Museums **p. 235** Calderdale District Archives **pp. 238–39** Hulton Archive/Getty Images **p. 240** Private collection, Tamara De Lempicka © ADAGP, Paris and DACS, London 2006 **p. 241** Photo Bartsch, Berlin, Jeanne Mammen © DACS 2006 **p. 242** *Die Freundin*, August 1929 **p. 243** *Garçonne*, 1931 **p. 244(t)** from *Broadway Brevities*, 6 June 1932 **p. 244(b)** Lesbian Herstory Archives, Brooklyn, New York **p. 245** Buddy Kent Collection, Lesbian Herstory Archives, Brooklyn, New York **p. 248** Smithsonian Institution, Washington, DC **pp. 252–53** from Théodore de Bry, *America* (1590) **p. 256** National Museum of American Art, Smithsonian Institution, Washington, DC, 2004. Photo Smithsonian American Art Musuem/Art Resource/Scala, Florence **p. 258** from E. E. Evans-Pritchard, *The Azande: History and Political Institutions* (Oxford 1971) **p. 259** from Eva L. R. Meyerowitz, *The Sacred State of the Akan* (London 1951) **p. 260** from Victor Turner, *The Forest of Symbols: Aspects of Ndembu Ritual* (New York 1967) **p. 261** from Victor Turner, *The Forest of Symbols: Aspects of Ndembu Ritual* (New York 1967) **p. 263** Musée de l'Homme, Paris **p. 264(l)** Musée d'Art Moderne, Liège **p. 264(r)** Private collection **p. 266** Rex Nan Kivell Collection, National Library of Australia, Canberra **p. 268** Ronald Grant Archive, London **p. 270** Private collection **p. 272** The Metropolitan Museum of Art, New York Purchase, Francis M. Weld Gift, 1950 (50.164) **p. 276** Photo RMN – © Franck Raux **p. 279** Private collection **p. 281** Courtesy Sotheby's, London **p. 283** Rex/Sipa Press, London **p. 287** Courtesy of Arab Film Distribution **p. 288** Private collection **p. 289(t)** Ronald Grant Archive, London **p. 289(b)** Ronald Grant Archive, London **p. 292** Sterling and Francine Clark Art Institute, Williamstown, MA **p. 293** Private collection **pp. 294–95** Courtesy Galerie de Nourmont, Paris **p. 296** Private collection **p. 297** Bridgeman Art Library/Archives Larousse, Paris **p. 298** Imperial War Museum, London **p. 299** Courtesy Sotheby's, London **p. 300** © Allen Ginsberg/CORBIS **p. 302** Private collection **p. 305** Collection Ferdinand M. Bertholet **p. 306** Kinsey Institute for Research in Sex, Gender, and Reproduction, Inc. **p. 307** Collection Ferdinand M. Bertholet **p. 308** Collection Ferdinand M. Bertholet **p. 310** from *Hsing-Ming-Kuei-Chih* **p. 311** Private collection, Shanghai **p. 312** Collection Ferdinand M. Bertholet **p. 315** Aberdeen University Library **p. 316** Jingoji, Kyoto **pp. 318–19** Achenbach Foundation for Graphic Arts, Prints and Drawings, Department of The Fine Arts Museum of San Francisco **p. 319(l)** Mann Collection, Highland Park, Illinois **p. 319(r)** Mann Collection, Highland Park, Illinois **p. 320** Collection Ferdinand M. Bertholet **p. 321** Private collection, Tokyo **p. 322** Photo akg-images, London/Jean-Louis Nou **pp. 324–25** Photo David Haberlah **p. 326** © Zen Icknow/CORBIS **p. 327(t)** Photo akg-images, London/Jean-Louis Nou **p. 327(b)** V & A, London **p. 328** Private collection **p. 330** © Raymond Burnier, Courtesy of Jacques Cloarec, Paris **p. 331** © Raymond Burnier, Courtesy of Jacques Cloarec, Paris **p. 332** Courtesy Dyke Action Machine **p. 334** Photo Jan Carel Warffemius **p. 335** © 2005 The Alvin Baltrop Trust. Used with permission. **pp. 336–37** Photo Jan Carel Warffemius **p. 339** Photo Rich Lipski, *The Washington Post* **pp. 340–41** © Jeffrey Markowitz/Corbis **p. 344** Courtesy NAMES Project Foundation **p. 345** Photo Jan Carel Warffemius **p. 346** Photo by Stephanie Houfek, Heartphotography@aol.com **pp. 348–49(t)** © Mike Stewart/Corbis Sygma **p. 348(b)** Time Life/Getty Images **p. 352** Collage poster by John A. Wooden, www.whitehouse.org **p. 353** © 1993. United Feature Syndicate, Inc. Reproduced with permission **pp. 354–55** Private collection **p. 359** © EMPICS **p. 360** Private collection **p. 361** Schwules Museum (Gay Museum), Berlin.

INDEX

Page numbers in *italic* refer to illustrations and the content of related captions.